W9-CDC-423

Depression Decade
FROM NEW ERA THROUGH NEW DEAL
1929–1941

THE ECONOMIC HISTORY OF THE UNITED STATES

Edited by Henry David, Harold U. Faulkner, Louis M. Hacker,
Curtis P. Nettels, and Fred A. Shannon

DEPRESSION DECADE

DECADE

From New Era through New Deal
1929–1941

By BROADUS MITCHELL

VOLUME IX

The Economic History of
the United States

M. E. SHARPE, INC.

Armonk, New York   London, England

Cover photo: Breadline. Culver Photo.

Copyright 1947 © renewed 1975 by Broadus Mitchell.

All rights reserved. No part of this book may be reproduced in any form without written permission from Holt, Rinehart and Winston, Inc.

This book was originally published as volume IX of The Economic History of the United States series by Holt, Rinehart and Winston in 1947. It is here reprinted by arrangement with Holt, Rinehart and Winston, Inc.

Library of Congress Cataloging-in-Publication Data

Mitchell, Broadus, 1892-
     Depression decade : from new era through New Deal 1929-1941 / by Broadus Mitchell.
       p.   cm.—(The Economic history of the United States ; 9)
     Reprint. Originally published: New York : Rinehart, 1947.
     ISBN 0-87332-097-2 :
     1. New Deal, 1933-1939. 2. Depressions—1929—United States. 3. United States—Economic conditions—1918-1945. I. Title. II. Series.
     HC106.3.M54   1989   89-10693
     330.973′0917—dc20   CIP

Printed in the United States of America

∞

ED   10 9 8 7 6 5 4 3 2 1

Contents

List of Illustrations

xi

List of Tables and Graphs

xiii

Foreword

WHEN this series of nine volumes on the economic history of the United States was first conceived, the nation's economy had reached a critical stage in its development. Although the shock of the depression of 1929 had been partially absorbed, the sense of bewilderment which it produced had not yet vanished, and the suffering and the bitterness of its first years were being transformed into less substantial, though still anguished, memories. Reform measures, either in operation or proposed, were being actively debated, but with less sense of urgency than earlier.

To the Editors of this series a fresh consideration of America's economic history was justified by more than the experiences of the recent past or the obscurity of the future. Rich contributions to the literature of American history had been made through cooperative series dealing with the political, social, and cultural aspects of American life. Numerous single-volume surveys of the country's economic development had been written. But, as late as the end of the fourth decade of the twentieth century, the world's foremost economic power had not yet produced an integrated, full-length, and authoritative treatment of its own economic history.

Scholarly concern with American economic history has been constantly growing during the past half century, and chairs of economic history have been established in leading universities. A more profound understanding of the role of economic forces in the nation's history has not only been developed by historians and economists, but has also won some measure of popular acceptance. The earlier thin trickle of monographs has broadened in recent years into a flood of publications. At present, such specialized studies, the many collections of documentary materials, and the mountains of government reports on different facets of American economic life are staggering in their richness and scope.

This series has been planned to utilize these available sources in the preparation of a full-scale, balanced, cooperative, and readable survey of the growth of American economy and of its transformation from one of primitive character to world pre-eminence in industry, trade, and finance. Clearly, in nine volumes all aspects of the nation's economic life cannot be treated fully. But such a series can point the way to new fields of study and treat authoritatively, if not definitively, the main lines of economic development. Further, the series is intended to fill a present need of those professionally concerned with American economic history, to supplement the economic materials now available in general school and college histories of the United States, and finally to provide the lay reader with the fruits of American scholarship. If these objectives are attained, then the efforts which have gone into the creation of this economic history of the United States will have been amply repaid.

Contributors to the series have been chosen who have already established their competence in the particular periods they are to survey here; and they are, of course, solely responsible for the points of view or points of departure they employ. It is not intended that the series represent a school of thought or any one philosophical or theoretical position.

In *Depression Decade* Dr. Broadus Mitchell provides both the historical data and a theoretical approach for an understanding of the character, course, and consequences of the severest economic dislocation that American society has experienced in the twentieth century. The focus of the volume is world-wide, rather than narrowly national, and Dr. Mitchell emphasizes the causal bonds which link World War I and its results with the catastrophic depression of the thirties. In presenting the significance of economic collapse in full detail, he never permits the statistical data to obscure the people who were caught in and lived through the depression.

With good reason, much of *Depression Decade* is concerned with the role of government in the economy. After 1929, the state assumed economic and social functions which went far beyond what it had earlier undertaken during years of peace. Dr. Mitchell describes the significant transformations in the realities of a "free enterprise" economy produced by new state functions and purposes. His account of the response of the Hoover administration to the depression underlines the kinship between its economic policies and many phases of the New Deal. The financial, banking, agricultural, and labor policies and reforms of the Roosevelt administrations, the National Recovery Administration, and the public works and social security programs are treated fully and critically. Dr. Mitchell calls attention to the contradictions and weaknesses in the New Deal policies, evaluates their ameliorative and recovery accomplishments, and concludes, finally, that the Roosevelt administrations did not come to grips with the central problems of American capitalism. Only World War II, he maintains, could put an end to large-scale unemployment.

Although some readers may question Dr. Mitchell's major conclusions, they are not likely to deny his success in avoiding the pitfalls of passion and prejudice frequently inspired by the developments with which he deals. Distinguished by clarity, balance, and critical acumen, *Depression Decade* is a lively, dispassionate treatment of a complex, bewildering, and debated period of American economic history.

THE EDITORS.

Preface

THE years of our national economic life here described were crowded with emotion and event. They registered the crash from 1929 superconfidence and the descent into the depression—at first dismaying, then disheartening, then desperate. Came hope in a New Deal, with new men and new measures. Though some had severe misgivings, most accepted eagerly the experiments of government to meet the emergency. As we shall see, few of these devices were altogther as novel as critics would have had the country believe; some were extensions of proposals made by the Hoover administration, others were as old as distress of the public purse. But all were invested with urgency and drama. Moreover, the plight of the American economy was linked with that of the world, both as cause and as effect.

Promising improvement turned to woeful relapse in 1937, and recurrence of hard times brought reversal of certain policies and renewal of others. Despite all efforts, millions of unemployed remained a national reproach. Then loomed war—first in local conflicts in Europe, Africa, and Asia, next in foreign rearmament orders, followed by the outbreak of the general struggle and leading us to a defense program, to endeavors to make ourselves an "arsenal of democracy," to the attack on Pearl Harbor and our entry as a frank belligerent.

This "rush of history" means that a brief account, unless it is to be a mere chronology, must select the more significant events and develop ments for scrutiny. Only in this way is interpretation possible. The most significant feature of this depression period was the unexampled intervention of the federal government in the economic life of the country. Measures of relief and reform increased in variety and scope. The depression was proof that the self-sufficiency of the economy had broken down. Few economic forces continued independent of government assistance or correction. Autonomous economic developments were in a peculiar degree suspended. Therefore emphasis has been given to public policy as expressed in legislation and administration.

This being a volume in a series covering the whole of American economic experience, it seemed proper to take time, here and there, to relate the period to earlier history. This procedure was suggested by the fact that the volume, coming almost up to the present, necessarily lacked the wisdom of hindsight. While the outbreak of war in Europe in September, 1939, foretold the end of business stagnation, the period of defense production belongs in an account of the depression in the United States; the story has been stopped at the attack of the Japanese on Pearl Harbor.

B. M.

New York City
August, 1947

xvii

Depression Decade
FROM NEW ERA THROUGH NEW DEAL
1929–1941

World Economy between Wars

THE depression following 1929 was world wide. The United States made contribution to the causes as to the course of the disturbance, which in turn reacted in every part upon this country. What happened in America becomes clearer on looking at the picture of continents in distress. This will serve to put the experiences in America in perspective. Incidentally, it will appear that a number of devices commonly regarded as American improvisations were adaptations of policies used elsewhere.

Economic processes are continuous. The period from World War I to World War II was integral. We are apt to think of the two decades from Versailles to Warsaw as distinct, broken at the stock market crash of 1929. But American ebullience of the "New Economic Era," 1921–1929, had no counterpart in Europe. There the effort until about 1925 was to restore war losses; when this was more or less achieved, the next four years went into tenuous and doomed attempts to maintain the newly established equilibrium. However, even in America the two dreams, good and bad, as pronounced by Joseph, were one.

Though many of the social dislocations of 1919–1939 were due to World War I, certain long-time developments, important for this story, were in train before the war. Industrialism was spreading and maturing. Not only was industry domesticated in the United States, Germany, northern France, Belgium, and Japan, but it was getting a foothold in countries producing raw materials and hitherto depend-

3

ent on others for manufactured goods, such as China, India, and Australia. In the older established centers, and in some of the newer, large-scale methods and "rationalization" were again stepping up capacity much as the application of power machinery had done in the first place. Further, petroleum and electricity were taking the place of coal in the generation of power.

This evolution operated to the relative hurt of Britain as "the workshop of the world." Her pre-eminence had been built on colonial empire, merchant marine, insular position, early start, and coal. But Germany, in technical skill and selling success, and the United States in both proficiency and magnitude of industry, were surpassing her. This development meant two things: (1) Britain was left weaker after the war, and was unable to take industrial leadership or impose European peace as she had after the Napoleonic struggles a century earlier; (2) industrial competition and economic nationalism were taking the place of the world division of labor which Adam Smith had projected and Cobden had tried to realize in Britain's interest.

These tendencies were on the side of production. Others were on the side of consumption. The rate of population growth in developed countries was declining, while increasing urbanization was adding to the standard of living. At a time when demand was preparing to shift from heavy clothing and cereals to lighter fabrics and vegetables, fruits, and meat, staple agriculture, worse luck, was further endangered by soil chemistry, mechanical power, improvements in transportation, and development of synthetics such as rayon.

These trends were intensified by World War I, but are not to be charged to its account. The war itself had to answer for enough. Four years of absorbed destruction of life and productive resources, with moral devastation, and redrawing of political and economic boundaries, amounted to a revolution in most human spheres. Probably World War I should be called instead a devolution, because, except in Russia, it did not lead to a higher plane of achievement, but rather to frustrated attempts to revive old institutions, and abortive efforts to create new ones. In technology, the war put the world forward, but in ability to realize upon this advantage, not so. International cooperation, despite the League of Nations, was rendered more difficult through collapse and uncertain repair of currencies, and through competitive trade restrictions. All led on to unchecked economic imperialism and militarism, the introduction to another and bigger war.

The tragedy was made more poignant by moments of seeming alleviation or even of improvement. Such were the subsidence of inflation, England's return to the gold standard, progressive forgiveness of reparations, free flow of loans from victors to vanquished, and a last trial at restoration in the fated World Economic Conference. Each time the dawn was false.

ECONOMIC AFTERMATH OF WAR

The war itself was responsible for what has been termed, with restraint, "disequilibrium." The effects were registered in every field, but particularly in those of production, trade, the exchanges, and finance. The result everywhere was to impair or destroy the self-acting controls, and to substitute emergency management. That the private property, price, and profit system survived where it did was testimony to its toughness or evidence of the unreadiness of collectivist advocates.

The war caused shifts in production. Wheat that had been supplied from Russia must now be grown in the United States, Canada, and Australia. Sugar that had come from Germany and Russia must now be furnished by Java and Cuba. Peace found the world as a whole with overcapacity to produce those things specially required for war, such as cereals, steel, copper, nitrates, oil, rubber, textiles. Destruction of farms and factories in certain areas was not so hurtful in itself, but such loss prolonged swollen production in other parts of the world. The speed with which the physical damage of war is repaired has always been remarkable, even before the industrial era. This time the problem rapidly became not that of lack, but of surplus. The war distributed German patents, developed critical industries in new countries, frightened nations into adopting plans of economic self-sufficiency. At the peace table the old promptings of a scarcity economy still held. But it turned out that reparations, if a penalty upon Germany in the payment, were equally punishment to the Allies in the receipt.

The treaty "Balkanized" Europe, cutting up larger trade areas to ensure political autonomy to peoples supposed to be culturally and racially homogeneous. When America led the way with high protection, the natural temptation of these small states to surround themselves with tariff walls received added impetus. The result was a restriction of markets which became almost a stoppage of international trade as it had been known before. The eagerness to be autarchic seemed in direct proportion to economic incompetence. The slenderer and more specialized the little nation's resources, the more determined was it to shut itself off from its neighbors. Dismemberment of the Austro-Hungarian Empire was bad enough in leaving the parts of a body without a head, but was worse in leaving the head, Vienna, without a body. For much of the period Russia was excluded from world trade; later she alternately spread a blessing by her orders for steel and machinery, and spread a curse by her dumping of wheat.

The most exasperating limitations on international trade—embargoes, quotas, and bilateral barter agreements—followed derangement of the exchanges. During the war all countries except the United States left the gold standard. On the Continent, especially in Germany, Austria, and Russia, followed such inflation as rendered exchange mere guesswork. The Dawes plan of 1924 ended the inflation in Germany. England's return to the gold standard the next year gave assurance in all the countries linked to sterling, and in two years more the depreciation which had continued in Belgium, France, and Poland was stopped by devaluation in those countries. Order in the world's monetary systems, which may be said to have existed by 1928, endured briefly. The drain of gold to the United States and France, consequent on debt payment, fear of other currencies, and attraction of our stock market, had so ill distributed this metal that any shock would knock important countries off the gold standard. England left gold in 1931. Up to this time each country had given at least lip service to the ambition of supporting the exchange value of its own currency. Now commenced the shameless race for depreciation in order to gain export advantage. Countries went on from mere exchange control to the most direct interferences with the flow of trade.

The United States entered the war a net debtor to foreign countries to the extent of $3 billion, and emerged a net creditor, exclusive of Allied debts, to the extent of $6 billion. Britain's foreign assets had fallen by a fourth, and those of France by half; those of Germany had been destroyed. The world's financial center shifted from London to New York. Because of Allied orders, the United States had gained gold during the war; in 1913 she had less than a fourth of the world's gold reserves, but by 1921 she had nearly 40 per cent. Debt payments to the United States increased her share of gold because the high tariff kept out goods. By 1926 the United States and France held more than half the world's monetary gold. In this situation Europe's return to the gold standard, even with drastic devaluation in most instances, was hazardous. The policy of the Federal Reserve Board from the middle twenties was to check the flow of gold to the United States. But a low interest rate, which was the means chosen, contributed to the stock market rise, and that in turn sharply reduced the foreign lending of American investors and increased the receipt of gold in the United States.

Maldistribution of gold in the world rendered capital exporting countries reluctant to make long-term loans and investments abroad. England and France, the great sources of foreign loans before the war, became mere loan brokers. The United States loaned to them long term, they reloaned short term. American supply in combination with the experience of European bankers in parceling out funds might have worked better except for disabilities of ultimate borrowers and of original lender. Germany was not relieved of interest charges by the short-term character of nearly half her loans, and her constant need to reborrow endangered stability. The United States, as world banker, was callow. On critical occasions the nation did not so much shirk its new responsibility as it proved ignorant of what that responsibility was. The United States was capricious, unreliable, unwilling to show the patience and accept the penalties of leadership. Just as Americans withdrew funds, their own and others', for the stock market, so five years later the United States turned national instead of remaining international and wrecked the World Economic Conference. A decade after this conference, when war was closing the scene, the United States swore to make herself the "arsenal of democracy." Perhaps she might have prevented the new war by accepting a world position earlier. Certainly democracy in Europe disappeared as economies crumbled.

GOLD-PLATED STANDARD

Now to mention the most important features of the twenties, and then follow in outline the course of the world depression, 1929–1939.

Say that by 1925 Europe's physical production had been restored to prewar level, and world trade was for the first time greater than in 1913, though the trade of Europe was about 10 per cent below what it had been before the war. After 1925 the indexes of physical recovery continued to rise, though Europe was far from enjoying such a "New Economic Era" as invested America from 1921 to 1929.[1] In the whole period economic improvement was deceptive.

Reparation and Allied debt payments bore no relation to movements of trade and investment. These were political commitments, contracted and imposed in bland indifference to economic requirements and feasibility. The war left Germany prostrate; the punitive peace loaded her with debt while robbing her of means of payment. Germany had an adverse balance of trade; she could get the gold to deliver to her creditors only by borrowing abroad at short term. The pound of flesh cost the spectacular German inflation: the mark fell from prewar parity of 4.2 to the dollar to 60 to the dollar in December, 1921, to 49,000 to the dollar two years later when French and Belgian troops had marched into the Ruhr; stood at 1,100,000 to the dollar in the summer of 1923; and the next year was "pegged" at 4,200,000 million to the dollar. The value of the money was destroyed and exchanges were made in foreign currencies and in terms of staple commodities.

This inflation was brought to an end by the Dawes plan, 1924; Germany returned to the gold standard with the reichsmark at the old parity. But this return was made possible only by means of the Dawes loan of 800 million gold marks to help Germany to pay the first annuity. Further, foreign commissioners were appointed for state railways and the Reichsbank, and creditors had the responsibility of translating marks into their own currencies. The Young plan, 1929, tried to cure defects in the Dawes plan and reduced the payments during the period of sixty years for which reparations were to run. Someone has said, in effect, that the Dawes plan made reparations no longer preposterous, but merely ridiculous, while the Young plan changed them to impossible. The economic drain on Germany for a dozen years, until the Hoover moratorium ended reparations and all other European debt payments, bore peculiar responsibility for dragging the world into the long depression.

Restoration of the gold standard in Europe was incomplete except in Britain, and there the honesty of the action was more danger-

[1] League of Nations, *Report on Enquiry into Course and Phases of the Present Economic Depression*, in League of Nations Commission of Enquiry for European Union, C. 284. M 134. 1931. VII. Ser. L. o. N. P. 1931. VII. 3 (Geneva: 1931), pp. 128–143.

ous than the dissembling practiced elsewhere. Britain returned to the gold standard in April, 1925, at the old parity, because of her sense of obligation as financial center, but the pound was overvalued. The gold reserve of the Bank of England now had to support a banking world grown so heavy that it might at any time crush the Atlas. The Cunliffe Committee on Currency and Foreign Exchanges after the War, which made its final report in 1919, is excused for insisting upon Britain's early return to the gold standard at the old parity, because at that time the economic effects of the war in inflation and in distortions of trade were not apparent. But those who followed might have recognized that the business of the world was too relaxed to be braced in that fashion.

Other countries which returned to the gold standard admitted in one way or another that their action was partial. They borrowed abroad for the purpose, or sharply devalued their currencies, or both. The international gold standard was reinvoked rather than revived. Circulation of gold coins disappeared, and countries took pains to avoid internal conversion of their paper currencies into gold. Such measures afforded illusory protection against the real dangers. These lay in the maldistribution of gold throughout the world and failure of this condition to correct itself because huge blocks of debt were political rather than commercial. Deflation was hindered by price and wage rigidities introduced by cartels and unions. While the gold-exchange standard economized the metal, it laid the scanty central hoards open to raids from countries which fell into difficulties. It is not surprising, in the uncertainty of the times and under the prevailing pressures, that the new gold values assigned to currencies were in some cases too high and in others too low. But this made maintenance of the international exchange system awkward and tentative. Also, though men might pretend that this refurbished gold standard would control in the old automatic fashion, it was clear that this was no longer possible, since gold itself had been subjected to deliberate management.[2] Demonetization of silver combined with other factors to produce the spectacular decline in the value of that metal from more than 7s. an ounce in 1920 to 1s. in 1931.

Imperfect as was return to the gold standard, it combined with an increase in postwar productive capacity to bring a fall in com-

[2] See the excellent account in H. V. Hodson, *Slump and Recovery, 1929–1937* (New York: Oxford University Press, 1938), pp. 13 ff.

modity prices. The results were unfortunate. Countries producing raw materials found that the demand for their products was inelastic and did not increase as the price declined. This inelastic demand was largely because, with the improved standard of living in industrialized countries, the character of consumption had changed to embrace relatively fewer staples and more luxuries and services. Wheat might be cheaper, but the worker with more real wages wanted not more bread but a motorcar, a radio, travel, or a permanent wave. Overproduction of primary materials called out experiments in price control, governments taking the initiative to improve the value of copper, grain, cotton, rubber, diamonds, coffees, and oil, usually by restricting the supply. Substitutes came forward, output was stimulated by any rise in price, but no scheme could long quarantine one commodity against world deflation.

Overproduction of raw materials was matched by surplus output, or surplus capacity, in important industrial fields. High tariffs and other expressions of economic nationalism were the consequence. Governments were ever readier for such interference in economic life. Momentum gained during the war was increased in the efforts at reconstruction. Alliance between business and government, and, after depression struck, between unemployed and government, was prepared.[3]

WORLD DEPRESSION

The easy-money policy of the Federal Reserve System after 1925, intended to turn back the flow of gold from Europe to the United States, was mainly responsible for the speculative rise in the stock market. The collapse of that market in October, 1929, is ordinarily taken as the beginning of the world depression. In fact, however, the speculative boom had obscured downward tendencies in production and prices of manufactured goods and raw materials. In the United States construction had fallen off from the summer of 1928. Distressed farmers had been clamorous for years. Elsewhere in the world stock prices began to decline months before the decline began in New York. Even without the market crash in the United States, industrial recession, deflation of prices, and financial strains that

[3] See League of Nations, Economic Intelligence Service, *Memorandum on Production and Trade, 1925 to 1929–30* (Geneva: 1931).

Europe found ever harder to meet would soon have made economic decline evident.

Following the stock market break, degenerative forces which had been latent became active. Stock prices everywhere fell on the signal from New York, with bond prices to follow after a period of resistance. Production, commodity prices, profits, employment, world trade, and international lending all dropped away. Sharp reduction of interest rates and release of huge sums from the stock market could not give borrowers credit or lenders confidence.

The comfort which was taken, especially in the United States, in relative business improvement early in 1930 and again in 1931, had little excuse. In 1930 in the United States, Britain, Germany, France, and Italy, some 6 million were thrown into unemployment. The economic frustration led to political recklessness, most conspicuously to the rise of Hitler in Germany. The false signs of improvement were mocking. They arrested discouragement temporarily, only soon to make it deeper. However, the slump beginning in 1929, making itself felt by degrees, was the preliminary anesthetic that merely dulled the patient before he passed entirely under with the financial crisis of the spring of 1931.

On May 11, 1931, it was announced that the Kreditanstalt, largest bank in Austria, would have to be reorganized to protect the depositors. The dangers to be expected from the collapse of this institution were evident in the aid offered by many agencies—the Austrian government, the national bank, the Rothschilds, the Bank for International Settlements, the Bank of England, and many other central banks. The losses of the Kreditanstalt, which carried such dismal portent for the whole of Europe, ran back to the treaties that had shorn Vienna of her empire. The bank, left in the position of responsibility without domestic resources, had been obliged to borrow heavily in other countries until it owed $76 million abroad, mostly to England and the United States. Failure of the Kreditanstalt meant the failure of Central Europe; the financial strain was communicated everywhere because important banks must bring home other foreign assets to compensate for funds tied up in Austria. Repercussions were political as well as economic, awakening French suspicion of Germany and English suspicion of France.

Though the customs union of Austria with Germany had been forbidden, the two were linked in credit weakness. Promptly, Germany became the second victim of European panic, for she had run deficits for six years. In spite of heavy withdrawal of foreign loans, Germany still owed debts, short term and long term, on which the service was beyond her exertions when to it were added reparations, making in all $800 million annually. Germany's industry was depressed, political discontent was rising. Foreign creditors drew out of Germany two fifths of her gold, $230 million worth. Extraordinary devices to allay alarm only excited it higher. President Hoover's proposal of a year's moratorium on all intergovernmental debts arising from the war came in the nick of time, June 20. But even so, France delayed consent for dangerous weeks while the largest central banks poured $100 million into Germany. The end was not yet. Failure of a large industrial enterprise (North German Wool Combing Corporation) dragged down its chief creditor, the Darmstädter und Nationalbank ("Danatbank"). This failure roused the government and the Reichsbank to measures of protection of the banking system as a whole that anticipated in many ways the emergency banking legislation of the New Deal in the United States two years later. A bank holiday, restriction of bank payments to the most necessary items, monopoly of foreign exchange, and maximum mutual assistance between German banks could not prevent further bank failures before the situation improved in August. A legacy from the crisis, however, was control of foreign exchange by the Reichsbank in such a way as to favor some imports and hamper others.

Bank failures spread to Rumania and Hungary, requiring extraordinary measures on the part of those governments. German banks remained in a parlous state even after restrictions on them were removed, and German weakness was reflected in financial attacks on Amsterdam, which had loaned heavily in Germany. To cover losses, Amsterdam drew heavily on London.[4]

Britain now paid an undeserved penalty for having tried to bolster the economy of Central Europe. She had loaned to Germany in the spring at long term, herself borrowing from France and the United States at short term. At a time when Britain could not liquidate foreign assets, when her export trade and earnings from shipping were down, when public commissions of inquiry revealed

[4] For all these developments, see League of Nations, *Commercial Banks, 1925-1933* (Geneva: 1934).

that a balanced budget could be achieved only at risk of deepening the depression, withdrawal of gold from the London market became strong and persistent. Something very like mutiny in the navy, started by announcement of pay cuts, was all the touch that was needed to turn impaired confidence into frank panic. The Bank of England used its utmost resources to support the pound. A National Government was formed, sinking political differences in the resolve to reassure a frightened world by a solid front.

DEPARTURE FROM GOLD

At the end of August, New York and Paris made emergency loans to the British Exchequer, but when these were almost exhausted, further frantic appeal to the same quarters brought sympathy only. Since the middle of July more than £200 million had been taken from London, and the day when the Bank of England could no longer meet the drain was clearly approaching. Nothing was left but for the Prime Minister, Ramsay MacDonald, to beseech the world to preserve its own interest and England's honor by forbearing to drain off the last of the gold. His pleas were unheard. On September 21, 1931, England left the gold standard and private purchase of foreign exchange was forbidden.[5]

Within six months, of the principal countries only Belgium, France, Italy, Holland, Switzerland, and the United States remained on gold. In others, such as Germany, the gold standard was nominal only. The rest, including most of the British dominions, the Scandinavian countries, and those of South America, had followed England to a paper standard. After wide fluctuation, the pound settled at a discount of about 30 per cent. In the United States, the sterling crisis was the occasion rather than the cause of hoarding, an abrupt drop in the bond market, and new bank failures that led to formation of the National Credit Corporation to lend to institutions in distress.

However, the chief effect of Britain's departure from the gold standard was to widen and sharpen tariff wars and competitive exchange depreciation. Hardly had Ramsay MacDonald stopped sobbing over the international radio that Britannia should not be

[5] League of Nations, Economic Intelligence Service, *World Economic Survey* (Geneva: 1931–1932), pp. 77–78.

forced to sacrifice her honor, than he began to smile broadly because the fall of the pound gave her marked advantage in exports. One thought of the country girl who returned from the city with fine clothes that astonished her old friends, explaining, "Why, you know, I've been ruined." Debtor countries that could get no more loans felt they must expand their exports and contract their imports. Invasion of others' markets and defense of their own alternated in speeding restrictions on world trade. Britain entered the lists with the Import Duties Act of March, 1932 (reaching 33⅓ per cent), and the later Ottawa Agreement establishing empire tariff preference spurred other countries in the process of retaliation. Sterling losses of so many countries spread deflation through the struggle for liquidity. The contest between economies that remained on gold and those that had left it became acute. Destruction of the only international exchange standard inevitably accelerated monetary management, which contributed to economic nationalism.

Professor Lionel Robbins has remarked that "the various mercantilist expedients were once again adopted. Tariffs, exchange restrictions, quotas, import prohibitions, barter trade agreements, central trade-clearing arrangements—all the fusty relics of medieval trade regulation, discredited through five hundred years of theory and hard experience, were dragged out of the lumber-rooms and hailed as the products of the latest enlightenment." It was hard to know where economic inducement ended and political motive entered. Exchange control was responsible for more international disequilibrium than were tariffs; it was more eccentric and productive of rigidities that thwarted flow of goods and funds across frontiers. The countries remaining on gold were placed at a disadvantage, and their misfortune limited the gains to be reaped by those which chose to depreciate their currencies. Professor Robbins said as early as 1934, "Whether or not it be welcomed as a solution for certain very pressing domestic problems, no really impartial observer of world events can do other than regard the abandonment of the Gold Standard by Great Britain as a catastrophe of the first order of magnitude." And he went on to ask, "Will European democracy in the form we have known it survive the repercussions it has engendered?" [6]

[6] Lionel Robbins, *The Great Depression* (London: Macmillan & Co., 1934), pp. 114 ff.

Attempts to restore international monetary unity, or at least some workable means of communication, continued to be made for a while, but England's departure from gold was the beginning of the end of any stability. The world of trade and trust was thenceforth to be compartmented until it looked like an egg crate. If England forswore gold reluctantly, others were to repudiate it gleefully. Instead of supporting the national currency when it was suspected abroad, a nation now entered the race for its depreciation.

All obstacles to trade intensified the difficulties of debtor countries in making payment. The Hoover moratorium did not cover other than intergovernmental debts; those of public bodies and of corporations owing to private creditors now became subject to standstill agreements, adjustments of interest, payment in scrip, and blocked currencies. Even in these compromises with creditors, debtor countries tried to incorporate in the concessions means of forcing out exports and of furthering internal deflation. So many national reputations suffered that humiliation became expected, regular, and respectable. Reconstruction loans issued under sponsorship of the League of Nations to Austria and Baltic countries had fallen, in the decade since the first were made, into the same sorry plight as others. The standing of the League was damaged. Charges were that its experts had not accurately estimated ability of debtor countries to pay; had not, in supervising the loans, warned of the necessity of budget economies; and had failed to calculate on the possibility of deep and general depression. The League at length offered advice that came too late. It has been said that the Financial Committee of the League played an important role "in the evolution of a technique of default." [7]

What should be the policy when the Hoover moratorium expired now became the occasion of suspicion between governments. Popular opinion in the United States, ignorant more than anything else, demanded payment of debts owing by allies. President Coolidge had opined, "They hired the money, didn't they?" England was willing to forgive reparations if war debts were similarly expunged. France was afraid that if the Young plan were suspended she would never be able to collect from Germany, and was acutely sensible of the likelihood of being held to accountability, notwithstanding,

[7] Hodson, *Slump and Recovery*, p. 136.

by the United States. In Germany, Chancellor Bruening was earnestly appealing to the world for the wiping out of reparations before his country collapsed utterly into a defiant dictatorship that would be fatal for the family of nations.

DEFAULTING DEBTORS

Talks at London and Basel by progressive concessions prepared the way for the Lausanne Conference, in July, 1932, which scrapped reparations and provided for a closely guarded loan to Germany. The chief reparations creditors refused to ratify until they had reached agreement with their own creditors—which meant, mainly, until the United States dropped claims to war debts. Obduracy in the United States, hardened by this decision, could make no more difference to the situation than the forlorn hope of reparations creditors that they could yet extract their due from Germany. The Lausanne agreement was never ratified but, in the sequel, became nonetheless binding. In December, 1932, only Britain, Finland, Czechoslovakia, Italy, and Lithuania paid the United States their debt installments, while France, Belgium, and four other governments were in default and three more had secured postponements.

Hoover went out of office, and Franklin Roosevelt held conversations with Ramsay MacDonald. The promise of a lenient, or realistic, attitude on the part of the United States toward its war debtors was vaguer than had been given in intimations by the Hoover administration, and resulted, after delay, in American demand for the installment due June 15, 1933. Britain now made a token payment, in silver at an artificially high valuation allowed by Congress, and President Roosevelt announced that he personally did not consider Britain in default. Other governments that had previously paid now used the method of silver tokens, except Finland, which paid in full, in silver. The others defaulted again, though France called her action postponement. The same history was repeated on December 15, 1933, but after this the last pretense of reparations claims and of European solvency (except for Finland) had come to an end. Germany, now under Hitler's control, had passed from financial to political default.

While several multilateral conferences looking to reduction of tariff restrictions and stabilization of exchange proved abortive, agreements between particular countries were more successful. The Ottawa Conference, 1932, ending in a preferential tariff system within the British Commonwealth, partook of the character of both the wider and the narrower efforts. The mutual lowering of tariffs was of benefit to an important group of countries, but whether this helped or hampered recovery of the remainder of the world is a question. One effect of Ottawa seems clear: Britain and her dominions entered the World Economic Conference committed on both of the main issues which came before that gathering. These were general tariff reduction and currency stabilization on the basis of a gold standard. In effect, these devices for restoring the world's economic activity came to be regarded in the conference as alternatives; the British Commonwealth could not, consistently with its own recent conduct, advocate either; hence it advocated both and made confusion worse confounded.

The World Economic Conference had been proposed by the Lausanne Conference which ended reparations, but it was the League of Nations which convoked the larger gathering to consider further means of promoting world recovery.

If the bearing of Britain in the conference was equivocal, intervention of the President of the United States was fatally hostile to the agenda and put an end to the effort. Earlier, when the conference was preparing, it had seemed that the United States would help to remove arbitrary impediments to trade, stabilize exchanges, reform and as soon as possible return to the gold standard, and adjust debts. These had been the assurances from Washington and were the ardent aim of Secretary of State Cordell Hull and his American delegation to the conference. In the middle of May, a month after the United States went off the gold standard, President Roosevelt still approved such objects of the conference as "the stabilization of currencies, the freeing of the flow of world trade, and international action to raise price levels."

However, by the time the conference assembled in London, June 12, 1933, the United States was launched on "New Deal" policies of stimulation of the national economy without regard to, or in opposition to, the rest of the world. The conference had no more than got under way when Secretary Hull presented to the delegates a message from President Roosevelt that was so sharp a lecture as to amount to a dismissal.

Reasons for this turn of President Roosevelt will be explained in describing the course of the depression in the United States. The conference lingered briefly, with no result except an agreement between certain countries for measures to improve the price of silver. The conference had been the effort of a distraught world to restore trade and lending—and so production, employment, and national solvency—by the cherished means of accessible markets and exchangeable currencies. Cooperation of the United States was indispensable to success. It might have failed from other causes, but the United States' choice of a national rather than an international program was the death of the undertaking. As tired and disgruntled statesmen dispersed to their countries it was to devise plans, uninspired except by suspicion or fear, which could not prevent another war.

United States departure from the gold standard, devaluation of the dollar, ample power given the President for inflation, plus the schemes for restriction of output (AAA and NRA), were all expected to raise domestic prices. But the domestic results of monetary debasement were slight. The increase in American prices was not so great as the fall in the value of the dollar on the foreign exchanges. Of course this gave a distinct advantage to American exporters and forced countries on gold to deflationary measures so that their goods could compete with those of America in world markets. Countries not on gold were spurred by the United States in the race for currency depreciation. Perhaps these international consequences were in President Roosevelt's mind when he took the decision to turn from collaboration to isolation. Perhaps not. In any event, from the time of the collapse of the World Economic Conference the centripetal tendencies that it expressed were in the discard, and centrifugal economic motion was pronounced. Each country was looking out for its own interest first, and made agreements with other countries only because joint action was necessary to selfish purpose. Economic war conducted easily to military war.

The United States had led in insistence that the nations most concerned should "do something for silver." The silver-producing states were alert to the chance now presented to increase the demand and the price for silver. Inflation would be served by turning countries toward bimetallism. Countries holding much silver were to limit the amounts they sold, and silver-producing countries were to buy up newly mined silver.

The United States played the most active role in what followed. The artificially high price that the United States maintained for silver forced China by degrees off the silver standard, and both Nanking and Canton governments went on an inconvertible paper basis. Similarly Mexico was forced by the high price of silver to call in all silver coins and give inconvertible paper in return. The silver purchase policy of the United States was futile at home and mischievous abroad.

ECONOMIC AUTARCHY AND REARMAMENT

In the first half of the thirties, the New Deal had its counterparts, more or less complete, in several countries. Restriction of production in some quarters of the economy, encouragement of output in others, raising of some prices and insulation of higher domestic from lower world prices, public works and more direct subsidies were all undertaken by governmental intervention. These efforts in England, Germany, France, Italy, Australia, Canada, and elsewhere were matched by international and national schemes for control of principal raw materials and agricultural products such as rubber, nitrates, tin, copper, oil, wheat, cotton, and coffee. In spite of measures that ranged all the way from mild admonition to the burning of 35 million bags of coffee by Brazil between 1930 and 1935, prices were not always raised nor was national credit always saved. Areas outside the agreements seized the invitation to increase their output, thus adding to the total productive capacity with which the world had to deal later. Brazil had this experience with coffee, the United States with cotton.

While all programs of economic nationalism tended to starve intercountry trade, Germany was most conspicuous, after the National Socialists came into power in 1933, for her autarchy. For her own industry she had to have imports of raw materials, but she paid for these as far as possible in blocked marks; when this treatment caused complaint, Germany turned to reclaiming scrap of all sorts and devised ersatz materials. Much of this effort was uneconomic, though only a trifling by-product of a partitioning of the world which was stultifying. In two countries more than others—Germany and Italy—internal economic betterment hung on the most harmful substitution of large standing armies and munitions factories for the legitimate industries which were lacking.

The countries of the gold bloc—France, Belgium, the Netherlands, Italy, Switzerland—were compelled to deflate as fast as those off gold were able to inflate. But the process was far more painful for makers of state budgets, for businessmen, and for workers. High protectionism and trading agreements among themselves were consequences. When virtue ceased to be its own reward in Belgium, the belga was devalued and the country practically left gold. Italy, facing a situation which was industrial and commercial as well as financial, could not escape from depression by invading Ethiopia, but petulantly threw good money after bad.

France and the other countries of the gold bloc had long endured the penalties of deflations. Restricted budgets, low wages and prices, long hours, defense against imports had been their only means of competing with neighbors that embarked on paper currencies. In 1936 pressure on the franc combined with deeper causes to end the unequal contest. The Popular Front had come into power under Léon Blum, who announced the French equivalent of the American "New Deal," with the forty-hour week, collective labor contracts, assistance for farmers, the aged, and those on small fixed incomes. In a word, the economy was to be released from confinement. For a brief interval credit reflation was the program. But this was abandoned when, September 25, 1936, the French, British, and United States governments announced that the franc would be devalued between 25 and 35 per cent. Every effort would be made to stabilize the currencies of the three countries in relation to each other. Soon the Netherlands, Belgium, and Switzerland adhered to the agreement and took suitable action, Italy devalued the lira, and minor countries in the gold bloc either tied their currencies to sterling or intimated that they might soon do so. Hope had been expressed that the effort to bring currencies closer together in purchasing power would relax trade restrictions and facilitate interchange. Germany kept to her old gold parity, because devaluation would compel her to pay more for raw materials imported, but this parity was nominal, being maintained only by rigid exchange controls.

Exchange equalization funds, built up of the gold "profits" from devaluations, were used to counteract currency fluctuations. Developments in late 1936 and the first half of 1937 seemed to bear out the trust that revival of world trade would bring international and national recovery. The League of Nations *World Economic Survey* could say by the spring of 1937 that confidence and enterprise had been stimulated to the point where "at the present time, economic activity in all but a few countries has definitely passed out of the depression into the boom phase of the business cycle." During 1936 and the early months of 1937 world trade increased in amount and value, but the increase was mostly accounted for by movement of raw materials to industrial countries where manufacturing was revived by rearmament programs. Heavy industry went ahead of raw materials production and of production of consumers' goods. There was a tendency to relax restrictions on movement of raw materials, because the countries producing them were eager to sell and the industrial countries wanted a full supply. However, as revival came, manufactures were further protected. In spite of technological advances, shortages of skilled labor appeared, and the League of Nations *World Economic Survey* in 1937 hoped that countries would get rid of all but the "hard core of unemployment due to special causes." World industrial production reached in 1937 a peak slightly above what it had been in 1929,

But this betterment proved artificial and temporary. A substantial part of it was owing to Russia's advance, which reached an output four times what it had been in 1929, and Russia's economy was no indicator of revival in the rest of the world.[8] World expenditures on rearmament were two to two and a half times in 1936 what they had been in 1933. War was added to preparation for war, Italy invading Ethiopia in 1935, the Spanish "civil" war commencing in 1936, and Japan attacking China in 1937. Britain announced her armaments program in February, 1937. The world never did get out of the depression except through rearmament and war.

RECESSION AND WORLD WAR

Further, revival in the United States, which had reflected itself beneficially to the rest of the world, changed to recession in the

[8] League of Nations, *World Economic Survey*, 1937–1938, pp. 69–72.

late summer of 1937. The American boomlet had been based on government spending, which came to an end with the President's belief that prices had risen unjustifiably; legal reserve requirements of member banks in the Federal Reserve System were raised by 50 per cent in August, 1936, and the first half of 1937; the Treasury sterilized gold by putting its new purchases in an "inactive gold fund"; government securities were sold to reduce deposits. The veterans had about exhausted their $2 billion bonus. Sitdown strikes became epidemic, Europe feared that the United States would lower the dollar price of gold to reduce prices. In March-April, 1937, commodity prices reached their peak. The undistributed profits tax had caused a sudden increase in dividend payments, the lapse of which combined with deeper causes to start a sharp market decline in the United States and in other countries. Widespread industrial recession soon became evident, failure of demand from the United States contributing to the general drop. After the middle of 1937, with both quantity and prices falling, total value of world trade declined seriously, particularly to the disadvantage of countries exporting raw materials.

This fresh depression helped reverse the hopeful tendency toward liberalizing international trade. Raw-material countries retreated from freer trade policies because of the effects of the fall in price of their exports. Restriction schemes that had been relaxed to satisfy the rearmament demand were reimposed, but not in time to prevent the piling up of surplus stocks. In 1937 170 clearing agreements were in force, intended to balance trade between pairs of countries only, and sacrificing much of the benefit of international specialization. Japan, in the autumn of 1937, put quotas or prohibitions on certain nonessential imports in order to conserve exchange for foreign goods made necessary by the war on China. Germany's autarchic Four-Year Plan effectively insulated her against world commercial fortunes, whether in recession or revival. France had never enjoyed recovery. Steady excess of imports over exports and the prospect of rising internal prices and more budget deficits had combined with political and military apprehension to cause a flight from the franc. In May, 1938, the exchange value of the franc was depreciated 10 per cent with the consent of England and the United States. Not till the end of the year, with further devaluation of the franc and easing of internal credit, did business in France begin to improve; nevertheless, production in 1938 was still little more than three quarters of what it had been in 1929.

The most important effort to free trade from quotas and tariffs was that of the United States through reciprocal agreements, sixteen of which, covering one third of American foreign commerce, had been concluded by the end of 1937, with others embracing an equal volume in the stage of negotiation. The beneficial effects of these agreements were spread because they contained the most-favored-nation clause. This policy of the United States strongly influenced the report of M. Paul van Zeeland on means of removing obstacles to international trade, made public in January, 1938, in the midst of the world recession. Reciprocal commercial agreements with the most-favored-nation provision were urged as the best means of restoring activity. Nations should agree not to raise duties, and gradually to lower exceptionally high ones, suppress quotas on industrial goods, and relinquish exchange controls. A return to the gold standard on some basis seemed the best solution of exchange fluctuations, but meantime countries should agree to preserve limits in the movements of their currencies on the exchanges. Restrictions on transfer of funds for imports were most serious impediments to world trade, because these had led to clearing agreements between particular countries. A solution might be found in multilateral clearing of claims falling due in each currency.

These considered proposals, purposeful yet tempered with patience, outlined such a scheme for restoration as perhaps the World Economic Conference would have framed had it been permitted. Intelligent as they were, they came too late, for their peaceful message was overwhelmed by German invasion of Austria and Czechoslovakia, by Polish and Hungarian annexations, and by redoubled military preparations in England and France. The economic drama had nearly played itself out to its warlike denouement.

About the middle of 1938 the recession reversed itself by virtue of resumed public works expenditures in the United States and huge armament orders elsewhere, with further revaluation of monetary reserves. But the fundamental economic derangement of the world was shown in the greater disparities of production curves of different countries after the depression than were evident in the period before 1929. Production increases before the great depression ranged in different countries from 12 to 55 per cent, and after the depression from 14 to 120 per cent, with similar divergence in periods of decline. The economic life of the world was no longer integrated, but had been sundered into jealous, isolated units, or at best into competing empire blocs. Long-term lending by developed countries did not revive; instead, nervous, speculative money flitted from one center to another, seeking hazardous, quick gain.

There was business hesitation, particularly in the United States, in the spring of 1939, but the fortunes of legitimate commerce no longer mattered much. The United States bartered cotton with England for rubber, and soon it was revising neutrality safeguards and entering on its defense program. From this point on, the economic story, the world around, becomes a military one.

It is difficult to review this history of twenty years from Versailles to Warsaw without being convinced that the convulsion of one war led to the tragedy of another. The international economic constitution never sufficiently recovered in all its parts to resist relapse.

CHAPTER I

Descent and Deficit

DEPRESSIONS have characteristically taken the country by surprise; else speculation, the confident counting on continued expansion, would not have marked the preceding phase. The downturn of 1929 was conspicuous in this respect, as the elation which came before was extraordinarily uncalculating. Striking evidence of complacency shortly before the collapse is furnished by the report on *Recent Economic Changes*,[1] made by a committee of the President's Conference on Unemployment. The survey of the years 1922–1929, on which the committee's findings were based, was under the auspices of the National Bureau of Economic Research "with the assistance of an unprecedented number of governmental and private agencies." The underlying investigations were carried out between January, 1928, and February, 1929, and the conclusions of the committee were drawn in the spring of 1929, about six months before the stock market crash and eight or nine months after indexes had shown declines in construction and important heavy industries. The chairman of the committee was Herbert Hoover; other members were leaders in finance, transportation, labor, science, and education.

Though "directed to make a critical appraisal of the factors of stability and instability"[2] and to suggest recommendations, the com-

[1] Conference on Unemployment, *Recent Economic Changes in the United States* (New York: McGraw-Hill Book Company, Inc., 2 vols., 1929), 950 pp.
[2] *Ibid.*, p. v.

mittee showed a nearly complete infatuation with prosperity and the promise of its continuance. "Acceleration rather than structural change is the key to an understanding of our recent economic developments" [3] was the opening sentence of the report, which went on to congratulate the country upon price stability due, among other things, to "prudence on the part of management; . . . skill on the part of bankers . . . and the expansion of foreign markets." [4] An assurance soon to be disappointed was that "with rising wages and relatively stable prices we have become consumers of what we produce to an extent never before realized." [5] Its attention attracted casually to the dips of 1924 and 1927, the committee failed to see that the whole span 1922–1929 was a gigantic upswing, for it reported that "no serious cyclical fluctuations have characterized the period under review. . . ." [6] Technological unemployment was noted but discounted in the general esteem for inventions. The broadening influence of America's creative minds was largely responsible for "the maintenance of our economic balance." [7] Our degree of economic stability was high, and later strophes of the hymn praised "the dynamic equilibrium of recent years," [8] and "the organic balance of economic forces." [9] "Our situation is fortunate, our momentum is remarkable." [10] Hopefully, organic balance of the economic structure would be preserved by persistent, intelligent effort.

The introduction to the essays of the specialists, by Professor Edwin F. Gay, while more mindful of the danger signals, was unaware of impending panic and depression. Dr. Gay spoke of "an increasing professional spirit in business, which springs from and entails recognized social responsibilities." Codes of ethics were helping in the "self-policing" of business. "The strength and stability of our financial structure, both governmental and commercial, is of modern growth." [11] With the wisdom of hindsight one remarks that Professor Gay and those working with him omitted to study the interaction of the American economy and world forces; their scrutiny was too far national. The individual studies of recent changes in important areas of American economic life presented ominous as well as prideful tendencies. But in conferences with the committee, in

[3] *Ibid.*, p. ix. [4] *Ibid.*, p. xiii. [5] *Ibid.*, p. xiv.
[6] *Ibid.*, p. xvii. [7] *Ibid.*, p. xx. [8] *Ibid.*
[9] *Ibid.*, p. xxii. [10] *Ibid.* [11] *Ibid.*, p. 11.

which the disclosures of the studies were discussed, no doubt was inserted into official confidence in the future. Nowhere was there a Joseph to set seven as the number of the fat years.

It is not necessary to give a detailed recital of the stock market crash of October and November, 1929, including a full account of the phenomenal volume of shares traded, the drop in quotations, and the number of hours the ticker ran behind. After the first break in September, October days made records for deluges of selling—over 4 million shares on the New York Stock Exchange on the 16th, over 6 million on the 23rd, almost 13 million on the 24th, nearly 16.5 million on the 29th; the highest number of shares poured out on any day in November was less than 8 million on the 13th. In a few weeks of "the greatest stock market catastrophe of all the ages," some $30 billion in supposed values disappeared.[12]

The stock collapse may be called the exciting force of the depression. It was merely the spectacular signal of the end of the "New Economic Era" of the prosperous twenties. But the determining cause, or causes, of hard times lay deeper. The business cycle is a continuum, and it is a mistake to regard high or low points on a chart as beginnings. The fever is reaction from the chill, but both follow from the organism that has lodged and is regenerating in the system. In this instance chief responsibility may be ascribed to World War I, with its international and national results. In the world at large were credit, trade, and currency derangements, intensifying and exaggerated by the ambitions of new and old countries. Political demands were blended with economic policies.

If national signs may be separated, the United States as a result of the war became a creditor that at once required and refused the only practicable means of payment. Her protective tariff, with consequent drain of gold from Europe, must bear heavy blame. The troubles of staple agriculture followed, and communicated themselves slowly but surely to the entire economy. Accompanying were technological improvements on farm and in factory that made for instability, evident in warning dips in the business curve in 1924 and 1927. Unheeded warning was in the sudden increase of unemployment. In various ways, prosperity was forced from about

12 See New York Stock Exchange, *Report of the President,* 1929–1930 (New York: 1930) and New York Stock Exchange, *Year Book,* 1929–1930 (New York: Committee on Publicity, 1930).

1926, convenient proof lying in the growth of consumer credit through installment sales. A further influence was the low interest rate maintained by the Federal Reserve Board, with international motive better than the result at home. Withdrawal of funds loaned in Europe brought in its train a proliferation of investment trusts and the last and most specious phase of prosperity—mounting stock market speculation. Ironically, this overlapped with the sag in the index of general industrial production between May, 1927, and June, 1928,[13] from which building construction, with its many connections, did not recover; bituminous coal and cotton textiles, though basic, were disregarded as chronically depressed. But this summary touches upon only the most prominent features, to the neglect of many that would make plainer the evil interaction of forces.

STOCK MARKET COLLAPSE

The first impact of the depression was less sudden and pronounced on industry and business generally than in the stock market, where the blow fell with concentrated force. This fact, coupled with partial though temporary recovery of stock prices early in 1930 and aided by wishful thinking, led many, from President Hoover downward, to believe that basic progress was to continue, and that trouble had been confined to securities speculation, where liquidation, though severe, was probably salutary. We may see first what happened to stocks, and then to business broadly, in the final quarter of 1929.

The index of security prices compiled by the Standard Statistics Company (1926 = 100) showed a movement of a group of 404 stocks from 183.6 in January, 1929, to 225.3 in September, the peak, with a fall to 153.8 in December.[14] The course of 337 industrials was from 191.4 in January to a high average of 216.1 in September to 146.9 in December. For 33 rails, the history was 141.0 in January, 168.1 in September, and down to 136.0 in December. Public utilities figured conspicuously in the market; 34 of these went from an average of 188.3 in January up to the peak of 321.0 in September, and fell off

[13] *Federal Reserve Bulletin*, XV, No. 3 (March, 1929), 191.
[14] *Ibid.*, XVI, No. 1 (January, 1930), 14. For shrinkage in dollar values see U. S. Senate, Banking and Currency Committee, Report on Stock Exchange Practices, 73 Cong., 2 Sess., p. 7.

to 200.9 in December. In the case of each group of stocks, the quotation for December 28 was lower than the average for the month. Naturally bonds, with fixed interest return, had a contrary trend, 40 issues falling steadily from an average price of $96.12 in January to a low of $92.29 in September, and recovering to $94.09 for December. Rates on new call loans in the stock exchange reached the monthly peak of 9.80 in March, averaged 8.62 in September, fell to 6.10 in October, and further to 4.88 in December.

A corollary of the decline in stock prices was the shrinkage in brokers' loans. Loans on securities by member banks in leading cities, after rising from $6 billion to $7 billion in 1927, and gaining a half billion more in 1928, reached the peak of over $9 billion about November 1, 1929.[15] The *Federal Reserve Bulletin* for December commented: "After the recent liquidation security loans still showed a large growth during the past year. The growth was not in loans to brokers, however, but in security loans to others, chiefly customers who had transferred their borrowings from brokers directly to the banks." All other loans showed a constant growth from February, most rapidly during November. The increase after the middle of October, $300,000,000, was contrary to the usual seasonal trend, and included, besides loans for commercial purposes, a variety of investment operations.[16]

A spectacular decline in the volume of funds loaned by member banks in New York City to brokers accompanied an even greater liquidation of brokers' loans for the account of nonbanking lenders; $3,450,000,000 on loan to brokers and dealers November 27, 1929, represented a reduction of almost half, as compared with the maximum ($6,634,000,000, October 23), being back to the level of two years earlier.[17] About 60 per cent of this decrease occurred in loans for nonbanking lenders, which decreased $1,840,000,000 in the five weeks after October 23, but were still $1,420,000,000 above January 6, 1926. As was true of member banks in the country generally, those in New York increased the volume of their credit as they took over the loans of nonbanking lenders, the total funds used in the security market decreased by a large amount, and the credit situation improved—a result which continued for a time to be reassuring.

Issues of domestic corporate securities, exclusive of refunding,

---

15 *Federal Reserve Bulletin*, XV, No. 12 (December, 1929), 758.
16 *Ibid.*   17 *Ibid.*, p. 756.

had increased steadily from $3,332,000,000 in 1924 to $6,015,000,000 in 1928, and then shot up in the first ten months of 1929 to $8,130,-000,000. Miscellaneous issues, including those of investment trusts, in 1927 had been only $883,000,000, in 1928 were $1,577,000,000, and in the first ten months of 1929 were $3,396,000,000.[18] Investment trusts were the principal single factor in the growth of total security issues in 1929, particularly in the later months; they were also a source of brokers' loans for the account of nonbanking lenders, since the trusts loaned on call at the high interest rates of early autumn 1929 part of the funds they had obtained from the public through sale of their own securities. Thus investment trusts figured doubly in the speculative rise. When security prices fell, investment trusts withdrew some of their funds from the call loan market to use in buying securities at lower prevailing prices.

The country's stock of gold had increased by $250 million during the first ten months of 1929, mostly through imports; it began to decline at the beginning of November, following the break in the stock market and with the comparatively more attractive money rates abroad, and at the end of December had been reduced by $100 million.[19] The Federal Reserve Board's wholesale price index for all commodities (1926 = 100) dropped from 97.2 in January, 1929; went up to 98.0 in July; fell to 94.4 in November.[20] The index of industrial production (1923–25 = 100) fell from 117 in January, rose to a peak of 126 in June, fell to 106 in November.[21] Production in basic industries decreased 9 per cent in that month, standing at a point 5 per cent lower than a year before.[22] Prior to November, the decline in production that began in midsummer was confined to industries which had expanded rapidly earlier in the year, such as iron and steel, automobiles, and rubber. But in November came declines also in copper, cotton and wool textiles, shoe manufacture, coal, petroleum, and building contracts.[23] Carloadings in November showed a more than seasonal loss.[24] Decrease in factory pay rolls and in physical volume of production were larger than the decrease in factory employment. Department store sales, adjusted for seasonal variation, fell from 123 in September to 108 in November.[25]

[18] Ibid.
[20] Ibid., p. 37.
[22] Ibid.
[24] Ibid., p. 15.

[19] Ibid., XVI, No. 1 (January, 1930), 1.
[21] Ibid., p. 15.
[23] Ibid., p. 16.
[25] Ibid.

WHISTLING IN THE DARK

Public statements at the New Year on the business outlook for 1930 damaged more reputations of forecasters than they bolstered. In the midst of the stock market debacle two months earlier, prominent persons whose word was apt to be taken—bankers, industrialists, economists, government officials—had declared their confidence in stocks, not to mention underlying business soundness. At the beginning of the year more perspective might be looked for. The optimism expressed, however, was hardly representative, for most of those with serious misgivings about the future did not offer their opinions or find them published. Secretary of the Treasury Andrew W. Mellon committed himself blithely: "I see nothing . . . in the present situation that is either menacing or warrants pessimism. . . . I have every confidence that there will be a revival of activity in the spring and that during the coming year the country will make steady progress." [26] The White House reported the President as considering "that business could look forward to the coming year with greater assurance." [27] Willis H. Booth, president of the Merchants' Association of New York, saw "no fundamental reason why business should not find itself again on the up-grade early in 1930." [28]

The Guaranty Trust Company of New York expressed qualified hope: "Although there is no failure to appreciate the importance of the collapse of stock prices as an influence on general business or to ignore the historical fact that such a collapse has almost invariably been followed by a major business recession, emphasis has . . . been placed on certain fundamental differences between the conditions that exist at present and those that have usually been witnessed at similar times in the past." Inflation in stocks had not been matched by an advance in commodity prices. It was recalled that there had been no crucial credit strain, though this assurance disregarded expansion of federal reserve credit in the last quarter of 1929 by half a billion dollars and the lowering of the discount rate to 5 per cent and then to 4.5 per cent to prevent deflation from bringing down the banks. There was little accumulation of inventories, though "the most important factor in the present business recession was over-production in the most important industries.

[26] *Commercial and Financial Chronicle*, XXX, No. 3367 (January 4, 1930), 21.
[27] *Ibid.*   [28] *Ibid.*, p. 24.

. . . The movement of stocks registered an effect rather than a cause of this condition." Commodity markets were not glutted. This, it might have been remarked, was more apparent than true, for wheat had fallen 17 cents a bushel and cotton $7.50 a bale during October, and the Federal Farm Board had made loans on these staples to prevent panic among farmers. The Guaranty Trust feared the Greeks though bearing gifts: "The vigorous measures undertaken by the Government to combat the downward tendency in business have also injected an element of uncertainty. . . . Never before have public agencies interceded in such a direct and intensive way to alter the course of business, and the results [are] necessarily unpredictable."[29]

Secretary of Commerce Robert P. Lamont contented himself with listing the gains that the year 1929 as a whole had registered over 1928, and with predicting prosperity and progress "for the long run."[30] He did not say how long the run was to be. Carl Snyder, speaking to his colleagues of the American Statistical Association, was wisest in concluding: "What repercussion the collapse will have upon the industry and employment of the country remains to be seen."[31]

FLUCTUATIONS DURING DEPRESSION

A profile of the depression is well supplied in *The New York Times* "Weekly Index of Business Activity," adjusted for seasonal variation. The component series are carloadings; steel, electric power, automobile, lumber, and (beginning with 1938) paperboard production; and cotton mill activity. The estimated normal, rather than any one period of years, is taken as the base, or 100. The index uses only figures of physical volume, thus avoiding distortions caused by price fluctuations.[32]

The high point in 1929 was reached in the week ending June 29, when the index stood at 114.8. Though this was closely approached more than eight years later (for the week ending August 14, 1937, the index being 111.2), and was virtually equaled soon after the outbreak of World War II (week ending November 18, 1939, being 113.7), the peak of business activity was not actually regained until

---

[29] *Ibid.*, p. 21.   [30] *Ibid.*, pp. 20–21.   [31] *Ibid.*, pp. 56–57.
[32] See *The New York Times* (January 2, 1942).

after the middle of November, 1940. We may speak, then, of the course of business as revealed in this index in the whole intervening period of eleven years and four months.

Without an attempt to describe or to explain the relatively minor ups and downs, it may be said that there were three major trends of roughly equal duration. The first was a fairly steady decline for three years and nine months, until the low point was reached on March 18, 1933, with the index at 63.7. The second phase, covering three years and ten months, was that of apparent recovery, to the middle of August, 1937. The third period, three years and three months in length, began with precipitate "recession" becoming irregular improvement. Thus, in terms of topography, the traveler through the depression went down a long, tolerably smooth hill to the bottom of the valley, then climbed a slightly longer and considerably rougher hill on the other side until he had almost regained his original height. Here he fell over a precipice, dropping to a new valley floor lower than any he had experienced since the end of 1934, the index being 79.6; from this depth he toiled upward again, through exceedingly broken country.

Three lesser movements, while incorporated in the larger ones, had characteristics that call for comment. The first was what President Hoover and his party contended was the beginning of true recovery in the summer of 1932, when the index went from 66.2— or two thirds of normal—on August 6, to 73.8—or about three fourths of normal—on January 7, 1933. According to this version, the election of Roosevelt and the fear that he would abandon the gold standard broke the uptrend and dipped the curve downward to the new low of March, 1933. Nothing can be proved one way or the other. A somewhat similar upward movement had occurred in the first four months of 1931, when Hoover was in the middle of his term, and yet half the whole decline came after this propitious sign. Other and greater rises, with subsequent falls, occurred under the New Deal. For example, the curve of business activity in September, 1934, after a marked climb, sank below where it had been almost a year before and, indeed, back to its position early in 1932.

The second of these partially distinct movements came on the heels of the first. It was the sharp and continuous upswing immediately after the New Deal took over, from 63.7 in the middle of

March, 1933, to a peak of 93.4 in the middle of July, only to fall again by early November to 76.5. This was the longest unbroken improvement in the whole history of the depression, and one of the most precipitate drops. The movement was associated with the prevalent hope and resolve ushered in with the new administration, and particularly with the speeding of industry in anticipation of the higher costs that NRA would soon impose. The decline from the peak activity registered roughly the degree of this anticipation or forcing.

The third movement, which began in the middle of May, 1939, when European armament orders became heavy, rose from 91 at this time to almost 100 at the outbreak of war at the beginning of September, reached the top, 113.4, at the end of December, and then lost, in a similarly short period, all the gain since the war started. The fall was temporary, for the ascent began immediately and continued. The figure reached by the index the week of the attack on Pearl Harbor was 132.7. However, even then, be it remembered, the United States still had some 4 millions unemployed.

PUBLIC PURSE FLATTENED

The course of the depression, and of governmental policy toward it, may be accurately read in the public finances of the period. The federal gross debt increased between 1930 and 1941 from $16 billion to $58 billion.[33] The depression did not strike the Treasury instantly. In the fiscal year July 1, 1929—June 30, 1930, the debt was reduced by $745 million. However, this year marked the close of a decade in which Treasury surpluses had permitted debt reduction. This prosperity had brought the debt down from the 1919 peak of $26 billion by more than $10 billion, or to 60.9 per cent of the top figure.[34] The portent of the depression penetrated slowly to men's minds, even where observers were in the most responsible official and business positions and had every aid of experience and information. President Hoover, in his budget message of 1929, considered that "with an estimated surplus of over $225,000,000 this year and $122,000,000 next year, it is felt that some measure of reduction in

[33] *Statistical Abstract of the United States, 1942* (Washington: Government Printing Office, 1942), p. 237.
[34] *Ibid.*

taxes is justified." [35] And Francis H. Sisson, Vice-President of the Guaranty Trust Company, New York, said with what afterward appeared as restraint, "Some doubt has arisen as to the ability of the Treasury to maintain the rate of debt retirement that has been shown during the last decade." [36]

In December, 1930, President Hoover was not disturbed by the "moderate deficit for the current fiscal year," explaining that it was mostly due to world-wide depression accentuated by expenditures made necessary by relief at home. He proposed temporary borrowing that could be absorbed with recovery. [37] At the end of that fiscal year (June 30, 1931), the debt was more than $616 million larger than the year before; most of the last reduction had been wiped out. The main cause of the increase in debt was decline in revenues, which were $3,189,639,000 as compared with $4,177,942,000 in the fiscal year 1930. [38] Income and profit tax receipts had fallen 23 per cent and custom receipts 36 per cent. [39]

The next year, 1931, President Hoover thought the country's finances would do well, with prudence, to hold their own:

> It will not take much to exhaust the expected surplus. . . . This is not a time when we can afford to embark on any new or enlarged ventures of Government. It will tax our every resource to expand in directions providing employment during the next few months upon already authorized projects. . . . The plea of unemployment will be advanced as reasons for many new ventures, but no responsible view of the outlook warrants such pleas as apply to expenditures in the 1932 Budget. I have full faith that in acting upon these matters the Congress will give due consideration to our financial outlook. I am satisfied that in the absence of further legislation imposing any considerable burden upon our 1932 finances we can close that year with a balanced Budget. [40]

The gloomy prospect for the fiscal year 1932 was partly due to the moratorium on intergovernmental debts which President Hoover had proposed in the summer of 1930 but which was not officially accepted until August, 1931. This cut Treasury receipts by about $250 million. France lost $175 million; Britain $80 million. Germany,

[35] U. S. President, Message . . . transmitting the Budget for the Service of the Fiscal Year ending June 30, 1931.
[36] *American Year Book, A Record of Events and Progress, 1930* (New York: D. Appleton-Century Company, 1931), p. 167.
[37] . . . Budget . . . 1932, p. xviii.   [38] *Statistical Abstract*, 1942, p. 195.
[39] *Ibid.*   [40] . . . Budget . . . 1932, p. xix.

of course, was the chief beneficiary, with a saving of $427 million
at no sacrifice. For a short time comfort was taken in the provision
that the suspended payments were to be made over a ten-year period (July 1, 1933–July 1, 1943) with interest at 3 per cent, but
Hoover and Laval realized there might have to be postponement
because of the continuance of the depression.

In December, 1931, Hoover tried to explain how an estimated
surplus of $30,000,000 in the previous year's budget became a deficit
then estimated at $2,123,000,000 [41] and which at the end of the fiscal
year (June 30, 1932) turned out to be $2,473,000,000.[42] Receipts had
fallen below expectations because of the severity of the depression;
expenditures had increased by $355,000,000 above Hoover's esti-
mates of the previous year. He thought not enough taxes could be
imposed to balance the budget in 1933, but perhaps a balance could
be achieved in 1934.[43] In 1931–1932 Congress received sixty mes-
sages from President Hoover, a third of which urged strict economy.
On May 31, 1932, he addressed Congress in person, begging it to
reduce expenditures, pass needed revenue legislation, and—in accordance with his recent conversion—provide for relief against the
distress of unemployment. "In your hands at this moment," he reminded solemnly, "is the answer to the question whether democracy
has the capacity to act speedily enough to save itself in emergency." [44]

The most important measure this year was the creation of the
Reconstruction Finance Corporation (approved January 22, 1932)
with government-subscribed capital of $500,000,000; it was at once
set up with Charles G. Dawes at its head. After long wrangling, the
home loan banks were begun with $125,000,000 from RFC, the
Federal Farm Loan System was allotted $125,000,000 of new capi-
tal, and $2,100,000,000 was appropriated for relief and public
works, $1,800,000,000 of this amount being used to expand the
capital of RFC.[45] Hoover urged that $200,000,000 be saved by an
administrative consolidation that eliminated useless bureaus, and
something was accomplished, though less than he hoped. At the
close of the fiscal year June 30, 1932, the gross debt of $19,487,-
000,000 represented an increase of $2,685,000,000 over the year

[41] *Ibid.*, 1933, p. vi.   [42] *Ibid.*, 1934, p. vii.   [43] *Ibid.*
[44] *The New York Times* (June 1, 1932), p. 12.
[45] *American Year Book*, 1932, p. 194.

before.[46] The greatest single cause of the deficit was the drop in receipts. Total receipts for the fiscal year 1932 were only $2,005,000,-000 as against $3,189,000,000 in 1931 and $4,177,000,000 in 1930. The increase in expenditures was smaller than the decrease in receipts; they were $4,885,000,000 for 1932 as compared with $4,-091,000,000 in 1931 and $3,994,000,000 in 1930. The budgetary deficit for the fiscal year 1932 was $2,880,000,000 as compared with $901,959,000 for 1931.[47]

ECONOMY ENJOINED

In January, 1932, Hoover appealed again for retrenchment, saying, "We cannot squander ourselves into prosperity." He called for balancing the budget for the fiscal year 1933. Mellon and Mills, of the Treasury, in describing a few days later their plans for more income and less outgo, revealed that higher income tax rates, lower exemptions, and excises were in their minds. The government could make its best contribution toward prosperity by putting its own house in order. In the ensuing bitter budget struggle in Congress, the administration charged legislators with incompetence; they answered that the President showed no leadership.

When, in December, 1932, Hoover came to transmit his budget for the fiscal year ending June 30, 1934, he was hopeful that the worst of the depression had been passed, and that 1934 would be as good a year as 1929. Continuation of the federal gasoline tax and enactment of a manufacturers' excise tax would balance the budget. He exhorted as before: "I can not too strongly urge that every effort be made to limit expenditures and avoid additional obligations not only in the interest of the heavily burdened taxpayer but in the interest of the very integrity of the finances of the Federal Government." [48] He was in his third deficit year. Economies he projected for the fiscal year 1934 would, to be sure, find him out of office, but there is no reason to question the sincerity of his proposal that appropriations be cut some $830,000,000; "unavoidable increases" of $250,000,000 would make the net reduction $580,000,000. Much of the recommended decrease was in federal salaries and in benefits to

46 *Statistical Abstract*, 1942, p. 237.
47 *Ibid.*, pp. 195–196.
48 . . . Budget . . . 1934, p. xvii.

veterans. The President did not favor public works to stimulate employment, thinking self-liquidating projects financed by RFC were sufficient.[49]

But this was the "lame duck" session. The scene was one of utter futility. A Congress partly rejected was besought by a President wholly repudiated to enact measures unequal to the crisis. Politics was blamed for the procrastination, but perhaps it was as well that power, along with responsibility, be reserved for the incoming administration. The gross public debt at the end of this fiscal year, June 30, 1933, was $22,538,000,000 as against $19,487,000,000 the year before.[50]

NEW DEAL DEFICIT FINANCING

In sketching the fiscal operations of the New Deal it is useless to try to compare depression public finance under Hoover and under Roosevelt, for the two periods were different in duration and in policies. A few rough generalizations, however, may be made. Hoover incurred deficits mainly from falling revenues; Roosevelt was to experience rising revenues, but had deficits because his expenditures mounted yet higher. Hoover tried to cure the depression by parsimony in government, Roosevelt by public promotion of business. Hoover—although much could be cited to the contrary—bled the patient, while Roosevelt offered blood transfusions. One believed in negative, the other in positive remedies.

From the time Roosevelt assumed office in March, 1933, to the attack on Pearl Harbor the gross direct debt of the federal government increased from $20,935,000,000 to $55,040,000,000.[51] The gross is used rather than the net figures because important unrealized assets of the Treasury, such as funded bonds of foreign governments, were in fact unrealizable, and unexpended funds in the general account seem to have resulted from appropriations in excess of even the enormous requirements. The New Deal, whether by way of excuse or conviction, embraced the doctrine of deficit financing. This was in some sense as old as Hamilton, to go no farther back,

[49] *Ibid.*, p. v.
[50] *Statistical Abstract*, 1942, p. 237.
[51] *Federal Reserve Bulletin*, XX, No. 1 (June, 1934), 355; *ibid.*, XXVIII, No. 1 (January, 1942), 47.

but had currently sprung from John Maynard Keynes in England and had ardent advocates in this country. Deficit financing, for many of the New Deal, was not simply accepted as a necessary evil, but became, at such a time, a normal instrument of public policy. In any event, to these, deficit financing was not the reproach, not to say the heresy, that the National Economy League and others of similar orthodoxy declared. Government expenditure in excess of current income and accumulated revenue found fiscal sanctions. But support was brought to the device by the whole principle which invested the New Deal: government must take a creative part by invigorating and supervising the economy. So this financial method, though important for itself, was part and parcel of the strategy that had been adopted.

Yet Roosevelt made a concession to the older habit of mind by separating, beginning with his first budget, "regular" from "extraordinary" expenditures. The regular were, of course, for the maintenance of customary civil functions, while the extraordinary or special expenses were those incurred because of the peculiar needs of the depression. The argument was that military disbursements in time of war were always regarded as separable, and that the present emergency in the economic life of the country justified a similar practice. Of course, the President's Republican opponents, and a conservative faction among the Democrats, disputed the existence of an emergency. Also, the argument was weakened in proportion as the nation found itself in a "permanent emergency." Indeed, as time wore on, President Roosevelt himself transferred certain objects of expenditure from the extraordinary to the regular category—such as public works and the Civilian Conservation Corps—urging that these would be needed for a long period or indefinitely. If the distinction between usual and special expenses had as its design to persuade the people that the budget was being balanced, it failed in that purpose. The division might stand in the Treasury accounts, but not in the public mind. The Director of the Budget, Lewis W. Douglas, must have flinched later at his part in the "double budget," but he did say, justly, that "the test of a balanced budget is whether or not there is an increase in the national debt." [52]

The New Deal in the beginning incurred less deficit than Hoover

[52] *American Year Book*, 1933, p. 215.

had encountered toward the end of his term. In the opening five months of the New Deal's first fiscal year, the deficit was $772,465,-000 [53] as against $1,151,000,000 in the opening five months of the previous fiscal year under Hoover. Excluding emergency expenditures, the New Deal in this period came within $79,638,000 of balancing the budget.[54] In this period the Roosevelt agencies had not begun to spend. The National Economy League, however, saw with alarm what was coming, petitioned the President to balance the budget, and foretold that without a mighty effort the public debt would increase by $4 billion in the fiscal year 1934.[55] Small economies accomplished by reorganizing governmental departments were far more than offset by the new alphabetical agencies that were to spend billions.

The Economy League was restrained in its forecast. The deficit on June 30, 1934, was $6,631,240,000, giving an increase in the public debt of $6,141,297,000; the whole debt then was $27,053,000,-000.[56] The main spending agency at that time was RFC. By January, 1935, Roosevelt had restored to federal employees the final 5 per cent of the 15 per cent pay cut that had been made to redeem the economy pledge in his 1932 platform. That of 1935 was called the "Ten Billion Dollar Congress," and enemies complained of "the administration's profligate spending policy." Representative Roy O. Woodruff of Michigan calculated that the $8,851,069,000 appropriated for the fiscal year 1935, with the sums appropriated in the current session, made a sum greater by $1.5 billion than was spent by the United States in the 124 years from Washington to Wilson. On February 8, 1935, Roosevelt signed the work relief bill for $4,880,-000,000. In his next radio "fireside chat" he tried to still outcries in numerous quarters by explaining to the people that this huge sum was necessary to put to work 3,500,000 employables then on the relief rolls. To say that public works offered real jobs was more amiable than accurate.

Expenditures in the fiscal year 1935 for all sorts of "recovery and relief" amounted to $3,068,803,053.20. Of this, relief took $1,906,-230,820.53 and public works $1,020,411,840.50. Under relief, the

[53] *Statistical Abstract*, 1935, p. 162.
[54] *Ibid.*
[55] *The New York Times* (December 18, 1933), p. 1.
[56] *Statistical Abstract*, 1935, p. 201.

Civilian Conservation Corps received $435,508,643.05. Aids to home-owners amounted to $103,554,093. RFC received $135,384,933.[57] In spite of this volume of spending, Treasury operations in 1935 were smooth in the main. In April Secretary of the Treasury Henry Morgenthau, Jr., said that the average interest rate on all government securities in the hands of the public was only 2.86 per cent, and that the interest cost of the public debt was $800,000,000, or less than when the debt was $8 billion smaller in 1925. In the six months thereafter the interest rate fell to 2.57. There being few private capital issues, government securities offered the chief means of investment.

DEEPER INTO DEBT

In this period there were very few months in which the debt did not increase. The main reason for the fact that the deficit in 1936 was larger than ever was the order to pay immediately, over what was held to be the "not very vigorous protest" of the President, the veterans' adjusted service certificates; this gave the Treasury an additional burden of $1,673,500,000, without which the deficit would have been about equal to that of the two previous years.[58] Despite the loss of processing taxes on farm products in the fiscal year 1936, revenues continued to increase because of high taxes and improvement in business; income taxes, for example, brought 35 per cent of the revenue as against 29 per cent in 1935.[59] The editor of *The Annalist* looked forward to a federal revenue of more than $7 billion in the fiscal year 1938, though Roosevelt had warned that any such result must depend on the continuing expansion of business "at the present rate," which many thought impossible. In December, 1935, *The Annalist's* index of business activity was 92 per cent of normal; in November, 1936, it was 107.5 per cent. In December, 1935, the Bureau of Labor Statistics' index of factory employment, adjusted for seasonal variation, was 89 per cent of the 1923–1925 average; in November, 1936, it was 96.4 per cent. The factory pay rolls index in the same period went from 78.2 to 90.6. RFC was getting increased repayment of its loans. In spite of this improvement, or helping to account for it—depending on one's point of view

[57] *Ibid.*, p. 170.   [58] *Ibid.*, 1937, pp. 165–167.   [59] *Ibid.*

—federal spending on WPA and relief hardly diminished to the end of the year 1936.

No long-term bonds were maturing until the end of 1941. The Treasury had handled its problems well, including the soldiers' bonus. Changes had occurred in the form of the debt. The percentage of the debt represented by bonds declined, 1930–1936, from 75–80 per cent to 55–60 per cent.[60] Notes had formed 17 per cent when Hoover left office, but were 31.4 per cent at the end of 1936. Certificates of indebtedness dropped to a fractional percentage under Roosevelt, but bills went up from 3.1 per cent, when the New Deal took office, to 6.4 per cent by the close of 1936. At that date bonds aggregated $20,500,000,000, notes nearly $11,000,000,-000, bills $2,200,000,000.[61] The interest-bearing total was $33,700,-000,000. The average yield of Treasury bonds fell, January, 1935—December, 1936, from 2.83 per cent to 2.27 per cent.

The budget for the fiscal year 1938 provided for a decrease of about a third in recovery and relief expenditures, increases in costs of the "regular" government departments, and a billion for national defense. The social security taxes, which began to be collected in January, 1937, were eagerly calculated by the Treasury to yield about $300,000,000 that year and about $774,000,000 the next year. The President thought that with "regular" expenditures of some $6 billion he might "balance the budget." [62] He may have been persuaded to this promise partly by the fact that interest rates, while continuing phenomenally low, were higher in the last half of 1936 than in the corresponding period of 1935. But less subtle forces were at work upon him. Business, which had been abjectly grateful for federal subventions, direct and even indirect, when the depression was deeper, was resentful of the primary role that government had assumed in the economy, and smarted under high business taxes, especially that on undistributed profits.

The premature optimism of the President and his advisers was a factor of equal importance. In his budget message, January 5, 1937, Roosevelt, with some precautions, was prepared to turn over to business the responsibility for continuing recovery,[63] while government would concern itself with forwarding social justice, mindful of the still unanswered challenge—as the President expressed it—of "one

[60] *Ibid.*, p. 200.   [61] *Ibid.*
[62] . . . Budget . . . 1938, pp. v–vi.   [63] *Ibid.*, p. vi.

third of a nation ill-nourished, ill-clad, ill-housed." But recovery had gone beyond the need for further pump priming; the emergency was over. There were to be dismissals from the relief rolls, canceled commitments of RFC and PWA were to be eliminated, RFC was to make no new commitments, farm subsidies should be reduced, and certain agencies erected in the crisis were to be discontinued. The President did want from Congress $1,500,000,000 to carry relief through the fiscal year 1938, he asked for extension of PWA for two years, and CCC was to be made permanent. The buying of gold and silver went on.

Secretary Morgenthau underlined the call for economies in relief and recovery charges, saying that the budget could be balanced only "by focusing attention on the several classes of expenditures that have been mainly responsible for our past deficits, namely, public highways, public works, unemployment relief and agriculture. . . ." However, the President warned that balance would not be achieved at the expense of necessary relief. Business must speed up employment. "This government does not propose . . . to allow American families to starve."

Total expenditures in the fiscal year 1936 were $8,476,000,000; in the fiscal year 1937 they dropped to $8,001,000,000. The deficit in 1936 was $4,361,000,000; in 1937 it was down to $2,708,000,000. The increase in federal government receipts in the fiscal year 1937 over the previous year must have encouraged the President to conclude that the "spend-lend" program had accomplished his purpose. The figures were $4,116,000,000 in 1936, and $5,294,000,000 in 1937.[64] The individual income tax in 1937 produced a billion, the corporate income tax another billion, and by this time social security taxes were seventh in order of proceeds.[65] Early in 1937 the Treasury had felt obliged to bolster prices of government bonds by federal reserve and trust fund purchases, because, with the improvement of business, banks had increased their commercial loans and sold government bonds. The Federal Reserve Board, fearful of commodity price inflation, raised reserve requirements of member banks. The budget message of January, 1938, declared that deficits must be reduced, since the income of the government was so high. But by this time the country was in a business relapse, which had begun in

[64] *Statistical Abstract,* 1938, pp. 171–173.
[65] *Ibid.,* p. 181.

September, 1937, in which all the declines, particularly in employment, were unprecedentedly swift. This was a slap in the face of
official optimism, a rebuke to the boasts of businessmen that they
could take over if only government would withdraw. The recession
discredited New Deal policies. The administration was at a pause.

RECESSION AND RENEWED SPENDING

So far as public finance was concerned, there was a brief span
in which to decide on the next policy. During the second half of
1937 and the first quarter of 1938 the Treasury lost no revenue from
the business depression, though afterward taxes and customs yielded
less. The social security payments were increasing, and in April,
1938, the general working balance received $1,200,000,000 released
from the inactive gold funds. Similarly, in the nine months following June, 1937, federal expenditures were much reduced. The actual
increase in the gross public debt in the fiscal year 1937 had been
$2,647,000,000, while in the fiscal year 1938 it was only $740,000,-
000.[66] Appropriations for WPA declined from $689,000,000 in the
first quarter of 1937 to $495,000,000 in the first quarter of 1938;
almost $80,000,000 was lopped from the agricultural adjustment
program, though $40,000,000 more was spent for defense.

However, in the last nine months of 1938 there was a spirited
return to heavy government spending in the attempt to lift the
country out of the new depression. WPA, in the last six months of
1937, had cost $1,019,000,000, but in the same period of 1938 its
cost rose to $1,502,000,000, while expenditures for AAA went up
almost four times. Extraordinary expenditures in the fiscal year
1938 (ending June 30) had been $1,996,000,000, but in his budget
message in September, 1938, the President estimated for this category an expenditure of $2,741,000,000 in fiscal year 1939 and $2,-
019,000,000 in fiscal year 1940. The net deficit for the last six months
of the calendar year 1937 was only $607,000,000, while for the last
six months of 1938 it was almost six times as large. Chairman Marriner S. Eccles of the Federal Reserve Board defended public spending as the means to business prosperity, and the President considered
an increase in national income more important than reduction of
deficits.

[66] *Statistical Abstract*, 1942, p. 368.

The President banked heavily on new military expenditures. The year before, in a speech in Chicago, he announced that international anarchy compelled the nation to abandon its position of isolation and "statutory neutrality." He urged a quarantine of "aggressor nations," and the next day the State Department branded Japan as an aggressor and treaty violator. The United States had done little or nothing to hinder Mussolini in Ethiopia or Germany and Italy in Spain. Now the growing arrogance of Hitler and the East-Asia presumptions of Japan undoubtedly stirred Roosevelt to preparation. But, as his policies to meet the nation's domestic misfortunes unfolded, it is hard to escape the conviction that an excuse for growing defense spending was welcome. The defense cost in the fiscal year 1938 had been $980,000,000; for the next fiscal year this was estimated to rise to $1,017,000,000, and for 1940 to $1,126,000,-000. Ever since 1931 the nation had been spending on military maintenance and preparations almost a fifth as much ($5,876,000,000) as the government got in taxes ($30,844,000,000) in that period. During the calendar year 1938 the interest-bearing direct debt increased by $2,200,000,000, and the outstanding obligations of federal agencies increased by $350,000,000. By the beginning of 1939 the direct debt was $38,889,000,000, and, in addition, the total of guaranteed obligations of government agencies was $4,992,000,000.[67]

The administration, in its revived spending policy, did not have the same support of the people, if one could believe the polls of public opinion, as it enjoyed in 1934. Now most persons considered the spending to be excessive.

Ever since the refunding of the First and Fourth Liberty Loan bonds in 1935, the Treasury had been able to make greater use of long-term securities, and the absolute and relative volume of outstanding notes and Treasury bills declined. The interest rate on the public debt fell to new low levels in 1938, because of refunding, an influx of gold, and the absence of competition from private capital issues. The average interest on the whole debt at the end of 1930 was 3¾ per cent; at the end of 1934 it was 3 per cent; and it continued to fall to between 2½ and 2⅝ per cent at the end of 1938. Decline in interest rate was most spectacular on short-term obligations. The rate of 3–5 year Treasury notes went down steadily from a high

67 *American Year Book*, 1938, pp. 218–222.

of 1.59 per cent reached in April, 1937, to 1.13 per cent in January, 1938, and to 0.67 per cent in December of that year. Between April, 1937, and December, 1938, the interest rate on new issues of Treasury bills declined to one seventieth of the former level, the average for December, 1938, being at the yield of .01 per cent.[68] On two issues of 90-day bills the government had offers to buy the bills at a slight premium, i.e., the interest rate was negative, or the Treasury was paid to borrow. Protracted deficit financing had its dangers, but, after a long trial, rise in the interest rate was not among them.

The table below shows distribution among the holders of the total public debt, direct and guaranteed, by types of investors, at different dates:

HOLDERS OF PUBLIC DEBT, VARIOUS DATES

	June 30, 1930	June 30, 1935	June 30, 1938
Total obligations	$15,138,000,000	$31,033,000,000	$38,316,000,000
Holdings of member banks	7.6%	12.3%	9.8%
Holdings of all commercial banks	36.3%	46.0%	43.6%
Holdings of Federal reserve banks	3.9%	7.8%	6.7%
Holdings of U. S. government agencies	1.3%	4.3%	5.5%
Holdings of life insurance companies	1.7%	6.0%	10.3%

Source: *American Year Book*, 1938, p. 224.

At the end of the period over half the debt was held by banks. Toward the end member banks increased their holdings less rapidly than the debt increased, but the reverse was true of nonmember banks and mutual savings banks; life insurance companies and government agencies were taking over the debt at a rapid rate.

A letup after four years of full federal spending had shown that the government was rewarded not with exit from the depression but with plunge into a "recession." President Roosevelt was not deterred from resuming the old method. Early in 1939 he said defiantly in his budget message: "We have been buying real values. . . . The greater part of the budgetary deficits that have been incurred have gone for permanent tangible additions to our national

[68] *Ibid.*, p. 225.

wealth. The balance has been an investment in the conservation of our human resources, and I do not regard a penny of it as wasted." [69]

DEFENSE AS OBJECT OF SPENDING

The year 1939, in public finance, marked a continuance of the policies of 1938; large spending went on, with a good part shifted from work relief and aid to youth into defense. In the fiscal year 1939 revenue decreased, the deficit increased ($3,542,000,000 as against $1,384,000,000 in 1938), and the gross public debt grew from slightly more than $37 billion to almost $40.5 billion. However, public borrowing was easier than ever, average yield of long-term bonds being down to 2.35 per cent. Life insurance companies increased their holdings of government obligations by more than a billion dollars.

The defense program began in earnest in 1940, claiming expenditures in the fiscal year of $1,579,000,000, though work relief still received a larger amount ($1,861,000,000) and aids to agriculture were $1,375,000,000. Receipts were slightly larger than in the previous year, because of business improvement and better yield of income taxes. Government spending was the largest in the decade, $9,127,000,000; the deficit was larger than in the past year; and public grumbling against relief expenditures, particularly for youth, was loud and persistent.[70] The gross debt at the end of the fiscal year 1940 was $43,000,000,000. A few months later the Secretary of the Treasury urged that the debt limit be raised by Congress, a meaningless procedure since continued at intervals while the debt increased to six times what it was at the beginning. In addition to the figure for the debt given above, the guaranteed obligations of the Federal Farm Mortgage Corporation, HOLC, RFC, Commodity Credit Corporation, and so forth, added another $5,528,000,000, though there were offsetting assets for much of this. Though many government agencies borrowed, others loaned to the Treasury, or bought the debt; such were old-age insurance, unemployment compensation, and civil service funds, the postal savings system, and Federal Deposit Insurance Corporation, which in a decade absorbed about $6 billion of public securities. Holdings of the debt by banks,

69 . . . Budget . . . 1940, p. x.
70 *Statistical Abstract*, 1942, pp. 195–196.

insurance companies, and federal agencies accounted for three
fourths of it by the middle of 1940. The average yield on long-term
bonds declined to $1.89, the average price being $111.8. The rate
of interest on new Treasury bills was negative.[71]

Opposition to the accumulating public debt had all along been
vigorous, not to say defamatory. That most of it was contracted to
restore business seemed to make no difference with business critics.
The part spent to save lives and to rescue self-respect and skills had
even less excuse in the minds of objectors. All such expenditures
drew concentrated fire and continuous sniping. There is every reason to believe that the real protest was not fiscal, but broadly economic and political in character. It wore thin to keep proclaiming
that disaster would overtake the Treasury, while private financing abdicated, and interest rates on public loans fell as the debt
increased. The true fear was that government, intervening in the
crisis, would weaken the claims of the system of private enterprise.
What began as succor to private business threatened to supplant it.
The most powerful elements in private industry and finance being
attached to the Republican party, and those which were Democratic choosing to speak through the anti-New Deal faction of
their party, did nothing to reduce the onslaughts on administration
spending. All of these groups, however, were now in a hopeless case.
When the government reduced spending in 1937 and invited private business to take over, the economic collapse was spectacular.

Of course, the answer was given that the large spending of
the middle thirties and the piling up of the deficit, along with the
undistributed profits tax and other distasteful fiscal policies, had
alarmed and oppressed business to the point where it could not
function. But this argument, as election results kept on showing,
was not convincing to most people. Besides, there were the millions
of unemployed, who could not be banished by any sophistry, to be
cared for. Still, the die-hards clamored.

But little or no protest arose from these quarters when far larger
deficits were run up for war. The economy cry was stilled; those
who had viewed with alarm now saw with approval. Food for the
nation's destitute had been dangerous, but eggs, milk, meat, fats for
faraway peoples seemed the part not only of tenderness but of wisdom. Bread was cast upon the waters with a cheer, though it gave

[71] *American Year Book,* 1940, pp. 251, 254.

small promise of ever returning. Those who had been so insistent upon a *quid pro quo* for government spending seemed to have lost all sense of accounting. The relief that had been given by FERA and WPA now looked petty and its managers parsimonious. The United States would provision a great part of the world, and never reckon the cost. Building of schools had been condemned as extravagant, but bombers, for all the dollars and lives they took, were approved. Money to clear slums had been deprecated, but money to devastate distant cities was eagerly voted. Digging cellars under Farm Security homes had been called extravagant, but shell holes pocking ten thousand countrysides were all right. Salvage of democracy in America, through measures of health, education, recreation, and purposeful work had been heinous, while defense of doubtful democracy around the world, though with every engine of destruction, was called merciful.

In his budget message to Congress in January, 1941, the President said that total expenditures in that fiscal year, ending in June, would be $13,202,000,000; in the following twelve months they would be $17,486,000,000. The expected gross deficit in 1941 to be financed by borrowing was $6,290,000,000; the next year it would be $9,310,-000,000—this deficit alone being larger than all expenditures a short two years before.[72] These modest amounts, soon to be exceeded, were heard without a flinch.

DEFENSE DEFICITS ACCEPTED

Why were the arts of peace so narrowly questioned, and the arts of war given such license? Why did the sharp pencils that had tried to pare deficits in the domestic betterment phase turn suddenly to great brushes that splashed much bigger debts on the nation's books? To be sure, threat to survival as a people bore its part, though conviction of that came more slowly than votes for defense appropriations. Also, there was an interval in which American business as a whole drew back from the prospect of war preparations, wondering whether its last case would not be worse than its first. But these doubts, which may have been prudent, soon passed. It was seen that the new government spending was not for the purpose of building up a market by the uncertain means of enlarging the purchasing

[72] . . . Budget . . . 1942, p. xvii.

power of underpaid workers and indebted farmers. The indirect methods of reviving the economy had been abandoned. Here was demand—immediate, enormous, uncalculating. The vexing problem of consumption was solved by prodigious destruction. The whole tortuous system of securing profits by drawing the dimes and the dollars of ill-provided and fickle citizens was to be short-circuited.

Spokesmen of property and profits and the price mechanism, who had been so critical of the relatively orthodox efforts of the New Deal to reanimate the economy that they defended, were now avid for abandonment of the old rules. Where is the money coming from? The echoes of that ancient, anxious query died in the shouts of "Aye!" for mounting deficits. Moreover, patriotism was as convenient a cover for fiscal heresy as it was for political jealousy. Republicans could stand shoulder to shoulder with Democrats in promoting munitions and not lose face. Indeed, any tardiness of the President in preparing the country for war was turned to the uses of party reproof. Roosevelt's political opponents pointed out with asperity that planes and ships "on order" could not fight battles.

Further, the mere magnitude of the new defense spending was exhilarating. The old broken homeopathic doses of the New Deal had been disapproved as slow and debatable in effect. But the new therapy would drench with the drug. The tablespoons of mild teasing stimulant had provoked complaint from the patient, but here business was given in its hands the quart of whisky, the gallon, the barrel, and invited to get drunk. The fatigue of the long depression, with its hope deferred, had prepared the cautious for a spree.

In any comment on the conversion of critics to the virtues of defense deficits, the primary part of the administration itself must not be forgotten. The President before long was to announce that the New Deal was dead, and that the war economy had taken its place. Some doubted whether the chief devices of the New Deal were so much discarded as put to magnified uses. It was a bitter saying sharply resented by the President that the New Deal, which had plowed under crops, was now intent upon plowing under young men, but the sting of the allusion was not solely in its spite. Artificial scarcity had been a specific of the New Deal. But try as it might to frustrate potential plenty, efforts had been in vain. Now the President laid firm hold on all the mightiest weapons of destruction.

High purposes that had nothing to do with the mean matter of recovery? Yes, that was declared and believed.

What remains of the outline of the nation's public finance from the onset of the depression to the attack on Pearl Harbor may be told briefly. The fiscal year 1941 was the first full year of the defense program. The depression had been so deep and prolonged, and the recession was so recent, that general economic conditions did not improve markedly at once, even in response to large new armament orders. Still, business apprehension for the reasonable future was over, for all knew that surplus stocks would be wiped out and expanded streams of production would be required. Total receipts of the government were $8,269,000,000, or $2,345,000,000 more than in the previous fiscal year. Of total expenditures of $12,775,000,000, the sum of $6,301,000,000 was for defense. Work relief still claimed $1,451,000,000, aids to agriculture $1,094,000,000, and aids to youth $347,204,000. The gross deficit in the fiscal year was $5,167,000,000, and the public debt became $48,961,000,000.[73] Whereas the calendar years 1938 and 1939 had shown increases in the public debt of about $2 billion, 1940 showed nearly $3 billion, and 1941, to the end of November, over $9 billion, to the total of $55,040,000,000, not including more than $6,370,000,000 of guaranteed debt of federal borrowing agencies.

However, reservations current in certain important business quarters were expressed by the *Guaranty Survey* for November 25, 1940:

Not only are the foreign orders very large and the demands of our own defense program rapidly increasing, but the prospect of capacity operations in strategic industries for some time to come has led to a wave of forward buying in anticipation of possible shortages, priorities and price advances. Activity of this kind obviously can not be regarded as constituting a normal business recovery. Huge expenditures for war equipment designed, not for production but for destruction, however necessary such outlays may be at times, can represent only an economic burden in the long run. And inventory accumulation by private business can not continue indefinitely. Already the prospect of new taxes and new borrowing to meet the staggering cost of defense is taking shape.[74]

[73] *Statistical Abstract,* 1942, pp. 197–199.
[74] Quoted by permission of the publishers.

RESPONSE IN HEAVY INDUSTRIES AND EMPLOYMENT

When government launched the defense program, industry was decrepit, investment expanding little in spite of the encouragement offered by public spending for relief and other purposes. New corporate financing in 1940 continued in the stagnation of the previous five years, having fallen to less than half the amount of 1936 and 1937 and to a mere fraction of that of 1929.

From federal reserve figures, increase in the production of certain war items was marked and in the next year became spectacular. Comparing October, 1941, with the same month of 1940, one notes that the index of iron and steel production increased from 172 to 191, locomotives from 160 to 378, tin consumption from 109 to 166, beehive coke production from 266 to 413, textiles from 123 to 151, leather 107 to 121, bituminous coal from 98 to 127. There were large increases in other lines, while production of automobiles, plate glass, and other items fell, because of the interference of priorities. The federal reserve index of total industrial production (1935–1939= 100) rose from 130 in October, 1940, to 168 in December, 1941.

From autumn of 1940, when effects of defense production showed themselves, employment rose steadily. By October, 1941, advances were apparent in nearly all important lines, the index of employment having increased in a year in iron and steel from 116 to 138, machinery production from 126 to 179, transportation equipment from 139 to 201. At the same time that employment and pay rolls were expanding in war industries, "priorities unemployment" was temporarily conspicuous in some important consumer goods industries. The Bureau of Labor Statistics' index of factory employment showed a steady upward trend in 1941 in both durable and nondurable goods. The average for all manufacturing in 1939 (1923–1925=100) had been 99.9 and for 1940 was 107.5; in January, 1941, the index stood at 115.5, by June had climbed to 127.9, and in October was 135.1.[75]

In the second year of the defense program, half of which turned out to be a war economy, it was expected that there could be only limited contractions in nondefense expenditures, while in the following year there would be substantial reductions in public works, work relief, and aids to agriculture, in order to prevent inflation, if

[75] *Federal Reserve Bulletin*, XXXVIII, No. 1 (January, 1942), 58; *ibid.*, No. 2 (February, 1942), p. 156.

not because of war production demands. The President, in his 1942 budget message, said: "Total receipts from existing tax legislation will triple under the defense and war programs. They are expected to increase from 6 billion dollars in the fiscal year 1940 to 18 billion dollars in the fiscal year 1943. . . . As we approach full use of our resources, further increases in revenue next year must come predominantly from new tax measures rather than a greater tempo of economic activity."[76] One cannot help remarking on the prevalent notion that destruction of resources was considered use of them.

The Lend-Lease Act of March 11, 1941, and the Ship Warrants Act of July 14 completed preparation for official commercial and financial controls, "which during 1941 developed into a closely integrated mechanism of economic warfare."

American merchandise exports in 1941, through November, were $4,492,000,000, and imports in the same period were $3,002,000,000, making the total value of the nation's foreign trade the largest since 1929. [Lend-lease and not gold inflow made possible the export balance of almost $1,500,000,000. Exports to Axis and Axis-controlled countries fell to low levels by 1941, British gold reserves were exhausted by the end of 1940 and British-owned American securities were being rapidly liquidated.] In 1941 some $450,000,000 of British-owned securities were pledged for a generous RFC loan of $425,000,000. The net gold inflow in 1941 was below $1 billion. American exports shifted from the Continent of Europe to the United Kingdom. In the first nine months of 1940 goods worth $581,000,000 were shipped to the Continent, but in the same period of 1941 only $117,000,000 worth went to that area. Assets in America of all Continental countries were frozen in the middle of June, 1941. American shipments to Japan, particularly of petroleum and scrap to be used in the war against China, had continued after the nation had assumed its role as the arsenal of democracy. However, shipments to Japan came to a virtual standstill with the freezing of Japanese dollar assets on July 26, 1941, following the Japanese occupation of French Indo-China. Before that date these most important war exports had been embargoed. Exports of the United States to Japan, January–September, 1941, were $58,000,000 in value compared with $165,000,000 in the same period of 1940.[77]

[76] . . . Budget . . . 1943, p. xi.

[77] Amos E. Taylor, of U. S. Department of Commerce, in *American Year Book*, 1941, pp. 393–395.

In the first nine months of 1941, American exports to the United Kingdom were $1,024,000,000, compared with $698,000,000 in 1940 and $370,000,000 in 1939. Exports to Canada, January–September, 1941, were $875,000,000, as against $511,000,000 in the same period of 1940 and $336,000,000 in 1939. To a greater or less extent American exports increased to Egypt and South Africa. The trade of the United States with Latin America, particularly the former's imports, grew rapidly, and government agencies made large loans to enable Latin-American countries to hold surpluses that would otherwise have been a loss because of the British blockade of the Continent of Europe, or would by some means have reached the Axis powers.[78]

By the end of November, 1941, when lend-lease was getting under way, the value of lend-lease actual exports was only $710,-000,000, though total lend-lease aid—including building and repair of ships, training of airplane pilots, and the like—was $970,000,000. By this time, however, lend-lease appropriations already amounted to nearly $13,000,000,000. Before December 7, 1941, over $7,265,-000,000 of lend-lease funds had been allocated for the manufacture of arms and ships, and nearly $800,000,000 for new facilities. The lend-lease administrator reported "this stimulus to United States war production was in addition to British, French and Dutch munitions orders placed before the passage of the [Lend-Lease] Act and totalling over $3,000,000,000, paid for in cash."[79]

[78] *Ibid.*, 1941, p. 394.
[79] U.S. Lend-Lease Administration Office, *Report on Lend-Lease Operations, March 11, 1941, to December 31, 1942* (Washington: Government Printing Office, 1943), pp. 9, 15.

CHAPTER II

Hoover's Depression Policies

FOR a year after the depression struck, President Hoover seems to have had no other notion than that our hard times were engendered by our own economic recklessness. Then he began to speak of overproduction of staples in other countries as having led to foreign slump and decreased demand for American exports. There was world-wide depression, but at this stage he felt that measures being taken for American recovery would help extricate the others. His optimism in early months of the depression is well remembered; some said later that he was naïve and self-deceived, others that he was disingenuous in minimizing the destructive forces in order to save the credit of his administration. In any event, it was not until the depression not only failed to show natural recuperation or to yield to remedies adopted, but deepened, that President Hoover laid blame for American misfortunes at the door of foreigners.

Accusing this country first was what was to be expected. The initial crash was here. Hoover took too long to see that the stock market debacle was leading into industrial stagnation, but it is to be remembered that nearly all shared his surprise at the collapse of speculation, and that few, for months afterward, would admit the dismal sequel in general economic breakdown. His substantial fault was in not recognizing, after most others did, that the American depression started the active contagion, and that American high tariff policy spread and intensified it and delayed world recovery.

President Hoover's first theory of the depression—that it was

55

homemade—was typically expressed in his first annual message to Congress, December 3, 1929. Apologists have said that he "reviewed . . . the economic situation in a very restrained manner, in order not to alarm the country."[1] The President assured Congress that "during the past year the Nation has continued to grow in strength. . . . The problems with which we are confronted are the problems of growth and of progress."[2] He dealt with foreign relations, national defense, government finances, tax reduction, foreign debts, and alien enemy property, before coming to the stock market crash, the "hesitation" in business, and the threatened serious unemployment. His description of this major development was: "The long upward trend of fundamental progress . . . gave rise to over-optimism as to profits, which translated itself into a wave of uncontrolled speculation in securities, resulting in the diversion of capital from business to the stock market and the inevitable crash. The natural consequences have been a reduction in the consumption of luxuries and semi-necessities by those who have met with losses, and a number of persons thrown temporarily out of employment. Prices of agricultural products dealt in upon the great markets have been affected in sympathy with the stock crash." He referred to the planned expansion of public construction, and to the encouragement he had given to voluntary efforts of business, saying that by these means he was convinced that "we have re-established confidence," and that "the measures taken must be vigorously pursued until normal conditions are restored."[3]

By the time Hoover addressed the American Bankers Association, October 2, 1930, he was shifting part of the blame to untoward economic events in other countries: "This depression is world-wide. Its causes and its effects lie only partly in the United States. Our country engaged in overspeculation in securities which crashed a year ago with great losses. A perhaps even larger immediate cause

---

[1] William Starr Myers, and Walter H. Newton, *The Hoover Administration, A Documented Narrative* (New York: Charles Scribner's Sons, 1936), p. 33. With the permission of Herbert Hoover.

[2] William Starr Myers, ed., *The State Papers and Other Public Writings of Herbert Hoover* (New York: Doubleday, Doran & Co., 1934, 2 vols.), I, 138.

[3] *Ibid.*, pp. 145, 146. This account of the collapse showed little progress beyond the President's public statement on the heels of the spectacular market declines, October 25, 1929, that "the fundamental business of the country, that is, production and distribution, is on a sound and prosperous basis."—Myers and Newton, *The Hoover Administration*, p. 23.

of our depression has been the effect upon us from the collapse in prices following overproduction of important raw materials, mostly in foreign countries. . . . These major overexpansions have taken place largely outside of the United States. Their collapse has reduced the buying power of many countries" and resulted "in slowed-down demand for manufactured goods from Europe and ourselves, with inevitable contribution to unemployment." Then he went on in hopeful vein: "Because the present depression is world-wide, does not require that we should wait upon the recovery of the rest of the world. . . . We are able in considerable degree to free ourselves of world influences and make a large measure of independent recovery because we are so remarkably self-contained. Because of this, while our economic system is subject to the shock of world influences, we should be able, in large measure, to readjust ourselves. . . . Any forward movement in our recovery creates a demand for foreign raw materials and goods and thus instantly reacts to assist other countries the world over." [4] From this intermediate position—partly of national self-reproach, partly of accusation of outsiders—he went on in later months and years to place whole responsibility, at least for continuance of the depression, upon happenings abroad against which this country had little or no defense.

President Hoover, as will be seen in later pages, did much, through domestic measures, to allay the effects and even to reverse the course of the depression; as indisputable need dictated, he more and more laid aside his inhibitions for direct, forthright government action. His policies, explicit and implied, came closer to the program of the New Deal than has been generally recognized. And he was more mindful of the need of international treatment of the depression than the New Deal was. A number of features caused Hoover's attack on the depression to fall short, in success and in public acclaim, of that of his successor in the White House. One cause was his double concern with domestic and with world recuperation. Roosevelt, after a brief interval in which it seemed that he would throw his force into the World Economic Conference, abandoned international responsibility, even disparaged it by fostering nationalist devices, though not without the face-saving afterthought that a prosperous America would do most to produce a prosperous world. Later the reciprocal trade agreements partly repaired the damage.

[4] *Hoover State Papers,* I, 376, 377.

But Roosevelt placed the task on a simpler basis than Hoover was ever willing to allow himself. The progress of events, here and in Europe, had played their part in the New Deal decision. Yet the fact was there, and it gave the New Deal a tactical advantage which is not to the discredit of the Hoover administration.

AMERICA'S PART IN WORLD DEPRESSION

President Hoover was elected as the possessor of precisely the qualities which the swift-ensuing depression belied. He was "the great engineer" who in the Commerce Department had promoted the efficiency of American business. He was the "great humanitarian," having fed the Belgian babies and the peoples of the Near East. In his case it was prestige which goeth before a fall, but with some mixture of pride too, for he had boasted of the early abolition of poverty, had heralded two chickens in every pot, and, even with his own failure upon him, predicted direr days for the country if his opponent should become President.

The depression, bringing business disruption and consequent suffering for millions, was not Hoover's fault. But shocked, confused, distressed people are not given to scrutiny of economic history, and find that to blame a discredited leader is simpler and more satisfying than to reflect on the way the world has been wagging. The contrast between prosperity under Coolidge and collapse under Hoover was too patent to be far out of mind. It was most natural, therefore, that Hoover should try to shoulder off responsibility for the national misfortune. He could not put the onus on conduct of the country during the two previous administrations without indicting his party and himself, for he had sat in those carefree Cabinets. His initial protest was that the depression was a luckless illusion, a bad dream. Then when it was clear that the woeful signs were no conjured phantasmagoria, but a waking, horrid reality, he groped for excuses until he hit upon the plausible plea that the depression, engendered outside the United States, had spread to it in a worldwide contagion. His stress upon international forces in the cause and continuance of the depression undoubtedly owed something to his long residence as a businessman and administrator in many foreign countries. To a greater extent than any other American president he had firsthand knowledge of the world economically.

In all of his mining operations Hoover had never followed a vein more eagerly than this one of exculpation which referred the depression to foreign causes. This line had its strategic advantages, it being easier to assure the people that they had been victims and take station as their defender than to tell them that they had been vicious and deserved to be reformed. For the time being, if an explanation short of the truth was to be found, this one—that the depression came upon the United States from without—served tolerably. However, there were refutations at hand from the beginning, and they accumulated and crystallized as statistical proof. After a decade and a half, the evidence against Hoover's contention seems conclusive. America was far from innocent in the inception and fostering of the world depression.

This is not to go to the other extreme and say that America was solely at fault. Without going to remoter origins, blame may be placed upon World War I, from which disorganization followed inevitably. The opening review in this volume of interwar years must make this apparent. World war brought in its train much else that belonged to the world, and no longer to individual countries. After that general upheaval, particular national economies might be wiser or more reckless, but all were involved together in uneasy revival and in certain descent. Connected causes, elaborately and fatally contingent, bound them all. The American stock market crash in the autumn of 1929 precipitated the world depression about in the sense that one more man climbing onto a crowded raft sinks it, but the weight of previous comers must not be forgotten.

A study by the Department of Commerce [5] has ascribed many of the world's economic and political troubles to depression in the United States and to its behavior before and after 1929. The falling off of industrial production abroad came at about the same time as in the United States, but was more gradual. As compared with 1929, the decline in the United States was greater and lasted longer than in other countries. By the last quarter of 1930 American industrial production was 26 per cent below the 1929 average as compared with a drop of only 13 per cent abroad; by the last quarter of 1931 American decrease from 1929 was 40 per cent and that abroad only

[5] Hal B. Lary and associates, *The United States in the World Economy: The International Transactions of the United States during the Inter-War Period* (Washington: Government Printing Office, 1943).

21 per cent. By June–August, 1932, this country had dropped 51 per cent below the 1929 level, but industrial production abroad was only 31 per cent below 1929. These were the low points. However, the revival which commenced abroad in the autumn of 1932 proved to be steady, while that of the United States was interrupted and retarded. Even in the Central European countries, the worst hit of those abroad, industrial production did not drop as rapidly as in the United States. The depression did not reach its deepest in Germany, Austria, Poland, for example, until these countries had been subjected to severe external financial and monetary pressure. The Scandinavian countries had no depression to compare with that in America.

In contrast to the case of the early twenties, the United States did not recover quickly and so could not serve as a source of capital and of goods. When depression struck the United States it prolonged and complicated bad times throughout the world. American loans to Europe and South America in the twenties were lavish and reckless, and accustomed foreign countries to levels of consumption which required a continuing volume of foreign exchange. The international lending function demands, in its way, quite as much responsibility as the borrowing function, and the United States had never sufficiently counted the consequences of the creditor position. Americans felt that it was their privilege to lend when they liked, withdraw when they chose. Thus, when their own stock market became so attractive, they suddenly reduced foreign lending in the middle of 1928 and, except for some reopening of their purse in the first half of 1930, discouraged foreign flotations thereafter. New issues for foreign account rose to $1,114,000,000 in 1927, were still $1,019,000,000 in 1928, then fell to $415,000,000 in 1929, recovered to $775,000,000 in 1930, dropped to $190,000,000 in 1931, and to $51,000,000 in 1932. After 1929 the power of the United States to lend was lessened, and her citizens would not lend what they could because of defaults and other discouraging developments abroad; instead, after 1931 they repatriated loans.

RESTRICTED IMPORTS LESSENED DOLLAR EXCHANGE

Not only did the United States fail to furnish dollars which the world needed, in the form of loans and investments, but she shortened her payments by contracting merchandise imports. From $4,399,000,000 in 1929 these fell to $3,061,000,000 in 1930, to $2,-091,000,000 in 1931, and to $1,323,000,000 in 1932. In the four years 1926 through 1929 America furnished foreign countries, in new investments and purchase of goods and services, from $7,300,000,000 to $7,500,000,000 a year, which sustained foreign incomes and stabilized the debt structure. Then in three years following 1929 the supply of dollars declined by 68 per cent. To illustrate more sharply how the rest of the world was put on short rations, the United States supplied in 1929 some $7,400,000,000, but cut this supply by 1932 to $2,400,000,000, or a reduction of $5,000,000,000. During these years the dollars required to meet fixed debt-service payments to the United States were $900,000,000 each year. Deducting these payments from the dollars which Americans supplied, foreigners had available for other purposes in 1929 the sum of $6,500,000,000, but in 1932 had only $1,500,000,000.[6]

Since European nations clung to the gold standard, they were obliged to meet external demands with internal economies which were at first rigorous and then became ruinous. As to this deflationary pressure, the Commerce Department study judged that "while in many countries the immediate force was exerted by the wild flight of capital, the basic strain emanated largely from this country's crippled economy and the drastic cut in the supply of dollars." To escape, countries depreciated their currencies, raised their tariffs generally or preferentially, used trade and exchange control through quotas and licensing—all of which tended toward economic nationalism. The Hawley-Smoot Tariff of 1930 in the United States, which President Hoover so mistakenly defended, bore as definite blame in these melancholy developments as any single happening. In spite of this woeful mistake, Hoover sincerely wanted to promote economic restoration abroad and thereby in this country.

As favorable a view as should be taken of the effects of this tariff is expressed by Hal B. Lary:

Part of the decline in imports was undoubtedly caused by the new and heavier duties embodied in the tariff of 1930, but how large a part is difficult to say. Several general facts suggest that the restrictive effect of the new duties was relatively far less than that of the depression. For one thing, the

[6] *Ibid.*, p. 24.

fall in quantity of imports was somewhat less than that of industrial production. Moreover, the drop in imports subjected to heavier duties was not impressively greater than that in other commodities. Nevertheless, the unfortunate consequences of this additional barrier to trade at a time when foreign countries were already undergoing a heavy loss of gold to the United States should not be minimized.[7]

In further extenuation, it may be added that the decline in United States exports began earlier than that in the nation's imports.

Ironically, since Europe's recovery was on nationalistic lines, the United States could benefit little. As compared with America, the depression was less severe and recovery came faster. In dollar value, national income of the United States fell to its low point in 1932 and did not recover until a new world war intervened; physical volume of industrial production reached its low at the same time, but returned to the 1929 level by 1937. On the other hand, in eleven foreign countries dollar value of national income never reached so low as it reached in the United States, and returned to predepression high early in 1934; the physical volume of industrial production in all foreign countries, excluding the Soviet Union, fell slightly more than half as much as in the United States, and recovery was complete by mid-1935. As indication of nationalist policies abroad, in foreign countries imports fell farther below their domestic activity and thereafter increased less rapidly; of sad significance for its citizens, their imports from the United States dropped far below their imports from elsewhere and continued lower. In other words, all international trade was reduced, but that with the United States particularly. From 1934 to 1939 the United States had a net inflow of gold amounting to $10 billion, mostly European capital fleeing from gold-bloc countries in crisis; in the main this gold was not invested here, but was held as a useless mocking hoard.

The study quoted above, deprecating a repetition of narrow nationalist devices that accentuated instability and, it may be added, helped lead to war, sagely observed: "What is emphatically not possible is to have it both ways—a large volume of dollar receipts against a small volume of dollar payments. Yet United States foreign economic policy in the past has been largely predicated upon this manifest impossibility, most notably when the tariff on

[7] *Ibid.*, pp. 171–172.

imports was sharply increased on two occasions in the face of continued efforts to collect war debts and promote exports."[8]

If President Hoover admitted too little of this country's responsibility for the depression here and in the world, and put too much emphasis on European origins, it must be said that he exerted himself to cure the financial crisis that developed in Central Europe in the spring of 1931. His proposal, made public June 21, for a year's moratorium on intergovernmental debts, was economically intelligent and morally courageous, and was handled with political skill at home and diplomacy abroad. The action had to encounter the cupidity of France, the danger that the President's stand would be interpreted as unjustified dictation in European affairs, and fears in the United States that foreign war debts legitimately owing and legally separable from reparations, would by this means be forfeited.

But the pressure on the Austrian banks and government, rapidly communicating itself to Germany and, not remotely, to Germany's many creditors, was accentuating depression in America and, more important, was promising complete collapse in Europe. France was brought into line only after delays that threatened the good effects of the moratorium proposal, and only after she was convinced that she would be isolated and have to yield up, in what she owed to others, the pound of flesh she was demanding of Germany. Hoover's plan deserved a better success than it enjoyed. But no sooner were the intergovernmental debts dealt with than the billions of short-term credits extended to Germany by private bankers pressed for moratorium also, else the economic and political crackup of Germany, which Hoover's plan sought to avoid, would follow anyhow. Hoover's detailed scheme for maintenance of private credits to the German economy, communicated on July 17, 1931, became the "standstill" agreement accepted by foreign statesmen and financiers meeting in London on July 23, American Secretaries Stimson and Mellon participating under the President's instructions. The situation in Germany, as it turned out, both economic and political, had been too far damaged to be saved, but Hoover's wise leadership at a dangerous juncture stayed the danger, and led on to the Lausanne Agreement the next summer reducing German reparations to a minimum. It similarly prepared the way for the World Economic

[8] *Ibid.*, p. 24.

Conference in London in 1933, the collapse of which was the fault
not of Hoover, but of Roosevelt.

FARM RELIEF BADLY NEEDED

The first recommendations of President Hoover, both promised
in his campaign, were farm relief and upward revision of the tariff,
particularly on agricultural products. He spoke of these briefly in
his inaugural and made them the subjects of the special session of
Congress that opened April 16, 1929. In his address to this session
he referred to the numerous causes of the farmers' troubles, said
that no one line of attack would be enough, and urged "the creation
of a great instrumentality clothed with sufficient authority and resources to assist our farmers to meet these problems . . ." The Federal Farm Board would begin with help to farmers in reorganizing
the marketing system, but should go on to investigate and promote
a variety of correctives that included most of the objects later associated with the Agricultural Adjustment Administration of the New
Deal. However, the whole reform should be kept on a voluntary
basis; no fee or tax should be imposed on farmers, the government
should not engage in the buying and selling and price fixing of
products, and encouragement should not be given to increasing
surplus output. The worst of the results which he warned against
were not avoided, and his "new day in agriculture"[9] refused to
dawn.

Four days later, in a letter to Senator Charles L. McNary, he
gave excellent reasons why he condemned the export debenture
plan. It would be a costly direct subsidy from the Treasury which
would go chiefly to speculators, but to the extent that it reached the
farmers would stimulate further overproduction and lead to dumping. By mid-July he was congratulating the Farm Board at its first
meeting on its prospects for usefulness, and said it was invested
"with responsibility, authority and resources such as have never
before been conferred by our government in assistance to any
industry."[10] His first annual message to Congress, December, 1929,
repeated his optimistic view of the work of the Farm Board.

The same calamities that continued to plague the farmers fell

[9] *Hoover State Papers,* I, 33, 35.
[10] *Ibid.,* p. 75.

with full force at the beginning of the depression. They were sharper because newer; alleviations were few, and remedies were only in the minds of hesitant administrators and legislators. Surplus of farms, surplus of farmers, surplus of staple crops formed the loud complaint. Productive capacity was so great that six months of drought in 1930 was a minor help. The Middle Atlantic states and the Ohio and Mississippi valleys were the worst hit, with crops less damaged in larger areas to the West and Northwest. Farm incomes from the production of 1930 for the country as a whole were lower than for any year since 1921 and 16 per cent below 1929; in the drought area the reduction below 1929 was 25 per cent. In August, 1930, a conference of governors of the drought-stricken states agreed to set up a committee of various federal agencies, with subordinate state committees to devise aid. The railroads gave reduced freight rates on hay, feed, and water going into the dry districts and on cattle shipped out. Several hundred counties designated by the central committee received this assistance. To give employment, federal roads authorized for the fiscal year 1932 were scheduled for earlier construction. Seed loans helped farmers plant fall gardens and pasture crops.

But the 1930 wheat crop was 840 million bushels compared with 806 million in 1929 and the 1924–1928 average of 833 million. Farm prices of wheat for the first four months of the marketing season averaged 71 cents a bushel as against $1.09 in the same period of 1929. In spite of the feeding of much wheat to livestock because of the shortage of corn, 1930 wheat prices were the lowest in thirty years. The cotton crop was slightly under 1929, with the price at the end of the marketing season only 11 cents a pound. The corn crop was 22 per cent below that of 1929, but prices of all livestock dropped severely.

Exports of agricultural commodities in the year ending June 30, 1930, were the lowest since 1915; in value they were 19 per cent below 1928–1929. World competition cut demand for American crops. Agricultural products formed only 32 per cent as against the usual 40 per cent of all exports. Cotton exports were particularly low, though exports of tobacco increased in volume and value.

The Secretary of Agriculture was constrained to point out that the increase in technical efficiency in fifteen years had all gone to benefit consumers. Science had made two blades of grass grow where one grew before, only to have the second blade depress the price of both. The attempt to outdo competitors in efficiency was hopeless, for agricultural production was increasing all over the world. Every country knew that reduction of staples was necessary, but no country wished to start. The Secretary's diagnosis of the farmers' plight was as candid as his remedy was cautious: "By this time it is evident that supply-and-demand conditions cannot be set aside by legislation, that the dumping of surpluses abroad is not feasible, that the indefinite storing of surpluses tends to prevent rather than to cause a rise in prices, that tariff duties are not effective on commodities produced largely for export, and that subsidies would increase rather than restrain production." He counseled voluntary restriction: "Comparatively small changes on a sufficient number of farms, have in the aggregate a great beneficial effect [in reducing acreage and therefore surpluses]. All that is necessary to set this constructive force in motion is team play. Farmers must recognize their common as well as their competitive interests." [11]

He went on to lament the fall in farm real-estate value, with the large number of forced sales. Tractors had eliminated the demand for millions of tons of feed crops, and food habits of the people had turned from cereals to milk, pork, sugar, fruits, and fresh vegetables. Not only had European farming recovered from the war to damage U.S. exports, but production had been stepped up in many semi-arid areas of the world through technical advance. The Argentine had become a dangerous rival in exports, while Australia, New Zealand, and Russia were more serious competitors than they had been a few years before. The Secretary reflected that submarginal lands should be diverted to other than agricultural uses and public reforestation should be pushed. While he recognized that the land reclamation policy of the United States should be "reconciled" with need for crop restriction, he did not expand on a tariff policy that was more inconsistent.

The Hawley-Smoot Tariff had gone into effect June 18, 1930. Schedule 7, agricultural products and provisions, went up in import duties from 19.86 per cent to 33.62 per cent, or an increase of 69.28 per cent, the greatest advance in rates of any schedule in the act. Increase of duties on sugar, tobacco, wool, and wines was less.[12]

[11] Arthur M. Hyde, in *American Year Book*, 1930, p. 378.
[12] Milton S. Eisenhower, *ibid.*, p. 380.

The year 1931 brought farmers no relief. Crops of tobacco, cotton, and winter wheat were large, though on the whole the year's agricultural production was average. But returns to farmers were much lower than in 1930 or even in the depression year 1921. Prices of farm products fell more than those of other goods, the index (1909–1914=100) being 68 in October 1931. In the same period the prices paid by farmers fell only from 137 to 126. A wheat crop 8.5 per cent above the 1925–1929 average, with an increased world wheat carry-over, was ruinous to wheat farmers. The farm price of wheat October 15, 1931, was 36.1 cents per bushel compared with 65.6 cents a year before. The prewar price had been 26 cents better. Some countries reduced their wheat acreage, but not Russia.

BUMPER CROPS OR DROUGHT, BUT ALWAYS MORTGAGES

The cotton crop was nearly 17,000,000 bales, the second largest ever produced. Ten million acres had been added to the nation's cotton area after the war, and the boll weevil was being successfully combated. Cotton acreage had increased in other countries. Exports of cotton from the United States in 1930–1931 were 6,760,000 bales contrasted with 8,044,000 in the 1928–1929 season. Producers in 1931 received 28 per cent less for livestock slaughtered than in 1930. Dairymen and poultrymen had heavy reductions in income.[18]

The farm population showed a net increase of 206,000 in 1931, the first since 1922. Unemployment had reduced the movement from farms to cities, and persuaded city people to move to rural districts.

More aid was offered to distressed farmers in 1931 by the government. Over 385,000 applicants borrowed from funds of the Department of Agriculture in the winter and early spring to buy seed, fertilizer, and feed in consequence of the drought of the year before; loans were made in 1,646 counties in 31 states. Other relief similar to that later used by the New Deal on a larger scale was invoked. The sum of three million dollars was added to the regular fund for building forest roads and trails. Where unemployment was severe, men were rotated on the construction crews. In the first half of 1931 the miles of highway under construction doubled. Extra surveys were made of wild life refuges and for control of injurious

13 Hyde, *ibid.*, 1931, pp. 395–397.

rodents and predatory animals. A law approved in March, 1931, authorized the appropriation of $1,000,000 for the fiscal year 1932 and the same for nine years thereafter, for "investigations and experiments to ascertain the best methods of controlling mountain lions, wolves, coyotes, bobcats, prairie dogs, gophers, ground squirrels, jackrabbits, and other animals injurious to agriculture and forestry." So long as the bears and bulls of Wall Street were on the rampage, fang and claw of the wilderness had not drawn attention, but what injured agriculture was not lions or gophers.

Guardians of the farmers' welfare thought they detected "the first sustained improvement" in June–September, 1932, with a slight rise of the purchasing power index. Agricultural prices in the first half of the year had declined to 52 per cent of the prewar average. The cotton crop was only two thirds of that of 1931, wheat production was extremely short, and tobacco was below the average crop. The Secretary of Agriculture, preparing city dwellers to favor appeals of farmers for government help, observed that "sustained farm production, though it depresses farm commodity prices, makes life easier for wage earners with reduced incomes and lessens the burden of unemployment relief. It is necessity and not philanthropy that makes agriculture fill this role. Nevertheless, it does so to the substantial benefit of the community. . . ."[14]

The New Deal was to embody the opposite view that the welfare of the industrial population was promoted not by the misfortunes of the farmers but by their revived buying capacity.

Farm real estate continued to fall in value in all parts of the country except New England and the Pacific coast. Forty per cent of all farms in the United States were mortgaged, compared to 30.8 per cent in 1925. The general property tax was an unequal burden on farmers. Congress appropriated $25,000,000 to permit hard-pressed farm borrowers more time to pay their debts. The land banks loaned to help organize agricultural credit corporations and livestock loan companies. Lending power of the intermediate credit banks was increased. The Reconstruction Finance Corporation was the instrument of much assistance.

Anyone following the history of the depression must often remark how often the actions of the New Deal were present in the assumptions of the previous administration. A good illustration is in

14 Hyde, ibid., 1932, p. 399.

the observation of Secretary of Agriculture Hyde in 1932: "Agriculture's present situation draws attention to the necessity for a better economic utilization of our land resources, and shows that it is necessary to control erosion, to make farsighted provision for future timber and public recreation needs, to preserve wild life, to divert lands submarginal for farming to other uses, to guide land settlement, and to make certain adjustments in governmental organizations so that tax burdens may be reduced." In speaking of taking out of use lands not suited for agriculture, Mr. Hyde went on in the strain of his successor, Mr. Wallace: "Broadly, the idea is to transform marginal farm land and idle cutover land into forest, wild life, or recreational land; . . . to substitute paying for non-paying uses. . . . Other land may be a better playground than a workground. It is not always a question of getting immediate cash returns." [15]

The Secretary warned against talk of concerted effort to place unemployed of the cities on the land. "Such projects should not be undertaken lightly. Merely to shift the problem of relieving want is not necessarily to solve it. . . . A movement large enough to diminish urban unemployment materially would create serious rural problems." Farming was an arduous business, hard enough for those who knew how.[16] Agriculture could better help the unemployed in other ways. Thus in March, 1932, Congress authorized the Farm Board to deliver wheat up to 40,000,000 bushels to the Red Cross for relief of distress; a later law increased the wheat distribution and added 500,000 bales of cotton.

Highway construction was of increasing importance as an aid to farmers. An appropriation of $120,000,000 for emergency extension of the federal highway system was to pay the shares ordinarily borne by the states.

ABORTIVE EFFORTS OF FARM BOARD

The Farm Board, trying to carry out the purposes of the Agricultural Marketing Act of June 15, 1929, was in trouble from the start because, in effect, it put a premium on production. The act itself was broad enough to admit of the restrictions on output later practiced by the Agricultural Adjustment Administration, but President Hoover was opposed to such intervention. The object of the

[15] *Ibid.*, p. 402.   [16] *Ibid.*, pp. 403–404.

law was "the placing of the industry of agriculture on a basis of economic equality with other industries." One suggested method was by encouraging organization of producers into associations of marketing cooperatives; another, as phrased by the board, was "by aiding in preventing and controlling surpluses in any agricultural commodity, through orderly production and distribution, so as to maintain advantageous domestic markets and prevent such surpluses from causing undue and excessive fluctuations or depressions in prices for the commodity." As a result of its experience in the first year the board reported that "the objectives of cooperative organization among farmers must be indeed not only control of the marketing of their own products but also the exercise of some influence on the quantity and quality of commodities produced for the market." The board saw that "production [must] be brought in line with consumer demand," but doomed its efforts to disaster because it chose not to prevent surpluses but to control them.[17]

The act appropriated $500 million as a revolving fund to be used by the board in making loans to cooperative associations beyond what these could get from commercial banks and the federal intermediate credit banks. The cooperative associations so assisted could appoint commodity advisory boards that would help in advising producers on "suitable programs of planting and breeding in order to secure the maximum benefits"[18] under the act. This permissive and indirect system proved unable to limit output.

The first work of the Farm Board was a vigorous and successful campaign to bring local farmers' cooperative marketing associations together in regional and national organizations to handle grain, wool, cotton, dry beans, livestock, pecans, and other products. It was explained that "the board exercises no control over them [the associations] beyond what is incidental to their indebtedness to the revolving fund."[19] The associations in each commodity were combined in a national sales agency. The first of these was the Farmers' National Grain Corporation, which soon had 25 stockholding associations representing some 250,000 producers. National cooperatives in wool, cotton, and livestock soon followed. This represented, at least on paper, a closer organization of farmers than the AAA ever

[17] *First Annual Report of the Federal Farm Board* (Washington: Government Printing Office, 1930), pp. 1, 4, 5.
[18] *Ibid.,* p. 5.   [19] *Ibid.,* p. 6.

attempted, and reminds one of the method to be used in industry by the National Recovery Administration.

The board made loans to the cooperative associations to allow these to give larger advances to their members than could otherwise be done. With the help of the board, wheat producers received advances amounting in all to 90 per cent of the current sale price. The board thought that the decline of wheat prices was unwarranted, and that they would recover, but had to admit that "this view was not borne out by actual developments. Facts eventually proved it wrong." The Grain Stabilization Corporation bought wheat at the loan value. Good money was thrown after bad, the board announcing on March 6, 1930, that "the Grain Stabilization Corporation will continue buying wheat at the market and remove from the market whatever additional quantity may be necessary to relieve the pressure and prevent any considerable decline in wheat prices. The Farm Board is prepared to advance to this farmers' organization whatever funds are necessary for this purpose." [20]

This was the kind of invitation to uncontrolled production which loaded the board up with unsalable surpluses. "It proved undesirable," the board reported, "to market during the year all of the wheat taken off the market, and it was carried forward under self-imposed restrictions against early sales, into a year of large carry-over and of larger world crops." Assurances against selling could not prevent depression of prices, since so much hung over the market. The physical problem of storage was serious, and other vexations beset. The story of the board's support of cotton prices was much the same. Producers got more, but "unfortunately, this was not the end of the matter. Cotton prices did not show sustained advances. Under the influence of the developing business recession, cotton consumption by domestic mills was greatly curtailed. Exports . . . declined. . . . Stocks of American cotton consequently rose above the usual seasonal proportions . . . and the situation grew worse instead of better." [21]

The board approved over half the applications for loans, and at the end of its first year had $148,616,194 outstanding. Contemplating the bear which it held by the tail, the board was brought to declare that it regarded "measures for prevention of surpluses, through control of excessive production, as absolutely essential to

[20] *Ibid.*, pp. 28, 30. [21] *Ibid.*, pp. 33, 38.

stabilizing farm prices and farm incomes. Cooperative associations and stabilization corporations, supplemented by other devices, may prove able to deal with temporary or occasional surpluses. But none of these, nor all together, nor any Government agency can protect farmers from the consequences of repeated or continuous production in excess of market requirements. Adjustments of production to market requirements are indispensable, in agriculture as in industry, to the solution of surplus problems." [22] Other strong expressions showed the board's disillusionment with temporizing methods.

INJURIOUS HAWLEY-SMOOT TARIFF OF 1930

The Hawley-Smoot Tariff Act of June 17, 1930, was a blunder, national and international. It was disingenuous in its construction, and President Hoover, having failed to give it guidance during its passage, added to his error by defending it afterward. There was no demand for this general upward revision of rates in either long public proposal or in fresh party mandate. The tariff had played no part in the presidential election of 1928. The economic crisis of the autumn of 1929 did not occur until the character of the measure had been determined. It began to be framed in the special session of Congress called in June of 1929; while this session dragged into the regular one the tariff bills disregarded the "limited revision" which had been Hoover's intention.

The Coolidge administration had been opposed to bounties to farmers, and Hoover had eliminated the export debenture feature, designed by an indirection to "make the tariff effective for farmers," from the agricultural relief law of 1929. Thus repeatedly disappointed, growers of staple products were resentful and ready to demand higher import duties even though these must be futile and signified nothing but sullen rage. Republican tariff makers seized the opportunity to make an empty gift to farmers while claiming, as a pretended *quid pro quo,* generous concessions to industry. Whatever scruples had been shown in the House committee were abandoned in floor debate where the bill was amended into a hotchpotch. The chairman of the Senate committee, Reed Smoot, was a reckless protectionist clamorous to increase the rate on Cuban sugar

[22] *Ibid.,* pp. 25–26, 45–46.

for the advantage of western beet interests. He was in no way averse to corresponding favors to manufactured goods, and in this found an able ally in the newly appointed Senator Joseph R. Grundy from Pennsylvania.

Democrats threw in their votes on the side of agriculture, were at length obliged to accede to rival demands of industry and were not above improving the chance to secure what they could for manufactures in their own areas. In this situation the trading of favors was shameless. The duty on Cuban raw sugar was raised from the 1.76 cents a pound of the Fordney-McCumber law of 1922 to 2 cents, which was far beyond the difference in costs of production of the Cuban and domestic crops. An increase in the duty on wheat from 30 to 42 cents a bushel was supported by a more than questionable calculation of Canadian costs. A 7-cent duty on long staple cotton was for the exclusive benefit of the Imperial Valley of California. On some meats the rates were more than doubled, and the farmers got what they wanted on dairy items. The duties on hogs and corn were perfectly futile, except politically, because these products were exported, and increases were granted on other agricultural commodities imported hardly at all. Agricultural products and provisions were raised from the 19.86 per cent of 1922 to 33.62 per cent in 1930. There was no reduction to hurt any domestic manufacturer and many, from smallest to largest, received advances. The depression in cotton textiles was due largely to rivalry of the South, but the duty on these products was raised from 40.27 per cent to 46.42 per cent and woolen manufactures did even better.

President Hoover and others in their statements relied on the "flexible provision" of the law, which continued the authority of the Tariff Commission to recommend increases or decreases in rates up to 50 per cent to equate foreign and domestic costs.[23] But the commission's researches in a decade had been largely irrelevant, and its decisions had been marked by a strong bias in favor of protection. The 1930 law made no changes in the rules of the commission, but the President did have power to change its personnel, who were now to receive higher salaries.

The effect of the Hawley-Smoot Tariff is seen in the fact that the average ad valorem rate of duties on dutiable imports for 1921–1925 was 25.9 per cent, and in 1931–1935 was 50.02 per cent, while

23 *Hoover State Papers*, I, 317.

the average rate on total imports increased from 13.99 per cent to 18.45 per cent.[24]

Hoover thought the Hawley-Smoot Tariff nationally justified and that it by no means deserved the blame heaped upon it for causing retaliations abroad and being instrumental in producing an economically compartmented world. Roosevelt, in his 1932 campaign, was steady and vigorous in criticism of this tariff, and the general condemnation of it that followed is inseparable from the long continuance of his administration. In spite of the objection of more than a thousand members of the American Economic Association that the bill was most inopportune because at that juncture the commerce of the world needed to be opened, not hampered, Hoover approved the measure for several reasons. It embodied his recommendations of increased agricultural protection, "limited revision of other schedules to take care of the economic changes . . . since the enactment of the 1922 law," and reorganization of the Tariff Commission and alteration in the method of executing the flexible provisions. He took satisfaction in the statement of the Tariff Commission that of the increases, about 94 per cent were on agricultural products, measured in value, and only about 6 per cent on articles of nonagricultural origin. The average rate on agricultural raw materials showed an increase from 38 per cent to nearly 49 per cent.[25] He constantly cried up the law for its preservation to American farmers of the American home market, ignoring the fact that farmers producing exported products could not get such benefit.

Figures quoted by Hoover and his critics compared the Hawley-Smoot with previous tariff acts. The public was confused by seemingly conflicting figures that were all accurate if taken with their particular qualifications. It was plain that the law involved changes in about a third of the dutiable items in the tariff list, 890 of the 1,125 changes being increases, including 47 transfers from free to dutiable list, and 235 being decreases, including 75 transfers from dutiable to free list. Thereafter figures did not clarify. The President pointed out that whereas the average duties collected under the Fordney-McCumber Tariff of 1922 were 13.8 per cent of the value

[24] U.S. Department of Commerce, Bureau of the Census, *Foreign Commerce and Navigation of the United States for the Calendar Year 1941* (Washington: Government Printing Office, 1944), p. xv. See also F. W. Taussig, *The Tariff History of the United States* (New York: G. P. Putnam's Sons, 8th ed., 1931), pp. 489–526.

[25] *Hoover State Papers*, I, 314–315.

of all imports, both free and dutiable, if the new law had been applied it would have increased the percentage to 16 per cent only.[26] This argument omitted the possible effect of the new law in reducing certain imports or excluding them entirely. Hoover went on to show that "the average level of the tariff" had been higher under all previous laws since the McKinley Act except for the Fordney-McCumber and Underwood schedules. This was true enough, but if the average ad valorem rate for dutiable articles only was the basis of comparison, the Hawley-Smoot Tariff was the highest of any recent ones except the McKinley and Dingley laws, being 53.2 per cent.[27]

A good part of the fifteen months of congressional consideration of the Hawley-Smoot Tariff was against a background of declining imports and exports. The nation's foreign trade had begun to fall off in December, 1929; in the fiscal year ending June 30, 1930, the whole amounted to $8,543,000,000, a drop of 11.6 per cent from the high level of the preceding year. Customs duties collected for 1930 were $584,759,605, but for 1931 were only $378,781,494, or a decline of 35 per cent.[28] An accidental reason for this reduction was that the new tariff was passed just before the end of the fiscal year 1930, so that a large quantity of imports entered in haste to get the benefit of the old lower rates. How much of the continuing contraction was due to the stiffer Hawley-Smoot duties, and how much, both in volume and in value, to the effects of the depression, is impossible to say. Defenders said one thing, accusers the other.

President Hoover, in the campaign of 1932, scoffed at Governor Roosevelt's charges that "the Hawley-Smoot Tariff is one of the most important factors in the present world-wide depression," and that "it has destroyed international commerce." [29] Many of the high tariffs in other countries, said Hoover, were established by new states, set up after the World War, in order to develop their economies, and long before the American 1930 tariff was passed. Others, en-

26 *Ibid.*, pp. 314, 315.

27 U.S. Tariff Commission, *Computed Duties and Equivalent ad Valorem Rates on Imports into the United States from Principal Countries, 1929 and 1931* (Washington: Government Printing Office, 1933), p. 5.

28 *Eighteenth Annual Report of the Secretary of Commerce 1930* (Washington: Government Printing Office, 1931), p. xx; *Annual Report of the Secretary of the Treasury, 1930* with appendices (Washington: Government Printing Office, 1931), p. 469; *ibid.*, 1931, pp. 64, 426.

29 *Hoover State Papers*, II, 342.

acted later, were not directed at the United States, but were designed, at times of financial crisis, to reduce or prevent all foreign
purchases. With arithmetic which yielded something to the demands
of debate, he showed how trifling was the American increase in the
duties on world commerce, and continued: "So they would have us
believe this world catastrophe and this destruction of foreign trade
happened because the United States increased tariff on one-fourth
of one-third of one-eighth of the world's imports. Thus we pulled
down the world, so they tell us, by increases of less than one per
cent of the goods being imported by the world." [30]

The truth was that as a leading commercial nation the United
States set a bad example at a peculiarly inauspicious juncture, and
so contributed, directly and indirectly, to constriction of trade. The
country's leadership in a liberal international economic policy,
which was handsomely exhibited in the debt moratorium, was prevented from applying in the more important realm of exchange of
goods. Hoover prided himself on his loyalty to the Republican protectionist principle. It was a poor proof of patriotism. It will be seen
later how the New Deal introduced the partial corrective of reciprocal trade agreements.

RECONSTRUCTION FINANCE CORPORATION

While many instruments of the New Deal were anticipated in
the Hoover administration, the chief institution to be taken over
bodily and given functions beyond the boldest thought of the author was the Reconstruction Finance Corporation. Hoover proposed
it in his annual message to Congress on December 8, 1931, when
two years of deepening depression had belied his hopes of swift
recovery, and attempts at verbal exorcism had been followed by
expedients that relied ever less on private effort and ever more on
public support and initiative. The RFC thus marked a stage, though
not the final one, in Hoover's plans for overcoming the depression.
Modeled on the War Finance Corporation, the RFC was at first
thought of by Hoover as another emergency agency, which might
not have to be used extensively. "The very existence of such a bulwark will strengthen confidence," he said, and it should be liquidated in two years. With its capital subscribed by the Treasury, and

[30] *Ibid.*, II, 343.

with power to issue its own debentures, its purpose should be "by strengthening the weak spots to . . . liberate the full strength of the nation's resources." It should facilitate exports, and lend to agricultural credit agencies, but its main object, as soon appeared, was "to make temporary advances upon proper securities to established industries, railways, and financial institutions which cannot otherwise secure credit, and where such advances will protect the credit structure and stimulate employment." [31]

A few days later the President explained that the RFC would "give confidence . . . against further paralyzing influences and shocks, but more especially by the re-opening of credit channels . . . will assure the maintenance and normal working of the commercial fabric." [32] The bill creating the RFC met Democratic opposition in Congress that delayed and crippled the President's program. In spite of Hoover's earnest personal pleas to scores of members, the Senate eliminated the right of the RFC to make loans to public bodies and industries, the conference committee did not restore this power, and it was not until another fight eight months later that the wider authority was conferred. The bill passed both houses on January 16, 1932, the President announced that Eugene Meyer would be chairman of the RFC and Charles G. Dawes president, and he signed the act January 22. The entire capital of $500,000,000 was advanced by the government, the corporation was allowed to borrow up to $1,500,000,000 in government-guaranteed, tax-free obligations, and it could continue for ten years. Hoover tried to counteract the criticism that the new huge lending agency was a breadline for big business at a time when direct federal relief to the unemployed was refused. "Its purpose," he said, "is to stop deflation in agriculture and industry and thus to increase employment by the restoration of men to their normal jobs. It is not created for the aid of big industries or big banks. Such institutions are amply able to take care of themselves. It is created for the support of the smaller banks and financial institutions. . . ." [33] Among the seven directors named one was Jesse H. Jones, who afterward became head of the RFC and guided its great expansion beginning a year later under Roosevelt. At the outset, however, Hoover enjoined on the directors that their first object must be to stop bank failures under Section 5 of the act, which provided for loans to aid in liquidating or reorgan-

---

[31] *Ibid.*, II, 50.   [32] *Ibid.*, II, 84.   [33] *Ibid.*, II, 106–107.

izing financial institutions. The National Credit Corporation, set up in the autumn of 1931, through which banks were supposed to help each other, had proved disappointing.

The corporation was promptly organized with loan agencies in thirty cities, and issued no fewer than twenty-two circulars addressed to various groups of borrowers, explaining, with urgent solicitude, how each could get its help. During 1932 total authorizations were $1,939,199,172; actual disbursements were less, $1,524,-747,138; in the heaviest month, June, authorizations were $388,-254,246, disbursements were $298,276,816, and repayments were $48,684,900; loans outstanding at the end of 1932 were $1,224,798,-685. Operations during the remaining months of the Hoover administration, January and February, 1933, did not differ in character or amount. Under Hoover the largest beneficiaries were banks and trust companies, which got three times as much as the next largest class of claimants, the railroads. Smaller disbursements were made to building and loan associations, mortgage loan companies, relief and work relief, insurance companies, and less to a variety of agricultural credit agencies.[34]

UNWELCOME PUBLICITY FOR BIG BORROWERS

It is impossible to say how seriously publication of Reconstruction Finance Corporation loans contributed to the bank crisis in the spring of 1933. President Hoover was sure that calling attention to emergency borrowings of large numbers of particular banks precipitated runs upon them, though they were inherently sound and had sought help for the good of their communities. Lists were furnished Hoover of banks, building and loan associations, insurance companies, and so on, said to have been the innocent victims of suspicion thus drawn to them. When an amendment by Speaker Garner to the Unemployment Relief Act, at the close of Congress in July, 1932, calling for the publication of RFC borrowers, was modified and passed, it was understood by Senate leaders and President Hoover that, in practice, reports would be received by Congress in confidence. After the election in November, Garner, not feeling himself bound by any gentlemen's agreement, insisted that the current reports be given to the public; this was followed by a resolu-

[34] R.F.C. Quarterly Reports (Washington: Government Printing Office).

tion of the House in January that loans prior to July 21 be similarly treated. President Hoover and influential Democrats appealed to the House in vain. However, the wisdom of their protest would seem to be borne out by action of the New Deal, later, in repealing publication.

The best-publicized loan of the Reconstruction Finance Corporation was to the Central Republic Bank and Trust Company of Chicago, known as the "Dawes bank" because General Charles G. Dawes had organized and built it up to a position of national importance and continued, at least nominally, to be one of its officers. Dawes had been president of the Reconstruction Finance Corporation from the beginning in January to June 6, 1932, when he resigned to apply himself to the rescue of the affairs of the bank. More than others in financial circles, Republican politics, and the administration, General Dawes was regarded as "hard-boiled" and competently self-sufficient. He had been Vice-President, revamper of German reparations, ambassador to England. He had a stern jaw, clamped between his teeth a singular underslung pipe, wore with Spartan endurance a high stiff collar with sharp points that would have impaled the thorax of one less tough. His pictures showed him habitually frowning. A little more than a year before, he had written to Hoover from London, commending the President's resolute rejection of public relief in favor of reliance on private charity for the unemployed. "To veto a bonus bill," Dawes praised, "in a time of National prosperity is both commendable and courageous. To veto one during the worst of an unprecedented business depression, at a time when the bill prompted by dogmatism could be represented as one to relieve suffering, is an heroic thing. . . . Your steadfastness—when so many from whom it was not expected have weakened—in defense of our American system of relief as distinguished from the dole principle . . . [was] all the more difficult for the same reason. Your opponents were able to use a public calamity as an excuse for the violation of a fundamental principle of good government." [35]

This was the same Dawes whose bank received at one clip a public dole of $90,000,000. President Hoover, a few months later in a campaign speech at St. Louis, felt obliged, in a long explanation of the incident, to meet Democratic insinuations that Dawes used

[35] Myers and Newton, *The Hoover Administration*, p. 70.

his recent position as president of the RFC to bail out his bank. Hoover described the bank runs in Chicago, crucial financial center, which at closing time Saturday, June 27, 1932, threatened to continue with disastrous effect Monday morning. The problem on Sunday was to find means of saving the Dawes bank, and its 122,000 depositors, including 755 correspondent banks with 6,500,000 depositors scattered over fifteen states, not to speak of the 21,000 banks which were depositors in the 755, and which had a total of 20,000,000 depositors! Hoover drew out the ramifications of the Dawes bank to the farthest limit, or something beyond it, for the double purpose of exculpating Dawes from unworthy private motive and to illustrate the little-suspected public beneficence of the help RFC extended in critical quarters.

The boards of two federal reserve banks, and President Hoover with his anxious advisers, had sat long and late that Sunday, telephoning back and forth their hopes and fears, while bank examiners hastily verified the assets of the kingpin financial institution in Chicago. Knowing such action would be turned by Democrats into "calumny," Dawes demurred at asking the RFC for the huge loan that was the sole means of salvation. But, supported by prominent Democratic banking colleagues, he did so, and braved the abuse against which President Hoover later tried to defend him. Hoover praised the loan and the courage which sought and granted it, to rescue not one man or a few stockholders, but the solvency of a metropolis and many dependent communities, and the well-being of millions of citizens, including, inevitably, an appropriate complement of widows and orphans. Said Hoover: "The situation demanded broad vision and comprehensive understanding of the problem, instant decision, bold and courageous action. Only by this was a major disaster averted."

Dawes and Hoover and the RFC acted correctly. The loan was a proper one. The clamors against it, so far as they impugned motives, were unworthy. Comment is of a different sort. Hoover and his advisers were shortsighted in so long confining direct public financial relief to great business corporations, and in putting too much dependence on the percolation of public funds from these banks, insurance companies, and railroads to the needy millions of the people. When it came to immediate relief of the unemployed, Hoover failed to recognize that "the situation demanded broad vision and comprehensive understanding of the problem, instant decision, bold and courageous action." The national economic calamity entailed wider acute suffering, and had deeper causes than he grasped. At such a time private relief was insufficient for great and little alike.

CHAPTER III

Evolution of Relief

PRESIDENT HOOVER'S statement, on the heels of the great stock market collapse, is naturally the best remembered of many made by business and governmental leaders, intended to forestall economic depression. He said (October 25, 1929): "The fundamental business of the country, that is, production and distribution, is on a sound and prosperous basis."[1] At this critical juncture, when the country needed to be reassured, the statement was inevitable, and, besides, was undoubtedly sincere. Though strongly solicited, Hoover refused to urge on the public the purchase of stocks.

Within three weeks, the President knew his error of optimism. A confidential report from federal reserve officials had said: "The situation is far from liquidated . . . it is honeycombed with weak spots . . . it will take perhaps months before readjustment is accomplished."[2] On November 15 Hoover announced a series of meetings with business leaders designed to expand construction, maintain employment, and sustain wages. His reliance was on voluntary, but concerted, action of industry and finance, in which government—federal, state, and local—would aid with building projects. He regretted that "one of the results of the speculative period through which we have passed in recent months has been the diversion of capital into the security market, with consequent

[1] Myers and Newton, *The Hoover Administration*, p. 23.
[2] *Ibid.*, p. 24.

lagging of the construction work in the country. The postponement of construction during the past months, including not only buildings, railways, merchant marine, and public utilities, but also Federal, State, and Municipal public works, provides a substantial reserve for prompt expanded action." He did not say that he thought industry was sound at the moment. He was more guarded: "Any lack of confidence in the economic future or the basic strength of business in the United States is foolish. Our national capacity for hard work and intelligent cooperation is ample guaranty of the future." He promised that enterprises pledging themselves to "legitimate business expansion" would have the help of ample federal reserve credit, general tax reduction with assent of both political parties, and governmental bolstering of agriculture.[3]

In the next fortnight the President summoned to the White House the magnates in the industries which could undertake new construction—railroads, public utilities, and building. The preliminary conference with railway presidents, those of the eastern territory, issued a statement that they were "unanimous in their determination to cooperate in the maintenance of employment and business progress. . . . The railways which they represented would proceed with full programs of construction and betterments without any reference to recent stock exchange fluctuations; . . , it appeared that the total volume of such construction work already indicated an increase during the next six months over the similar period of last year." [4]

The President's outward optimism, whatever its motive and duration, was abandoned in his meeting with leading industrialists November 21. Among others present were Henry Ford, Julius Rosenwald, Walter Teagle, Owen D. Young, E. G. Grace, Myron C. Taylor, Alfred P. Sloan, Jr., Pierre du Pont, Walter Gifford, and Julius Barnes. The inside story is given by Myers and Newton.[5] Hoover "said that he would not have called them were it not that he viewed the crisis more seriously than a mere stock market crash; that no one could measure the problem before us or the depth of the disaster; that the depression must last for some time; and that there were two or three millions unemployed by the sudden suspen-

[3] *Hoover State Papers*, I, 133–134.
[4] *Ibid.*, p. 134.
[5] Myers and Newton, *The Hoover Administration*, pp. 26–27.

sion of many activities. He warned them that we could expect a
long and difficult period at best; that there must be much liquidation of inflated values, debts and prices with heavy penalties on the
nation; that no one could at this time measure the destructive forces
we must meet. . . ." The first duty was to prevent unemployment
and distress. "He explained that immediate 'liquidation' of labor
had been the industrial policy of previous depressions; that his
every instinct was opposed to both the term and the policy, for
labor was not a commodity. It represented human homes." Wages
should be maintained for the present, to protect both people and
purchasing power, but could be stepped down later as the cost of
living inevitably fell. "Thereby great hardships and economic and
social difficulties would be avoided. In any event the first shock
must fall on profits and not on wages." [6]

The press statement of this meeting, however, disclosed no fears:
". . . it was the unanimous opinion of the conference that there
was no reason why business should not be carried on as usual; that
construction work should be expanded in every prudent direction
both public and private so as to cover any slack of unemployment."
The American Telephone and Telegraph Company proposed in
1930 to spend more on construction than the $600,000,000 of 1929;
other utilities would follow suit; the automobile industry was less
confident, but steel companies would replace obsolete plants. "The
President was authorized by the employers who were present . . .
to state on their individual behalf that they will not initiate any
movement for wage reduction, and it was their strong recommendation that this attitude should be pursued by the country as a
whole." As a counterpart to this last pledge, labor leaders would
make no new demands for wage increases, and would discourage
strikes.[7]

The promises of industry for expanded employment, spelled out
in dollars when leaders had canvassed their colleagues, were not
borne out in the event. Instead, contractions were the rule. The obligation not to cut wages was, if possible, more widely dishonored,
while distributions to holders of corporate securities were maintained for two years.

[6] *Ibid.*, pp. 26–27.
[7] *Hoover State Papers*, I, 135–137.

EMBARRASSING REPUTATION

Two days later, November 23, Hoover wired governors and mayors begging them to cooperate in a program of public works expansion. The responses were cordial but vague. It is curious to note that Governor Franklin D. Roosevelt of New York was in effect discouraging: ". . . expect to recommend to legislature . . . much needed construction work program . . . limited only by estimated receipts from revenues without increasing taxes. . . ."[8] The Farm Board, to prevent collapse of prices of staples in the hands of growers, was extending generous emergency credit, and the Postmaster General promised more contracts for ocean mail carriage on condition of new ship construction.

When the President came to his first annual message to Congress, December 3, 1929, he wanted not to alarm the country about its economic situation, with the result that he treated the subject casually and gave superficial, false assurances. He dealt with a variety of topics, some of them remote, before broaching the one burning issue of the day. His preparatory remarks looked to strict ¬vernment economy with tax reduction. "Every dollar so returned ᴊrtilizes the soil of prosperity." He went on to say that "the long upward trend of fundamental progress" had bred overoptimism as to profits, resulting in the stock market crash. The economic consequences seemed minor. Business agencies had "paused," "hesitated" in their plans for continued expansion until the federal government "instituted systematic, voluntary measures of cooperation with the business institutions . . . to make certain that fundamental businesses of the country shall continue as usual, that wages and therefore consuming power shall not be reduced. . . ." He was convinced that through these measures confidence had been reestablished. The President certainly underestimated, in his report to the country, the seriousness of the crisis. That he was confused in his own mind may be indicated by the gratuitous assurance that "there has been no inflation in the prices of commodities."[9] Social services should remain the charge of local government and private effort, with mere organizational aid from the federal authority. It was important not to endanger the balanced budget. The budget

---

[8] Myers and Newton, *The Hoover Administration,* p. 29.
[9] *Hoover State Papers,* I, 145–146.

message carried recommendation for only a trifling increase in the expenditure on public works.

When he had been out of office almost three years Mr. Hoover contrasted his relief policies with those of his successor. He thought himself no less the humanitarian. He reminded that, before the depression, it had become his task "to organize and administer relief to over 150,000,000 people who had been reduced to destitution by war or by famine or by flood, both at home and abroad. I gave some years to that service in the aspiration to save life, to allay suffering, to restore courage and faith in humanity." Then he went on, "It also became my duty in 1930 to see that relief was organized for our unemployed." [10]

However, rejection of Hoover after four years of a depression presidency was due in good part to mass resentment against his relief policies. The anger came from experience here with hunger, cold, homelessness; with confusion, futility, abandonment. The bewilderment in some and near hatred in others were not helped by the reflection that Hoover's world renown had been won for his rescue of the distressed. His colleagues, Ray Lyman Wilbur and Arthur M. Hyde, said accurately, "Herbert Hoover had had the largest experience in relief of any human being." [11] And the distinguished social worker, Jacob Billikopf, said in 1931: ". . . there is no man in American life for whom I have a greater sympathy than for Mr. Hoover. He came to the presidency heralded as one of the greatest humanitarians of all time. Hailed as an engineer and administrator of the highest constructive genius, he was not only going to consolidate all the then existing elements in our prosperity but to usher in a new era of unprecedented prosperity. Few presidents before him can have suffered so many slings of outrageous fortune." But fortune was more outrageous for the millions of unemployed, whose burdens would have been lightened, said Billikopf, if Hoover had abandoned an outmoded individualism and rejected empty optimism. [12]

Further, Hoover's persistent objection to direct federal money relief to the millions of unemployed did not prevent him from cre-

[10] Ray Lyman Wilbur and Arthur Mastick Hyde, *The Hoover Policies* (New York: Charles Scribner's Sons, 1937), p. 384.

[11] *Ibid.*, p. 370.

[12] National Conference of Social Work, *Proceedings*, 58th annual session, 1931 (Chicago: University of Chicago Press, 1932), p. 33.

ating, with alacrity, the Reconstruction Finance Corporation, which gave enormous immediate aid to the largest business enterprises. Earlier, the Farm Board had taken as its aim the artificial raising of prices of prime essentials of life, had subsidized exports of wheat, and pondered outright destruction of food and fibers. So the sincerity as well as the wisdom of Hoover's professed preference for individual, voluntary, and local aid to the needy was called sharply in question. Hoover himself, and his apologists, with all their reasoning, were not able to make his tenderness for railroads, banks, and staple agriculture consistent with his obduracy toward the unemployed. The springs of private enterprise, for the purity of which he held such solicitude, would not be polluted by direct national grants. The funds were furnished and the machinery was erected with ample provision for expansion. The work of federal direct relief to business in many forms was carried on in semi-secrecy, with alarmed resistance to demands for public reporting of loans; at the same time, help for the unemployed must be without effective governmental organization. Indeed, the dire dangers of federal money going immediately to the jobless were explained *ad nauseam*. On the one hand was the revolving fund of $500,000,000 for the Reconstruction Finance Corporation, with more to be had by borrowing; the RFC was swift, open-handed, silently generous. On the other hand, was the institution of the up-ended crate with its little pyramid of apples, mocking in ruddy neatness.

BREAD LINE FOR BUSINESS

The President's explanation of this contrast was more pat than convincing. He said (August, 1932): "It is not the function of the Government to relieve individuals of their responsibilities to their neighbors, or to relieve private institutions of their responsibilities to the public, or of local government to the states, or of state governments to the Federal Government. . . . It is vital that the programs of the Government shall not compete with or replace any of them but shall add to their initiative and their strength. It is vital that by the use of public revenues and public credit in emergency the Nation shall be strengthened and not weakened. . . . It is only by this release of initiative, this insistence upon individual responsibility, that there accrue the great sums of individual accomplishment which carry this Nation forward. . . ." Then he went on to teach how lending to what appeared as the powerful few was really largesse for the powerless multitude: "It was in accordance with these principles that I first secured the creation by private initiative of the National Credit Association, whose efforts prevented the failure of hundreds of banks, and loss to countless thousands of depositors who had loaned all their savings to them. As the storm grew in intensity we created the Reconstruction Finance Corporation with a capital of $2,000,000,000 to uphold the credit structure of the Nation, and by thus raising the shield of Government credit we prevented the wholesale failure of banks, of insurance companies, of building and loan associations, of farm-mortgage associations, of livestock-loan associations, and of railroads in all of which the public interest is paramount. This disaster has been averted in the saving of more than 5,000 institutions and the knowledge that adequate assistance was available to tide others over the stress. This was done not to save a few stockholders, but to save 25,000,000 of American families, every one of whose very savings and employment might have been wiped out and whose whole future would have been blighted had those institutions gone down." [13]

This was the "percolation" theory of the RFC, regularly offered by Hoover and his advisers. Classes of corporations, selected for abundant help, were mere conveyors to the multitude. The irreverent said it was "the theory of feeding the sparrows by feeding the horse." As Louis Hacker has justly observed, President Hoover did not hold with the traditional do-nothing policy which in previous depressions had accepted, as an inevitable therapy, the reduction of capital claims. Instead, Hoover intervened to prevent wholesale bankruptcy which, at this point in the country's development, "would have been attended by too much risk; for the great investors now were the institutional savers—the savings banks, life insurance companies, building-and-loan associations. These were holding the farm and urban mortgages and the railroad and public utility securities of the country; and the failure of such institutions might have been fatal to capitalism." [14] The New Deal was hardly less anxious to preserve capitalism, albeit shorn of the most dangerous abuses. The distinction of the New Deal was that it accepted

[13] *Hoover State Papers*, II, 250–251, 254.
[14] *American Problems of Today* (New York: F. S. Crofts & Co., 1938), p. 192.

logically the implications of a mature capitalism. Enterprise, through growth of population, advance of technology, and use of the corporate form, had become socialized. The United States had a *de facto* business collectivism. As Berle and Means put it, the private corporation had become in effect public property. Hoover, by and large, was content with socializing the "public" losses of corporations because these would reach to the private losses of individuals. The New Deal properly went farther and was willing to socialize the private losses of unemployed individuals on the ground that, unless aided, these would destroy the public, including corporate, welfare. The Hoover analysis stopped cruelly short. Though in answer to events it made progress, the Hoover administration was accused of lack of humanity when its real fault was failure to carry through in scrutiny of the problem. The New Deal, by contrast, endeared itself for its sympathy with individual misfortune, when equally deserved thanks might have gone to it (but did not) for its industrious attempt to preserve capitalism.[15]

SCHOLARS HAD FEW SOLUTIONS

However, President Hoover, in his view of the depression, was not far behind economic opinion held in the universities. The second survey of the President's Conference on Unemployment was completed in October, 1932, and published early in 1933 as *Recent Social Trends in the United States*. It was prepared under the direction of an academic committee of which Professor Wesley C. Mitchell was chairman. This report made progress over the pre-depression one in recognizing the true import of developments. But actually recognition of the depression could not have been avoided, for it was by this time a stark fact. The academic experts went beyond President Hoover in recognizing that more and more the varied economic interests would be invoking government aid. The trend had been toward transfer of the work of private social agencies to public budgets. The breakdown was social, so the treatment must be collective. The quasi-government corporation, the government-owned corporation, the mixed corporation loomed. President Hoover may have squirmed a little when his savants affirmed:

15 For a running account of Hoover's relief activities and views, see Wilbur and Hyde, *The Hoover Policies*, pp. 370–401.

"Those who reason in terms of isms or of the theoretical rightness or wrongness of state activity may be profoundly perplexed by the range of governmental expansion or contraction, but the student of social trends observes nothing alarming in the widely varying forms of social adjustment undertaken by government, whether maternal, paternal, or fraternal from one period to another." [16]

The committee seemed appalled by the universal economic and social breakdown, was reticent in analyzing the causes of the depression and in recommending means of recovery. While declaring that planning was necessary for avoidance of the business cycle in the future, the task called for such elaborate procedures that the committee was sure it did not know where to begin. The possibility of economic misery leading to war was insufficiently contemplated. This prospect, could it have been foreseen, might have persuaded the committee to overcome its inhibitions and to urge, before war could strike, some of the swift if rough planning that would so quickly be undertaken in the cause of destruction. The diffidence of the committee in the midst of the depression was a pity. If the earlier committee of business leaders—that of the report on *Recent Economic Changes*—was too uncritical, this of academic men was so led by its curiosity that it could never stop for conclusions. Their indecision is dwelt upon here because it distinguished the earlier treatment of the depression from the attitude adopted by the New Deal administration.

It was perhaps inevitable that the President of the United States —whether Hoover or Roosevelt—would try, in public statements, to minimize the numbers of the unemployed. Unemployment all along was bound to be the chief barometer in the public mind for economic conditions. Mass unemployment, with attendant misery and frustration, was in cruel contrast to the New Economic Era of prosperity and was equally disgraceful, later in the thirties, in contrast to plentiful production and the means taken to destroy "surpluses" of life necessities. Hoover was more blamed for trying to put a good face on the extent of unemployment—shall we say for specious reports?—than was Roosevelt. Hoover had the excuse that the facts were newer, less well determined. By the time Roosevelt was

[16] President's Research Committee on Social Trends, *Recent Social Trends in the United States* . . . with a Foreword by Herbert Hoover (New York: McGraw-Hill Book Company, 2 vols., 1933), I, lxiii.

analyzing the figures, as in radio broadcasts, the totals had grown to the point where there was additional temptation to understate them, or to interpret them to the advantage of the administration. In retrospect it is significant to notice that in Roosevelt's analyses the numbers of the "unemployable" were swelled by contrast with the subsequent war period, when practically all in that category and many besides were put to work. It is true that all of the elements in unemployment were and remain relative: the young, the old, the handicapped who may be called unemployable in slack times become eagerly absorbed man power when production is furious.

COUNTS OF THE UNEMPLOYED

Dr. Julius Klein, Hoover's Assistant Secretary of Commerce, was persistently apt in presenting unemployment reports in a pleasing light. Of course this was an effort that could succeed only if conditions soon improved, and they did not. An example of the false impression received by the public came in the middle of February, 1930, when the President announced that the Department of Labor index of employment, which had dropped from 93.3 in October to 86 at the end of December, had increased to 92.8. Governors' reports and independent surveys showed that in thirty-six states no important distress had developed from unemployment, and that in the remaining twelve states private and local relief efforts were meeting the situation.[17] This analysis was less reassuring when it was realized that the three fourths of the states where unemployment was hardly felt were agricultural and grazing areas, while the populous industrial states were in trouble.

At Hoover's direction, an attempt was made to tabulate unemployment for the first time in the regular decennial census of 1930. At the end of April he announced the results: those out of work, but able to work and looking for employment, numbered 2,429,000, and those temporarily laid off were 758,000, or a total of 3,187,000.[18] The census embraced only the last working day preceding the enumerator's visit. Young persons who had never worked were not enumerated, though they might be available for work. As the

17 Myers and Newton, *The Hoover Administration*, p. 35.
18 Wilbur and Hyde, *The Hoover Policies*, p. 374.

census showed that about 1,200,000 of those unemployed on the day in question had been unemployed less than a month, this number, in official interpretation, was comfortably assigned to the category of those assumed to be normally "between jobs," or "frictionally" unemployed, so that the number unemployed due to the depression was supposed to be reduced to less than 2,000,000. However, Robert R. Nathan, of the Department of Commerce, estimated that the outside official figure would have to be increased by about 30 per cent, or to some 4,500,000, to give a reasonably accurate total for unemployment in April, 1930. Farm people working for members of their own family without wages, though included in the "gainfully employed," were not considered as subject to unemployment. There was reason to believe that numbers of those reporting themselves as voluntarily idle in April, 1930, were later ready to admit that their idleness had not been entirely voluntary. Also, apparently many who had recently lost their jobs did not regard themselves as unemployed and did not report themselves as such. This 1930 decennial census, with its few questions covering unemployment, and its broad and therefore fallible classifications, furnished a chief basis for later running estimates of unemployment.

BASIS OF UNEMPLOYMENT ESTIMATES

The United States has never had a regular census of unemployment. Thus, during the great depression, though unemployment was the overweening social fact, it depended, for knowledge of the volume of unemployment, on estimates. The actual counts made had their own elements of uncertainty, and their results were useful chiefly as furnishing checks on the continuous estimates. The estimates were arrived at by assuming a figure for the total labor force, another for existing employment, and subtracting the second from the first.[19] Each of the primary magnitudes involved debatable questions and degrees of exactness in method. For instance, in estimating the labor force, a lower figure for number of workers was

[19] On this whole subject see the excellent article by Russell A. Nixon and Paul A. Samuelson, "Estimates of Unemployment in the United States," in *Review of Economic Statistics*, XXII, No. 3 (August, 1940), 101–111; also National Resources Planning Board, *Security, Work and Relief Policies* (Washington: Government Printing Office, 1942), pp. 552–556.

obtained by those who simply calculated increase in total population than by those who recognized that the numbers in the working ages increased more than a third faster. Further, should wife and young people in the family, forced to look for work when the father lost his job, be included in the labor force? (The answer to this would seem to be yes, an instance of the fact that unemployment causes unemployment.) Then the question came whether unpaid family workers in agriculture were "employed." Other problems presented themselves.

Chief estimates by responsible agencies were those of the National Industrial Conference Board, the American Federation of Labor, the Congress of Industrial Organizations, Robert Nathan for the President's Committee on Economic Security, and the Alexander Hamilton Institute. Though these estimates differed at times by several millions, all showed the same turning points. Nixon and Samuelson concluded that the N.I.C.B. estimate was the most sensitive, while that of the Federation was probably nearest the actual figure. Of course the curve of unemployment was the reverse of that of production or of other indexes of economic activity. The peak of unemployment was reached in the first quarter of 1933 and the lowest point in the third quarter of 1937. Significant features were the increase in unemployment, between the last of 1929 and the beginning of 1933, of about four million a year, then a drop of four million in six months when NRA was anticipated and getting under way. There was violent fluctuation between early 1936 and the middle of 1938, because of the "recession" in the autumn of 1937, following which unemployment increased by about six million in nine months. There was the usual winter increase in unemployment of about a million and a half in 1939 despite the outbreak of war in Europe, with resumption of the decline in the spring of 1940. However, when the United States entered the war it still had, after a year of preparation for defense work and a like period of defense production, some four million unemployed.

VOLUNTARY AND DECENNIAL CENSUSES

To finish with this subject of estimates of unemployment, it is necessary to go ahead of the chronology and speak of the National

Unemployment Census in November, 1937, and the decennial census of 1940. President Roosevelt had previously resisted all importunings to allow such a census to be made, and now insisted that the report cards declare: "The Congress directed me to take this census." The questions asked were more numerous and more discriminating than in 1930: the inquiry was not limited to a single day, a better definition of unemployment was arrived at, young people looking for work for the first time were included, and emergency work was not classified as genuine employment. The great mistake was in the method of securing the information. Instead of using special enumerators, mail carriers left cards for heads of families and assisted in the correction of questionnaires obviously wrongly answered. Administration was not by the Bureau of the Census alone but by a special committee representing several government departments.

Results of this census were announced in a preliminary report by John D. Biggers, the director, on January 18, 1938. The number of cards actually filled out and returned was 7,822,912. However, a house-to-house canvass made in 1,864 areas selected at random and distributed throughout the country in proportion to population indicated that an addition of 3,047,088 should be made, and that the voluntary census was only 72 per cent accurate. Mr. Biggers considered the corrected total too high, and that the true figure was about 9,500,000. His reason was that the check census reflected more borderline cases than the regular census, of housewives, young and old people who did not normally belong to the labor force. Mr. Biggers, referring to these discrepancies, said, "We do not claim provable accuracy for any one figure. The true number of those who considered themselves totally unemployed, able to work and wanting work, in our opinion, lies between 7,822,912, the number who responded to the registration and 10,870,000, the number indicated by the enumerative census." [20] The fact was, however, that these people were able to work and looking for work; it was not possible to rule out the effect of the depression in increasing the numbers needing to work. Moreover, while the supposed subtrac-

---

[20] *Monthly Labor Review*, XLVI, No. 2 (February, 1938), 357–358. See also U. S. Census of Partial Employment, Unemployment, and Occupations, *Preliminary Report on Total and Partial Unemployment. United States Summary by States, Counties, and Cities* (Washington: Government Printing Office, 1938), pp. v–vi.

tions were being made as of a given date, the volume of unemployment was undoubtedly growing.

The decennial census surveyed unemployment in the last week of March, 1940. The definitions of classes into which those interviewed were divided were sharper than in the 1930 census and the results were correspondingly more reliable. Those on federal, state, and local unemployment relief projects and those who were able to work and seeking work but had no job were counted as unemployed. Among the employed, however, were included those laid off for less than four weeks with instructions to return to their jobs at a specified time. The census showed 3,042,000 on emergency relief projects and 4,919,000 others looking for work, or a total of 7,961,000 unemployed, representing 14.9 per cent of the labor force. More than 767,000 of the unemployed were newcomers to the labor force who had not worked for as much as a month.

The United States Department of Labor did not report the estimated number of the unemployed for months before April, 1940, when the figure was 8,800,000 including persons on public emergency work projects. The total estimated labor force then was 53,-900,000. Unemployment among male workers was 16.2 per cent and among female, 17 per cent.[21]

The number unemployed in September, 1939, at the outbreak of World War II had been greater. A conservative estimate was that of the National Industrial Conference Board, which placed the unemployed in August, 1939, at 8,838,000 and in September, 1939, at 8,192,000.[22] Marked improvement in employment coincided with the beginning of the war. During September and October, 1939, nearly 400,000 workers were returned to jobs in nonagricultural operations. There was a greater than seasonal gain of almost 270,000 workers in manufacturing industries, largely in the durable goods group, with substantial increases in wholesale and retail trade, mining, and on Class I steam railroads. The period September–October, 1939, showed increases in employment for 74 of the 90 manufacturing industries surveyed and for 8 of the 16 nonmanufacturing industries. Pay roll gains were shown by 75 of the manufacturing and 10 of the nonmanufacturing industries. For all manufactur-

21 *Ibid.*, LN, No. 1 (January, 1942), 266.
22 National Resources Planning Board, *Security, Work and Relief Policies*, p. 556. While the government estimated the unemployed in April, 1940, at 8,800,000, the Conference Board gave 9,017,000 for that month.

ing industries combined, the gains were 3.4 per cent in employment and 8.3 per cent in pay rolls; the addition to weekly wages was $14,800,000. Factory employment and pay roll indexes were both at the highest level since the autumn of 1937. The average hours worked per week in manufacturing gained 2.9 per cent. The current gains were larger than those reported for October in any of the preceding twenty years. On the average, employment in October had shown but little variation from the September level, while pay rolls had shown an increase of 1.2 per cent. Only 4 of the durable goods industries and 12 of the nondurable goods industries reported employment declines in October, 1939. The important declines were all seasonal. Industries feeding war experienced increases in employment. Steel gained 56,900 workers, automobiles 35,800, cotton goods 21,600, foundries and machine shops 21,400, woolen and worsted goods 15,700, electrical machinery 11,300, brass, bronze, and copper products 10,300, and sawmills 10,000, among others. The aircraft industry reported a gain of 6.1 per cent, or 2,500, in the number of wage earners, the thirteenth consecutive monthly increase. The industry had three times as many people employed as in 1929.

These figures of gains in employment did not include emergency public employment. Employment on construction projects financed by the Public Works Administration decreased by 26,000 during the month ending October 15, 1939, leaving 221,000 still on the pay roll of $20,827,000. However, there was an increase of 106,000 in the Work Projects Administration, 8,000 in CCC camps, and 13,000 on projects of the National Youth Administration.[23]

The estimated number of unemployed decreased fairly steadily from the 8,800,000 of April, 1940, to 3,800,000 in December, 1941, the month of the Japanese attack on Pearl Harbor. In 1941 every month except two showed a net decline in unemployment. The numbers given as unemployed included those on public emergency work projects. However, the numbers entering the armed forces (1,100,000 from January through November, 1941) were not included in the labor-force figure, which in January, 1942, was 52,400,000, or 400,000 less than in January, 1941.[24]

[23] *Monthly Labor Review*, XLIX, No. 6 (December, 1939), 1522 ff.
[24] *Ibid.*, LIV, No. 3 (March, 1942), 821.

CHARACTER OF UNEMPLOYMENT

While the mass unemployment in the depression of the thirties embraced those of every calling and condition, age, and place of residence, surveys in different parts of the country and in different periods showed a pattern of incidence.

Employment declined more in the durable goods and construction industries than in others. In the nondurable goods group the index of employment (1923–1925=100) fell from 105.9 in 1929 to a low of 79.2 in 1932, and in the durable goods group the drop in the index was from 106.2 in 1929 to a low of 52.8 in 1932. The value of all building construction fell from $2,933,212,041 in 1929 to $383,-363,271 in 1933, and the value of new nonresidential building construction declined from $1,147,796,781 in 1929 to $183,241,951 in 1933.[25] The index of employment in the machine-tool industry was 167.2 in 1929 and only 42.1 in 1932.[26]

The capital, other durable goods, and construction industries being so hard hit, it was not surprising that engineers should suffer peculiarly from unemployment. At the end of 1932 more than one tenth of the engineers were simultaneously unemployed; at one time or another between the beginning of 1930 and the end of 1934 more than one third of the engineers had some period of unemployment, and half of those who became unemployed were out of work for more than a year. This experience was common to all professional classes of engineers. The greatest frequency of unemployment was among the engineers entering the profession after 1929, half of whom were unemployed at some time from 1930 to 1934. While older engineers were less frequently unemployed, when they were out of work their unemployment lasted longer, cumulatively producing a higher percentage of unemployment among older engineers. Nearly half of the engineers unemployed at the end of December, 1934, had work relief.[27] Figures are not available for architects, draftsmen, and other allied professions, but their experience of unemployment was undoubtedly similar to that of the engineers.

Unemployment fell more heavily on unskilled than on skilled workers, only partly because many of the skilled were down-graded

[25] Bureau of Labor Statistics, *Chart Series* (July, 1942), pp. 7, 9, 44.
[26] *Ibid.* (March, 1941), p. 13.
[27] *Monthly Labor Review*, XLIV, No. 1 (January, 1937), 37–38.

and given jobs of the unskilled. The 1937 unemployment census showed that unskilled workmen constituted 42 per cent of all male workers unemployed, though the census for 1930 showed only 27 per cent of all male workers as unskilled. Of the 2,028,041 women registered as totally unemployed, 421,191 were seeking their first jobs and were not classified as to occupation. Of the remaining women, the three classifications of semiskilled, clerical workers, and servants included 88.3 per cent, though these classes embraced only 74.3 per cent of all female workers in 1930.[28]

Incidence of unemployment was less among women than among men, because there was less unemployment in the clerical and service occupations in which women predominate, and because women tended to secure jobs formerly held by men. However, the proportion of women unemployed increased as the depression were on, partly because unemployment of men forced women into the labor market. The duration of unemployment was less for females than for males.[29]

Unemployment among young people, particularly those who were first offering themselves for jobs, was one of the cruelest features of the depression. Surveys, local and national, and made at different times demonstrated that unemployment of 15 to 19 year-olds was about twice as great as for all ages; those 20 to 24 years old had unemployment a fourth to a third greater than the average. The percentage of unemployment among boys was greater than among girls. Constant accessions to the ranks of unemployed youth kept up the percentages of unemployed. At the other end of the age grouping, once older workers lost their jobs it was harder for them to find new ones.[30] The depression lasted so long that large numbers who lost their jobs never worked regularly again.

The percentage of employable persons unemployed appears to have been largest in small towns and villages. Thus a Michigan survey in 1935 found that in places of 3,000 population and under, 25.6 per cent of the employables were reported as unemployed, compared with 17.8 per cent in cities of 40,000 or more population. However, half of the total unemployed were reported in the most populous cities.[31] Slightly more than half of those voluntarily regis-

[28] *Ibid.*, XLVII, No. 2 (August, 1938), 322–323.
[29] *Ibid.*, XXXIX, No. 6 (December, 1934), 1335.
[30] *Ibid.*, XLIII, No. 5 (November, 1936), 1160 ff. See also Chapter VII.
[31] *Ibid.*, p. 1159.

tering in 1937 as totally unemployed and wanting work (not including persons on emergency work) were in eight states: New York (763,322), Pennsylvania (566,437), Illinois (338,055), Ohio (304,682), California (258,005), Massachusetts (248,484), Texas (229,254), and New Jersey (217,176).[32]

"Last hired and first fired" as an expression to describe Negro workers seemed to be borne out as to accuracy. A census in Massachusetts in January, 1934, showed that 19 per cent of employable white persons were totally unemployed, but 32.3 per cent of Negroes were in this category. The proportion of Negroes on government projects was slightly higher than of whites, as was the proportion of black employables on part-time work.[33] In the nation as a whole it was found in the 1937 census that the proportion of skilled Negroes unemployed was twice as high as of skilled whites, while the proportion of all Negroes unemployed was only a third higher than of all whites.[34]

The problem of partial unemployment was of great but unknown magnitude. In the 1937 national voluntary census, 3,209,211 persons registered as partly employed and wanting more work— 2,641,660 males and 567,551 females. The subsequent test census indicated that this voluntary registration of the partially unemployed was only 57 per cent complete.[35]

BANKRUPTCY OF PRIVATE PHILANTHROPY

Mass unemployment, magnifying all of the ills of destitution, necessarily had an impact upon social work supported by private philanthropy. Broadly, the result was to transfer auspices and transform methods. Public funds took the place of private charity not only in relief but in many of the preventive and health services. Equally or more important, cure by organized society of socially caused misfortunes appeared in the place of individual amelioration. Public welfare departments of states, which had been largely in the stage of proposal before, were established in increasing numbers. Social workers, answering the demands for administration of relief, strove to preserve discriminating family services (case work)

[32] Ibid., XLVI, No. 2 (February, 1938), 355.
[33] Ibid., XXXIX, No. 6 (December, 1934), 1332–1333.
[34] Ibid., XLVII, No. 2 (August, 1938), 325.
[35] Ibid., XLVI, No. 2 (February, 1938), 355.

but were unable to do so. For a time they lamented the overwhelming of these devices, but came to see that the problems of their clients could be met only by publicly fostered adjustments. Relief in billions, jobs in millions, extended education, public health, and social insurance offered the only hopeful solution. Social work in the treatment of poverty, like much before it—education, police, and fire protection—substantially passed over during the depression from private effort to governmental responsibility.

For several years social workers, while more aware than others of the proportions that unemployment was assuming, believed that local agencies could cope with it. They fell in with President Hoover's national campaigns of "Mobilizing for Human Need" as a welcome means of filling community chests, and to this extent delayed effective provision for the disaster. However, the most experienced and wisest of their number, after full test of local private and public resources, led the way in calling for ample federal appropriations. Dread of the dole, they said, was not in the minds of relief recipients, but of politicians who feared to impose taxes.

Successive annual meetings of the National Conference of Social Work showed the more prescient turning to the national government for aid in a crisis so different in degree as to be different in kind from anything known before. Thus H. L. Lurie, director of the Bureau of Jewish Social Research, said in June, 1931:

> If we previously believed that . . . economic insecurity of the individual was largely a condition of personal maladjustment best served by the case work method, preferably exercised by private benevolence, the exigencies of the present period of depression have radically altered our assumptions. . . . We are beginning to see that we have too long been dominated in case work by an economic philosophy remote from the actualities of our highly complicated industrial and economic organization.[36]

And Jacob Billikopf, after describing how the utmost local effort had failed to meet the problem of Philadelphia's unemployed, observed:

> The President's Emergency Committee . . . has come . . . with a project involving the national mobilization of social welfare and fundraising resources, so that the nearly four hundred community chests throughout the country may, next October or November, raise amounts

[36] National Conference of Social Work, *Proceedings,* 1931, p. 212.

sufficient to care for the vast army of the unemployed. We will certainly cooperate with the president's Committee. Certainly, we are happy to have the president's blessing. . . . But . . . I want to warn you, my fellow social workers, that we will be guilty of duplicity; we will be betraying the interests of the millions of unemployed . . . if . . . we should give the impression . . . that all a community has to do is to raise its chest quota. . . . As a result of the policy of drift . . . our government will be compelled, by the logic of inescapably cruel events ahead of us, to step into the situation and bring relief on a large scale. . . . Private philanthropy . . . is virtually bankrupt in the face of great disaster.[37]

In the next year, 1932, C. A. Dykstra, then city manager of Cleveland, considered that the conclusion of Colonel Arthur Woods, first director of the President's Emergency Relief Organization, had been shortsighted, and that of Mr. Walter S. Gifford, his successor, even more so, for they placed federal responsibility in the problem-atical future.

More and more we have recognized that we are in the midst of a national crisis. Many of our economists and statesmen agree that it is . . . international. . . . In the face of some such common agreement we have acted upon the assumption that the whole impact of unemployment disaster logically must be thrown upon local communities. . . . Valiantly . . . local organizations [public and private] . . . have wrestled with the relief problem. They have tried to make four hundred million dollars play substitute for twenty or more billions of dollars, formerly paid in wages.[38]

Julia Lathrop, chief of the Children's Bureau, in testimony before a Senate committee in February, 1933, showed by charts how federal relief had increasingly outdistanced local help, and went on to characterize the weaknesses of private charity.[39] But others who should have known better—Newton D. Baker and Harry L. Hopkins, for example—continued to talk, at least for effect, the old language. Baker in July, 1933, as national chairman of the "Mobilization for Human Needs" drive, was pushing the slogan "122,000,000 Partners of the Poor."

[37] *Ibid.*, pp. 38–39.
[38] *Ibid.*, 1932, pp. 65 ff. See also remarks of Arthur Dunham, director of special studies, Family Welfare Association of America, *ibid.*, p. 464.
[39] Edith Abbott, ed., *From Relief to Social Security* (Chicago: University of Chicago Press, 1941), pp. 121 ff.

DISAPPOINTED RELIANCE ON LOCAL RELIEF

The "Give-a-Job" campaign of 1931, addressed to the private citizen, was the most primitive form of work relief. It had been preceded by the sweeping injunction of Hoover to the largest American corporate employers, but that plea had been without notable result. Now the householder was urged to have his yard cleaned or his cellar whitewashed and so give someone a few hours' or a day's work. Nothing more haphazard and trivial, in view of the magnitude of the need of the unemployed, could have been proposed, but this formless device showed how unprepared America was to grasp the proportions of the crisis. "Block aid" was rather more systematic: volunteer committees collected small sums weekly for which an unemployed man would be given work in the block, removing ashes, and so on. Newly appointed municipal commissions on unemployment, well intentioned but groping, endorsed the scheme, but sentimental enthusiasm weakened, collections were irregular and dwindled to nothing.

Relief expenditures of family welfare agencies mounted abruptly in the winter of 1930–1931, and some could take no more applicants. The foolish self-assurance that there was no unemployment had been flung back in the country's teeth; the "conspiracy of optimism" was obviously a delusion. Then cities across the continent began work relief projects, variously administered and financed, and of many sorts from artificial to substantial, but showing on the whole every evidence of haste and uncertainty. That these plans avoided money relief from the public purse, which even Governor Roosevelt of New York at this time abjured, had to be their chief claim to common acceptance. Few men—and, of course, fewer women—got work for any length of time. There were defects enough in the great nationally organized public works programs later, but these short-time municipal efforts were vastly less adequate to the emergency.[40]

After defeat of the Costigan-La Follette bill for federal relief, in the winter of 1932, continued reliance had to be placed, perforce, on local and state funds and on private charity. How these resources had dwindled or been exhausted was told in May and June, 1933,

[40] See Joanna C. Colcord and others, *Emergency Work Relief* (New York: Russell Sage Foundation, 1932), pp. 286 ff.

in hearings on a new bill (La Follette-Lewis) providing that the Treasury might borrow $500,000,000 to supplement assistance from state and local governments. The American Association of Social Workers sent an impressive letter reiterating that large-scale aid from the federal government was overdue. The "situation . . . was beyond local control and local experience and one which needed the utmost which the whole Nation could give from its material resources and from its great capacity for guidance and leadership." H. L. Lurie showed how philanthropic funds, even when increased by the special relief mobilization campaigns in which Mr. Hoover placed such confidence, used up the year's budget in three or four months. Public appropriations had the same history. In order to cover relief needs even to this extent, other essential social services, such as health and child welfare, had been dangerously curtailed.

With demands increasing and public and private funds running out, relief was spread thin.

The amount of relief given to individual unemployed families is daily diminishing. In few of the cities is there any pretense at the present time of offering to families in need the budgetary standards which have been considered . . . as the minimum for the barest essentials. Few cities are providing shoes or clothing to destitute families. No money is available for necessary medical or dental care. No payment is made for gas or electric light and increasingly . . . relief agencies are unable to pay rents. Relief has been continuously and gradually reduced so that whole families are getting an average of $2.39 a week relief as in New York City, with $3 and $4 and at the most $5 a week . . . in other cities.

In Toledo the commissary was able to allow only 2.14 cents a meal for each person. Dallas had a 40 per cent increase in applications in the face of a mere 10 per cent increase in funds. Nearly everywhere landlords went unpaid until, on threat of evicting a family, they would be given part of that month's rent; landlords themselves came on relief. Houston reported, "Applications are not taken from unemployed Mexican or colored families. They are being asked to shift for themselves." [41] (Discrimination in relief, though not as callous as this, continued throughout the depression, even when federal funds were the main reliance; Negroes and certain foreign groups were kept on lower allowances on the theory that they had

[41] U S. Senate Committee on Manufactures, "Federal Cooperation in Unemployment Relief," Hearings on Senate Bill 4592, May 9, 1932, 72 Cong., 1 Sess., pp. 11–12.

always managed with less than others, or to prevent relief from approximating the miserable wages offered them.)

The deputy secretary of the Pennsylvania Department of Welfare said that at least 3 million people, a third of the population of the state, were "entirely without income from their wage earners"; 250,000 families, or a million persons, were on relief. Some small rural counties still had resources, but "in the coal counties the picture presented is that of a patient already suffering from a chronic progressive disease who has contracted an acute malignant infection." [42] The great industrial communities were similarly beset. The legislature at a special session had appropriated $10 million for relief, available in April, but, where grants were big enough to keep families in health, the money would be gone by July. In a typical western county of diversified industries, the seven private relief societies were almost out of pocket and could not continue over the summer; the government flour, distributed by the Red Cross, had been a help.

STARVING IN THE MIDST OF SURPLUS

It is not necessary to sift printed testimony to rehearse miseries from the lack of local relief before federal funds were furnished. In the summer of 1932 some saw the people abandoned when West Virginia bituminous mines were no longer worked. The miners occupied the mine shacks, had coal enough, walked miles to Morgantown for Red Cross flour when issued, started gardens from charity seed, lived to a large extent on blackberries. Some had almost no furniture, and slept on straw ticks on the floor. In one camp with several hundred people, including many babies, there was no soap, the women making a sort of suds from soap weed. The one cow in the settlement was half starved herself, and gave blue milk. The Quakers were generous and ingenious, and sent members of their Society to live and work on the spot, but far more than even Quaker conscience and fidelity were needed. Making homespun fabrics and mountain furniture occupied hands and heads, and yielded a few dollars, but formed no solution for the problems that overwhelmed coal as only the worst hit in a general calamity.

[42] *Ibid.*, pp. 14, 17–18.

Karl de Schweinitz, secretary of the Philadelphia Committee for Unemployment Relief, in May, 1932, reported that private funds had given out until a new drive could be conducted, no money could be had from the city, state funds were problematical beyond the next month. For eleven days when there was no relief many families had been penniless, and he recited typical cases of homes with small children and pregnant mothers with no food for a day or more, and then scraps which were begged, or dandelions—this in a country which was plagued with a surplus of food. "The hospitals have had definite cases of starvation." Federal funds offered on condition of state contribution would help move a reluctant legislature. Even the most experienced at that time thought the states, if sufficiently bribed, would pitch in; they were to find later that the federal government must assume responsibility if people were not to starve. De Schweinitz was asked whether he thought relief recipients would be more demoralized by national than by state help. He answered truly: "I think the real demoralization is not relief, it is unemployment. What really hurts people is being out of their jobs. . . . As far as Federal or State aid goes, it does not make any difference." [43] Mr. Hoover could have saved a lot of suffering, and perhaps his own political fortunes, if he had understood that simple statement.

In May, 1932, Chicago had 700,000 unemployed, 40 per cent of the total of the possible gainfully employed. Two years earlier, 13,000 families had received $167,000 in relief; the load had increased to 130,000 families requiring $2,612,000 in relief, not counting others in shelters. Chicago's relief had mounted from less than $11,000,000 in 1931 to an estimated $35,000,000 in 1932. A witness told how private relief had been foreshortened, and the same testimony could have been repeated in substance for many places: "Chicago quite generously raised about $11,000,000 . . . for unemployment relief, from private funds. A committee that corresponded to the Gibson Committee in New York, the Lloyd Committee in Philadelphia, and so on, raised these funds. That money presumably was to last from October 1, 1931, to October 1, 1932. It was completely exhausted February 1, 1932—completely gone." The "attrition" of privately supported relief had not only cut off food from people, but hospital services and other necessary social aids. [44]

Edward F. McGrady, later Assistant Secretary of Labor, said

[43] *Ibid.*, pp. 21–25.   [44] *Ibid.*, pp. 27–32.

for the American Federation of Labor: ". . . it was not our intention to be represented here today. The leaders of the trade-union
movement in this country have lost their patience after coming
down here repeatedly . . . to appeal to the committees . . . to do
something to stop millions of our people from starving, only to be
met with utter indifference on the part of the administration and
leaders of the Congress." If the administration did nothing to provide work for the millions of unemployed, or did not give food to the
people, before Congress adjourned, "I would do nothing to close
the doors of revolt if it starts. I say that as a man, as a citizen of
the United States. It would not be a revolt against the Government
but against the administration." [45]

The plight of the city of Chicago in the summer of 1932 came
in for special discussion. A reassessment of property four years
earlier had caused a delay in the collection of taxes of from one to
two years since then, and municipal employees had gone for long
periods unpaid, hundreds of public school teachers being on relief.
To pay back salaries of teachers would require a loan from the federal government of $20,000,000, with $25,000,000 more to permit
the schools to reopen in the fall with a prospect of continuance. [46]
As the city had no funds for its own workers, of course it could
contribute nothing to relief of the unemployed. The Illinois Emergency Relief Commission had been taking care of 111,000 families
in Chicago, or some 600,000 destitute persons. A fund of $23,000,-
000, less than half of it privately given and the remainder from sale
of State of Illinois notes, was exhausted. Some millions of dollars
worth of remaining state notes could not be sold. Relief stations
were on the point of closing. The mayor, other city officials, and
leading businessmen were appealing to have the RFC make advances to the state for emergency relief, the amount to be deducted
from future federal aid for highways. [47] In the testimony the RFC
was blamed for confining its direct help to railroads and banks and
other credit institutions. Further, banks were properly accused because they had taken money from the RFC and, instead of lending
it in the community where desperately needed, had applied it to
make themselves more liquid. Objections were raised—constitutional, political, fiscal—against making available to the unemployed

[45] *Ibid.*, p. 37.   [46] *Ibid.*, Part 2, pp. 44, 47.   [47] *Ibid.*, p. 57.

federal resources which were confessedly ample, and which were
the only resources in sight. In the case of Chicago, the country's
granary, hunger seemed especially ironical.

RURAL IDYLL

Concerning the problem of taking care of the millions of unemployed, the most naïve notion was that private charity, especially
if assisted by local public funds, would suffice. Though a puerile
idea in retrospect, it was not unnatural, and most well-informed
people held it until the mass proportions and probable duration of
the relief load became evident. The country had not experienced
unemployment of such relative magnitude before, and the New
Economic Era had made long-drawn depressions seem almost fan-
tastic. National administrations had proclaimed the sufficiency of
business, never considering central governmental responsibility for
so automatic a blessing as bread and cheese. The phase of local
reliance passed, but the frontier tradition and agricultural recollec-
tion of America died hard. Those who contended that the puzzle
would be solved if only the unemployed of the cities were urged
and enabled to move into the country remained vocal.

In the cities unemployment emphasized crowding, squalor, and
cold; the bread lines were visual reproaches. In the country, on the
other hand, was ample room. Further, in the cities, workers won
bread by an indirect process which for some reason had broken
down. But life in the rural setting was held to be synonymous with
raising family food. The thing was simple, direct, individually and
socially wholesome. The objections escaped most advocates, who
forgot that productive farms were also crowded; that a great part
of agriculture was commercial, not for subsistence; that typically
the urban unemployed knew nothing of working the land; and,
lastly, that the government was already embarked on a program of
limiting production of foodstuffs. Though the proposal, in its more
ingenuous form, was soon discredited in all but private quarters,
something of the idea lingered and reappeared in the subsistence
homestead colonies of PWA and even in some of the work of the
Farm Security Administration.

The original suggestion of "back to the land," without benefit
of second thought, was pressed on a House committee in the spring

of 1932.[48] The bills under consideration applied to destitute unemployed persons with previous agricultural experience. Inspired by Bernarr Macfadden, in the double purpose of giving calories to hungry people and copy to his publications, the bills bore every mark of ignorant haste. One proposed selling farms to the unemployed through the federal land banks, without explaining where the man from the bread lines was to get his considerable share of the investment. Another would appropriate $10 million to put the urban idle on abandoned farms where they would grub subsistence in the emergency. Professor John D. Black, serving as economist of the Farm Board, showed the evident dangers in both plans, and favored no more than small allotments near cities, to which men might go daily in trucks or for a week at a time. Representative Oscar B. Lovette of Tennessee and others of the committee who knew agriculture referred to the amount of relief already being given in rural areas. But no objections, however well founded, discouraged Macfadden and his friends, who had demonstrated, in "one-cent restaurants" in New York City that men could be fed at trifling cost on cracked cereals. Once move men from park benches to the land and they could not fail to grow what they needed to eat. Besides all else, they would be dispersed beyond the danger of revolutionary ferment and, praise God, would be out of sight.

A little later a Senate committee heard from General Pelham D. Glassford and other District of Columbia officers why $75,000 should be appropriated to help care for the "bonus army" that had descended on Washington. Senator Edward P. Costigan, with his usual intelligence, showed that the problem of the transient unemployed was nation wide and needed a new treatment, but his observations seemed lost on those who thought only of the menace to Congress.[49]

SHAME OF ANACOSTIA FLATS

A symbol of the national distress, in the summer of 1932, when the depression was at its depth, was furnished by the "bonus army"

[48] Hearings before the Committee on Labor, House of Representatives, 72 Cong., 1 Sess., on House Resolutions 11,055, 11,056, and 12,097, April 29, 30, May 2, 6, 1932, 112 pp.
[49] Hearing before the Committee on the District of Columbia, U. S. Senate, 72 Cong., 1 Sess., on S. 4,781, June 1, 1932, 27 pp.

in Washington. Fifteen thousand or more of the destitute, mostly veterans, some with their families, had collected in the capital, beginning in May and June, demanding immediate payment of the face value of the "adjusted service certificates," which were to mature in 1945. Active agitation for anticipating the redemption date had begun in the winter of 1930 at the first onset of unemployment, the argument being that putting several billion dollars in the hands of the veterans would not only relieve their plight but, by supplying needed purchasing power, would help restore business and agriculture. In February, 1931, Congress, over Hoover's veto, passed the bonus loan law providing that veterans might borrow, at a reduced rate of interest, up to half the value of their certificates. By September, 1931, when the American Legion met at Detroit, the demand, led by Democratic Senator Wright Patman of Texas, was for cash payment at once of the remaining half of the certificates' face value. Hoover made a hurried trip to Detroit to oppose this, and the resolution was defeated.[50]

However, on June 15, 1932, the House passed the Patman Bonus Bill, providing for payment with $2,400,000,000 of fiat money. The "bonus army," now swelled to its maximum size, was hopeful of similar action in the Senate. The veterans were camped, in shelters improvised from old tin signs and other scrap materials, on the Anacostia flats near the Potomac, and smaller numbers were living in vacant buildings, government property, near the Capitol. Each day many were on the Capitol grounds, vainly hoping the Senate would receive a deputation. In their camp and in their visits to the Capitol the veterans were in every way orderly.

President Hoover was preoccupied with his demands for economy and balancing the budget. Prices of industrial stocks and staple produce had turned more steeply downward, banks were failing fast, currency was being hoarded again. In nine months, more than $1.5 billion of gold had been withdrawn by Europe from the United States or earmarked; all French holdings had been withdrawn, and the dollar was at a 7.5 per cent discount in Paris. Hoover was obstinately fighting a variety of congressional proposals for inflation and spending for the benefit of the unemployed. These means he regarded, at that juncture, as more dangerous than ever, though increasing numbers in the country felt that they were necessary and

50 *The New York Times* (September 20, 22, 25, 1931).

were not just Democratic party weapons. Hoover had said shortly before, on May 27, 1932, "The urgent question today is the prompt balancing of the budget. When that is accomplished I propose to support adequate measures for relief of distress and unemployment." [51] More generous appropriations to the states for relief and a larger public works program were excoriated, while increased use of Reconstruction Finance Corporation credit for private business enterprise was pushed.

The bonus bill was defeated in the Senate on June 18, three days after the House had passed it. The veterans assembled before the Capitol that night took the blow quietly. Soon after the adjournment of Congress a month later, some 5,000 of them, using travel funds which Hoover asked Congress to appropriate, had left for their homes. An equal or larger number remained. President Hoover, being jittery, threw an extra guard around the White House. General Glassford, the Washington superintendent of police, had treated the bonus seekers with every consideration, and could not have liked his assignment, on July 28, to clear out those who were camped in the condemned buildings along Pennsylvania Avenue. The official statement was that the buildings were about to be torn down to make way for new construction, though actually they stood for some time afterward.

Early in the afternoon, when brickbats had been thrown at the police, a policeman shot and killed two of the veterans. On request of the Commissioners of the District, President Hoover called in from Fort Myer a sizable force under General Douglas MacArthur —four troops of cavalry, an equal number of infantry companies, a machine gun contingent, and some tanks. The soldiers, with bayonets, drawn sabers, and tear gas, dispersed the veterans and burned the shanties of their Anacostia camp. Hoover, in extenuation, claimed that a considerable part were not veterans, that many were "Communists and persons with criminal records." Most were undoubtedly veterans, but whether heroes or not, they were hungry in the nation's capital. The spectacle of cavalry and tanks driving and burning them out confirmed public doubts about the heart of the Great Humanitarian, or at least about the wisdom of the Great Engineer. General MacArthur's approval of his conquest was sooner forgotten.

[51] *Hoover State Papers*, II, 195.

Stock Market Crash

Clerks in Wall Street brokers' offices worked late into the night posting records of unprecedented volume of sales. (*Acme*)

Begging Business

Large numbers of the unemployed sold apples on the streets. Many big enterprisers knew subtler ways of securing public help. (*Underwood-Stratton*)

A Bread Line

This one was in New York City, but smaller places had theirs, too, before home and work relief was organized. (*Acme*)

Coal Dole

When destitute families could no longer buy coal, even a few pounds at a time, a relief bureau had to furnish it. (*Photo by New York Emergency Relief Bureau, courtesy New York Public Library*)

Right of Petition

Ten thousand unemployed men, demonstrating at the national Capitol in January, 1932. (*Acme*)

Camp of the Bonus Army

Anacostia Flats, Washington, D. C. United States troops drove out these veterans and fired their shelters in July, 1932. (*Acme*)

Bread Line for Business

Senator Carter Glass, Chairman Eugene Meyer, Jr., of Federal Reserve Board, and General Charles G. Dawes conferring on plans for the RFC, January, 1932. Dawes became head of RFC. (*Acme*)

Bank Holiday

During authorized suspensions, crowds like this one in a Cleveland bank came to ask about recovering their money. (*Brown Brothers*)

New Devices for Depression

President Herbert Hoover and President-Elect Franklin D. Roosevelt leaving the
White House for inauguration ceremonies, March 4, 1933. (*Wide World Photos*)

Planning for the "Forgotten Man"

Professor Raymond Moley, of Columbia University, conferring with President-Elect
Franklin D. Roosevelt before the first inauguration. (*Press Association, Inc.*)

Oil Code Completed

General Hugh S. Johnson, Administrator of the National Industrial Recovery Act (*center*), and Secretary of the Interior Harold S. Ickes (*right*). (*Underwood-Stratton*)

New Deal for Farmers

Secretary of Agriculture Henry A. Wallace (*seated*) with Undersecretary Rexford G. Tugwell. (*Harris & Ewing*)

Civilian Conservation Corps, 1936

CCC boys sawing wood at their camp on Isle Royale in Lake Superior. They protected against forest fires, made roads, and improved recreation areas. (*Wide World Photos*)

Shared Boll Weevil, Not Government Benefits

By taking land out of cultivation, the Agricultural Adjustment Act had the effect of dispossessing large numbers of sharecroppers. A family of New Madrid County, Missouri, 1939. (*Acme*)

"The Wailing Wall"

In spite of the angry laments of Big Business, the New Deal had for its chief object the rehabilitation of private capitalist enterprise. A cartoon by Harold M. Talburt. (*By permission of the Scripps-Howard Newspapers*)

Orderly Collective Bargaining

The National Industrial Relations (Wagner) Act gave unions legal status. Julius Hochman (*standing*), manager of the New York Dress Joint Board of the I.L.G.W.U., presents the union's case before Harry Uviller (*center*), impartial chairman. (*Photo by Harry Rubenstein*)

PORTENTOUS FORECAST

The men calling themselves Technocrats furnished the country a seriocomic interlude in 1932–1933. At first a small number of unemployed engineers, architects, and scientists led by Howard Scott, they found asylum in the Industrial Engineering Department of Columbia University while they commenced an energy survey of North America. All went smoothly until they announced some of their conclusions in 1932. Scott and the others had been fascinated by Veblen's thesis in his *Engineers and the Price System*, which had waited a decade to be converted into a set of slogans to scare the wits out of the satisfied. Veblen had drawn attention to the hostility between proficient production under engineers on the one hand, and scarcity as its maintenance was attempted by manipulative business enterprisers on the other. The observation was far from new when Veblen acidulated it and his sudden apostles made it caustic.

The Technocrats—recommending control of economic life by technicians—began by describing remarkable laborsaving methods in the power age. Human muscle, long the reliance in production, had been economized by machines, and now even men to mind the machines were being eliminated. A straight-line brick-making unit produced 4,000 bricks per day per man, instead of 400 as by the old manual means. A plant in Milwaukee, with 208 men to operate mammoth drop forges, could turn out 10,000 automobile frames a day, enough for the whole industry. A rayon plant in New Jersey virtually dispensed with human labor. The turbines in a modern huge hydroelectric installation, running through the twenty-four hours, generated a fourth as much energy as all the human and animal power in the country was capable of. Whereas in 1904 the manufacture of a second-rate automobile had required 1,291 man-hours, a better car was produced in 1929 with only 92 man-hours.[52] The "electric eye" was as infallible as fast in reading and sorting millions of cards that had formerly demanded laborious clerical patience, and this was only one of its innumerable tricks. The Roto-lactor, soon to be exhibited at the New York World's Fair, permitted 60 cows standing at machines on a turntable to be washed, dried,

[52] See Paul Blanshard, *Technocracy and Socialism* (New York: League for Industrial Democracy, 1933); he reduced extravagant claims of Technocrats to hardly less astonishing accuracy.

and milked in 12 minutes with minimum labor. Casual labor in the wheat fields had been driven out by combines which headed, threshed, and sacked the grain, covering 40 acres in a day.[53]

These triumphs of mechanical power and contrivance were but illustrations of a determined tendency exhibited in a study published in 1932 by Frederick C. Mills of the National Bureau of Economic Research.[54] Before World War I, in the years 1901–1913, the physical volume of production in manufacturing industries grew at the rate of 3.9 per cent a year, and the volume of employment in those industries at the rate of 2.7 per cent a year. In the postwar period, 1922–1929, while the annual increase of manufactured goods was greater, 4.5 per cent, the annual increase in volume of employment was only 1 per cent. Some Technocrats predicted that the unemployed would reach 20,000,000. This was because mass purchasing capacity could not keep up with the flood of goods and services. Again they could find support in Professor Mills's survey. To permit the increase in all production by 3.8 per cent per annum in 1922–1929, investment in new equipment had grown by 6.4 per cent a year, net income of all corporations by 7.3 per cent, their dividend payments by 12.8 per cent, and the profits of financial institutions by 16.2 per cent a year. But the average earnings of employees in manufacturing establishments in the period increased only 1.6 per cent. In contrast, dividend payments of all corporations in that period had increased from $3,437,000,000 to $8,356,000,-000.[55]

The Technocrats charged that facility in production in the power age had invalidated the price and profit system founded on scarcity. As costs of production were radically reduced, prices were destined to decline conspicuously, with repercussions throughout the economy. Debts—representing hardened outmoded prices—would never be paid. Money as it had been known would have to be replaced by an energy unit of value. Society, as R. H. Tawney had said, must become functional; engineers and their fellow specialists, serving collective efficiency rather than private acquisitiveness, must be substituted for bungling businessmen. The public, in a mood of self-

[53] See Graham A. Laing, *Towards Technocracy* (Los Angeles: The Angelus Press, 1933).

[54] Frederick C. Mills, *Economic Tendencies in the United States* (New York: National Bureau of Economic Research, 1932), especially pp. 292 ff.

[55] *Ibid.*, p. 490.

torture, clamored for the Technocrats' articles, speeches, and books.[56] It was reported that Yugoslavia's leading newspaper was explaining the Technocrats' doctrines to Serbian peasants.[57]

Economic frustration, with unemployment, industrial stagnation, and pressing debts, whetted the demand for accusation. The Technocrats offered a commanding combination of the concrete and the abstruse. Their soothsaying, which one did not understand, must be true, for their illustrations, which he did grasp, were appallingly familiar in his own experience. The Technocrat presented the fascinating apparition of a ghost with a slide rule.

Once Technocracy became a sensation, respectable opinion hastened to dissociate itself from the heresy. President Nicholas Murray Butler protested that Columbia University had no academic connection with the group, and Professor Walter Rautenstrauch, who was known as their friend if not sponsor on the faculty, confirmed the disavowal.[58] A split occurred in the coterie, Rautenstrauch, Leon Henderson, Basset Jones, and others withdrawing; the energy survey was taken over by Columbia's Industrial Engineering Department.[59] Howard Scott and his loyal adherents were in effect rolled down from Morningside Heights into the river, but clambered out, vowing to redouble their advocacy. A Columbia University commission soon published a volume giving its plan for *Economic Reconstruction*, more pedestrian than the spirited sallies of their erstwhile guests. Virgil Jordan, of the National Industrial Conference Board, called the doctrines of Technocracy "paralyzing superstitions."[60] Professor Irving Fisher, in no very good position for attack since he had foreseen the indefinite continuance of prosperity till the hour of debacle, found Technocracy backed by neither authority nor reason,[61] and ten days later declared it a dangerous sophistry.[62] The prompt negatives did not conceal an ele-

---

[56] As examples, Howard Scott and others, "Technocracy Smashes the Price System," in *Harper's Magazine* (January, 1933); Scott, *Introduction to Technocracy* (New York: John Day, 1933); Frank Arkright, *The A.B.C. of Technocracy* (New York: Harper and Brothers, 1933); Stuart Chase, *Technocracy, an Interpretation* (New York: John Day, 1933); Harold Loeb, *Life in a Technocracy* (New York: The Viking Press, 1933).

[57] *The New York Times* (January 17, 1933).

[58] *The New York Times* (January 18, 1933).

[59] *Ibid.* (January 24, 1933).

[60] *Ibid.* (January 10, 1933).

[61] *Ibid.* (January 15, 1933).

[62] *Ibid.* (January 25, 1933). President Nicholas Murray Butler, in an article, "Appraising Technocracy," in the *Woman Republican*, warned against rushing to conclu-

ment of naïveté. Accepted observers of American economic developments were able to overcome shock at the Technocrats' revelations barely in time to refute them. Simeon Strunsky, of *The New York Times* editorial staff, and others, took what comfort they could by pointing out exaggerations and arithmetic errors in the indictment, but these were touches that left the antagonist unhurt.[63]

After 1933 the furore died down, though the original Techno-crats showed by wide propaganda, particularly in the West, that they were not discredited in their own eyes or with a section of the public. The fact was that their vivid portrayal of the disparity between production and consumption, and their call for social planning instead of dependence on the profit motive and the price mechanism, were pertinent. By contrast, their constructive proposals were partial and confused. But it was the analysis that they had the wit and courage to make which counted. Technocracy undoubtedly played its part in public response to the New Deal which immediately took the stage. Demonstration a dozen years later of atomic energy gave fresh meaning to the Technocrats' predictions.

HOOVER'S INHIBITED PUBLIC WORKS

With notable exceptions, such as support of the protective tariff, Reconstruction Finance Corporation, and the Farm Board, President Hoover acted on the principle that the role of government in prying the country out of depression must be secondary to that of private business initiative. In this he was Jeffersonian, nearly as dogmatic as the old French Physiocrats. The part of government was the indirect one of putting its own financial house in order, and by this exhibit of virtue inspiring normal enterprise and industry. His position was well illustrated in his firm opposition to the many calls for generous federal relief through extraordinary public works.

One such appeal had come from the American Society of Civil Engineers, and Hoover replied, in May, 1932:

It is generally agreed that the balancing of the Federal budget and unimpaired national credit is indispensable to the restoration of confidence

---

sions.—*Ibid.* (January 28, 1933). Professor K. T. Compton had earlier taken issue with the Technocrats' predictions and conclusions—*Ibid.* (December 20 and 25, 1932). Professor Willford I. King had likewise replied to the theory—*Ibid.* (December 30, 1933).

[63] *Ibid.* (January 2, 22, 1933).

and to the very start of economic recovery. . . . A "public works" program such as is suggested . . . through the issuance of Federal bonds creates at once an enormous further deficit. What is needed is the return of confidence and a capital market through which credit will flow in the thousand rills with its result of employment and increased prices. That confidence will be only destroyed by action in these directions. These channels will continue clogged by fears if we continue attempts to issue large amounts of government bonds for purposes of non-productive works. Such a program as these huge Federal loans for "public works" is a fearful price to pay in putting a few thousand men temporarily at work and dismissing many more thousands from their present employment. . . . It will . . . fool no one to try to cover appearances by resorting to a so-called "extraordinary budget." That device . . . brought the governments of certain foreign countries to the brink of financial disaster.[64]

"Income-producing" or "self-liquidating" works—whether waterworks, toll bridges, or similar projects undertaken by states and political subdivisions, or construction executed by private industry —were preferable. With these the intervention of the RFC was temporary, the government loans would be repaid, no burden would be loaded on the taxpayer, as many or more men would be put to work, and building would not be in excess of need. On the other hand, "public works" in buildings, highways, and river and harbor improvements brought no tangible income and added to the deficit or oppressed the taxpayer; furthermore, these projects increasingly tended to be of remote usefulness. Much of the public construction authorized for the future would bring no advantage to employment if begun at once, being outside the continental United States, needing years for preparation, or being designed for places where the jobless were few.

President Hoover was far from able to envisage such public works as the later Tennessee Valley Authority, which gave large employment, furnished a permanent national asset, and promised multiplying financial returns far into the future. Depressions are cyclical, having nothing to do with budgets demanding to be balanced in fiscal years. Not enough spring was left in the economy to respond to exemplary federal bookkeeping. The true deficit that needed to be wiped out was the social one of idle resources and an admitted eight millions of unemployed. Wise economy required

64 *Hoover State Papers*, II, 194–195.

that solicitude be extended beyond the point of the accountant's pen, beyond the calendar to the country.

Later that same month of May, 1932, as the depression was sinking to its depths, the President's fears were intensified by long-continued congressional refusal of more revenue and less spending; new "pork-barrel" bills would raid the Treasury, and foreign fears of American fiscal stability had sent the dollar to a discount. Hoover appealed first to the public for patience with hunger while he made balancing of the budget his primary care. The situation was "degenerating" in foreign drafts of gold, currency hoarding, a major decline in industrial stocks, and a drop in prices of wheat and cotton. He then went in person before the Senate with his plea. He begged for "drastic reduction in expenditures" and for "adequate revenue legislation" which should "declare to the world the balancing of the Federal budget." [65]

However, at this time, as noted elsewhere, President Hoover was prepared, though reluctantly, to urge federal aid to states for relief, through loans to a total of $300 million by the RFC. Further, the RFC should be allowed to double its borrowing authority to $3 billion to permit it to aid employment and agriculture. He did not make these concessions until after reiterating his general objection, which by now had become a formula with him: "I hold that the maintenance of the sense of individual and personal responsibility of men to their neighbors and the proper separation of functions of the Federal and local governments requires the maintenance of the fundamental principle that the obligation of distress rests upon the individuals, upon the communities and upon the States." [66]

The results of Hoover's efforts with this Congress were on the whole gratifying to him. He staved off, only by veto of a relief bill July 11, 1932, proposals to broaden the lending powers of the RFC enormously, to make immediately public the names of all RFC borrowers, and to allocate federal relief aid to states without regard to the financial competence of those states. He secured the Home Loan Bank Act, which provided an initial capital of $125 million to be subscribed by the RFC but which was to be gradually assumed by the building and loan associations, savings banks, and insurance companies which joined and used the system. There was question whether this was an institution for the relief of home-

[65] *Hoover State Papers*, II, 198–199.　　　[66] *Ibid.*, p. 201.

owners or of home-financing agencies, though it was plain that President Hoover looked upon the two objects as the same. What the President regarded as "pork-barrel" bills had been defeated. He got an increase in revenues of about $1 billion and a reduction in expenditures of some $300 million. Inflationary measures had been eliminated or rendered relatively harmless. Needy states would receive federal aid for relief, and self-liquidating public works would be financed. The Red Cross would distribute in relief the flour from 85,000,000 bushels of wheat, and cloth and mattresses from 350,000 bales of Farm Board cotton. This proved an awkward business, but it was vastly better than destroying the products while people were in want, and the device of giving surpluses to the unemployed was returned to under different forms by the New Deal administration after grievous sins.

SAVE OR SPEND?

There was later much Republican complaint that Congress, with a Democratic majority in the House and control in the Senate, had thwarted President Hoover's recovery plans. The charge was at variance with the even louder administration lament that the winning of the election by Roosevelt three months after the adjournment of Congress had turned evident economic improvement into relapse. This came shortly after Hoover had congratulated himself and the country that the President's Emergency Relief Organization was protecting the people against the worst ravages of enforced idleness. The organization was the expression of President Hoover's belief in local private charity as the chief means of meeting destitution caused by mass unemployment. Creation of it was announced October 21, 1930. The first administrator was Colonel Arthur Woods, who had directed unemployment relief activities under Hoover in 1922. Through the governors, Woods secured the establishment of over 3,000 relief committees of leading citizens. Woods served until August, 1931, when he was succeeded by Walter S. Gifford, who continued for a year. Fred C. Croxton was then administrator until Hoover went out of office. The organization functioned economically, perhaps too economically, with volunteers at the central office in Washington and a small paid field staff.

Hoover had insisted on keeping the $300 million of RFC aid to the states separate from the drive to coordinate private giving. The organization, said the President, was "to maintain the bedrock principle of our liberties by the full mobilization of individual and local resources and responsibilities. . . . Personal feeling and personal responsibility of men to their neighbor is the . . . essential foundation of modern society. A cold and distant charity which puts out its sympathy only through the tax collector, yields a very meager dole of unloving and perfunctory relief." [67] The event was to prove the contrary. The New Deal "dole" was neither meager nor perfunctory, and, however unloving or loving, brought bread which private charity was never able to give.

President Hoover's disappointments—or frustrations, as he regarded them—multiplied in the last session of Congress in his administration. His continued proposals for increased revenue and decreased appropriations encountered much purely political opposition from a Congress controlled by the Democrats, but it is to be remembered that the legislature, so far at cross-purposes with the President, was elected by the country, and also that the virtue of retrenchment as the sovereign means of whipping the depression was being seriously questioned. The need of positive rather than negative recovery measures, though they would add to the deficit, was making ever stronger appeal.

Hoover took Democratic campaign assurances of the desire for a balanced budget at face value, and supposed that he could count on cooperation from Congress to this end. The Democratic platform had favored "maintenance of the national credit by a Federal budget annually balanced," and Governor Roosevelt used words of which he was to be reminded when President: "Any government, like any family, can for a year spend a little more than it earns. But you and I know that continuance of that habit means the poorhouse." [68]

In his annual message, December 6, 1932, Hoover recommended reductions in appropriations by more than $830 million and increase in revenue through a general sales tax "to cover practically all manufactures at a uniform rate [2 per cent], except necessary food and possibly some grades of clothing." [69] He would use his authority

[67] Wilbur and Hyde, *The Hoover Policies*, pp. 380–381.
[68] Franklin D. Roosevelt, *Public Papers and Addresses* (New York: Random House, vols. I–V, 1938; The Macmillan Company, vols VI–IX, 1941), I, 661, 663. With the permission of the publishers.
[69] *Hoover State Papers*, II, 499.

to group or consolidate more than fifty government agencies to save expense. Prominent Democratic leaders in Congress came out for a balanced budget and the general sales tax. But this approval was withdrawn when Roosevelt, from Albany, condemned the sales tax and, by report, Hoover's scheme for reorganization of bureaus, and called influential Democratic congressmen to meet him early in January to discuss federal finances. Agreement, at this meeting, on increases in income tax in the lower brackets, as a substitute for the general sales tax, met public protest and destroyed the prospect of a revenue bill during that session of Congress.

Hoover was not easily discouraged. In a special message he again enjoined revenue through a general sales tax, reduced appropriations, and elimination of overlap in government agencies. "One of the most helpful contributions," he said, "which the Congress and this administration would give to the next administration would be to enable them to start with the Federal budget in balance and the Federal finances in order." [70] He believed this objective was "definitely within reach."

The House defeated the plan for reducing the number of independent offices, and ran up appropriations, according to Hoover's calculations, to $161 million above his recommendations. A week after taking office, President Roosevelt in a message talked budget balancing as Hoover had done: "For three long years the Federal Government has been on the road toward bankruptcy. . . . Our Government's house is not in order. . . . Upon the unimpaired credit of the United States Government rest the safety of deposits, the security of insurance policies, the activity of industrial enterprises, the value of our agricultural products, and the availability of employment. . . . National recovery depends upon it. The effect of the failure to balance the budget upon the growth of the banking crisis is undoubted." [71] The New Deal was full of swift reverses. Unless we are to accept the logic of separation of federal expenditures into regular and "extraordinary" budgets, this call for fiscal devotion on the eve of an adventure in deficits was one of the startling cases.

[70] January 17, 1933; *Hoover State Papers*, II, 581.
[71] *Roosevelt Public Papers and Addresses*, II, 49–50.

CHAPTER IV

Banking and Currency Crisis

FRANKLIN DELANO ROOSEVELT (1882–1945) was elected President on the Democratic ticket in 1932 and was three times re-elected. He was born on his father's estate at Hyde Park, New York, and in education, travel, and outdoor sports made good use of the opportunities offered by wealth and social position. He graduated from Groton School, Harvard, and the law school of Columbia University. His marriage to Anna Eleanor Roosevelt, a distant cousin, gave him a partner whose enlightened mind and warm social sympathies were to be of utmost importance in his public career. While practicing law in New York City he succeeded to his father's responsibilities in Dutchess County, where he was elected and re-elected to the state senate. Here he earned a reputation for political independence and progressive social legislation. In 1911 he championed Woodrow Wilson for the Presidency, worked hard for his nomination and election, and accepted the post of Assistant Secretary of the Navy, which he held from 1913 to 1921. He was the "unwearying advocate" of naval preparedness, espousing policies which he later magnified. A vocal proponent of American membership in the League of Nations, he was nominated for the Vice-Presidency and defeated with James M. Cox in 1920. The next year Roosevelt was stricken with infantile paralysis; his recovery was due as much to his courage as to the therapy of Warm Springs, Georgia.

Now began a cordial association with Alfred E. Smith of New

York. Roosevelt placed Smith in nomination for the presidency at the Democratic conventions of 1924 and 1928. In the latter year, at Smith's insistence, he ran for governor of New York and carried the state while Smith lost it. He was overwhelmingly re-elected in 1930, partly by virtue of differences among the Republicans over prohibition. Chief features of his administration were provision for public development of the water power of the St. Lawrence River and an old-age pension law.

Smith, a candidate for the presidential nomination in the Democratic convention of 1932, bitterly opposed the nomination of Roosevelt, who had three times as many votes as he. Roosevelt was nominated when Texas and California delegates were released by John N. Garner, Speaker of the House, who was named for the Vice-Presidency. Roosevelt at once flew from Albany to Chicago to make a confident acceptance speech in which some naïve promises were unimportant compared to the display of magnetism and enthusiasm in the candidate. The Republicans had renamed President Hoover and Vice-President Charles Curtis, standing with Spartan fortitude on the administration's record.

The campaign was an unequal contest despite or because of Hoover's possession of the office. Roosevelt excoriated Republican failure to attack the depression vigorously. He promised ingenious corrective measures, many of which he later put into effect, though conspicuously absent in practice were the economy and balanced budget which stood high on the campaign list. Hoover's replies were defensive, sincere, statistical, and uninspired; his occasional sharp retorts were extravagant and recoiled upon him. Prominent Republicans deserted Hoover for Roosevelt, who was elected by a popular majority of 7 million, carrying all but six states; the electoral vote was 472 to 59, and the Democrats won a majority of 191 in the House and 22 in the Senate. Roosevelt was re-elected over Governor Alfred M. Landon, of Kansas, the Republican, in 1936 by the completest victory in presidential history. He was less easily successful against Wendell Willkie in 1940 and again over Governor Thomas E. Dewey of New York in 1944.

Roosevelt recognized that America had arrived at a stage where government must play a larger, more persistent, and planful part in its economy. This was necessary for stability, fuller use of resources, and a higher standard of living for a majority of the population.

Corrective and supporting measures of government, however, would be diminished or discontinued as private economic effort revived and showed promise of contributing to national welfare. Roosevelt's reliance, as a permanent American policy, was upon individual enterprise and the forces of the market to determine prices and the shares in the national product. This he repeatedly declared. After the autumn of 1935, when he assured business of a "breathing spell" from government direction, his program increasingly showed his intention to reduce control. However, he made it clear that the previous action of government in imposing high protective tariffs must be gradually undone, and that new fields had been entered permanently, such as the policing of stock promotion and exchanges, social security, and federal development of water power and other regional resources.

At least half the members of Roosevelt's original cabinet were known as liberals favorable to governmental undertakings for rescue and reform of the economy. Cordell Hull, Secretary of State, made chief contribution in negotiation of reciprocal trade agreements. Henry Morgenthau, Jr., who in December, 1933, succeeded William H. Woodin as Secretary of the Treasury, constantly assisted progressive policies from a powerful quarter. Henry A. Wallace, Secretary of Agriculture, at once became conspicuous, by action and utterance, and remained hardly second to Roosevelt as emblem of the New Deal. Frances Perkins, Secretary of Labor, had been Industrial Commissioner of New York when Roosevelt was Governor; though she never succeeded in attracting the personal loyalty of organized labor, her conduct of her department, except in a few instances, enlarged labor's rights and welfare. Harold L. Ickes, Secretary of the Interior, was a man of vigorous independence within the New Deal orbit. Daniel C. Roper, Secretary of Commerce, belonged natively to the New Freedom of Wilson rather than to the New Deal of Roosevelt, but was friendly to current tenets.

James A. Farley, Postmaster General, was chairman of the national and New York State Democratic committees, and had been Roosevelt's campaign manager; as chief dispenser of patronage he showed political loyalty with only incidental commitment to principle. Claude A. Swanson, Secretary of the Navy, George H. Dern, Secretary of War, and Homer S. Cummings, Attorney General, by deserts or accident were less defined in the public mind.

NEW DEAL "BRAINS TRUST"

More prominent and more influential than most of the cabinet officers were presidential and administration advisers composing what was called the "Brains Trust." These, with deletions and substitutions as time went on, had been grouped about Roosevelt from his first bid for the Presidency. Chiefly university professors and their protégés, especially of Columbia and Harvard, they devised proposals, assembled data, prepared speeches and legislation, and in numerous instances occupied important official positions. They represented the first large-scale entrance of academic persons into government councils. The opposition of conservative business and political interests, accurately considering the Brains Trust as a reproach to "practical" wisdom, made this company the target of sarcastic but futile assault.

Conspicuous in the list of "Brain Trusters" were Raymond Moley, Professor of Public Law in Columbia University, who became Assistant Secretary of State and seemed for a time to be the person closest to the President; Rexford G. Tugwell, Professor of Economics in Columbia, later Undersecretary of Agriculture, whose humanitarian services continued longer but still were relinquished too soon; Felix Frankfurter, Professor of Law in Harvard, and afterward appointed a Justice of the Supreme Court, who was a chief recommender of ideas and of disciples; Professor George F. Warren, of Cornell University, whose star as monetary adviser rose rapidly and set as suddenly; and A. A. Berle, young lawyer and economist, later Assistant Secretary of State, whose knowledge and social good will were long employed. Many other academicians and professional men could be mentioned, such as Harry L. Hopkins, Relief Administrator and later Secretary of Commerce, Isador Lubin, Commissioner of Labor Statistics, Jerome Frank and Robert Nathan, who played their parts in early or later stages of the administration. Others of the Brains Trust advised on more purely political matters or on publicity. The charge that those of this circle were "radicals," regularly offered by haters of "That Man in the White House," was inaccurate. On the other hand, critics who thought fundamental institutional changes necessary considered the President's advisers too opportunist. They were in varying degrees left of center. Another constant cry from numerous and not all unfriendly quarters was against bureaucracy, which these men were held to personify. It was meant that they disregarded democratic processes, and sought to make law instead of executing it. This description was often deserved, but it did not take sufficiently into account the economic crisis in which the Roosevelt administration found the country, with consequent necessity of prompter action than Congress could give. Moreover, Congress had formally conferred on the President emergency powers.[1]

Enough admirers and antagonists have attributed to President Franklin Roosevelt an economic philosophy. The variety of these imputed systems suggests that in truth he had no reasoned design founded in analysis and issuing in deliberate articulated actions. If anything, he moved less with the fervor of an innovator than with the assurance of a conservative. He had the Tory tolerance for change. Accustomed all his life to the power bestowed by position, earned by ability, and exercised unselfishly, he knew the difference between shallow opportunism and hopeful experiment. Possessed of tradition, its dogmas did not awe him. Rules, for him, were the result of reasonable assent of society; if they no longer served, or required to be reinterpreted, they could be set aside or modified in the same way in which they had been formed. The master craftsman in politics has a fidelity, but no fetishes. In Gladstone's phrase, "Nothing is so conservative as progress." And Samuel Gompers once remarked, "Men do not know how safe a thing freedom is."

Roosevelt had a belief in the vitality of the American economy and confidence in the sturdiness of American democracy. He honored these qualities of the country by applying their strength to meet new needs in new ways, certain that he would find a sufficient following. Without technical economic learning, he was sometimes attracted to suggestions hastily, but abandoned them as readily rather than be forced into an untenable position. His political perception, in which he did not need to take lessons from anyone, prevented him from being importunate; he did not draw on his last reserves.

Modesty is not thought of as one of his attributes. But he had a responsive humanity, which is better. His enthusiasm had the defect of its virtue, tending to infatuate him and those who came in

[1] See *The New York Times* (April 23, June 17, 1933).

his wide magnetic field. This led him into mistakes, but his own generosity won forgiveness from most.

Nor is it to be forgotten that institutional changes of the New Deal were in many cases overdue in the United States. England and several Continental countries had long made measures of social amelioration familiar, and further efforts impended. Roosevelt and his supporters in good part simply caught this country up to the procession. The brisk advance in economic production and accumulation, until rudely checked in protracted depression, had averted eyes from millions of men, women, and children too long forgotten. Too long not only for their own sakes, but for the health of the society.

Historians will later discern forces at work in this time which now, so close to the events, do not reveal themselves. We shall be wiser in that knowledge. But also something will be lost when the influence of vibrant personalities is obscured as it is bound to be by distance and philosophy. While acknowledging the limitations of present judgment, one makes no apology for ascribing potency to leaders. The future, in substituting pattern for persons, will miss, if not the truth of these times, then much of their spirit.

A patron saint of the more academic of Roosevelt's advisers in the New Deal was the British economist, business executive, and government counselor John Maynard Keynes (1883–1946). Educated at Eton and Cambridge, he acquired experience in the India Office and Treasury. He was the principal representative of the Treasury at the Paris Peace Conference, and deputy of the Chancellor of the Exchequer on the Supreme Economic Council, January–June, 1919. He first came to general American attention with his dissent from Versailles in The Economic Consequences of the Peace, 1919. In the next decade his comments on policy were as frequent as his contributions to doctrine, but he rose to full stature as economic theorist in his Treatise on Money (two volumes, 1930). This was followed by revision and amplification of his principles in The General Theory of Employment, Interest, and Money, 1936. These intricate works were unintelligible to the layman and, in fact, in their fine points, to all but a small coterie of economists. But fortunately for Keynes's influence, his compound reasoning, excruciating mathematical formulas, invented terminology, and perplexing diagrams were only the overlay for a display of common sense.

Keynes's preachment was obviously arrived at from knowledge of nearly a century of socialist protest plus the spectacle of the breakdown of laissez-faire capitalism. Keynes said in effect—what was commonplace in less effete circles—that since consumers could not buy, savers would not invest. Therefore, in whatever disregard of supposed self-acting economic forces, government must spend in order to move the wheels of industry off dead center. While this involved increasing public debt, it was (a) more tolerable than allowing the economy to stagnate or degenerate, and (b) the "deficit financing," if it was so shocking, would hopefully be temporary until revived profit and employment could pay back.

Keynes's prescription for distressed capitalism contained little that was new. Two minds more unlike than those of Keynes and Herbert Hoover would be hard to discover, yet Hoover, by force of circumstances and with faint heart, had used the practical expedient which Keynes set forth boldly and would employ freely. Keynes became an exalted example to American experimental economists and public executives because he furnished a respectable rationalization. Men who had given scant or surreptitious attention to spirited socialist diagnosis and demand found in Keynes righteousness clothed with obligatory ritual. It required only encouragement from an eminent quarter to induce many to declare that economic equilibrium was not only damaged but for the nonce destroyed, and that planned government intervention on a new scale was inescapable. If those who had long made excuses for capitalist shortcomings were to be infected with collectivism, they preferred catching chicken pox from Keynes rather than the smallpox from Marx. Events were to show that Keynes's heresy was incomplete. Public works through deficit financing and the whole bag of tricks of state capitalism would not serve to put men back to work and end the depression. The all-inclusive public enterprise of war would be necessary.

So much for the President's official family and intimates and exemplars who greatly affected the government's economic course. Roosevelt himself was always the dominant figure. He had the virtues of perception and decision, plus the moral strength, cordial temper, and common touch necessary to leadership. Among his assets were a fine bearing, a handsome, alert countenance, and an unrivaled radio voice. Most serious among his defects was a tendency on occasion to substitute plausibility for candor. Where he tried to mislead the public he had first perhaps deceived himself. Instances were not lacking. Though his dissatisfaction with the Supreme Court for holding important New Deal legislation unconstitutional had been expressed in 1935, Roosevelt gave no hint in his 1936 campaign of his bill, soon thereafter introduced (February, 1937), for appointment of additional justices to the highest and to inferior federal courts. Furthermore, the reasons which he made prominent, as that additional judges were needed to clear the court dockets, were plainly not what inspired his action: the desire to change the composition of opinion on the bench. This was a capital error to be recorded against him. His private consummation of the exchange with the British of fifty American destroyers for Atlantic bases was another failure to take the public into his confidence. He pretended, when it suited him, that the Atlantic Charter, which he had promulgated and hailed, did not have formal validity. In asking for a declaration of war he described as a treacherous attack a stroke of the Japanese which he had anticipated and which, after a point in the degeneration of negotiations, he had desired.

These episodes, with whatever reflections they prompt, are destined to recede in the world's memory. A more serious comment upon Roosevelt's leadership of America may be offered more in sorrow than in anger. It is that plans which began so buoyantly for "the more abundant life" and the dignity of man ended in "total war." Praise or blame for this, and where either should be assigned, will be long debated. The melancholy fact remains that a national mobilization for construction brought up in international destruction.

PHENOMENAL BANK FAILURES

The prosperous twenties were oblivious of danger signs—the premonitory business slumps in 1924 and 1927, the forced expansion of consumer credit (installment buying), overextended agriculture with diminishing markets, and maintenance of high protection after the United States had become a creditor nation. However, neglect to take warning from these threats is more easily understood than disregard of the large number of bank failures in the decade. Nearly seven thousand (6,987) banks became insolvent in 1921–1930. Of these, nearly a fifth (1,181) were members of the Federal Reserve System, with deposits of $874,670,000, which should have given special cause for alarm. The suspended nonmember banks numbered 5,806, with deposits of $1,711,718,000. A total of 806 suspended banks, with deposits of $303,306,000, reopened.

The heaviest mortality was among small banks in small towns in areas (West North Central and South Atlantic states) of depressed staple agriculture. More than 60 per cent of the failures were among banks with capital of $25,000 or less, and 90 per cent among those with capital under $100,000. Almost 60 per cent of failed banks were in places of less than 1,000 population; less than 6 per cent were in places of 25,000 and over. The staple farm areas where bank failures were endemic were oversupplied with banks, the two regions cited having 25 per cent of the population of the country, but 38 per cent of the total number of banks. Hazardous practices of country bankers, encouraged by loose state banking laws and slack enforcement, needed only the collapse of crop prices and land values to render them fatal.

After the general business depression struck, bank suspensions suddenly more than doubled. In 1928, there had been 491; in 1929, the number rose to 642; but in 1930, to 1,345. Large city banks increasingly joined the procession into insolvency, an early conspicuous case being that of the Bank of United States, in New York, which failed in December, 1930. In 1931, a peak number of 2,298 banks suspended, with deposits of $1,691,510,000, and in 1932 suspensions were 1,456, with deposits of $715,626,000. Failures in September, 1931, were 305, and rose to the high point of 522 in October. The launching of the National Credit Corporation in this month had temporary preventive effect, more psychological than financial; suspensions in November, 1931, dropped to 175, but the number rose to 358 in December and was 342 in January, 1932.[2] England's abandonment of the gold standard in September, 1931, resulted in the loss by the United States of $700,000,000 in gold in six weeks; domestic withdrawals increased money in circulation in the United States by some $400,000,000 in the period. These

[2] Federal Reserve Board, *Annual Reports,* for the years referred to. See also C. D. Bremer, *American Bank Failures* (New York: Columbia University Press, 1935), pp. 40–57. His figures, constructed from several sources, differ slightly from those given here, because of varying interpretation of terms.

heavy withdrawals were both causes and symptoms of distrust in banks and in the whole economic outlook.

After the stock market crash, bank failures had become wholesale closings. The first bank "holiday" was declared by the Governor of Nevada in October, 1932. The banks of New Orleans were assisted by a shorter holiday in February, 1933. When the trouble of the Detroit banks became acute—February 10 of the same year—President Hoover worked assiduously to prevent their closing and later to end the Michigan bank holiday that the governor had proclaimed. He tried a succession of expedients based on local aid, national aid, and combination of the two, only to have one plan after another fail. From this time on to the early end of his administration—though the tortured days of accumulating bank closings seemed to drag heavily enough—the President virtually ceased to put hope in his independent efforts, and pitched his strategy on appeals to the President-Elect. Hoover became convinced that all of the alarming manifestations of the crisis—loss of gold stocks, hoarding, bank failures, and the epidemic of bank holidays to prevent more failures—were due to no neglect of his. Previous bank difficulties had been local and manageable. The present panic, he contended, was due to widespread fear, at home and abroad, that Roosevelt, when he came into office, would disavow the gold standard and indulge in monetary chicanery which could only be guessed at. Roosevelt's equivocal assurances during the campaign of attachment to "sound" money were followed by evidences that he was flirting with notions of an irredeemable standard. Conservative Democrats were remonstrating with him on this score, economists and financial editors voiced their apprehensions at the prospect.

Roosevelt returned from a ten-day fishing trip just as the Michigan bank holiday was proclaimed. Three days later, February 17, having decided that the only rescue lay in inducing the President-Elect to declare himself against inflation of the currency and in favor of supporting measures, Hoover sent him by secret-service messenger a long letter begging for such a public statement. Roosevelt discussed the plea with intimate advisers, and concluded that he should not fall in with it. The same decision would probably have been reached had not Hoover's letter been accusing. Roosevelt considered that runs on banks were not due to rumors about the future of the gold standard, but grew from well-founded fear of the safety of deposits. Hoover was worse than tactless in referring to "a steadily degenerating confidence in the future," and in urging that a statement by Roosevelt on several of his coming policies "would serve greatly to *restore* confidence and cause *a resumption of the march of recovery.*" (Italics mine.) Roosevelt was admonished to promise what Hoover had not performed—to balance the budget. There is clear evidence that Hoover, in addition to patriotic purpose, had the unworthy design of tossing Roosevelt on the horns of a dilemma—the President-Elect must make the statement and thereby endorse the Hoover program, or refuse to make it and incur responsibility for the storm about to break.

Thus on February 20 Hoover wrote to Senator David A. Reed: "I realize that if these declarations be made by the President-Elect, he will have ratified the whole major program of the Republican Administration; that is, it means the abandonment of 90% of the so-called new deal. But unless this is done, they run a grave danger of precipitating a complete financial debacle. If it is precipitated, the responsibility lies squarely with them for they have had ample warning—unless, of course, such a debacle is part of the 'new deal.'"[3]

Hoover made other appeals to Roosevelt directly, and indirectly through conversations with William H. Woodin, the incoming Secretary of the Treasury, but without result.[4] The Federal Reserve Advisory Council made a similar request of the President-elect.

BANK PARALYSIS

Bank holidays were declared in Indiana on February 23, in Maryland on the 25th, in Arkansas on the 27th, and in Ohio on the 28th. The Michigan closing, while a shock, was understandable, for Detroit's great automobile industry was one of the prime sufferers in the depression, but the Maryland bank holiday, in a state with a better balanced economy, was a more serious portent. As banking in successive states was suspended, the drain on resources of institutions in surrounding areas, and particularly on the New York banks, increased in intensity. By March 3, general protective clos-

[3] Myers and Newton, *The Hoover Administration*, p. 341.
[4] For Hoover's side of this episode see *ibid.*, pp. 329 ff., and for Roosevelt's side, Raymond Moley, *After Seven Years* (New York: Harper & Brothers, 1939), pp. 139 ff.

ings had occurred in seventeen more states, mostly in the South and West, and including California, Oregon, Texas, and Wisconsin. The Federal Reserve Bank of New York later reported:

> In the period of a little over three weeks between February 8 and March 3, the withdrawals of currency by the member banks from the Reserve Banks were over $1,700,000,000, the greater part of which occurred in the last week of the period. Out-of-town banks withdrew nearly $800,000,000 from their balances with New York City banks in order to meet the demands on them, and banks throughout the country found it necessary to draw more and more heavily upon the Federal Reserve Banks for additional credit. . . . The excess gold reserves of the Federal Reserve Banks declined to a little over $400,000,000, as compared with a high point of nearly $1,500,000,000 in January. The burden fell most heavily on the New York Reserve Bank which was called upon to meet not alone the demands from its own district but large demands from other districts as well.[5]

Besides losses of balances to the interior, New York banks were progressively depleted by demands of foreigners, these two outgoing streams amounting during the day of March 3 alone to more than $300,000,000.

Hoover to the last continued to pin hopes to a reassuring statement if this could be pressed from Roosevelt, and thereby diverted energies that should have gone into completion and execution of his own measures. He appealed repeatedly to the Federal Reserve Board for constructive advice, but got feeble response. He comforted himself with the observation that more than three fourths of the banks of the country, in volume of deposits, were still functioning. He rejected the proposal, though endorsed at the eleventh hour by the Federal Reserve Board, for a universal bank closing by presidential proclamation; he dallied with schemes of limited federal guarantee of deposits, of restricted withdrawal (to prevent hoarding and foreign shipment of gold), and of issue of clearinghouse certificates, but ended by resigning action to the state governors.

In the early morning hours of March 4, Inauguration Day, Treasury officials, old and new working together, appealed to the governors of all the remaining states whose banks were open, to close them. Finally Lehman of New York, the most reluctant, agreed, and so twenty-five more bank holidays were proclaimed.

[5] New York Federal Reserve Bank, *Monthly Review of Credit and Business Conditions* (April, 1931), p. 26.

The fate of the federal reserve banks only hung temporarily in doubt.

When Roosevelt stood that Saturday afternoon to take the oath as President, the economic heart of the country, as symbolized in the banks, had stopped beating. He had determined on emergency measures of resuscitation, swiftly to be translated into action. But at once he gave the nation a restorative in the courageous tone of his inaugural. This challenge to depression fears cleared the way for executive and congressional actions that were to come in unprecedented sequence. Despair, about to become terror, was replaced by resolve, as the President assured "the only thing we have to fear is fear itself—nameless, unreasoning, unjustified terror which paralyzes needed efforts to convert retreat into advance. . . . This Nation asks for action, and action now." If Congress failed, he would "ask . . . for the . . . broad Executive power to wage a war against the emergency, as great as the power that would be given me if we were in fact invaded by a foreign foe. . . . The people of the United States have not failed. In their need they have registered a mandate that they want direct, vigorous action." [6]

Thereafter means were still important enough, in all conscience, but the first crucial battle of reviving the nation's belief in its capacities had been won. Perhaps it is more accurate to say that the nation was given faith in the capacity of the new President to make imperative decisions and to lead the country in lines of action.

Roosevelt had determined to invoke emergency powers left over from World War I days to declare a bank holiday; he would call into conference such bankers as he could reach immediately, and with their help improvise a law, to be passed by a special session of Congress, which would give the banks first aid. The hectic discussions in the next days and nights between bankers, Treasury officials (including those of Hoover's regime), other presidential advisers, and congressional leaders produced the tactic of holding, as far as possible, to familiar institutions and practices. Radicalism was to be discountenanced. A minor decision was not to resort to scrip as a national expedient, but to rely on issues of federal reserve notes. A major decision was that the federal government would not possess itself of the banks, but, with maximum speed, would reopen, in the hands of their owners and managers, all that were sound. Some felt

<hr />

[6] *Roosevelt Public Papers and Addresses,* II, 11, 12, 15.

at the time, and have continued to believe since, that this was a moment when the country, and Congress, would have followed the President in making the banks national property. If that had been done, the other chief sectors of the economy could have been subsequently socialized. Such an action would have meant that the New Deal, instead of reforming glaring defects in order to preserve the capitalist system, would have set about superseding it.

The President scouted the idea. Wise decision or not, this was probably the inevitable one. Under emergency conditions the interests and training of all the responsible participants dictated that course. It would have required men long schooled in collectivist advocacy to put the country on a different tack.

MEASURES TO MEET FINANCIAL CRISIS

The early monetary and banking measures of the New Deal must be treated together: though often of contrary tendencies, the two were inextricably confused. The proclamation, issued Monday morning, March 6, under the old Trading-with-the-Enemy Act, declared a four-day bank holiday during which all banking functions were suspended, though such a minor service as the making of change was permitted. The proclamation really took the country off the gold standard by forbidding the export of gold and the redemption of currency in gold or gold certificates. Students of money, according to the preference of each, have chosen several later dates as marking the departure from the gold standard, but this original proclamation in fact put gold beyond reach, which is the practical test.

Congress was called in special session for March 9, and that very day passed the hurriedly drawn Emergency Banking Act. This law validated the national bank holiday and other measures that the President had already taken, furnished distressed banks with capital and currency, and provided a plan for reopening of all banks except those in hopeless condition.

Two days previously, March 7, the Secretary of the Treasury issued a regulation requiring that member banks should deliver all gold and gold certificates held by them to Federal Reserve banks in return for other forms of coin or currency. On March 8 the Federal Reserve Board directed reserve banks to forward to the board lists of all persons who had withdrawn gold or gold certificates from reserve or member banks since February 1 and who had not redeposited these by March 13. The Executive Order of March 10 did little more than formalize action already taken forbidding export of gold and dealings in foreign exchange except under Treasury permission. While motives are hard to assess, and the ostensible reason for forbidding hoarding and export of gold was to protect the credit of the United States, subsequent policy prompts the conclusion that the true purpose was to remove gold and gold dealings so as to prevent depreciation of the paper currency from becoming dangerously obvious.

This Emergency Banking Act permitted the Reconstruction Finance Corporation to supply capital to banks by buying their preferred stock (called "capital notes" in the case of state banks not allowed to issue preferred stock). Federal Reserve banks were empowered to make loans to nonmember state banks and, on security of United States obligations, directly to business enterprises. New currency was provided by issue of Federal Reserve bank notes which, as always, needed no gold reserve, but which were now supported not solely by government securities, but by any kind of business paper which the Federal Reserve banks thought fit, even though not ordinarily eligible for rediscount.

For the all-important purpose of reopening the banks, these were divided into four groups. Those considered fully sound (with assets equal to their deposits) were allowed to resume unrestricted payments to depositors; in this group fell half the banks of the country, with 90 per cent of the banking resources, and all were reopened by March 15. In a second group were banks (a fourth of the total number) in less good condition, which were allowed to pay out a percentage of their deposits. "Conservators" took charge of banks in the third group, whose assets were so depleted that they were allowed to make no payments from old deposits, though they might accept new deposits if these were segregated and kept in cash or government securities. About 5 per cent of banks, numbering a thousand, fell in the fourth group, in such bad condition that they were closed permanently. The President had extended the original four-day bank holiday.

Judging the soundness of the banks, especially those to be fully reopened at once, was demanding and ticklish work for Treasury officials already near physical and mental exhaustion. Calculations were necessarily as rough as they were speedy. Many decisions were tipped in favor of public convenience and morale, as most conspicuously in case of the Bank of California, with its 410 branches and one million depositors.

As soon as banks began to be reopened, fears were dispelled; in the first three weeks $1,185,000,000 of currency flowed back to the banks, which enabled them to retire more than $850,000,000 of Federal Reserve credit and to increase the reserves of member banks by more than $200,000,000. The President's first radio "fireside chat," on Sunday night, March 12, in which he explained what the government was doing and asked the people to return their money to the banks had much to do with the gratifying result. His words and tone of voice were more effective than any quantity of statutes and Treasury mechanism, and furnished the best illustration of the fact that the New Deal, in its pristine days, was a man even more than it was a group of measures.

Between March 4 and the middle of the month, $370 million of gold and gold certificates were turned in under government orders, or $50 million more than had gone into circulation since the first of the year. The flow continued heavy through March, was $175 million more in the second quarter, and $60 million more by the end of the year 1933. In addition, scrip of many sorts, which had been issued prior to the national bank holiday to the extent of perhaps a billion dollars in nominal value, was promptly retired. Though it had been considered that perhaps as much as $2 billion of the newly engraved Federal Reserve bank notes would be required, only a few hundred million were demanded.[7]

Still, the process of reopening the banks that were on a restricted basis was slow, and many small communities were entirely without banks for months. At the end of May, 1,163 member banks with deposits of $1,856,000,000, and nonmember banks with perhaps equal deposits, continued to be restricted. This situation was inevitable, and did not diminish the triumph of putting a speedy and unmistakable end to the banking crisis that had greeted the administration on the threshold.

Raymond Moley has written: "It cannot be emphasized too strongly that the policies which vanquished the bank crisis were

[7] Federal Reserve Board, *Annual Report* (1933), p. 15.

thoroughly conservative policies. The sole departure from convention lay in the swiftness and boldness with which they were carried out. Those who conceived and executed them were intent upon rallying the confidence, first, of the conservative business and banking leaders of the country and, then, through them, of the public generally. . . . If ever there was a moment when things hung in the balance, it was on March 5, 1933—when unorthodoxy would have drained the last remaining strength of the capitalistic system. Capitalism was saved in eight days. . . ." [8] One may be allowed to fear that an economic system which had come so near to self-destruction was scarcely worth the passionate loyalty expressed.

PREPARATION FOR INFLATION

The Emergency Banking Act gave the President authority over gold during the continuance of the crisis. He used this power on April 5 in an order requiring that all persons, by May 1, should deliver to Federal Reserve or member banks any gold coin or bullion, and gold certificates held by them, and member banks must in turn deliver gold and gold certificates to federal reserve banks. The order of March 10, though it prohibited the free export of gold, permitted the export, under license, of enough to meet "legitimate and normal business requirements." An order of April 20 took the United States unequivocally off the gold standard by forbidding gold export unless this was shown to be "necessary to promote the public interest." The President's statements at the time, and the reasons he gave later for his actions, indicated that he was convinced the country could not simultaneously hold to the gold standard and raise domestic prices, and he was determined to accomplish the latter. By this time an inner group of advisers was persuading the President of the need of a managed currency, while others not of that belief broke with him on this issue. Still, Roosevelt declared that it was the desire of the United States to return to the gold standard and "to get the world as a whole back on some form of gold standard." [9] This was for the future; at the time the dollar depreciated on the foreign exchanges and the domestic price level moved upward.

[8] *After Seven Years,* p. 155.
[9] *Roosevelt Public Papers and Addresses,* II, 140.

Just before this arbitrary gold embargo, inflationary demands in the Senate (the House was always ready for them) rose to formidable pitch. Senator Burton K. Wheeler came close to getting free coinage of silver at a ratio of 16 to 1. Senator Elbert D. Thomas of Utah at once introduced an omnibus inflationary amendment to the Emergency Farm Relief bill. The President promptly decided to accept, as permissive, powers that otherwise might later be thrust upon him as mandatory. Thomas would agree to a rewriting of his amendment. Plans for conversations with Prime Minister MacDonald looking to the London Economic Conference were at that moment being made, and especially for this reason State Department and other more conservative advisers were shocked at the President's acquiescence in domestic inflation. Lewis Douglas, Director of the Budget, lamented "the end of Western civilization." [10]

The Senate passed the Thomas inflation amendment three to one on April 28, and a week later the House approved it by a heavier vote. The President was given six methods of increasing the credit and currency of the country; any or all could be invoked whenever depreciation of foreign currencies adversely affected the foreign commerce of the United States, when necessary to maintain parity of currency issues of this country, when emergency required expansion of credit, or when credit expansion here was needed to secure international currency stabilization. The inflationary options were as follows: (1) to persuade the Federal Reserve banks to buy government obligations in the open market to the extent of $3 billion, without tax on reserve deficiency, in order to put more lending power in the hands of the banks. If the reserve banks refused, the Treasury might (2) issue $3 billion in United States notes (fiat "greenbacks") in exchange for government bonds, 4 per cent of these notes to be retired annually. These notes and all other coin and currency were to be full legal tender. Or (3) the President might adopt bimetallism, fixing the relative weight of gold and silver. Or (4) he could reduce the weight of the standard gold dollar (which was in fact not procurable) by not more than 50 per cent. These last three devices were to be used only in case the reserve banks refused to make the open-market purchases. Besides,

[10] Ernest K. Lindley, *The Roosevelt Revolution* (New York: The Viking Press, 1933), p. 119.

the President might (5), for six months, accept silver at not more than 50 cents an ounce—then 10 per cent above the market price—in payment of debts due the United States from foreign governments, to a maximum value of $200 million silver certificates to be issued against most of this bullion. Lastly, (6) in wording which bowed to restraint where all the rest of the measure embraced expansion, the Federal Reserve Board might increase or decrease reserve requirements.

His fears confirmed, Senator Carter Glass, who had refused the post of Secretary of the Treasury because he doubted that Roosevelt would hold to gold, now made a denunciation of the amendment as vehement as it was futile. Flinging the door wide to inflation helped boom industry and stocks for a time. The event was to prove, however, that powers to issue Federal Reserve notes and greenbacks would not be used, though the other devices, plus deficit financing, furnished means enough. In a radio speech on May 7 Roosevelt explained that the inflation amendment would permit the administration to embrace the object of a commodity dollar, "raising . . . prices to such an extent that those who have borrowed money will, on the average, be able to repay that money in the same kind of dollar which they borrowed." [11] This scheme was to be elaborated in a "fireside chat" in October.

Abrogation of the gold clause in public and private contracts, accomplished in a joint resolution signed by the President June 5, 1933, was a foregone conclusion from orders and acts that prohibited the paying out of gold. The resolution said that every obligation, past or future, with gold clauses or without, "shall be discharged upon payment, dollar for dollar, in any coin or currency which at the time of payment is legal tender for public and private debts." [12] The gold clause in contracts, as a protection to creditors, ran back to the time of the first issue of greenbacks during the Civil War. Some $100 billion of obligations, including most of the $22 billion of federal debt, carried the gold clause. The President's explanation, in support of abrogation, was that this country had only between 3 and 4 billions of monetary gold, and so if claimants "started in to demand gold," only one in twenty-five could be satis-

[11] *Roosevelt Public Papers and Addresses,* II, 166.
[12] Joint Resolution, No. 10, 73 Cong., 1 Sess., p. 112.

fied.[13] This did not go to the point, unless a situation of a universal gold panic is assumed.

The Supreme Court, in cases decided early in 1935, in effect supported the government all along the line. The gold clauses in private contracts were invalid because they attempted to interfere with the constitutional power of Congress to determine the value of its money. Further, gold could not in fact be had, and the demand for currency "equivalent" to the gold called for would have resulted in "unjustified enrichment" to the extent of some 60 per cent. True, said the Court, government exceeded its powers in abrogating the gold clause in its own bonds, but plaintiffs had no recourse because they had not shown that they had suffered any loss. The minority of the Court regarded "repudiation and spoliation of citizens by their sovereign with abhorrence. . . ." [14]

The foregoing decisions applied to American citizens, who, it was held, had suffered no loss. But foreigners owning American securities, public and private, containing the gold clause, did lose through international depreciation of the dollar. Therefore the President called for a law, approved August 27, 1935, closing the courts to suits against the government for damages in consequence of abrogation of the gold clause. Later decisions applied the Supreme Court's ruling to special cases that arose.

WORLD ECONOMIC CONFERENCE SCUTTLED

The most serious consequence of the administration's rapidly developing policy of currency management was in the destruction of the World Monetary and Economic Conference which met in London in June and July that summer of 1933. For the President to disappoint assurances of attachment to gold, which he was held to have given to his own country, was one thing; as a domestic matter the ends might justify the means. But the President had committed himself to supporting a last concerted international attempt at exchange and currency stabilization, and the domestic policy which he adopted flew in the face of promises to the rest of the world. In many ways, as has been seen in these pages, Roose-

[13] Franklin D. Roosevelt, On Our Way (New York: The John Day Company, 1934), p. 78. Quoted by permission.
[14] U. S. Reports, Vol. 294 (October term, 1934), pp. 240–381.

velt carried farther, and made truly effective, means which Hoover had inaugurated or proposed. But his monetary actions, in their international results, reversed his predecessor's efforts, and were intended to do so.

This decision was probably the most momentous one that Franklin Roosevelt made. One may speculate, with cause, whether in defeating the world's resolution to stabilize currencies and thereby promote trade, President Roosevelt did not contribute heavily to the international economic and political deterioration that led to fresh war. Even so, was his decision reasoned, did he seek earnestly to strike a balance between immediate gain and later loss? Or, infatuated with the prospect of rising prices at home, did he hastily condemn others to frustration, discord, and the appeal to arms? There was a lighthearted suddenness in his behavior which spoke of ignorance, or certainly of the little knowledge which is a dangerous thing. The London Conference, in its preliminary plans, was a holdover from Hoover. Currency and exchange stabilization, restoration of trade, and, hopefully, a general return to the international gold standard were the mutual objectives in conversations between President Roosevelt and European ministers in April and May. The countries trying to remain on the gold standard—France, Switzerland, Holland, Belgium, Italy—were desperately anxious for this solution, and Britain did not want deliberate depreciation of the dollar to destroy her export trade. But already, while Roosevelt was giving lip service to international stabilization, he was tasting the sweets of nationalist action by the United States to raise prices and so find exit from its depression. The two commitments overlapped —the one to national recovery through world cooperation, the other to national recovery through purely domestic means which, said pious afterthought, would really furnish the best prospect of international prosperity.

New Deal expedients—departure from gold, NRA, AAA—all looked to the raising of the domestic price level, and determined in advance the course which Roosevelt was to take in smashing the London Conference. It was increasingly apparent in talks with European statesmen that their countries would not continue to make more than token payments, if those, on their debts to the United States. Roosevelt was a ready pupil in the monetary theories of Professor George F. Warren, of Cornell, which had the moral endorsement of John Maynard Keynes. These influences were compelling enough, but the temptation to use home remedies was strong without them. Britain had found that her forced abandonment of gold was a blessing in disguise, for, with a depreciated pound, she had swelled her exports. If the countries still clinging to gold, in their pleas to the United States not to inflate its currency, were concerned for world welfare, Britain's concurrence in the entreaty was suspect, for she wanted to preserve her recent advantage. The competition in currency depreciation and trade restrictions had brought world economic condition to a sorry pass, but was it the command of the United States to be saint where others had been sinners? Anyhow, her citizens were self-contained enough to escape the familiar penalties encountered by the rest, big enough to impart a world benefit by whatever self-serving devices they adopted. It was politically intoxicating to the President to see stock and commodity prices rising. What if part of this was due to so bold a thing as speculation? That did not change the gratifying result. What if the dollar was falling on the exchanges? That, if bad at all, was an irrelevant incident.

The American delegation to the London Conference, headed by Secretary of State Hull, was heterogeneous in views, and several members were without experience in international negotiations. Over and above the divisions that developed in its own ranks, there was the difference between Roosevelt and Hull, the former tending toward domestic inflation, the latter bent upon stabilization of currencies and the renewal of world trade. A smaller group—containing Governor George L. Harrison, of the New York Federal Reserve Bank, O. M. W. Sprague, adviser to the Treasury, and James P. Warburg, financial adviser to the American delegation—sailed a few days later to confer with central bank officials with a view to temporary exchange stabilization while the conference did its work. These conversations turned into a contest on the part of the Bank of England and the Bank of France to have the dollar pegged about where it was (at $4.00 to the pound), rather than see it sink lower with a trade disadvantage to England and the feared result of pushing France, Switzerland, and others off gold. The Americans acquiesced, only to be sharply corrected by Roosevelt. The President said he attached little importance to stabilization of a few currencies with respect to each other, but that if such was attempted, he wanted more room for the dollar to depreciate. Governor Harrison thereupon hurriedly left for home, while the others of the bank negotiators cabled that they would try to drive a better bargain with the Europeans, but hoped that the President would not compel them to reverse their assurances of a satisfactory temporary stabilization.

Roosevelt had told Raymond Moley, Assistant Secretary of State, to be in readiness to go to London as his liaison officer. Moley was now rushed to the President, on a fishing cruise on the *Amberjack*, off Pollock Light, by plane and destroyer. Roosevelt, in giving instructions to Moley, was chiefly mindful of the success his domestic program was having in raising prices and lifting America out of depression. If the other nations would go along in his objective of raising the world price level, only then could the United States cooperate at the London Conference.

A DISCOMFITED MESSENGER

Moley sailed for England June 21, and the same day the President made another thrust at the conference in a cable to Warburg and Sprague. He turned down a new stabilization proposal, said that further attempts at temporary stabilization should be discontinued. This threw the American delegation into something between confusion and hopelessness. It was the hopelessness which communicated itself to the others at the conference, but the American delegation loyally issued a statement the next day explaining that efforts of its government to raise prices in the United States were the most important contribution it could make to the success of the conference; at the same time the delegation was moving for "ultimate worldwide stabilization . . . for the purpose of stimulating economic activities and improving prices." [15]

When Moley arrived in London, he found the delegates of the gold countries in a panic. They were losing gold fast, were afraid the President would use his inflationary powers in a way to make maintenance of the gold standard anywhere in the world impossible. They had vivid memories of the wild inflation as a sequel to the war, and were fearful that if it reappeared there might be revolutions in Europe. Representatives of the countries tenuously holding to the gold

[15] *The New York Times* (June 23, 1933).

standard had drawn up a declaration, in which Britain joined heartily. The Americans at the conference, particularly Moley, were besought to get President Roosevelt to agree to it. The statement was similar (except that it omitted provision for silver) to a resolution submitted to the conference by Senator Key Pittman of the silver-producing state of Nevada, ten days before, June 19. The brief document declared that stability in the international monetary field should be achieved as quickly as possible; it was agreed that an international gold standard should be re-established, "but the time at which each of the countries off gold could undertake stabilization and the parity at which each of the countries off gold could undertake stabilization must be determined by the respective governments";[16] countries still on the gold standard would maintain the free working of the standard at current gold parities; countries not on the gold standard undertook to limit exchange speculation, and all central banks were to work together for the objects of the declaration.

Moley cabled this statement to the President and did all possible to secure his approval. Moley and the other Americans in London considered that the document was in line with the President's wishes, in no way tying his hands, and at the same time it would have psychological value in Europe and permit the conference to continue and complete its work. Roosevelt was at his home on Campobello Island, off the coast of Maine, and without a telephone, so that his answer was delayed during anxious days. When it came, July 1, it was a refusal to accept the declaration. In the reply, Roosevelt apparently was influenced by a memorandum of Herbert Swope on the advantages of domestic price lifting, and by the personal advice of Henry Morgenthau, Jr., who had become a believer in the monetary theories of Professors George F. Warren and Frank A. Pearson. The President said that the United States must be left free in the manipulation of domestic prices. Taking exception to the promise in the declaration, he did not know how governments could check speculation. Efforts at stabilization would leave currencies unsound so long as national budgets remained unbalanced.

This message showed misapprehension of what the declaration

16 Arthur W. Crawford, *Monetary Management under the New Deal* (Washington: American Council on Public Affairs, 1940), p. 54.

proposed, imperfect understanding of monetary principles, and a reversal of his earlier action in encouraging the conference. If announced in that form, it would wreck the conference then and there. The substance of it leaked out, with profoundly disturbing effect. Moley and his friends hastily composed a solicitous explanation of the Roosevelt rejection for official release, but this was not used because that morning, July 3, came a fresh message from the President which amplified the previous one and employed a lecturing tone. The substance of the message was lamented by practically all at the conference, while the manner of it was resented by the Europeans. Roosevelt remonstrated that the conference should not be diverted from its broader object of greater prosperity for all countries by attempting temporary and artificial stabilization of a few currencies. "The sound internal economic system of a nation is a greater factor in its well-being than the price of its currency in changing terms of the currencies of other nations." National budgets must be balanced. Further, "old fetishes of so-called international bankers are being replaced by efforts to plan national currencies with the objective of giving to those currencies a continuing purchasing power which does not greatly vary in terms of the commodities and need of modern civilization. Let me be frank in saying that the United States seeks the kind of dollar which a generation hence will have the same purchasing and debt-paying power as the dollar value we hope to attain in the near future. That objective means more to the good of other nations than a fixed ratio for a month or two in terms of the pound or franc." Temporary exchange fixing was not the true answer to restoration of world trade; instead, existing embargoes must be mitigated. "The Conference was called to better and perhaps to cure fundamental economic ills. It must not be diverted from that effort." [17]

This deliverance of Roosevelt exploded the conference. Hull, Moley, and others worked desperately to save it, but the best they could do was to keep it lingering for three weeks, after which it "recessed," never to meet again. This result was inevitable after Roosevelt changed his stand from international cooperation to an experiment in purely national salvation. If world trade was to be

[17] *The New York Times* (July 4, 1933).

revived, currencies must be stabilized, and quickly. It was worse than idle to talk of postponing this work, for the President's statements portended a rivalry in currency depreciation, and, in throwing the remaining countries off gold, removed indefinitely the reconstruction of the gold standard. Not even time can give a verdict, for international collaboration, then so much desired by all other countries, might not have been effective either. It may be said, however, that the course which the President charted contributed to economic distress in Europe and Asia and thus helped conduct to World War II.

Roosevelt wrote five years later: "It is true that my radio message to the London Conference fell upon it like a bombshell. This was because the message was realistic at a time when the gold bloc nations were seeking a purely limited objective and were unwilling to go to the root of national and international problems." [18] John Maynard Keynes of Britain, not in agreement with his own government, called the President "magnificently right." [19] On the other hand, James P. Warburg in resigning July 6 as financial adviser of the American delegation, declared to Hull that the President "now has in mind a monetary and currency program which differs quite radically from that which formed the basis of his original instructions to us." [20] Professor Sprague, who resigned as economic adviser to the Treasury in November, 1933, published a forthright but good-tempered statement reviewing the whole New Deal program to that point. He approved parts of it, but declared "the decided opinion that neither further depreciation of the dollar nor inflation will be helpful as a means of bringing about a trade recovery and higher prices. . . . the best conceived monetary policies can do no more than support and facilitate those economic policies and developments which are required to convert the existing situation from depression into prosperity." [21] He thought the Warren scheme of further depreciation of the dollar through purchases of gold unnecessary, relatively unfruitful in raising prices, and dangerous as

[18] *Roosevelt Public Papers and Addresses*, II, 266.
[19] Irving Fisher, *Stable Money; A History of the Movement* (New York: Adelphi Co., 1934), p. 358.
[20] James P. Warburg, *The Money Muddle* (New York: Alfred A. Knopf, Inc., 1934), p. 121.
[21] O. M. W. Sprague, *Recovery and Common Sense* (Boston: Houghton Mifflin Company, 1934), pp. 70–71.

showing a willingness of the administration to resort to extreme measures.

WILLIAM JENNINGS BRYAN REDIVIVUS

The one tangible result of the London Conference was a resolution to lift the value of silver. The conference itself did no more than acquiesce in a plan formed by the chief silver-producing countries—the United States, Mexico, Canada, Peru and Australia—and the chief silver-using nations—India, China, and Spain. The pact, as worked out, provided that during four years beginning January 1, 1934, the silver-producing countries would absorb, for coinage, legal reserves, and so on, 35,000,000 ounces of silver annually, and the silver-using countries bound themselves not to dump surpluses on the market by melting and depreciation. As it turned out, the United States was to bear much the heaviest responsibility in the program. While the country produced, in 1932, about 20 per cent of the silver, the United States government was to buy up 70 per cent (24,421,410 ounces) of the amount to be absorbed by all.[22] The silver-using countries did not bind themselves to restrict their average sales.

The United States was assigned, and eagerly assumed, the chief role because the whole silver scheme was pushed through by Senator Pittman, who was chairman of both the silver subcommittee of the conference and of the Foreign Affairs Committee of the United States Senate. As a Democrat and as a silver advocate he had been unsuccessful in his persistent efforts under Republican presidents, except in keeping up a clamor as the price of silver dropped from $1.12 an ounce in 1919 to 29 cents in 1931.[23] He had advanced the contention that China's purchases from the United States had declined because of the low value of silver currency in terms of the United States gold currency. Ostensibly, his plan was, by putting and keeping silver in monetary circulation, directly and indirectly, to raise general prices, especially in the United States, but in this he only took advantage of what had become a popular demand for inflation. His real purpose, it was plain, was to give a handsome subsidy to the western silver-producing states.

[22] See *The New York Times* (July 23, 1933).
[23] Crawford, *Monetary Management under the New Deal*, p. 64.

Silver purchase formed an important feature of the New Deal program of inflation, and indeed continued after economy and price restriction were being officially cried up. This silver policy was grounded in the Thomas Amendment to the Agricultural Adjustment Act of May, 1933, the silver pact in connection with the London Conference in July, 1933, the Gold Reserve Act and devaluation of the dollar in January, 1934, and the Silver Purchase Act of the following June. In the main it was abortive, or worse—wasteful, and harmful to silver countries, particularly China; its one substantial effect was what was all along chiefly intended: the giving of a public subsidy to western silver producers.

Silver purchase was begun under an executive order of December 21, 1933, and was confined at this time to domestic newly mined metal. The authority was the Thomas Amendment, which permitted the President to provide for free coinage of silver at the ratio to gold which he might fix. He fixed the ratio in effect on the date of the order, 23.22 grains of fine gold and 371.25 grains of pure silver, or the old 16 to 1. With gold worth $20.67 an ounce, the currency value of the bullion in a silver dollar was one sixteenth of the gold price, or $1.29 an ounce. The silver producers wanted this price paid for their new metal, but the President objected, and the order took half the offered silver in "seigniorage," this silver to be retained as bullion. This gave the domestic producers 64.64 cents, which was 19 cents above the market. Seven months after the Silver Purchase Act was passed, the program entered on its second and broader phase, with nationalization of domestic silver and extension of United States buying to all the world.

Passage of the Gold Reserve Act spurred silver advocates to introduce bills. None met the President's wishes; and on May 22, 1934, he sent to Congress a silver message, and simultaneously a new bill embodying his views was presented. Enactment of this (June 19) was rushed. The Secretary of the Treasury was to buy silver at home or abroad until it amounted to one fourth of the monetary value of the government's metallic stocks, or until the market price of silver reached the monetary value of $1.29 an ounce. No silver previously produced in the United States should be bought at more than 50 cents an ounce. Certificates, legal tender and redeemable in standard silver dollars, should be put in circulation against all silver purchased. Furthermore, with minor exceptions, all silver was nationalized and must be delivered to the mints at a fair price, soon set at about 50 cents an ounce. No reduction was made in the weight of the standard silver dollar though, since devaluation of the gold dollar, the fine metal in the two stood to each other in the new ratio of 27 to 1, instead of the old 16 to 1. However, the Gold Reserve Act gave the President authority to devalue the silver dollar in the same ratio as he devalued the gold dollar, a devaluation which, if done, would mean a value of $2.19 an ounce instead of $1.29 an ounce for silver; full devaluation, to 50 per cent, would have meant, of course, $2.58 for silver. Under authority which it had, the Treasury issued $80 million of silver certificates against the 62 million ounces of unobligated silver it then held, which was on the basis of $1.29 an ounce monetary value; this was twice, or more than twice, its cost. Thereafter certificates were issued in correspondence with the cost, not the monetary value, of newly bought silver.

DOMESTIC INTENT POLITICAL, WORLD EFFECTS PERNICIOUS

During the first year and a half the Treasury bought foreign silver at successively higher prices, the President each time raising the price paid for domestic newly mined silver slightly to exceed that given foreigners. For a part of that time the Treasury was buying an average of 50 million ounces a month, or at a rate four times the current world production. The world price reached its peak of 81.31 cents on April 26, 1935.[24] By then China and other silver-using countries, instead of being benefited by the American program, were in distress because of it. Their silver money was worth more, their domestic commodity prices fell. Deflation in China had the effect of decreasing that country's imports from the United States to half what they had been. So the Treasury forbore to push the world price of silver higher. Lacking the former support, the price fell to 70 cents in June, 1935, and to the successively lower figures, reaching 42¾ cents, which the Treasury offered for the amounts it was willing to take. Thus by March, 1938, the world price of silver was back where it had been before the Silver Purchase Act. The Treasury kept up the price to domestic producers, to 77.57 cents to the end of 1937, and then to 64.64 cents to the

[24] *Ibid.*, p. 104.

end of June, 1939. Thereafter it paid only 35 cents for foreign silver, but the price of domestic newly mined silver, by a law of July, 1939, was fixed at 71.11 cents (that is, the nominal price was still $1.29, but the seigniorage charge was reduced from 50 to 45 per cent). By this time the fictitious price had no object beyond the frank one of subsidy to American silver producers.

From January, 1934, to June, 1940, the Treasury bought 2,360,-000,000 ounces of silver for $1,276,400,000;[25] the average price was about 54 cents an ounce, which made the profit or seigniorage about 75 cents an ounce (the difference between the cost and the "monetary value" of $1.29 an ounce). At the end of this period the professed aims of the program were as distinct as at the beginning. So far from a true world price of $1.29, it was 35 cents, or 21 per cent less than the average price in the year before the Silver Purchase Act. The United States was hardly closer to making silver equal one fourth of its combined metallic monetary stocks. At the beginning of the Roosevelt administration the percentage was 16.2; after six and a half years of enormous buying of silver, it was only 16.5. The reason for the latter failure was, of course, the Treasury's unexpectedly rapid acquisition of gold, from a value of less than 8 billion dollars in June, 1934, to nearly 20 billion in June, 1940. It is possible that the silver purchase program would not have been undertaken if the unprecedented accumulation of gold in this country could have been foreseen.

Contrary to hopes, purchase of silver had little effect in raising the general price level. Though other devices as well were employed, prices increased only slightly until 1937 (never reaching the desired 1926 height), and then dropped in the "recession" during which silver continued to be added to the country's money supply. In six and a half years from the beginning of 1934 outstanding silver certificates increased by $1,332,379,753, standard silver dollars by $7,070,973, and subsidiary silver by $102,306,822.[26] The silver certificates increased reserves of member banks by a billion and a quarter dollars, but their reserves were excessive without this addition.

Though expectation was that the United States policy would encourage use of silver as money, it led in fact to world abandon-

25 *Bulletin of the Treasury Department* (July, 1940).
26 U. S. Treasury, *Circulation Statement of U. S. Money* (June 30, 1940).

ment of the full silver standard and to reduced employment of silver in subsidiary coinage. China, after an unsuccessful appeal to the United States, put an export tax on silver, and when this was ineffective, nationalized silver and went over to a managed currency. Japan's invasion of the northern provinces of China was aided by her sales of seized silver, and Italy's invasion of Ethiopia profited similarly. Mexico was the chief of several Latin-American republics that lost silver coins because their bullion value became greater than their face value; Mexico substituted bronze and copper coins and paper for silver coins. Though foreign countries with silver to sell benefited from the high prices the Treasury offered, there was no evidence that their commodity imports from the United States increased or that the entrance of their products into the American market decreased. All in all, the silver program was a fiasco.

PICTURES IN THE EMBERS

In the six months after the United States definitely cut loose from gold—April 20, 1933—the dollar depreciated some 30 per cent in foreign exchange, but the corresponding price advance of industrial stocks and of cotton, wheat, and other basic products entering international trade, and the lesser advance of the general commodity price index did not hold up. It is not possible to say what part was played in foreign exchange and price movements by potential monetary inflation as such and what part by institutions for raising prices, such as the AAA, NRA, WPA, and FERA. Probably the combined effect showed itself in the initial price increases so gratifying to the administration. But by midsummer the economic boom collapsed, prices on the stock and produce exchanges falling suddenly in July. The general commodity price index, from 60.2 in March, rose to a peak of 71.8 in October, and declined during the remaining months of the year. Nor was the administration satisfied with the degree of depreciation of the dollar in foreign exchange.

Something must be done to redeem promises to keep prices going up and thereby benefit industrialists, farmers, debtors, and employment. The result was the positive program of dollar depreciation announced in the President's fireside chat the night of October 22, 1933. By this time he had absorbed the monetary theory of

his advisers, Professor George F. Warren of Cornell and Professor
James Harvey Rogers of Yale, and was able to repeat and apply it
himself. The idea was no more than a specialized interpretation of
the familiar quantity theory of money. Instead of comprehending
all the mediums of exchange, such as checks, notes, and so forth,
this notion was that prices, so far as the important role of money
was concerned, depended on the value of gold. The gold in the
world was held to be insufficient in quantity to support the prices
prevailing before the depression; in fact, the depression had been
caused by the scramble for gold after so many countries had departed from it during World War I. The obvious solution, said the
theory, was to make the available gold go farther by devaluing
currencies, or at least the United States currency, in terms of it.
Warren contended that an increase of 75 per cent in the price of
gold—from $20.67 an ounce, the old par of the dollar, to $36.17 an
ounce—would ensure return to the 1926 price level. This would
mean a 43 per cent reduction in the gold content of the dollar,
which had contained 23.22 grains of gold. He joined with apostles
in pointing out the superior advantages of a full 100 per cent increase in the price of gold to $41.34 an ounce, or a 50 per cent
decrease in the gold content of the dollar.

Roosevelt's radio broadcast that October evening was probably
the boldest attempt ever made to give the widest public a brief
instruction in complicated economic doctrine and maneuver. The
government's purpose, the President said, was to raise prices to a
level that would accomplish recovery—permit repayment of debts
at the value of money at which they were contracted, put workers
back in jobs, and restore purchasing power of farmers by bringing
back the price parity of their products with industrial products.
Thus, in addition to the Warren theory, appeared again the commodity dollar ideas of Irving Fisher and the emphasis on purchasing power associated with the name of Keynes. He concluded:

As a further effective means to this end, I am going to establish a Government market for gold in the United States. Therefore . . . I am au-
thorizing the Reconstruction Finance Corporation to buy gold newly
mined in the United States at prices to be determined from time to time.
. . . Whenever necessary to the end in view, we shall also buy or sell gold
in the world market.

My aim in taking this step is to establish and maintain continuous control.

This is a policy and not an expedient.

It is not to be used merely to offset a temporary fall in prices. We are
thus continuing to move towards a managed currency.[27]

Accordingly, three days later, October 25, 1933, an executive
order authorized purchase of newly mined domestic gold, and a
committee was named to set prices (Jones of RFC, Acheson of the
Treasury, Morgenthau, then of Farm Credit Administration). The
previous day the world price of gold had been $29.80, which meant
the dollar was worth 72 cents. The first price to be set was $31.36
an ounce, equivalent to a 66-cent dollar. Within ten days the price
had been advanced to $32.67. The world price increased, but since
it hung at $1.50 or more below the domestic price, foreign gold
began to be bought on the London market. The price of domestic
gold was raised to $34.45 and then, January 31, 1934, the price of
gold was put at $35.00 an ounce, which meant that the dollar was
devalued to 59.06 cents.

The President asked for legislation in a message to Congress on
January 15. Ownership of gold, basis of the currency, he said,
should be vested in the government, which would keep it in bullion. The Thomas Amendment gave him power to reduce the gold
content of the dollar by 50 per cent maximum; he believed that
the devaluation at that time should be to at least 60 per cent of
its former value. From the gold "profit" resulting from devaluation,
a fund of $2 billion should be created for stabilizing foreign ex-
change rates. The Gold Reserve Act, embodying these proposals,
was passed under strong administration pressure within fifteen
days, January 30, 1934. Federal Reserve banks were paid for the
gold they held in gold certificates, which became reserve against
federal reserve notes. Coins were to be melted into bars, which
could be released to pay foreign balances.

The Gold Reserve Act thus provided a monetary system answering to none of the tests of a true gold-standard currency, for
there was no definite gold content of the money unit, no gold coinage, no convertibility on demand, no unrestricted export. Avail-

[27] F. D. Roosevelt, *On Our Way* (New York: The John Day Co., 1934), p. 183.

ability of gold for foreign payments was all that saved the United States money from being on an out-and-out paper basis.

On January 31, 1934, the day following passage of the Gold Reserve Act, the President by executive order devaluated the dollar from 23.22 grains of fine gold to 13.71, or to 59.06 per cent of its old weight. This odd value was chosen in order to permit a round $35 an ounce as the price to be given for gold. The gold "profit," or "increment resulting from a reduction in the weight of the gold dollar," amounted at once to $2,805,516,060, and later, as more gold came in, to $2,817,150,670. Of this, only $200,000,000 was in fact ever used for stabilization purposes.

In his proclamation the President gave the justification that "the foreign commerce of the United States is adversely affected by reason of the depreciation in the value of the currencies of other governments in relation to the present standard value of gold and that an economic emergency requires an expansion of credit." [28] This was the familiar policy of competitive depreciation, which other countries followed before and after without benefit of the Warren-Pearson rationalization. Against increasing Republican opposition, successive extensions of the President's monetary powers carried them to June 30, 1941.

[28] *Federal Reserve Bulletin* (February, 1934), p. 69.

CHAPTER V

Financial and Banking Reforms

THE Emergency Banking Act was followed, in three months, by the Banking Act of 1933, signed June 16. This statute owed its character in only minor part to the New Deal. It developed from investigations of the Senate Committee on Banking and Currency, beginning in 1931, under Senator Carter Glass, into defects of the Federal Reserve System as they had contributed to the depression, and of the House Banking Committee, beginning in 1930, under Representative Henry B. Steagall, into the pros and cons of group banking. The Glass Bill, which formed the groundwork, passed the Senate in January, 1933, after a year of opposition which changed it for the worse. Senator Glass, after the stock crash of 1929 and the accumulating bank failures, had set about the mournful task of overhauling the Federal Reserve System. No thoroughgoing revision was attempted, but even so the additional controls introduced and the limitations placed on the member banks aroused the antagonism of the American Bankers Association, the New York Federal Reserve Bank, and the Hoover-dominated Federal Reserve Board itself. Valuable time was lost in the interval of passage of the Glass-Steagall Act of February, 1932, which permitted substitution of government securities for surplus gold in the backing of federal reserve notes. Glass himself, thinking he had a better plan for indemnifying depositors in closed banks, long fought off the deposit insurance scheme of Steagall. As it was, the general bank freeze had to intervene before differences were reconciled.

Passage of the Banking Act of 1933, with its divorce of investment affiliates from commercial banks and its insurance of deposits, was speeded by disclosures before the Senate Committee on Banking and Currency of abuses, particularly of leading investment bankers, which had led to and followed from the depression. Conspicuous witnesses were J. P. Morgan and partners, Otto H. Kahn of Kuhn, Loeb & Co., and Charles E. Mitchell, chairman of the National City Bank and National City Company. The grilling which these and others received from Ferdinand Pecora, special attorney for the committee, lent force to the President's inaugural anathemas on the money-changers, and put the financial fraternity in no position to object to discipline. Sharp public resentment carried over for a while, and facilitated later legislation, such as the Securities and Exchange Act and the more thorough banking law.

The Senate inquiry laid bare financial practices which were generally legally permissible but were morally wrong, not to say abhorrent to a people caught in the backwash of depression. Juggling of capital gains and losses by the enormously wealthy so as to avoid all income taxes, netting huge profits from the marketing of securities that later lost most of their value, granting favors to the powerful while the poor were fleeced—proof of these tricks made Wall Street a fair mark for public attack. As the *New Republic* remarked, the investigation showed less fault if investment banking were regarded purely as a private business for profit than if looked on as involving important public obligations. Recreant to their public function, the investment bankers could not complain that government proposed to police them in future.

But the public did not accuse because, prior to 1929, it had been deceived. People remembered that they had been too credulous. The bitter indignation was aroused by discovery that certain rich men had escaped income taxes while those of moderate and small means had been compelled to come up with theirs. The Senate inquiry showed that twenty Morgan partners paid no income taxes for 1931 and 1932, and only a trifling amount in the aggregate for 1930. The story was much the same with the partners of Kuhn, Loeb & Co. The committee said that "the methods of avoiding or minimizing the amount of tax payable were generally familiar to such persons as could afford to pay for expert advice. When confronted with these devices, the government bureaus charged with the duty of collecting taxes and enforcing the law appear to have been helpless to cope with them." Several methods of avoidance were laid bare. Witnesses who enjoyed trust and esteem testified to practices that were morally repugnant.

A scheme "exceedingly favored by leaders of American finance" was that of pretended sales of securities to near relatives at a loss. Charles E. Mitchell claimed a loss of $2,872,305.50 on 18,300 shares of his bank stock in 1929. The stock was sold to his wife and later repurchased by him, admittedly for the purpose of reducing his income tax. He paid no income tax in 1929.[1] On the strength of this evidence Mitchell was later tried in federal court, contention of the government being that the sale was not bona fide, but he was acquitted. Thomas W. Lamont, a Morgan partner, established losses of $114,807.35 in the sale of securities to his wife, December 31, 1930. The tax on the amount declared to have been lost would have been $20,365. Lamont bought the securities back from his wife the following April. Sale and repurchases were direct, without any broker. Otto H. Kahn, of Kuhn, Loeb & Co., was able to deduct $16,000 from his income tax for 1930 by a similar *pro forma* sale of securities to his daughter. In this case the daughter reassigned the securities to her father in a document dated the day after the sale, though it was testified that the document was not executed until after the 60 days required by law for repurchases.[2]

James V. Forrestal, a partner in Dillon, Read & Co., and later first Secretary of Defense, went to a great deal of trouble, through foreign and domestic corporations formed by him, to avoid a tax of $95,000 on 1929 profits of $864,396.41.[3] The tortuous manipulation was in contrast to the simplicity of the ignoble purpose. Albert H. Wiggin of the Chase National Bank set up three Canadian corporations "for the avowed purpose of minimizing the payment of income taxes in the United States."[4] Income taxes were avoided through short sales, family trusts, and through lax enforcement. The new administration, which had so scolded the bankers, was briefly embarrassed because it was revealed that the Secretary of the Treasury, the Assistant Secretary of the Navy, and an ambassador at large were on the "preferred list" of investment houses, en-

[1] U. S. Senate Committee on Banking and Currency, "Stock Exchange Practices," Report pursuant to Senate Resolutions 84, 56, and 97. 73 Cong. 1 Sess., pp. 321–322.
[2] *Ibid.*, p. 322.   [3] *Ibid.*, pp. 323–325.   [4] *Ibid.*, pp. 325–327.

titled to buy securities at less than market prices. The suspicion that this meant intended bribery was scouted by administration apologists.

MOURNFUL POST-MORTEM

The inquiry of the Senate Committee on Banking and Currency had shown, in painful detail, how the banks had been caught up in the speculative mania. They diverted Federal Reserve credit to the stock market, acquired assets which could not be promptly liquidated, established investment affiliates which injured depositors, and in too many cases became the minions of disingenuous bank holding companies. Besides checking these and other abuses, the Banking Act of 1933 had to give to depositors practical assurance that they would not lose their funds in the future.

The subcommittee hearings, held at intervals covering more than two years (from April 11, 1932, to May 4, 1934), formed an ominous obbligato to the early New Deal legislation embracing the Banking Act of 1933, the Securities Act of the same year, the Securities Exchange Act of 1934, and amendments to the Revenue Act of 1934 to prevent methods of tax avoidance which had been disclosed. The 12,000 printed pages of evidence were summarized, with the committee's comments, in the final report June 6, 1934.[5] Mr. Pecora was the fourth to serve as counsel for the committee, from January, 1933, to June, 1934, but it was his plan of campaign which gave the investigation its rigor. Bankers, brokers, and others who had long preserved secrecy of their operations, and made this the means not only to protection but prestige with the public, had to yield up their files and answer searching questions on the witness stand. Nothing was sacred against exposure. In effect, the New York sightseeing buses not only took passengers to the familiar haunts of Times Square, Grant's Tomb, and Chinatown, but invaded the financial and corporate sanctums, where every safe was turned out and every maneuver was rehearsed. Successively securities exchanges, investment and commercial banking practices, income tax avoidances, investment trusts, holding companies, and concentration of control of wealth were opened to popular gaze.

Even after the severe declines from 1929, thirty-four organized

[5] *Ibid.*, p. 394.

exchanges throughout the country on July 31, 1933, listed 6,057 common and preferred stock issues with a total market value of $95,051,876,259, and 3,798 bond issues with a market value of $49,080,819,993.[6] Establishing the concern of Congress with such enterprises, the committee observed: ". . . a business of such stature not only entails the use of the mails and other instrumentalities of interstate commerce, but itself constitutes an important part of the current of interstate commerce. Neither can it be doubted that the credit mechanism of the Nation is interlocked with transactions on exchanges, or that such transactions exert tremendous influence upon industry and trade. In retrospect, the fact emerges with increasing clarity that the excessive and unrestrained speculation which dominated the securities markets in recent years, has disrupted the flow of credit, dislocated industry and trade, impeded the flow of interstate commerce, and brought in its train social consequences inimical to the public welfare." The cost to the public of maintaining the securities markets had been "staggering." Total commissions and interest received by members of twenty-nine exchanges between January 1, 1928, and August 31, 1933, or the amount paid for effecting transactions, was $1,975,112,663. Total income of members was $2,440,311,397, and net income $999,428,938. These sums represented only a "fragment" of the cost of speculation on the exchanges. The shrinkage in the value of securities following the boom of October, 1929, had been "unprecedented." Total market value of stocks listed on the New York Stock Exchange fell from an all-time high of $89,668,276,854 on September 1, 1929, to $71,759,485,710 on November 1, a decrease of $18,-000,000,000; and on July 1, 1932, the figure sank to the low point of $15,633,479,577, a decrease of $74,000,000,000 from the high. Bonds sank from a high of $49,293,758,598 on September 1, 1930, to a low of $30,554,431,090 on April 1, 1933, a decrease of over $18,000,000,000.

Declared the committee: "The economic cost of this downswing in security values cannot be accurately gauged. The wholesale closing of banks and other financial institutions; the loss of deposits and savings; the drastic curtailment of credit; the inability of debtors to meet their obligations; the growth of unemployment; the diminution of the purchasing power of the people to the point

[6] *Ibid.*, p. 5.

where industry and commerce were prostrated; and the increase in bankruptcy, poverty, and distress—all these conditions must be considered in some measure when the ultimate cost to the American public of speculating on the securities exchanges is computed."[7]

The committee came promptly to the practice of buying on margin. It began with a little lecture, explaining that "margin purchasing is speculation in securities with borrowed money," the credit facilities in this country being unequaled anywhere and virtually automatic in their operation. During the year 1929, on twenty-nine exchanges the total number of customers was 1,548,-707, of whom the transactions of 599,237, or more than 38 per cent, were on margin. The percentage of margin transactions on the New York Stock Exchange was a little higher. The number of margin accounts increased in the speculative period of the first seven months of 1929 by over 51,000; again in the first six months of 1933, when speculation was rampant, margin accounts grew by 70,000. The uncontrolled speculations of margin customers injured the national economy out of all proportion to their numbers. Their actions resulted in wide fluctuations of security prices which imperiled the holdings of bona fide investors. "The celerity with which margin transactions were arranged and the absence of any scrutiny by the broker of the personal credit of the borrower, encouraged persons in all walks of life to embark upon speculative ventures in which they were doomed by their lack of skill and experience to certain loss. Excited by the vision of quick profits, they assumed margin positions which they had no adequate resources to protect, and when the storm broke they stood helplessly by while securities and savings were washed away in a flood of liquidation." Stricter margin limitations under the Securities Exchange Act of 1934 had been plainly called for.[8]

The dangers of excessive credit for speculation were reviewed. With unfavorable financial developments, brokers' loans were called, borrowers were forced to sell securities on a vast scale, and the resulting drop in market prices compelled further liquidation because accounts became undermargined. This process impaired the security of collateral loans made by banks and the value of securities held by banks in their own portfolios. Plentiful funds for brokers' loans led to speculation not only in securities but in com-

[7] *Ibid.*, pp. 5–7.   [8] *Ibid.*, pp. 9–11.

modities. Industry, overoptimistic, issued unnecessary securities, which reduced bank deposits and increased the cost of credit to legitimate business.

STOCK EXCHANGE MANIPULATION

The most perilous part of brokers' loans had come from non-banking corporations, individuals, and investment trusts, either through the agency of banks or directly. When these loans by "others" were suddenly withdrawn, the banks had to step into the breach, straining their resources beyond the point of safety in the effort to prevent a general collapse. With the call loan rate ranging from 15 to 20 per cent, nonbanking sources poured out funds to brokers, corporations sometimes issuing securities just for this purpose. Brokers' loans for the account of others were uncontrolled by the banks, needing no reserves. While the banks had made relatively small increase in their own loans to brokers, those from others had shot up. During 1929 the Cities Service Co., without interposition of bankers, had loaned in the New York call money market to the cumulative amount of $285,325,092, the peak amount on one day being $41,900,000 on September 25, 1929. By the end of the year this company had no call loans outstanding. Standard Oil of New Jersey had loaned much more on call—a cumulative amount of $17,662,520,000, the highest amount on any one day being $97,-824,000. Electric Bond and Share and Sinclair Consolidated Oil were other large lenders in the Street.

Charles E. Mitchell, formerly chairman of the National City Bank of New York, testified to the result: ". . . after the break . . . all those people who had been lending on call for their own account . . . rushed and took their money out; and then every bank in New York was obliged to make up that deficiency and was forced to go to the Federal Reserve bank for borrowing. So that following the period of the collapse . . . all New York banks leaned heavily on the Federal Reserve credit, and that was the only thing that saved the situation at that time. But prior to that time and while this speculation was going on we did not lean on the Federal Reserve credits at all, or for only a day or two here and there, to even our position up." [9] The Banking Act of 1933 forbade member banks

[9] *Ibid.*, pp. 12–16.

to make loans as agents for nonbanking corporations. Neither could they pay interest on demand deposits; this was to deter interior banks from sending funds to financial centers to be used in call loans.

The committee decided that "the true function of an exchange . . . to maintain an open market for securities, where supply and demand may freely meet at prices uninfluenced by manipulation and control" had "been fulfilled most imperfectly." Stock exchange representatives had not regarded as pernicious manipulative devices which gave a deceptive appearance of activity in order to profit at the expense of the unsuspecting. Pools raised the price of a security by concerted activity among pool members until insiders, who had lost nothing because they had bought and sold among themselves, could unload on the public. "A supply . . . of the security which is the subject of the pool manipulation is necessary to its successful consummation. . . . The pool sometimes depresses the price of the stock in advance through short selling or the dissemination of unfavorable rumors, and then accumulates substantial blocks at the reduced price." The whole discreditable performance was spelled out. Pools continued to operate after the commencement of the investigation.[10] After the committee's revelations the New York Stock Exchange adopted rules ostensibly to combat the evils of pools, but their phraseology left loopholes. The practices were bad, but more alarming was the exchange's unconcerned toleration of them. The attentive reader of evidence adduced by the committee on this abuse and other habitual ones wonders how Congress held hopes that later regulatory acts would reform the securities exchanges. The customary justification of speculation had always been that it served the public interest by ensuring an accessible and presumably a free market. If this rationalization was not broken down by abundant exposure of collusive artifice it was because the people did not hear or heed. The hope of Congress that it could sweep the stables must have been a part of its larger optimism that it could clean up the economy of which the exchanges were an offensive incident.

The committee reserved especially severe condemnation for the existence of "preferred lists" of persons to whom investment bank-

10 *Ibid.,* pp. 30 ff.

ers furnished securities at or slightly above cost, but in any event at less than the securities were then bringing on the market or were certain to fetch shortly. "The 'preferred lists,'" said the committee, "strikingly illuminate the methods employed by bankers to extend their influence and control over individuals in high places. The persons upon whom princely favors were bestowed in this manner, were officers and directors of banks, trust companies, insurance companies and other great financial institutions, executives of railroads, utilities, and industrial corporations, editors, lawyers, politicians, and public officials—in short, persons prominent in all the financial, industrial, and political walks of our national life. The granting of these preferential participations on the one hand and their acceptance on the other created a community of interest and similarity of viewpoint between donor and donee which augured well for their mutual welfare and ill for that of the public. . . . Implicit in the bestowal of favors on this magnificent scale is a pervasive assumption of power and privilege. Implicit in the acceptance of such favors is a recognition of that power and privilege. The 'preferred lists,' with all their grave implications, cast a shadow over the entire financial scene." John J. Raskob, chairman of the National Democratic Committee, bought 2,000 shares of the Allegheny Corporation privately offered him by J. P. Morgan & Co. at $20 a share when the high for the stock on the open market was $33⅛. In five months the stock reached 57. "Among others to whom allotments were offered at $20 per share were: Joseph Nutt, treasurer of the Republican National Committee—3,000 shares; Charles Francis Adams, Secretary of the Navy—1,000 shares; Edmund Machold, speaker of the Assembly of the State of New York and State chairman of the Republican Party in New York State—2,000 shares; Silas H. Strawn, president of the United States Chamber of Commerce and president of the American Bar Association—1,000 shares; William Woodin, president of American Car & Foundry Co. and later Secretary of the Treasury—1,000 shares." F. H. Ecker, president of the Metropolitan Life Insurance Co., who was in a position to return any favor, was another on the Morgan list. Kuhn, Loeb & Co. and National City Co. had their lists of friends able to reward a courtesy.[11]

[11] *Ibid.*, pp. 102–107.

BANK AFFILIATES AND INVESTMENT TRUSTS

Abuses of affiliation of investment banking companies with commercial banks were rehearsed at length. Through these affiliates commercial banks indulged in practices which were forbidden them by law and which had "the direst consequences." The banks, supposed to give disinterested advice, referred inquiring depositors to investment affiliates that were sponsoring securities. Acting through affiliates, the banks broke the law by speculation in their own stock. The National City Company, the investment affiliate, encouraged its salesmen to "switch" customers to stock of the National City Bank. Employees were sold stock of the Chase National Bank and Chase Securities Corporation at a fixed price at a time when officers of the corporations were speculating in the stock, manipulating it through pools.

The divorce of investment affiliates from commercial banks, demanded by the Banking Act of 1933, was in response to confessions wrung in the hearings. The multifold corporate guises in which bank officers and directors clothed themselves became the means of double dealing. The disclosures in the hearings showed that many had lost all sense of the trust imposed in them and which they were handsomely paid to discharge. The action of Albert H. Wiggin, executive head of the Chase National Bank, in selling the stock of the bank short for the aggregate sum of $10,-596,968 was but one culminating instance.[12]

There is no space to continue the sorry story of banking and investment malfeasance and chicanery. Investment trusts as perverted in America came in for woeful description. The investment trust was pronounced "the vehicle employed by individuals to enhance their personal fortunes in violation of their trusteeship, to the financial detriment of the public. Conflicts of duty and interest existing between the managers of the investment trusts and the investing public were resolved against the investor. The consequences of the operations of these management trusts have been calamitous to the Nation."[13] And again: "The investment trusts of this country, from their inception, degenerated into a convenient medium of the dominant persons to consummate transactions permeated with ulterior motives; served to facilitate the concentration of control

12 *Ibid.*, p. 189.   13 *Ibid.*, p. 333.

of the public's money; enabled the organizers to realize incredible profits; camouflaged their real purpose to acquire control of equities in other companies; and became the receptacles into which the executive heads unloaded securities which they, or corporations in which they were interested, owned." [14] Misplaced confidence "in the competency and integrity of purpose of the investment trustees" was exemplified by the Goldman-Sachs Trading Corporation, which in three years lost $60,000,000 in capital and surplus, the stock falling from an original purchase price of 104 to 1¾ at the time of the hearing.[15] It was recommended that further corrective legislation be passed.

This "Pecora" investigation,[16] as it was familiarly called, of the Senate Committee on Banking and Currency, showed the inside of the American capitalist cup. The uncleanness was laid by many to the speculative mania and its aftermath, in which institutional derangement and personal perfidy were joined. That was a shallow view. The boom itself, which nourished these fungi, was not an unhappy accident, but the result of accepted forces. The individual who had betrayed a trust or recklessly imperiled the public welfare was the minor criminal compared to the economic system under which he operated. It is hard to conceive a comprehensive review of a debacle more calculated to disillusion the candid mind with the private profit motive as a means to social health.

CORRECTIVE AND PROTECTIVE MEASURES

The act therefore undertook to curb use of Federal Reserve credit for speculative purposes by requiring that each Federal Reserve bank keep itself informed whether its member banks were making undue credit extensions for trading in securities, real estate, or commodities. An offending bank might be refused accommodations or be formally suspended from use of Federal Reserve facilities; indeed, the latter action might be applied to a whole district at a time. Member banks were forbidden to make loans for "others" (nonbanking businesses or individuals) in the stock or bond markets; such loans made through the banks had circumvented Federal

[14] *Ibid.*, p. 339.
[15] *Ibid.*
[16] The main results of the inquiry may be quickly grasped in Ferdinand Pecora, *Wall Street under Oath* (New York: Simon and Schuster, 1939).

Reserve control over speculative credit in 1928 and 1929. Member banks must not underwrite securities or buy nongovernmental securities for themselves beyond certain limits. Bank executives must not borrow from their own banks, and must report their loans from other banks. A year after passage of the act no member bank must retain any connection with an investment company, on pain of forfeiting membership in the Federal Reserve System.

Bank holding companies were regulated. These had tended to set aside democratic representation in the Federal Reserve System; further, the true condition of banks in a group was concealed from examiners by shifting assets from one to another in the combination; hence holding companies and the banks held by them were to be examined simultaneously, and another provision sought to check the spread of the bank holding-company device. On the other hand, chain or branch banking for national banks was encouraged. Branch banking had proved a stabilizing force in Britain and Canada, and the privilege enjoyed by state banks of extending their branches had prevented the formation of national banks and so had limited the influence of the Federal Reserve System. The act of 1933 permitted a national bank to establish branches within the state where it was located if the state law allowed state banks to have branches.

Insurance of deposits was included in the act only after a strenuous contest, for previous state schemes had proved unsuccessful, and there was question whether the federal government should assume the responsibility now assigned it. The Federal Deposit Insurance Corporation was created under management of the Comptroller of the Currency and two others appointed by the President; the stock would be subscribed by the Treasury ($150,000,000), by member banks (½ of 1 per cent of their deposits), and by Federal Reserve banks (half of their surplus on January 1, 1933). The corporation could issue its obligations up to three times its capital. Leaving aside an interim scheme soon superseded, the corporation would insure deposits 100 per cent up to $10,000, 75 per cent between $10,000 and $50,000, and 50 per cent beyond $50,000. All member banks must be members of the FDIC; state banks, to be insured, must become members of the Federal Reserve System within two years.

Where a participating bank failed, the FDIC was to be the receiver. It would set up a new bank without capital stock, but with the amount of the insured liabilities of the failed bank. These deposits could be withdrawn by their owners, but if left with the new bank were to be retained in cash or United States securities. The old bank would be liquidated. If the new bank succeeded in attracting stockholders, they would elect directors and the institution would proceed independently. If the new bank could not get stockholders, the FDIC could turn it over to another bank willing to take it, or, failing this, the affairs of the new bank would also be wound up.

A variety of provisions extended the scope of the Federal Reserve System and the authority of the Federal Reserve Board. No reserve bank was henceforth to carry on independent negotiations with foreign banks (as the New York Reserve Bank had done); the Board must consent in advance to any such conference, and must be informed of proceedings by its own representative or by a report. The Open Market Committee of one representative from each Federal Reserve district, which had been functioning informally, was recognized in the law. However, though members of the board could sit with the committee, the board could not initiate open-market operations, though it could disapprove the proposals of the reserve banks. Membership in the Federal Reserve System was opened to Morris Plan and savings banks. Federal Reserve banks were given new powers to make direct advances to member banks on their own notes, such loans to become immediately payable if the borrowing bank increased its loans for speculative purposes beyond allowed limits. Member banks could no longer pay interest on demand deposits, and the Federal Reserve Board might fix interest rates on time deposits. Any officer of a member bank who persistently offended against regulations or sound banking practice might be removed by the Federal Reserve Board after full hearing. Double liability for shares of national banks was abolished for stock issued in the future, but $50,000, instead of $25,000, became the minimum capitalization of national banks because so many failures had been due to the inadequacy of capital.

BAILING OUT THE BANKS, AND A NEW ACT

In the two years following the Banking Act of 1933 the banking crisis was "mopped up," to the accompaniment of huge government investment in and loans to banks of all sizes and descriptions. Having been summoned to the rescue, the administration chided while it comforted; its oft-expressed criticisms of the banking fraternity and of existing weaknesses of the banking system were tacitly assented to by the bankers themselves, keenly conscious of their ill odor with the public. The New Deal was preparing a measure which would further centralize authority over the banks in the Federal Reserve Board, and bring the board more closely under administration control. Not until a bill was introduced in February, 1935, did bankers and their allies rally to a resistance which succeeded in modifying administration intentions.

It may be remembered that in the three days following the banking crisis, 75 per cent of member banks, with 90 per cent of member bank resources, had been reopened on an unrestricted basis. This left 1,400 national banks and 221 state member banks, with 10 per cent of member bank resources, unlicensed. A month after the end of the holiday, nearly 30 per cent of nonmember banks remained unlicensed by the state authorities. By the end of the year 1933, unlicensed member banks had been reduced to 512, and unlicensed nonmember banks to about 1,400. Thereafter the remainder of the debris was cleared away: by the end of May, 1935, unlicensed member banks declined to 2, with deposits of $428,000, and unlicensed nonmember banks to 66, with deposits of $43,511,000. All of this was not accomplished without casualties. Between the middle of March, 1933, and the end of May, 1935, as many as 2,063 unlicensed banks, with deposits of $2,565,321,000, and also 289 licensed banks (supposedly sound) with deposits of $191,025,000 had been placed in liquidation. The bank failures since 1921 and the amalgamations and absorptions had reduced the total number of banks to 15,443, virtually half the number before that date.[17]

The Reconstruction Finance Corporation bought into banks, to permit them to be licensed, to provide certain communities with banking services, and to prepare banks for participation in deposit insurance. A special division of the RFC, with an advisory committee, to improve the capital position of the banks was formed in October, 1933; by the end of the year it had received applications from over 5,000 banks, a third of them members of the Federal Re-

[17] *Federal Reserve Bulletin* (June, 1935), p. 404.

serve System. Two years after the bank crisis, the RFC owned some half a billion of bank preferred stock, carrying voting privileges, or about a fifth of the total capital stock of licensed member banks. When (July 15, 1935) the RFC announced that it would stop buying bank stock, it held $1,009,420,034 in preferred stock, capital notes and debentures, and loans secured by preferred stock in 6,468 banks. Thus the degree of government involvement, aside from anything else, seemed to justify reorganization of banking in order to prevent repetition of breakdown.

The administration bill was formulated under the direction of Marriner S. Eccles, chairman of the Federal Reserve Board, who was guided by the principle that "*laissez faire* in banking and the attainment of business stability are incompatible. If variations in the supply of money are to be compensatory and corrective rather than inflammatory or intensifying, there must be conscious and deliberate control."[18] The House promptly passed the bill, but prolonged attack in the Senate led to substantial revisions in the act as finally approved. It was held that the original bill gave the President too much power over the board and so over the reserve banks and their credit policies. The deposit insurance scheme, even as modified to make $5,000 the upper limit of guarantee for any one depositor in a bank, and though a regular premium payment was substituted for stock purchase plus assessments, was assailed by the larger banks. These larger banks, with a small proportion of fully insured deposits, felt that premiums based on total deposits put an unfair burden on them for the benefit of the smaller banks, practically all of whose deposits were fully insured.

The Banking Act of 1935 (signed August 23) was described by the *Federal Reserve Bulletin* as "the most fundamental revision of the Federal Reserve Act since its adoption 22 years ago in 1913." It placed in the Federal Reserve Board powers which had previously been diffused—those over open-market operations, rediscount rates, and reserve requirements. The central authority (its name changed to Board of Governors) still consisted of seven members appointed by the President with approval of the Senate; terms, overlapping, were lengthened to fourteen years, and salaries were raised to equal those of cabinet officers. However, the chairman and vice-chairman, though designated by the President, were not

[18] *The New York Times* (February 9, 1935).

removable at will as the administration had proposed, and, to diminish administration influence, the Secretary of the Treasury and Comptroller of the Currency were dropped as ex officio members.

The head of each Federal Reserve bank (now called president instead of governor as before) was still to be elected by the directors of the bank, but he must be approved by the central board; he took over the functions of the Federal Reserve Agent, whose authority the banks had previously contrived to subordinate. Mandatory authority over rediscount rates was now given to the board, reserve banks submitting their proposed rates every fortnight for approval. Previously, changes in reserve requirements of member banks could be made only in emergency and with approval of the President of the United States, but now the board was empowered to order doubling of reserves. Formerly the Open Market Committee of the System was named entirely by the reserve banks and was merely advisory to the board; no reserve bank was obliged to participate in the purchase and sale of securities decided upon. Now the board was given majority control of the committee, and the reserve banks were compelled to follow its orders. However, to preserve the independence of the Federal Reserve System, government securities must be bought only in the open market, not directly from the Treasury.

MORE POWER FOR THE RESERVE BOARD

The act introduced changes which recognized the altered character of the investments and loans of member banks. Their holdings of short-term commercial and industrial paper had diminished to 12 per cent of the total in 1929 and to 8 per cent in 1935, while long-term obligations increased, partly because of different financing methods of business, partly because savings deposits held by member banks had increased tenfold in a dozen years. Real-estate investments of member banks had grown. Such assets could not be quickly liquidated, but if member banks were to borrow from the Federal Reserve in sufficient volume to permit the expansion of money and credit which the administration believed necessary to get the country out of depression, paper hitherto ineligible for rediscount must be comprehended in some way. Hence the board was empowered to approve loans on assets not of the old highly liquid character, even though the bank receiving the loan shall not have exhausted all other means of reserve borrowing. However, to hold such loans within limits, they must be made at an interest rate ½ of 1 per cent above the current rediscount rate and may run for not more than four months. This limitation would prevent the dumping of assets behind time deposits, such as had proved disastrous earlier in the depression. Also, under certain restrictions national banks might lend on real estate up to 60 per cent of its value for ten years, and all member banks might invest in real estate up to the total of their capital and surplus or up to 60 per cent of their savings deposits, whichever was greater; experience in the depression had shown that real-estate mortgages were as marketable as long-term bonds.

The act made $5,000 the limit of insurance for any one account, which was a doubling of the guarantee then in effect, for the interim scheme, with a $2,500 limit, had been continued, and the more generous plan of the Banking Act of 1933 never went into effect. The premium to build up the fund was fixed at 1/12 of 1 per cent, payable semiannually. No lower premium was allowed to larger banks or to banks supposed to be in an especially sound condition. In another particular connected with deposit insurance, the law of 1935 was less demanding than that of 1933. Only the larger state banks—those having average deposits of $1,000,000 or more during the year 1941—must become members of the Federal Reserve System by July 1, 1942, on pain of forfeiting the insurance. The earlier law would have brought into full membership the other 6,000 insured state banks, with one seventh of total bank assets, which now were permitted partial membership.

Seeing the spectacular increase in Postal Savings during the crisis in the spring of 1933, the banks were afraid of the continued growth of deposits with the government. The 1935 act therefore declared that the rate of interest on Postal Savings should not exceed the rate paid on savings by member banks located nearest the post office in question.

Any national bank was permitted to end double liability on its stock after July 1, 1937, by giving newspaper notice six months in advance; however, national banks must pass one tenth of their profits to surplus until surplus equaled capital.

The Banking Act of 1933 and more particularly that of 1935 were passed at a time when the administration and many outside it were placing emphasis on monetary and credit management as means toward broad economic recovery and thereafter stabilization. Thus the 1933 law tended toward more centralized control of open-market operations and dealings with foreign banks; it sought to restrict use of bank credit for speculation and so make it more amenable to manipulation with respect to the price level, and it contemplated bringing state banks into the Federal Reserve System. In 1934 and 1935 those who wanted government monetary and bank management introduced bills for a national monetary authority and for government ownership of the federal reserve banks. Representative Henry B. Steagall, sponsor of the administration banking bill in the House in 1935, included—it was said with the President's approval—a policy declaration, a mandate from Congress: "It shall be the duty of the Federal Reserve Board to exercise such powers as it possesses in such manner as to promote conditions conducive to business stability and to mitigate by its influence unstabilizing fluctuations in the general level of production, trade, prices, and employment, so far as may be possible within the scope of monetary action and credit administration." [19] He and Mr. Eccles felt that a large degree of control, and not mere "accommodation" of commerce, industry, and agriculture had become imperative. In line with this objective, members of the board should be "persons well qualified by education and experience, or both, to participate in the formulation of national economic and monetary policies." This was urged to supersede the old stipulation that the President, in making appointments, should have "due regard to a fair representation of the financial, agricultural, industrial and commercial interests, and geographical divisions of the country."

All of these proposals—for one central bank, for a monetary authority, for a policy declaration, and for new qualifications for board members—were turned down. But the Banking Act of 1935, though it had been modified, carried the intention and embodied new facilities for federal government control, through the Federal Reserve Board, of the country's economy. The question remained whether the reform had been sufficiently thorough.

19 House Resolution 7617, Sec. 204, 74 Cong., 1 Sess., p. 50.

POLICING PROMOTION OF SECURITIES

The Securities and Exchange Commission of five members was appointed the last day of June, 1934, to administer the Securities Act of 1933 and the Securities Exchange Act of 1934. It was the first federal monitor set over corporate finance as such. Thus, especially as it was charged with the administration of kindred laws, it became the most frankly regulatory body. Other agencies of the New Deal and earlier, however supervisory, had protective and even promotional features. The Federal Trade Commission guarded competition, supposed to be the life of enterprise. The Interstate Commerce Commission had antimonopoly aims. NRA and AAA gave industry and agriculture a voice, made government the partner rather than the proctor. But the Securities and Exchange Commission enforced a moral code against a group which, by power if not always by prestige, had until then succeeded in holding itself above the law. Ferdinand Pecora, who had been chief chastiser of wayward financiers and their minions, was made one of the first commissioners.

The regulatory powers of the commission were made effective through criminal, civil, or administrative sanctions. The commission had no power to institute criminal prosecutions itself, but must depend on the discretion of the Attorney General. Civil remedies were sought by injunction suits in which the commission appeared as plaintiff. Administrative sanctions were exercised through final orders of the commission, entered only after notice and hearing, and appealable to the federal courts.

The first annual report, 1935, was brief, formal, and somewhat tentative. Year by year, as the commission got deeper into its work, and was given wider scope, it gained self-confidence and matured its methods. Though it had been viewed with alarm, real and pretended, and prospectively stigmatized as utterly arbitrary, the record shows that the commission used judgment, patience, and leadership. In some respects it interpreted law with a reasonableness that Congress itself, resentful of recent abuses, had hardly intended.

The earliest and main functions of the Securities and Exchange Commission were to ensure truthfulness in the offering of securities and honesty and openness in trading on the exchanges. In order to have fair and full disclosure of material facts regarding securities offered for sale, the commission required the filing of registration statements and the issue of prospectuses containing the more important information presented in these statements. Further, it registered and regulated national securities exchanges and over-the-counter markets, compelling publication and prescribing rules of trading intended to prevent deceit and permit the average investor to be informed of the true condition of the companies involved. However, beyond these precautions the commission was not to go, as in passing on the merits of any security.

Other acts, later placed under the commission's control, invested it with more discretion as defender of the public interest. These gave the commission supervision of public-utility holding company systems, trust indentures, investment trusts and investment advisers, and permitted it to prepare advisory reports, for courts and investors, on corporate reorganizations. The laws assigned to the commission in this period, in addition to the original two—Securities Act of 1933 and Securities Exchange Act of 1934, as amended—were the Public Utility Holding Company Act of 1935; Chapter X, National Bankruptcy Act; Trust Indenture Act of 1939; Investment Company Act of 1940; Investment Advisers Act of 1940.

Innumerable illustrations could be given of ways in which the commission, over the whole enlarging field of its responsibilities, prevented misrepresentation and plausible subterfuge. These were important for the informed investor, but vastly more so, of course, for the novice who was attracted and solicited by a variety of means. The first annual report gave an instance: a large public-utilities system filed a registration statement containing a balance sheet showing a capital surplus of $111,000,000 and an earned surplus of $12,000,000. This balance sheet had whole pages of footnotes which even the trained analysts of the commission found difficult to understand and apply. The short of it was that when proper accounting methods were used, it appeared the company's assets were $153,000,000 less than had been claimed, and instead of large surpluses there was a corporate deficit of $30,000,000. In another early case a mining company was required to amend its prospectus to show that only a small percentage of its receipts from stock sales during twenty years had been used in development of its properties, the balance having gone for commissions, salaries, and the like. After a year the company asked to withdraw its registration statement, as it could not sell stock with the truthful prospectus. The commission worked out detailed reporting forms for many purposes; comprehensive rules for government of national securities exchanges were calculated to stop abuses that had long been scandals but had gone almost unchecked.

LIMITING UTILITY HOLDING COMPANIES

The public-utility holding company was one of the fanciest financial erections—one could hardly call it a structure—of the New Economic Era. It had its beginning earlier, in 1870, and became prominent just before and after World War I. But the New Era saw the many-tiered façades, with fullest embellishment. In 1926 almost half the output of electricity was controlled by five companies; twenty companies dominated four fifths of the power industry. The onset of the depression shook the holding companies, but soon was supplying further opportunities for concentration of control. The most conspicuous collapse was that of Samuel Insull's Middle West Public Utilities Company, in which large numbers of unsuspecting investors lost a stupendous aggregate, and which put Insull to ignominious flight.

One holding company, perhaps with a layer of several holding companies beneath it, may have been of use in coordinating the management and services of a number of otherwise disconnected operating properties. But the pyramids that were piled up, six, seven, eight, nine stories high, with special subsidiaries for promotional and engineering aid, were mostly inspired by nothing better than the cupidity and chicanery of their authors, the credulity of those who bought their securities, and the helplessness of consumers of gas and electricity who suffered under artificially high rates. It was the practice of the insiders to retain control of a majority or a sufficient block of the voting stock, unloading the remainder of the securities on the public; as one holding company was placed above another, the percentage of investment by the manipulators became less and less until it was trifling. Stock from top to bottom was abundantly watered, while fictitious charges of engineering and advertising affiliates and scandalous salaries ate up profits. Where the basic operating plants were geographically close together and physically linked, industrial efficiency and even consumer advantage may have resulted, despite the wastes. But in too many instances the "system" existed only in the machinations of promoters, their lawyers, and their bankers.

The Public Utility Holding Company Act of August 26, 1935, contained the hotly debated "death sentence" against useless intermediate corporations. The Securities and Exchange Commission was directed, broadly, to limit each holding company to a single integrated system, corporate and geographic, and to require fair distribution of voting power among security owners. Acquisition of securities and assets by holding companies, payment of dividends, solicitation of proxies, intercompany loans, and service, sales, and construction contracts passed under the commission's supervision. The commission could approve voluntary simplification and reorganization plans submitted by registered holding companies.

Prolonged study of the situation was necessary before the commission could begin regulation of holding companies. Thereafter the policy was one of firmness with patience: the commission wanted to proceed so that its actions might not cause undue hardships or confusion while protecting the public interest. Early administration of the Public Utility Holding Company Act was complicated by a large number of suits (45 by June, 1936; 13 more in the next year) brought by holding companies attacking the constitutionality of the law—in spite of public disclaimer by the commission, the Attorney General, and the Postmaster General of any intention to enforce the criminal penalties of the act until its constitutionality had been established by the Supreme Court. For this purpose the commission brought suit against the Electric Bond and Share Company, November, 1935, seeking an order requiring the 13 holding companies in this system to register with the commission. An exhaustive stipulation of facts, agreed upon by both sides, was filed with the Court in June, 1936. Not until March, 1938, was decision of the Supreme Court rendered, upholding the constitutionality of the law.

By June 30, 1940, there were registered with the commission 144 utility holding companies with total assets of nearly $14.5 billion; embraced were 55 holding company systems, including 1,493 holding, subholding, and operating companies. The commission concentrated on the integration and simplification provisions of the act. Disappointed in efforts to encourage filing of voluntary plans for compliance, the commission was obliged to begin formal proceedings for integration with respect to nine major utility systems comprising $8,359,000,000 or about 58 per cent of total registered assets, besides simplification proceedings in three instances. Legal delays were interposed, but at length overcome. The giants of the industry were brought on the carpet. The largest in point of assets ($2,853,400,000) was Electric Bond and Share Company, which controlled in the United States 36 utility subsidiaries operating electric facilities in 27 states, gas facilities in 12 states, and 45 nonutility subsidiaries, with total operating revenues of $346,000,-000. Others were of lesser but still huge proportions.[20]

UNDERPINNING INVESTMENT

The commission executed with zest the assignment given it, by Section 30 of the Public Utility Holding Company Act, to make a full study of the activities of investment trusts, investment companies, investment advisory services, and related organizations. If investment trusts and the like, which more than any other device had put Main Street in Wall Street, had been mysterious before, they were so no longer. If they had been regarded as too sacred for scrutiny while they paid, and too sordid to justify inquiry when they failed, neither scruple deterred the commission, which was pitiless in going into the business in all its bearings. The commission, by June, 1937, when its study was nearing completion, had received questionnaire replies from 495 management investment companies, 178 fixed investment trusts, 37 investment special plans, 16 common trust funds, 400 investment counsel organizations; had made field studies and taken more than 20,000 pages of testimony in public hearings. It was believed that there were a million and a quarter shareholders in investment trusts and plans of all types. Particular studies were made of the largest schemes and of typical smaller ones.

By summer of 1940 the results of these investigations had nearly all been submitted to Congress. The main recommendations were embodied in bills which, after hearings and substitutions, be-

[20] U. S. Securities and Exchange Commission, *Sixth Annual Report, 1939–40* (Washington: Government Printing Office. 1941).

came (August 2, 1940) the Investment Company Act and the Investment Advisers Act.

Expansion of the functions of the Reconstruction Finance Corporation under the New Deal, both in magnitude and in variety, was impressive as seen in the figures of the reports, and as known—with a mixture of gratitude and chagrin—to thousands of businessmen and their enterprises. The public was less aware of the broad support and initiative which the RFC was furnishing, for the tactic was to keep this huge governmental resource discreetly in the background, and permit the role of its beneficiaries to appear as far as possible original. As developments seemed to demand, the RFC created its own subordinate corporations, and became less a salvaging agent for private finance and business than a primary economic force. The completeness of RFC service is seen in loans that it made to state funds which had been created for the purpose of insuring repayment of deposits of public moneys! After the United States entered World War II, the RFC, with its subsidiaries, was to be the most powerful corporation in existence.

Probably for security reasons, since the RFC was an engine in the defense program, reports were not published after that for the first quarter of 1941. In the whole period from February 2, 1932, to March 31, 1941, the corporation had made loans, allocations, and commitments of $15,744,628,021, disbursements of $11,400,888,829, had notes outstanding of $1,356,408,442, and credits outstanding of $2,319,777,784. A partial list of recipients of aid includes banks and trust companies, including receivers, liquidating agents, and conservators; building and loan associations, including receivers; insurance companies, mortgage loan companies, credit unions, federal land banks, joint-stock land banks, intermediate credit banks, agricultural credit corporations, national and regional; livestock credit corporations; railroads, including receivers and trustees; processors and distributors subject to processing taxes; agencies financing exports of agricultural surpluses; public bodies for relief and work relief; rural electrification; corporations created by the RFC, and businesses aiding in national defense. In the period here reviewed, 15,847 loans were made to 7,581 banks and trust companies aggregating $2,724,611,376, including $1,389,806,215 to aid in the reorganization of closed banks, and 8,708 loans on and subscriptions for preferred stock, and purchases of capital notes and debentures, amounting to $1,342,814,189. Two hundred and twenty-one loans, to a total of $922,741,586, were made to 89 railroads. Under the act of June 25, 1940, authorizations to the number of 134 were made to 56 corporations, including 4 created by the RFC, totaling $1,009,-284,048 for defense purposes, besides 139 authorizations to 111 business enterprises and 3 loans to 2 public agencies for the same purpose.[21]

[21] RFC, *Quarterly Report,* 1st Quarter, 1941 (Washington: Government Printing Office, 1941).

CHAPTER VI

Agricultural Adjustment

IN the summer of 1933 a Negro farmer from Georgia stood on the grounds of the White House to receive a medal from the President of the United States. He was honored because he was the first to plow under his quota of cotton. At that very time some fourteen million workers were unemployed and, in the words of the same President, a third of the nation was ill clothed. It may have been that the farmer who symbolized the campaign to destroy growing cotton had to borrow money to buy a decent shirt in which to appear for his award.

Someday America will look back on that episode with unbelief. Only a decade later, the Secretary of Agriculture, who flanked the President on the White House lawn, became the chief champion of plenty for this country and the world. The medalist, for the moment the nation's model farmer, had obeyed the Agricultural Adjustment Act of May 12, 1933. This, with its successor laws, marked the extreme of irony, not to say imbecility, to which the depression had brought the nation's economy. Millions were hungry and naked, while food and fiber were turned back to the clods or fields were left untilled. The economy of scarcity never found franker illustration. There was never a governmental policy carried out with such mingled satisfaction and shame. Officials who devised the program of "crop control" (read curtailment) tried to avoid responsibility

179

by shifting blame to others or by pleading an exigency brought about by forces over which they had no control.[1]

Thus Secretary of Agriculture Henry A. Wallace confessed that "to have to destroy a growing crop is a shocking commentary on our civilization," and that he could "tolerate it only as a cleaning up of the wreckage from the old days of unbalanced production. . . . The plowing under of 10 million acres of growing cotton in August, 1933, and the slaughter of 6 million little pigs in September . . . were not acts of idealism in any sane society. They were emergency acts made necessary by the almost insane lack of world statesmanship during the period from 1920 to 1932."[2] George N. Peek, the first administrator, said that he accepted, did not shape, the plow-up and the kill. Grave professors, making their elaborate survey of the restrictive measures, found fault with details, but did not think it necessary to question the usefulness of the whole.[3]

It nowhere seemed to occur to them that an economy which, for its correction and preservation, demanded such violence to reason, had better be abandoned than revived. Though current thought was not so bold, was there ever a time when avowal of production for use, rather than for private profit, was more appropriate? The price mechanism had stalled; in the extreme case, grain in some sections could not be sold at all. Finding international participation too injurious, the country had embarked upon economic nationalism. The central government had become a universal supporter of enterpriser, capitalist, farmer, worker. It had been considered sacrilegious to impair the self-sufficiency of industry, and demeaning to the masses to give them public charity. But beyond such desperate expedients, it would be virtually impossible to supersede the historic individualism of the American farmer. Physical isolation had imbued him with a firm self-determination. He was devoted to the blessed office of furnishing the staff of life. He was a part of nature, and so was above artificial social contrivance. But all such inhibitions and taboos were set aside.

It was reported at the time that a real obstacle to the cotton

[1] George N. Peek, *Why Quit Our Own?* (New York: D. Van Nostrand Company, 1936), pp. 124–139.

[2] Henry A. Wallace, *New Frontiers* (New York: Reynal & Hitchcock, Inc., 1934), pp. 174–175, 200.

[3] Edwin G. Nourse, Joseph S. Davis, and John D. Black, *Three Years of the Agricultural Adjustment Administration* (Washington: Brookings Institution, 1937).

plow-up was the noncompliance of the southern mule. For generations he had been taught, with stick and trace chain, not to step on cotton. Now that he was urged to trample it, he refused. A policy which seemed good to the Secretary of Agriculture was declined by the mule in the cotton row.

It is not necessary to recount in any detail the unhappy history behind the demand of American farmers for "purchasing power parity." Trouble stemmed from World War I, which expanded agricultural output ("food will win the war"), and converted the United States from a debtor nation, owing foreigners $200 million annually, to the second largest creditor nation, claiming from foreigners $500 million a year. These developments called for a change in the nation's trade policy which it did not recognize, much less put into effect. Americans had paid their debts by a favorable balance of trade, and had maintained a protective tariff to that end. Though it was imperative that they shake off the habit, they did not.

The citizens of the United States indulged the belief that they could keep out foreign industrial products, sell their agricultural surplus overseas and collect debts, old and new, from countries drained of gold and whose goods they would not let in. They built their protective wall higher in the Emergency Tariff of 1921, the Fordney-McCumber Tariff of 1922, and, crowning stupidity, the Hawley-Smoot Tariff of 1930. The result was stunning. Beginning in 1920 farm prices plummeted in the midst of depression at home and abroad, when lending to Europe was reduced, and farming there was revived, all of which should have been a warning against the continued huge output of staples. The physical volume of United States agricultural exports remained nearly the same, but the value was cut in half in a year.

At this point, as many begged later, Americans should have chosen; they should have accepted their new international position, reduced tariffs, and taken payment in goods. Instead, they resumed foreign lending, forced a market for their farm surpluses, and deferred the evil day. For a time, in the middle twenties, the illusion seemed perfect. But when Americans stopped sending Europe money with which to buy from them, preferring to promote their own promising stock market, European demand sickened. Anyhow, European farms had more than recovered prewar production.

SHRINKING DEMAND FOR FARM STAPLES

Worse was in store, for the tariff of 1930 led to retaliation abroad. The crop surplus of the United States was fended off from every shore by hoisted duties and every sort of other restriction, ingenious and injurious. Economic nationalism, of which Americans had supplied a pattern, was intensified by world depression. In 1925 a fifth of all Italian imports had been wheat. The Fascist government, joining high duties to exhortation, increased home production after 1930 to 40 and 60 per cent above prewar levels, while Italian wheat consumption was reduced by the mounting price. Germany raised her tariff on wheat from $0.42 per bushel in 1929 to $2.11 in 1934, on lard from $0.65 per hundred pounds to $18.10. Other expedients were added. Millers must use 80 per cent German wheat, and no lard from the United States was permitted to enter Germany. Similar tactics became universal, Britain and her dominions decreeing "Imperial preference." Countries with export surpluses foisted them off by bounties or placed them through unilateral agreements. Fears of a new war determined nations to supply their own needs for agricultural staples if they could.

At the same time, the production of American farms continued under war momentum, augmented by the further development of tractors, combines, electric equipment, superior transportation and storage facilities, better seed selection, and knowledge of soil chemistry and animal husbandry. Agricultural output, 27 per cent larger in 1929 than twenty years before, was produced by 7.5 per cent fewer persons: the average worker on the land was raising 40 per cent more. The number of horses on farms fell rapidly after the war, soon eliminating the need for 20 million acres that had grown feed grains. Cotton of India, Argentina, and Brazil competed with that grown in the United States, cutting the proportion of the country's crop exported from nearly two thirds to something over half. Rayon and other synthetic fibers reduced the demand for cotton more than the automobile and similar new industrial uses expanded it. Other changes conspired against the great farm staples. Fall in the birth rate and restriction of immigration, plus prosperity of the twenties, raised the standard of living, and this reduced the per capita consumption of cereals by a third since the beginning of the century in favor of fruits, vegetables, meat, and dairy products.

American farmers even learned how to feed animals better on less. Their wheat carry-over began to increase after 1926, doubled in 1929, and continued upward at about the rate of imposition of foreign duties.

By 1925, after hard years for agriculture beginning with 1921, the ratio of prices received by farmers to prices paid by farmers returned almost to the prewar "normal." Thereafter the farmers' position worsened, irregularly through 1929, then drastically. Farm costs did not decline as fast as income. Though land values were falling, mortgage interest remained fixed at the enlarged postwar volume, and taxes, doubled during the war and immediately after, rose higher in the twenties. The "New Economic Era," after its midpoint was reached, was anything else for farmers, who cast resentful and envious looks on the gains of industrialists. It was natural, therefore, that plans which they offered for relief should aim to "make the tariff effective for agriculture." This goal could be accomplished, if at all, only with twisting and turning, since burdensome surpluses of farm staples promised to sink the whole of these crops to the low levels of world prices. Surplus was the bane. It was one thing to protect an industrial home market against imports, quite another to defend an agricultural home market against back-flooding from potential exports.

Attempts of the "farm bloc" in this direction in the earlier twenties—through emergency agricultural tariffs, market regulation, aid to farm cooperatives, and more farm credit—had proved abortive. Then came more tortuous schemes, all trying to realize a two-price system. They were based on attempted quarantine of the domestic supply, the price of which was to be raised, from contagion of the surplus which, offered on the world market, must bear a low price. These devices were broadly three in number. The McNary-Haugen bills, vetoed by Coolidge in 1927 and 1928, proposed to have farmers, through an "equalization fee," meet losses on the surplus marketed abroad while obtaining higher prices for the segregated home supply. Foreign losses were to be minimized by skillful marketing, total supply was to be reduced, perhaps, by making the equalization fee punitive. All in all, the domestic price was to be raised by the amount of the agricultural tariffs, or at least by enough to restore the "parity" between agricultural and industrial prices which existed in 1909–1914. The Farm Bureau Federation backed the McNary-Haugen scheme.

The Grange supported a second proposition, that for "export debentures." This plan amounted to a federal subsidy on agricultural exports to be paid out of tariff receipts. An account of the too-ingenious particulars is not necessary here, for the proposal never got beyond the stage of debate. The third expedient of "domestic allotment" was elaborated by M. L. Wilson, then head of the Agricultural Economics Department of Montana State College, and was backed by the Farmers Union. This plan was bolder, more thorough than the others because of its provision for reduction of output. While all of the proposals, plus the practice of the Federal Farm Board, entered in some degree into the amalgam of the Agricultural Adjustment Act of 1933, the domestic allotment became the stock of it. As finally framed, the domestic requirement in each major crop was to be estimated in advance. Each producer who accepted his pro-rata allotment would be given benefit payments drawn from taxes on processors. Thus the price of the domestic supply would be raised through reduction of output and by the amount of the benefit payments, the cost of which would be passed on by middlemen to consumers. If there were still a surplus it would be sold abroad at the lower world price. This scheme, in legislative development under the Hoover administration, was espoused by Roosevelt as candidate for the presidency, and after his election, but before he took office, it assumed, in declared purposes and in provisions, still more the shape of the final AAA.

This review of background has gone beyond the proper beginning period, and has omitted the one actual experiment in agricultural relief, that of Hoover's Federal Farm Board authorized by the Agricultural Marketing Act of June 14, 1929.

Beginning with 1929, even before the depression struck, the situation of agriculture became worse. Farm production continued unabated, then rose to a peak in 1932, and by 1933 had fallen a little below 1929, during all which time industrial production, and consequently consuming power, was declining disastrously. It was in this period that impediments to export became most pronounced. Good crops abroad, plus tariffs retaliatory to the Hawley-Smoot Act of 1930, gave the United States mounting carry-overs of the staples. From 1929 to 1933, the per cent of total gross income from farm production due to foreign demand fell from 14.7 in the previous four-year period to 9.6. Export of cotton and tobacco declined markedly, but that of wheat and pork was cut almost in half. In 1932, when crop acreage was greatest, farm income was the lowest on record; per capita farm income was cut even more, because in this year the movement of population from cities to farms exceeded that from farms to cities, increasing rural unemployment.

RESORT TO PLANNED SCARCITY

The main significance of the New Deal was moral rather than economic. Coerced by depression, the government resolved to drop inhibitions and to interfere with economic and social institutions on several fronts at once. The character and even the extent of the intervention were not novel. The objects and the means were not new or always wise. Under mercantilism and in the first decades of the laissez-faire policy, efforts of government to alter economic behavior had been as inclusive, though they had never before been so sudden. Few of the basic devices of the New Deal were unfamiliar. Dutch spice merchants had burned part of their crops, colonial tobacco planters had been forced to restrict production, widespread relief and ambitious public works were historic, sanction of combinations among manufacturers and traders had sufficient precedent, inflation was an ancient recourse. But previously these methods had been resorted to gradually. Now they were summoned simultaneously. The temerity was in the timing.

The New Deal was of mixed purposes. The conflict which it faced was that production was bursting the bonds of price. Plenty was routing the scarcity that seemed necessary to the maintenance of the accustomed economy. In some parts the New Deal accepted and furthered the forces of production. Such were the Tennessee Valley Authority, with its power dams, Rural Resettlement with its transfer of farmers from barren acres, public works, federal housing, aspects of social security legislation, and other features that might be mentioned. But at least half of the strength of the New Deal was given to restoring and bolstering scarcity. The main commitment was to usher in "the fuller life" by rehabilitation of a system that depended on scarcity. The attempt was doomed to disappointment because science and technology had so far overcome the ignorance and ineptitude which induced dearth.

The Agricultural Adjustment Administration was the agency which more than any other focused on restriction of output for the sake of driving up prices. The Agricultural Adjustment Act was passed on May 12, 1933, under frightening circumstances. Farm relief under Hoover, through the Farm Board and emergency agricultural credit of several sorts, had not only failed, but as a consequence had led on to desperate direct action. Within three years the number of farms changing hands because of foreclosure and other defaults had risen by over 150 per cent. Historically familiar defenses of embattled farmers were invoked. Chief agricultural states of the Middle West and Southwest passed mortgage moratoria running from six months to three years. The South Dakota governor called out the militia to enforce the ban on foreclosures. Farmers used the less formal method of assembling armed at sheriffs' sales and seeing to it that the owner bought his land back for a few cents. A recalcitrant judge in Iowa, a rope around his neck, was saved from hanging when the crowd was content with stealing his pants and smearing him with axle grease. The Supreme Court held that the mortgage moratoria represented a valid exercise of the police power. The defiant Farm Holiday movement, to prevent products from going to market at giveaway prices, resulted in overturned trucks and milk cans emptied into the ditches.

Within a week after the new administration took office, Secretary Wallace called farm leaders of all persuasions to Washington. The crisis had relaxed factional insistence on particular programs. "Do anything, but do something!" was the spirit. Parts or adaptations of all the old proposals reappeared in the measure now put together under pressure. However, domestic allotment with production control won main emphasis. Threat of still expanded output was the goad. Wallace has recalled that, during the hectic councils, "cotton was sprouting on an expanded acreage. Winter wheat was ripening. Spring wheat was going in. Hog and cattle numbers were reaching record levels, and the dairy industry was wrestling with more than its annual spring surplus." Delays while Congress debated were maddening. The combined backing of farm forces was not enough to persuade the Senate until recruits were brought up from other quarters by incorporating provisions to lighten farm mortgages and inflate the currency.

Though framers of the act, to overcome congressional objections, presented it as an emergency measure, there is abundant evidence that all along they intended it to be the basis of long-time policy. The President himself suggested that a two-year limit on the operation of the law be replaced by a provision that he should end it whenever he found that the emergency was passed, a substitution which gave much latitude. The same intent became increasingly evident in administration. The scheme was only well started when a new Program Planning Division, with an assistant administrator in charge, was assigned "to shape the entire program into a coherent whole which will constitute an advance through emergency measures to an established and lasting agricultural industry." The first AAA progress report said: "Far-reaching and fundamental production adjustment programs which already have been undertaken or are contemplated must be consolidated into permanent measures." And in October, 1935, the President declared: "It never was the idea of the men who framed the Act, of those in Congress who revised it, or of Henry Wallace or Chester Davis that the Agricultural Adjustment Administration should be either a mere emergency operation or a static agency. It was their intention—as it is mine—to pass from the purely emergency phases necessitated by a grave national crisis to a . . . more permanent plan for American agriculture." [4] If these proponents of the measure had been something less than frank with the public, they were still unshaken in their resolve when the crucial feature of the act was held unconstitutional by the Supreme Court in January, 1936, for, as will be seen, they were ingenious in building new structures on the wreckage.

The act undertook to "re-establish prices to farmers at a level that will give purchasing power . . . equivalent to the purchasing power of agricultural commodities in the base period." This period was, for most crops specifically dealt with, the five years just preceding World War I, 1909–1914. Four means of raising prices and adding to farmers' income were provided: (1) restriction of output and removal of surpluses from the market; (2) direct payments to

4 *Roosevelt Public Papers and Addresses.* IV, 432–433.

farmers for reducing their output; (3) levying of excise taxes on primary processors in order to get the money to pay these benefits; (4) marketing agreements between producers' cooperatives, processors, and distributors, permitted or required by government, for the purpose of raising or maintaining prices; these marketing agreements were to apply to any farm product, not simply to designated "basic" crops.[5]

At first only seven "basic commodities," the prices of which were depressed by large export surpluses, were made subject to production control—wheat, cotton, field corn, hogs, rice, tobacco, and dairy products. Later nine more commodities were added—rye, flax, barley, sorghum, cattle, peanuts, sugar beets, sugar cane, and potatoes, though several of these were "basic" to nothing more than political expediency; some of the added commodities were controlled not at all or only partially.

The base period, 1909–1914, referred to as "normal," in which the lost "parity" of agriculture and industry had last been achieved, as a matter of fact had been more favorable for farmers than any other in recent peacetimes.[6] The act, even in subsequent revisions, contained only slight protection for consumers who were to bear the burden; parity was to be approached gradually and not be exceeded. But it must be allowed that George Peek, in taking office as the first administrator, concealed nothing. "In the first place," he said, "the sole aim and object of this act is to raise farm prices. Generally speaking, it is to raise them to a point where farm products will purchase as much of industrial products as they did before the War, and to keep farm prices at that level." Consumers were morally exhorted with assurance that "what is to be done is to bring about economic justice—to right a social wrong—which grew up under our economic system in the false theory that the urban half of our population could enjoy the benefits of an artificial, protective system, leaving the rural half largely outside the benefits of that . . . device. . . . Lately it has resulted in taking the farmer's crop away from him without paying for it. Nobody wants to do

[5] U. S. Department of Agriculture, *Report of Administration of the Agricultural Adjustment Act,* May 1933–Feb. 1934 (Washington: Government Printing Office, 1934).

[6] Robert F. Martin, *Income in Agriculture, 1929–1935* (New York: National Industrial Conference Board, 1936), pp. 102 ff.

that." He went on to say that restoration of parity would be for the general welfare.[7]

THE "PLOW-UP" AND THE "KILL"

The program was to get producers of designated crops to agree to restrict output to something like domestic requirements; this restriction would lift prices, and the additional amount that farmers needed to bring them to parity would be given in benefit payments from the processing taxes. But wheat, corn, cotton, and tobacco were already growing, and livestock operations then under way would swell production in 1934 and beyond. Precious time was lost while the vast machinery of Agricultural Adjustment was devised and set in motion. Not to delay a whole season, therefore, the drastic step was taken of accomplishing "control" through outright destruction. Though this had been suggested before in the case of cotton, the proposal had been made on the part of the Farm Board only—a despairing *envoi*. Now it was to be embraced with stunning suddenness and vigor. The AAA did some better things, but it is fated to be remembered for the initial "plow-up and kill."

Deliberate destruction of wheat, though planned, was avoided. Secretary Wallace wrote: "Fortunately . . . the crop reports showed a sensational reduction in winter wheat prospects because of unfavorable weather. It would not be necessary to plow under growing wheat; nature had already done it—unequally, cruelly, to be sure, but decisively, and without provoking the resentment of consumers. Our press section breathed a sigh of relief; it would not be necessary to write about the logic of plowing under wheat while millions lacked bread." [8] But since many wheat farmers had little to sell even at the improved prices, they were given benefit payments in return for the promise to reduce their acreage for the following three years.

The cotton crop, on the contrary, promised to be bigger than ever. A million farmers, in August, 1933, began to plow up from a fourth to a half of their cotton—10,000,000 acres—receiving "rental payments" in cash or partly in cash and partly in options to buy government-held cotton. Corn and hogs had to be adjusted together, for if there were too many hogs with respect to corn the

[7] Peek. *Why Quit Our Own?*, p. 20.   [8] Wallace, *New Frontiers*, p. 171.

price of pork would drop beyond control, and if corn was relatively plentiful and cheap, a surplus of hogs would be bred. It was intended in 1934 to reduce corn by 10,000,000 acres and hogs by 7,000,000 head. But what to do in 1933, when both products were selling at ruinous prices and more sows had been bred to farrow than in 1932? It was decided to help present and future by slaughtering over 6,000,000 swine—222,000 sows soon to farrow, 5,105,000 little pigs, and 1,083,000 light pigs. Most of this pork, under agreements of the government with the packers, became fertilizer; less than a tenth was saved as food and distributed in relief. The irony of the pig kill did not end with denying the hungry. The fertilizer contributed to more production on farms, which, in the eyes of the AAA, was the one thing not needful. Sixty million pounds of butter were bought by the government and given away, incidentally to help the poor, primarily to help the price. Over 12,000 acres of tobacco were plowed under. California cling peaches were permitted to rot in the orchard.[9]

The men who managed this destruction considered themselves practical. But never did a theory take such precedence over common sense. Millions lacked food and clothing, but were told they could get these by perceiving a pretty paradox: less would really mean more, a restored "balance" between agriculture and industry would provide purchasing power and jobs and wages and so consumption goods. Two birds in hand were to be exchanged for one in the bush.[10] The public went along with marked revulsion, refusing to see how price was more important than pork. The angry protests taught the AAA that the complacency of the people had its limits, and after this episode increasing care was taken to distribute "surpluses" to the destitute, especially through a food stamp plan. More would have been accomplished in this direction had not owners of industry joined their objections to those of farmers. Thus when cotton was given to the unemployed to allow them to make their own mattresses, mattress factories demurred. And Upton Sinclair's bigger and bolder scheme for self-help for the unemployed in California was defeated by chambers of commerce, aided not a little by the New Deal in Washington.

[9] U. S. Department of Agriculture, *Agricultural Adjustment*, 1933–1934, pp. 22 ff., 74, 97 ff.
[10] *Ibid.*, p. 3.

INCREASING COERCION NECESSARY TO RESTRICTION

It was agreed from the start of the AAA that preservation of democratic methods, including local autonomy and, indeed, free choice by the individual farmer as to whether he would participate in a crop control program, was highly desirable. It was accepted that some sacrifice of efficiency and speed was justified if excessive bureaucracy could thereby be avoided. This resolve to cater to democracy was more than loyalty to laudable tradition. An army of agents controlled by the central administration would be expensive in salaries, and unless they participated actively in the scheme, farmers whom the AAA sought to help might sabotage it through ignorance or resentment. Chester Davis, then head of the Production Division, said early in the history of the AAA: "We want to avoid being placed in a position where we can develop a full-grown program and come out and say to you 'Here it is.' We think we are going to go further safely if we do not go too far in front of the army and get shot from behind." [11]

One would suppose that not much persuasion should have been necessary with farmers who were to get the same or a better income for raising less. The individualism of farmers did not stand in the way of their accepting a plan in return for a payment. A chief difficulty lay in the different situations of commercial farmers and those whose controlled crop was a by-product. The former reduced cost when they reduced output, while the latter, mostly operating on a small scale, saved little or no expense when they signed up with AAA.

The ideal was to have the farmers themselves plan the control programs with the central administrative officers. Except in a token fashion, this was not feasible, for the requisite statistical information and collective view was possessed only by the AAA at Washington. However, large numbers of county committees of farmers gave advice on local conditions, and checked contract statements and compliance of their neighbors. Since these local committees tended to be composed of large farmers, AAA had to be on the lookout to protect the interests of small men who were less well represented. By the terms of the law, a majority of the producers

[11] American Institute of Cooperation, *American Cooperation* (Washington: The Institute, 1933), p. 487.

must vote for a control program before it could be put into effect or be renewed. The personnel of the federal and state extension services was used to explain the designs of the central organization to local farmers and their committees.

In spite of sincere effort to keep the scheme decentralized and democratic, more and more coercion had to be employed.[12] Previous voluntary attempts at restriction of production had been defeated by the numerous individuals who preferred, since prices were to be raised, to stay outside the plan and grow as large crops as possible. Unless they could be persuaded, most of those composing the minority had to be forced into compliance in one way or another. Even those signing contracts could evade the purpose of control by taking their worst land out of use, planting it in alternative crops, or cultivating more intensively.

The principal coercive devices were in the Bankhead Cotton Control Act and the Kerr-Smith Tobacco Control Act of 1934. The first levied a tax of 50 per cent of the price of the standard grade, but not under 5 cents per pound. The smallest producers were given tax-exempt certificates for their entire production, but others received the certificates only to the amount of their assigned quotas. Since all considerable producers were forced to reduce output (for the tax was prohibitive) they made contracts in order to get the benefit payments. The tobacco tax was a third of the selling price. The Warren Potato Act of 1935 applied this same method to another commodity. Important opportunities, such as borrowing from the Commodity Credit Corporation, and getting federal seed loans, were confined to signers. It is fair to say that the effective pressure for the coercive measures came from complying farmers who did not want to see their agreements undone by a recalcitrant minority. Another form of coercion, more distant, was compensating processing taxes on commodities to which producers might shift in the effort to sidestep control. Creating and maintaining artificially high prices necessitated action all along the line; thus compensating duties were levied on imported processed staples where these imports threatened to undermine the control structure.

A brief description of other methods of price control will precede an examination of crop restriction. One method was that of commodity loans to permit producers to hold corn and cotton off

[12] Peek, *Why Quit Our Own?*, p. 25.

the market until prices improved. This was not a new device, as loans had been made to coöperative associations of producers under the Agricultural Marketing Act since 1929, and the buying up of surpluses by the Farm Board had had much the same effect. The policy of government holdings was briefly discredited because there was no limit to the accumulation while no power existed to limit output. The AAA had this power and, without hostile notice, encouraged enormous storage; these stored commodities were nominally collateral against loans, but would certainly be thrown on the hands of the government if control measures did not succeed. Funds came from several sources, mainly through the Commodity Credit Corporation, organized with exclusively government capital in October, 1933. In practice, the corporation guaranteed bank loans to the farmers.

The scheme of loans to permit holding corn and cotton was devised under pressure from producers, who were feeling the decline of prices after the first speculative advance when AAA was announced, who had not yet received benefit payments, and who clamored for inflation or outright price pegging. Just as the plan of loans on surpluses was adapted from the Hoover policies, and relied heavily on the Reconstruction Finance Corporation which he had sponsored, so it ran forward to become the basis of the "over-normal granary" and crop insurance which became important after the first AAA was invalidated. This is another illustration among many of the fact that the New Deal, in framework and mechanics, was not so novel as has often been supposed, but was, rather, a well-defined stage in a development.

Borrowers agreed to sign the corn hog and cotton contracts, which speeded and widened restriction and thereby safeguarded the held surpluses from becoming uncontrollable. The loans were "without recourse"—that is, if borrowers did not choose to repay the money and reclaim their collateral, the government must take the corn and cotton in full satisfaction of the obligations. The loans were at first 10 cents a pound on cotton and 45 cents a bushel on corn, which were the prevailing prices at principal markets; the interest rate was 4 per cent. Loans could be called if middling cotton rose to 15 cents at New Orleans and if No. 2 corn rose to 75 cents at Chicago. Cotton loans were on warehouse receipts, corn loans on corn on the cob in sealed cribs on the farms.

In 1933–1934, about $121 million was loaned on 271 million bushels of corn stored on 200,000 farms in ten states. The operation was a success from every standpoint. At the outset, prices on farms were substantially below the loan rate, but as prices rose, the loans were repaid and the corn was released for sale or for feeding on the farms at total gain of some $83 million or about 30 cents above the loan rate. Further, much stored corn was carried over to the season of 1934–1935 when there was a shortage of production, and was thus a general economic benefit. New corn loans were made in the fall of 1934 and 1935, but as the need for them had been diminished by the improved price, they were of less consequence than the first loan.[13]

The experience with cotton loans was less successful. In 1933, some $120,000,000 was loaned on 2,339,000 bales. Prices went above the loan rate, but by the following July only half the loans had been repaid, and the government was financing, including cotton inherited from the Farm Board, about 3,000,000 bales. This surplus was maintained not only by speculative hopes of borrowers, but by the AAA itself, which was convinced that the only way to extricate itself was to accumulate more cotton collateral, trusting to crop restriction to raise the price further. This scheme was easier to plan than to execute. But the South was delighted, cried for more of the same, and in the fall of 1934 a new loan was offered on better terms, 12 and 11 cents a pound. Prices fell in the spring of 1935 and the government found itself holding all told 6,200,000 bales—twice as much as ever under the Farm Board—in which it had invested 13 cents a pound.[14]

Finally, in 1936, partly to supply domestic and foreign markets, the Commodity Credit Corporation released a great quantity of cotton at a loss. Competent students have concluded that whatever gains the cotton loans gave to growers in support of prices were counterbalanced by the harmful effects of the operation.

Encouraged by the financial success of the first corn loan (the government made a net profit of half a million dollars) and by the use of impounded surplus in relieving shortage due to drought, Secretary Wallace began talking and writing about a permanent plan for an "ever-normal granary," later elaborated to form a crop

---

[13] U. S. Department of Agriculture, *Agricultural Adjustment,* 1933–1934, pp. 91–93.
[14] *Ibid.,* 1933–1935, pp. 122–131.

insurance scheme to be described in the discussion of the later aspects of agricultural adjustment.

OTHER DEVICES FOR RAISING PRICES

Every method which responsible administrators and hard-pressed farmers could devise for increasing agricultural prices in the face of surpluses was tried. One was subsidized export, or dumping abroad; related ways were diversion to relief or to lower commercial uses. All but the last had been used by the Federal Farm Board, and the AAA was quick to follow its example. With a loan from the RFC, China reluctantly took more than $15 million of wheat, flour, and cotton. The wheat "sale" was arranged by the North Pacific Emergency Export Association, which subsidized exports to the extent of more than 28 million bushels on which the loss was $6.5 million.[15] The AAA contributed part of the RFC loans to get foreigners to take tobacco, prunes, and nuts.

The relief population at home proved more absorbent of surpluses. The Federal Surplus Relief (later Commodities) Corporation was the means of assisting both depressed prices and depressed people. The surpluses distributed were made supplementary to regular relief donations, and included meat of all sorts, dairy products, wheat and flour, eggs, fruits, vegetables, salmon, cotton and much besides. This was a far more eligible program than that of putting surpluses to lower-value uses, as when $750,000 was spent in subsidizing the diversion of peanuts into livestock feed and oil to prevent their sale as nuts, and when larger sums were employed to have millions of yards of cotton cloth become reinforcement in highway construction [16] and to turn low-grade tobaccos into nicotine.

The first and third of these surplus disposal devices had distinct drawbacks. Dumping abroad gave cheap goods to foreigners at the expense of the American consumer while there were millions at home in want, and ran counter to the reciprocal trade agreements effort. Diversion to lower uses was only less repugnant to reason than outright destruction.

A last method of raising prices was through marketing agree-

15 *Ibid.*, 1934, p. 77.
16 *Ibid.*, 1933–1935, pp. 136–137.

ments. These were not confined to basic commodities, and were applied, under AAA, to twenty-eight products. Processors and distributors agreed to pay higher prices on condition that some kind of production limitation was used. Shipments from producers to processors might be confined to superior grades, the remainder being allowed to go to waste. In the case of perishable products, prohibition of any shipment for a few days would remove the danger of a price-destroying glut. Often the amount of the crop that could be profitably marketed was determined, and producers were given the quotas which they might ship.

Such methods had been used for a number of years by farmers' cooperatives, but the schemes tended to fail because some pro-- ducers refused to join in, and the example of their gains at the expense of others was apt to disrupt the effort. To cure this difficulty, the Secretary of Agriculture was empowered to license processors and distributors, and to withdraw licenses from those who did not enforce the rules. Among the more important products covered by marketing agreements were milk, tobacco, rice, prunes, peaches, citrus fruit, grapes, canning vegetables, and nuts. Some attempt— too little—was made under agreements to have marketing practices fairer and more efficient, and in this and other respects the agreements approached code provisions in NRA. Agreements and licenses were respected at first, but when some found that they could venture on violations with impunity, others followed, so that in 1934 clarifying amendments had to be added to the act. But the interpretation of interstate commerce was strained to embrace products originating and marketed wholly within a state if they should "in any way affect interstate . . . commerce." This overreaching definition defeated its objects and provoked more violations; the Schechter decision, reinstating the meaning of interstate commerce as before understood, destroyed the agreements except in a few cases where strong cooperatives hardly needed a law anyhow. Amendments in 1935 substituted for agreements "Secretary's orders," issued under safeguards but accomplishing much the same purpose and permitting a steady expansion of this means of price raising. On the whole, marketing agreements enjoyed limited success. They furnished another illustration of the eagerness of New Deal legislation at this time to abandon the antitrust acts and encourage collusion to restrict supply and increase profit returns.[17]

The primary purpose of the AAA throughout, but especially in its first incarnation—or up to January, 1936, when the processing taxes were killed by the Supreme Court—was crop control, which meant in practice crop restriction. As has been seen, the methods were various, but typically took the form of voluntary agreements of farmers to reduce output in return for benefit payments from the proceeds of taxes on the first processor of the product. How effective was this effort? An answer is hard to give even when an attempt is made to compare production in a year of control with that of the base period or of the preceding year, particularly because weather conditions and changes in output which would have occurred in the absence of the program were influential. But the more pertinent contrast would be between production in a year of control with what production would have been in that year without control, and here the truth is teasing and can never be known.

JUDGING THE SUCCESS OF AAA

The farmers' agreements covering the various included crops ranged from 50 to 75 per cent of the acreage; they were higher in areas of specialized commercial production and lower in those of small and scattered output. In the case of wheat, successive droughts did far more to cut crops, draw down the carry-over, and *increase* net *imports* than did the measures of human restriction. The contracts of 1933–1935 may have reduced output by 50 or 60 million bushels in all, which was slight as compared with the limitation caused by nature. For example, the deliberate restriction in 1934, maybe 25 or 30 million bushels, was a tenth of the damage due to adverse weather.[18] The Brookings study, *Three Years of the Agricultural Adjustment Administration,* concluded that, had weather been normal, the AAA methods could not have reduced the wheat crop by more than 160 million bushels a year, which would have left a production (700 million bushels a year) distinctly in excess of domestic requirements. The story was much the same for corn, weather being far more effective than wishes. The attempt to hold

[17] *Ibid.,* 1933–1934, pp. 6–7; 1933–1935, pp. 23–25.
[18] *Ibid.,* 1933–1935, pp. 152, 154.

rice acreage down to the point to which it had fallen in 1933 was broadly successful, though less so in the South than in California; however, average yield per acre in 1934 and 1935 was higher than ever, and carry-overs were reduced by large distribution in relief and by increase in exports. Eighty per cent of peanut acreage was pledged to reduction of planting to 90 per cent of preceding years, but nonsigners expanded, with the result that the crop of 1935 was the largest on record, and prices were kept up only by the diversion of nuts to oil and feed. While the pig-sow slaughter reduced hog production, the high cost of feed reduced it more—indeed, to below what AAA had intended. Cattle, after much opposition of breeders, were to be brought under a processing-tax and reduction program when the drought of 1934 made this superfluous; the government bought over 8 million head, thus saving owners from losses which would have been crushing.

Cotton was a different story. Acreage reduction in the three years 1933–1935 was more than a third, and production would have been from 10 to 13 million bales greater in this period without the drastic restrictions imposed. The world carry-over was cut, though the experiment did not last long enough to bring this down to normal. Tobacco output was also materially decreased, beginning with the plow-up of 12,000 acres of cigar filler and binder tobacco in 1933, and going on to reduce the production of flue-cured tobacco by perhaps 250 million pounds and Burley by somewhat less. In fact, restriction of these types worked so effectively that it had to be relaxed in 1935 to prevent loss of export markets.[19]

The AAA experiment with direct crop restriction showed that obstacles to success make the device measurably useful only in short periods of emergency. Plans, unless those of outright destruction, must be made months in advance, and calculations are likely to be undone by weather conditions. In the degree that the scheme is effective, price gains and benefit payments are reduced, a fact which makes farmers less eager to cooperate and prompts them to evasion, if not of the letter, certainly of the spirit of the program. Unless the nonsigner is coerced by methods repugnant to democratic professions, he remains a constant menace. The whole purpose of restriction runs counter to the growing demand to seize

[19] *Ibid.*, for rice, pp. 237–241; peanuts, p. 246; cattle, p. 266; cotton, pp. 119 ff; tobacco, pp. 198–200.

upon the economy of abundance which is plainly obtainable. The apologetics of reduction become less and less convincing. At the outset of the AAA it was possible to get public acquiescence by pointing to the habitual limitation of output practiced by combinations in industry. At that time the government, through NRA, was not only permitting businessmen to raise prices by restricting supply, but was urging on collusion with this object, and, once it was adopted by a majority of producers and dealers, was making it mandatory upon all. But with the disappearance of NRA, and the failure of other government-sponsored devices for raising industrial prices, government itself executed an about-face and took the public with it in a frontal attack on combinations in restraint of trade. The apostate confessions of Mr. Thurman Arnold, as Assistant Attorney General in charge of antitrust prosecutions, and the protracted probings of the Temporary National Economic Committee put business consolidation out of favor and elevated again the ideal of competition. Thus the Department of Agriculture was no longer so safe in using the excuse, "Industry limits output, why may not farmers do the same?" The farm control programs subsequent to the AAA had to be less open not only because of constitutional prohibitions, but because it was desired not to rouse a public suspicion which was ready to become hostile. All along the agricultural leaders had talked about the need of achieving and maintaining "balance" between farm and factory output, and had sought to show, with a patience worthy of a better cause, how under the capitalist system prosperity of one large sector of the economy is necessary to the well-being of all. But this approach always supposed more inclination to listen and understand than the American people possessed. Therefore this explanation of the Department of Agriculture came to play a smaller part in its strategy than some plausible methods which tried to make restriction of production look like conservation of resources. Those will be dealt with later.

Nearly a billion dollars in processing taxes were collected between the summer of 1933, when they began to apply, and January, 1936, when they were declared unconstitutional. On what classes—farmers, middlemen, consumers—they were burdens, to which they were benefits, and in what proportions, would be a hard enough problem in shifting and incidence. But the puzzle is complicated by other features of the AAA program, by the effects of droughts, and by monetary manipulation to raise prices. Total cash income from agriculture increased almost 24 per cent in 1933 and around 15 per cent in each of the next two years. Benefit payments were a fourth of this increase in cash income in 1933, more than two thirds in 1934, and over half in 1935. In this period farmers' expenditures increased less than cash income, so that net gains were greater than appear. It is supposed that the processing taxes on wheat (30 cents a bushel) and cotton (4.2 cents a pound) were passed forward to consumers, so that wheat growers in three years received some $326 million from this source, and cotton growers about $452 million. The processing tax on corn seems to have been passed forward to consumers; while the price of hogs rose somewhat, it would have risen more except that the main effect of the processing tax was to depress prices paid to producers. The processing tax on tobacco was probably borne mostly by the manufacturers.

SHARECROPPERS VICTIMIZED

The AAA, especially in the first three years, worked out no effective means for the equitable sharing of benefit payments between landlords and tenants. Abuses were worst in the cotton districts of the South. The theory was that cash tenants, regarded as farm operators, were to get the whole of the benefit payments for their crop reduction, as well as the increased price of the cotton; the AAA knew that when leases expired landlords would get a share by raising rents. "Managing share tenants," getting from the owner nothing but the land and controlling their own work, were to sign the contracts and receive separate checks for their part of benefit payments. Ordinary share tenants and croppers who contributed nothing but labor did not get separate checks, but were to be paid by the landlord according to their share of the cotton. The supposed category of "managing share tenants" was often ignored by the landlords, and where landlords got the checks the chances of fair treatment of any subordinate claimant were slim. Hired laborers were to get nothing of the benefit payments, and it was easy for owners to reduce share tenants and croppers to the status of laborers.

Studies by apologists of the program minimized the robbery

and displacement of tenants through acreage reduction, while findings of critics were exaggerated the other way. Displacement of the
lowest ranks of cotton growers was due not only to acreage reduction, but to other, connected, causes. Tractors, often bought by landlords with benefit payments, did the work of many men with mules
where tenants were expelled and the holdings were thrown together. Relief and public works had something to do with tenants
and laborers leaving cotton land. Also, since there was a surplus
of labor backed up on the farms even in the absence of crop restriction, bargaining was easy for landlords. All of these causes, but
chiefly the AAA reduction program with benefit payments, created
a scandal and a tragedy as thousands of the poorest cotton farmers
sought succor in the cities or, as jalopy Joads, headed for California,
there to be migrants on the barest subsistence. Rural Resettlement
(later Farm Security) stayed this result in large numbers of cases,
and where it could not hold the people in their old districts, provided some decent camps for the wanderers. The AAA in later
adaption was more successful with the tenant problem, but partly
because large numbers had already been eliminated.[20]

The AAA made some attempt, both in statute and in administration, to prevent the gouging of consumers, whether in favor of
producers or of processors. But where the whole purpose and effort
was to raise prices to producers by restricting output, and where
processing taxes were expected in the main to be passed forward
to retail purchasers, any plans, however sincere, for the defense of
consumers were foredoomed to failure. Consumers were going to
pay for the program probably in two ways, by receiving less goods
and by receiving these at higher prices. That much admitted, attempts to prevent abuse were at most afterthoughts. A Consumers'
Counsel set up in the AAA was for a short time militant, but later,
from whatever cause, contented itself with showing consumers,
through the publication called *Consumers' Guide,* how they could
make the best of a bad situation. Cajolery tended to take the place
of criticism. A special unfairness to consumers was in the pyramid-
ing of processing taxes, which was almost impossible to police. The
best excuse that can be offered for the architects of AAA, so far as
consumers were concerned, is their belief, or hope, that restoration

[20] U. S. Special Committee on Farm Tenancy, *Farm Tenancy* (Washington: Government Printing Office, 1937).

of farm income would give more work in industry, transportation, commerce and all the other lines, thus giving consumers the funds with which to pay the higher prices.

NATURE TAKES A HAND

The droughts of 1934 and 1936, the former being the more severe, were the worst in seventy-five years. Much of the area between the Appalachians and the Rockies was struck, cutting crops in 1934 by a third, in 1936 by a fifth. This result in general fell in with the crop restriction policies of the Department of Agriculture, and the second drought reduced yields the year after the control features of the AAA had been invalidated by the Supreme Court. The droughts increased prices of farm products, farm incomes, and the purchasing power of these incomes. The effects of the droughts on agricultural prices continued beyond the immediate reduction of products, for carry-overs were diminished. As a consequence, in 1937, with bumper crops, and despite the drop in prices of farm products toward the end of the year, farm income had a buying power equal to that of the predepression period 1924–1929. Farm prices themselves were above prewar level, but nonfarm prices had risen still higher.[21]

These features were on the credit side of the ledger, as the Department of Agriculture figured. But there were unfavorable results also. The droughts bore on some growers much harder than on others, and special drought relief and government efforts to adjust farm debt could not make up the difference. Some creditors refused to reduce their claims, believing that the calamity would bring government to the rescue to a greater extent. However, new loans by the federal land banks and the land bank commissioner dropped from the peak of $1,283,563,000 in 1934 to $445,067,000 in 1935, and to $186,428,000 in 1936. Also, a higher proportion of loans was used to buy farms and to make improvements rather than to liquidate old debt, partly because of the fact that so much farm debt had already been wiped out.[22] Government lending agencies were coming to feel that where accumulated debt burden

[21] Arthur P. Chew, of U. S. Department of Agriculture, in *American Year Book,* 1937, p. 429.
[22] *Ibid.,* p. 430.

was crushing and creditors were not amenable to adjustment, it was preferable to allow foreclosure and settle the farmer on a new place less highly capitalized.

The droughts, with their sharp limitation of output, cast doubt on the wisdom of the whole crop control project. The Soil Conservation and Domestic Allotment Act, which replaced the Agricultural Adjustment Act, nominally, at least, made crop reduction secondary. The benefit payments for planting soil-conserving crops were not made direct to farmers by the federal government as the result of contracts, but reached the farmers through the states after committees had checked performance against standards. At just the time when the Department of Agriculture had lost its most effective power to restrict output, many questioned whether the unpredictable intervention of nature did not invalidate human schemes of whatever sort. Wallace feared that "probably in a period of good crops and high yields the degree of crop control attainable under the new measure [Soil Conservation Act] will not be adequate. . . ."[23] Forebodings seemed justified when in 1937 crops were the largest in many years. The cotton crop was 18,-746,000 bales, an average of half a bale to the acre, an all-time high. Wheat production gave a good surplus for export. The corn yield, which had been 1,500,000,000 bushels in 1936, was 2,651,-000,000 in 1937. By November, cotton sold at the lowest prices in four years, wheat dropped below $1 a bushel in terminal markets, and livestock prices declined. High 1936 prices had encouraged the sowing of record acreage. The crops of fresh fruit and vegetables were so large as to cause marketing problems. Parts of the lower grades were not used, and some of the apple crop was not even picked. The Agriculture Department reported ruefully: "It was again evident that in years of normal weather the farmers can produce more than the market can be depended upon to take at reasonable prices."[24]

The overwhelming crops, together with cancellation of controls which had taken virtually mandatory effect, led to Wallace's advocacy of an "ever-normal granary" which was embodied in bills before both branches of Congress in the special session called by the President in November, 1937. The Department of Agriculture

[23] *American Year Book*, 1936, p. 421.
[24] *Ibid.*, 1937, p. 429.

had to meet a good deal of skepticism in protesting patiently: "Our agriculture is largely an export industry. . . . The Administration contends that there is no danger of a domestic shortage that cannot be obviated by maintaining an ever-normal granary, and believes crop adjustment involves no threat whatever to the domestic consumer." It involved, however, the delicate question of determining to what degree production for export may be limited without jeopardizing the country's competitive position in international trade. The dominance of the United States in the world cotton market had been lost, partly because of its policies of inducing high domestic prices and withholding from export. Also, former buyers of American cotton lacked dollar exchange and could not get their goods in over the tariff; they therefore had learned to look to Brazil, India, Egypt, and Argentina.

Wallace argued that export at any price, though below cost and with loss of soil fertility, was bad business. The United States needed to export 40 per cent of her cotton. Soil-conservation measures, with adjusted low-cost production, were expected to allow America to hold its place in world markets more effectively than could be done through reckless competition leading to alternate gluts and shortages. The same was true of wheat. Domestic requirements could be met from 55,000,000 seeded acres, which was 25,000,000 less than the area seeded for the 1937 crop, and 12,-000,000 less than the average for the 1928–1932 period. Probably 60,000,000 seeded acres would give domestic needs with 50,000,000 bushels for export. "With seedings held to that level, the ever-normal granary could stabilize the supplies and avoid burdensome carry-overs." [25]

The droughts withered crops and pulverized the exposed soil. Winds filled the atmosphere for miles above the earth's surface with the dense brown cloud and carried deposits all the way to the Atlantic. The parched central portion of the country in 1934 earned the name of "dust bowl." Conditions there were reported in terms of visibility—one block, a quarter mile, on good days a mile. The loose soil was drifted against fences, half buried buildings. If the people who did not move managed to survive somehow, cattle could not live without water and feed. Large numbers of livestock

[25] *Ibid.*, pp. 433 ff.

were bought by the government and shipped to more favored regions to prevent universal slaughter and ruin of meat prices. Even when the droughts were at their worst, some in the region had the hardihood to reflect that there had been similar curses before, and were confident that a normal season of rain would restore the area to its customary pursuits and productivity.

A committee was sent to examine into the causes of the extraordinary drought damage. Secretary Wallace explained its findings in considerate language because the people were not to be scolded while they suffered: ". . . the committee assigned primary importance to the attempt which has been made for several decades to impose on the Great Plains a system of agriculture not adapted to the region. Methods suited on the whole only to a humid region were introduced into a semi-arid region. This was largely the outcome of a mistaken public policy." The Homestead law kept allotments small and required that part of each be plowed, causing immeasurable harm in overcultivation and the poverty of cultivators. Overcropping and overgrazing must be checked. "In the long run the Great Plains will support more people on a higher standard of living if its agriculture is regulated intelligently than it can possibly support if present tendencies run their course." [26] Many of the farmers were suspicious of plans to induce a shift from cropping to grazing.

SOIL CONSERVATION AND THE "EVER-NORMAL GRANARY"

The Supreme Court, January 6, 1936, in the Hoosac Mills case, held the production control features of the Agricultural Adjustment Act of 1933 unconstitutional as an invasion of the powers of the states. Processing taxes, an integral part of production control, were eliminated. The act's provisions for marketing agreements, commodity loans, and the diversion of surplus were left intact.

The administration promptly secured a substitute for crop control and benefit payments in the Soil Conservation and Domestic Allotment Act of February, 1936. The droughts and dust storms, the effects of which were stressed in the official documentary film, *The Plow That Broke the Plains,* persuaded the nation that its

[26] *Ibid.,* 1936, pp. 420–421.

precious farm soil was being blown away. The old demand for conservation was reinvoked. The underlying motive in the new law,
however, was to re-establish "the ratio between the purchasing
power of the net income per person on farms and that of the income per person not on farms, that prevailed during the five-year
period August 1909—July 1914." With the elimination of processing
taxes, "parity income" took the place of "parity prices."

From an annual appropriation of $500,000,000, payments were
made to farmers: (1) for diverting 15 per cent of acreage in soil-
depleting crops (a higher percentage for cotton, tobacco, and some
others) to soil-conserving crops, such as pasture and legumes; (2)
for increasing the area planted in soil-conserving crops, usually
$3.30 an acre; (3) for adopting soil-building practices in great
variety, such as the use of fertilizer, contour plowing, strip cropping, and the like. Any farm could get at least $10 out of the pro-
gram. The scheme was really one for continuing subventions to
farmers, and lacked the precision of the previous act.[27] Relief demands were confused with agricultural policy. Nearly four million
participating farmers were paid increasing total amounts—$370,-
000,000 for 1936, $460,000,000 for 1937, and $494,000,000 for 1938.

The result was that the Agricultural Adjustment Act of 1938,
which drew on all previous experience, embodied proposals that
had been growing in official favor, and gave the central government a tighter control over farming operations than ever before.
The soil conservation plan was continued. Acreage allotments for
cotton, corn, wheat, tobacco, and rice were set to support prices
rather than to promote soil conservation. Producers of these crops
could receive soil conservation payments only if they held to these
quotas. Secretary Wallace, almost from the beginning, had been
developing the device of an "ever-normal granary," and this project
now appeared in several provisions of the law. Commodity loans
could be made to farmers for storing surpluses in big crop years,
thus making supplies available in years of dearth. If prices fell to
certain low points, loans were mandatory for wheat, cotton, and
corn producers cooperating in the acreage allotment program.

Further, two thirds of the farmers consenting, marketing quotas
might be imposed, with heavy penalty taxes on sales in excess of a

[27] U. S. Department of Agriculture, *Agricultural Conservation* (Washington: Government Printing Office, 1936).

farmer's quota. "Parity payments" could be made to producers of the five principal crops when prices were below 75 per cent of parity. Crop insurance was provided for wheat, farmers paying premiums in wheat in years of large crops, and receiving indemnities in wheat in years when the crop was reduced by drought, plant disease, insect pests, and so on. This, with other aspects of the "ever-normal granary," was presented by Secretary Wallace on the authority of Joseph of Egypt, no less, without regard for the fact that Joseph's world was a small one, and that in ours, taking all countries together, staple food output is much the same year after year. In other words, the "ever-normal granary" was a nationalistic scheme.[28]

This new act of 1938 brought few solutions. Through a low acreage allotment the cotton crop of that year was reduced, but the impounding of a third of it by the government, plus domestic prices (due to generous government loans) above world prices, cut the nation's cotton exports to the lowest point in sixty years. There had long been a danger in the price-raising program that the United States would lose its foreign markets. Synthetic fibers were displacing cotton anyhow.[29] In 1939 this country resorted to export subsidies, Egypt retaliated, and only the outbreak of war saved cotton from fresh confusion. As the result of a big wheat crop in 1938 the farm price fell to 57 per cent of what it had been the year before. The government took losses on loans, and gave heavy subsidies to export, which is to say it engaged in the wheat dumping practiced by others.[30] Drought in 1939 cut production, but the world carry-over depressed the price, and the government lost on wheat crop insurance, until war brought relief.[31] Not even the war could help corn, for the hybrid varieties placed output beyond control, and the rest of the world preferred other grains.[32] Tobacco suffered when Britain, to save dollar exchange for munitions, and to favor Turkey, bought leaf in the Near East instead of in the United States; government stepped in to buy the surplus.[33]

The first months of World War II raised agricultural prices and the volume of United States exports. Then German military suc-

---

[28] *Agricultural Adjustment*, 1937–1938, pp. 97 ff.
[29] *Ibid.*, pp. 148 ff.   [30] *Ibid.*, p. 34.
[31] *Ibid.*, 1939–1940, p. 71.   [32] *Ibid.*, pp. 34 ff.
[33] *Ibid.*, pp. 45–46.

cesses threw American agriculture back into distress. European crops failed, but, ironically, the British blockade shut out American food from markets eager to buy. Britain herself bought little in the United States besides war materials. As though the country's surpluses were not enough, the government felt obliged to promise to care for those of South America. Farmers had come to a bad pass. Agricultural adjustment had striven during seven fat years to make them lean, but nothing had served. War itself was proving a poor consumer.[34] Then lend-lease and the rally of allies changed the picture, and the formal entry of the United States into the struggle placed a premium upon agricultural output. Still, old inducements to scarcity did not vanish suddenly. Even after rationing began, the government was still paying farmers not to produce!

The AAA was intended to help primarily commercial farmers, those raising sizable cash crops. Many of these were sufficiently distressed, but generally they were distinguished from the five million families and single persons living on farms in near destitution. Among these were owners of exhausted or otherwise submarginal land, often in parcels too small to support a family; part-time farmers whose side occupations in lumbering or mining had disappeared; tenants of various grades running down to croppers; agricultural laborers, hundreds of thousands of whom had lost a better status because of debt, through the crop restriction program of the AAA, or from the competition of agricultural machinery, masses of them becoming migrants; and lastly a few million young people backed up on the farms because they could no longer find jobs in the cities.

RESCUE FOR DESTITUTE FARMERS

Only gradually was it realized, even by those who later devised long-range, constructive measures, that deep-rooted rural dependency was the problem of these people. As their poverty was not temporary, so it was not new. The picture of the typical American farmer, firmly fixed in self-sustaining plenty, was more and more in the imagination. In the period of World War I, large numbers of

[34] U. S. Agricultural Adjustment Administration, *Agricultural Adjustment; A Report of Administration of the Agricultural Adjustment Act* (Washington: Government Printing Office, 1941), p. 4.

farmers, invited by eager markets at home and abroad, turned commercial, and the depression found them bankrupt rural businessmen without the means of resuming their old subsistence methods. By the owners of the expanding large farms, and by the country banks and other mortgage holders, these little people of the land were treated like weeds, to be grubbed up, cut down, got rid of. Where they held on, tenuously, they exploited their few acres for what they would yield to desperate extraction, with no means of replenishment.

The New Deal organized rescue for these rural dispossessed in the Resettlement Administration of 1935, which with improved status and enlarged responsibilities became the Farm Security Administration in 1937. But a description of the work of these agencies must be preceded by a brief account of the emergency expedients used earlier before the condition was recognized as one likely to endure. Late in March, 1933, all agricultural loan agencies were collected under the Farm Credit Administration. In May was passed the Emergency Farm Mortgage Act and the following month a Farm Credit Act. Mortgage holders were paid off from $2 billion in bonds issued by the land banks, and land bank commissioner loans, which substituted humanitarian for financial criteria of soundness, were given to farmers who had no other resource; however, in both cases, a supposed "normal" value of farm property was made the basis of increasing the help extended. With all this, foreclosures came faster than willing public dollars could reach the scene, so that farmers with sheriffs turning in at the gate were invited to wire the White House collect for assistance. Of over 900,000 pleas for loans, 550,000 were granted, the FCA in twenty months refinancing a fifth of the total farm mortgage debt. More than half the applicants were in such plight that they received land bank commissioner loans. The debts of 40,000 farmers were reduced by a fourth through debt adjustment committees set up in 2,700 counties in 44 states. Following state debt moratoria, the Frazier-Lemke Farm Bankruptcy Act of June, 1934, gave the farmer a stay of five years and the right to buy his place back at the price fixed by a district court without regard to the size of the mortgage. Declared unconstitutional a year later, this act was replaced by another fairer to the creditor. Newly created agencies under the Farm Credit Administration made short-term loans for the raising of a crop and for the services of farm cooperatives. Though the government guaranteed the interest on farm loan bonds, private takers were too few, and the Reconstruction Finance Corporation had to furnish a great part of the funds. At the end of the thirties, a lenient collection policy had not prevented 25 or 30 per cent of the borrowers from being delinquent.

It turned out that much of the farm credit was charity, but relief agencies as such—the Federal Emergency Relief Administration and the Public Works Administration—were brought to the help of the rural people with doles and jobs on the roads. In two southern states relief officials tried to do something more constructive by lending destitute farmers money to buy seed and implements. The Emergency Relief Administration broadened this practice and early in 1935 was seeking to restore 250,000 farm families to self-support. But many belonged to the 650,000 families estimated to be stranded on 100,000,000 acres not worth farming. In 1934 the AAA and the FERA began buying up such submarginal districts, transferring the populations to better soil, and turning the old depleted lands into recreation areas or giving them back to the wild animals. The Subsistence Homesteads Division of the Department of Interior, with $25,000,000 from NRA, established small-farm communities near industrial centers; the people were to feed themselves from the land and supply their cash by factory earnings, but the results, from faults in planning, were disappointing.

In April, 1935, the several sorts of federal rural social work were combined under the Resettlement Administration, whose main duties were to relocate farmers from 10,000,000 acres of submarginal land, and to rehabilitate other impoverished farmers where they were if their land justified the effort, thus gradually getting them off relief. That 9,000,000 acres of submarginal land were taken out of cultivation and the people moved was remarkable, for the Resettlement Administration had no permanent status, it inherited unfeasible projects from defunct agencies, and many of its clients, understandably enough, were submarginal themselves, from age, ignorance, and ill-health, and hard to help to a fresh start. For many critics of the New Deal, the Resettlement Administration was the easiest mark because of its inevitable paternalism, and Rexford G. Tugwell, the head of it, became for these, undeservedly, the symbol of expensive and misguided federal philanthropy. Political animus and economic reaction paraded as sympathy for unfortunate small farmers torn from their loved homes and rudely transferred to government-supervised sites.

PROBLEM OF FARM TENANCY

Loans to farmers with prospects of rehabilitating themselves bought horses, cows, equipment, and fertilizer, on condition that borrowers followed good advice in reforming their practices. Groups of farmers could cooperatively secure major machinery and breeding stock, and organize to receive sorely needed medical attention. With these efforts at treatment, the problem of rural poverty continued to unfold; full exploration was necessary before plans of corrective action could be laid out. The President's Committee on Farm Tenancy, reporting in 1937, furnished the basis for what was done later. Tenancy increased from 25 per cent of all farmers in 1880 to 42 per cent in 1935; of 6,812,350 farmers, 2,865,-155 were tenants. Tenancy was found in all parts of the nation, with concentration in areas of cash crops, chiefly cotton, tobacco, corn, and wheat. More than half of the southern farmers, nearly a third of those in the North, and a fourth of those in the West were tenants. Less than a fifth of all tenants, mainly in the North and West, rented for cash and enjoyed the independence going with ownership of work-stock, equipment, and fertilizer. Of tenants paying in kind, those with lowest economic and social status were "sharecroppers," the term meaning that they had nothing but their labor to supply, having to depend on landlord or neighboring merchant for "furnish" (food and clothing) until the crop was grown and sold. Sharecropping became a widespread system in the South after the Civil War, when nobody had money for rent or wages. Always onerous and often outrageous credit terms for all items of "furnish" combined with dishonest bookkeeping and annual oral leases to press croppers into peonage. Nearly as many of the croppers were white as black.

A WPA survey in seven cotton states in 1934 [35] had shown an average net income of croppers, cash and "furnish," of $312, or $71 a person; in the lower Mississippi delta, where land was richest,

[35] T. J. Woofter, Jr. and others, *Landlord and Tenant on the Cotton Plantation* (Washington: Works Progress Administration, 1936).

income was lowest, $38 a person or 10 cents a day. In this area only 70 per cent of cropper families got any cash after "settling," and these averaged $33. Generally croppers were allowed little land or time for growing a garden, keeping chickens or a cow; this had much to do with the deficient diet which pulled down vitality and sometimes induced pellagra. Ramshackle tenant houses had an average value of $417 in North Carolina, the best state; those of Negro tenants were worth only $194 in Alabama. Absence of screens and privies made for typhoid, malaria, and hookworm, while the bottom standard of living and of education contributed to widespread venereal disease.

One of the few liberties left to tenants was to move. Nearly half of all tenants surveyed in 1935 had been on their places for one year or less. Most of the constant shifting resulted in net loss to the tenants, and to "mining" of the soil for maximum production in minimum time. Tenants on the move broke any community ties, worst of all those of children with the school, especially since the end of the crop year fell in the middle of the school term.

Another group, a fourth of all persons engaged in agriculture—the farm laborers—for years had suffered from conditions which were intensified by depression. In 1933 average cash wages were considerably below $300 a year, though in many cases these were supplemented by perquisites. Unemployment and underemployment were high. One in six or seven was a migratory farm worker, following the ripening crops on the Atlantic seaboard, in the Middle West, or on the Pacific coast. The ranks of farm laborers, including migrants, were swelled by hopeless debts that expelled small owners and tenants. AAA acreage restrictions tended to eliminate tenants directly and were accompanied by benefit payments that could be spent for tractors and other mechanical equipment, thus loosening the hold of little men on the land. Drought contributed its part. A mass of new migrants was first conspicuously noticed in the Farm Tenancy Report of 1937—the hundreds of thousands, usually in families, going from Oklahoma and Arkansas, and from "dust bowl" states northward, to California, Oregon, Washington, and elsewhere. These were the people soon to draw the sympathy of most of America through the picture of their lot in John Steinbeck's *Grapes of Wrath*. Their roadside camps were abominable, but at least gave more freedom than the shacks inside the high wire fences of the ranch owners. The growers, in handbills distributed in the most distressed areas, had solicited these people to come. It was hoped that they would respond in numbers so large that wages would be beaten down to a minimum, but the stream of Joads in jalopies far exceeded what was wanted, giving reluctant California an imported relief problem. Many migrants were illegally but effectively turned back. Numbers who entered California used their last remaining resources to return to their home districts where, though penniless, they were not despised. In California the migrant workers often struck against miserable conditions, to be met by the organized opposition of ranchers and law officers led by the Associated Farmers, nearly all of whose influence and funds came not from farmers, but from utility and financial corporations, as the La Follette Committee showed on the spot. The Southern California Branch of the American Civil Liberties Union was one of the few local forces maintaining the rights of the migrants as workers and as citizens.

The President's Committee on Farm Tenancy, viewing the scene of human dislocation and destitution in agriculture, in 1937 recommended a rounded program of relief and reform. The Resettlement Administration was to be renamed the Farm Security Administration, enjoy wider powers, and have a financial affiliate, the Farm Security Corporation, which should make loans to promote farm ownership. Families to be settled on federally purchased land should be selected with care, given a trial period further to weed out the unfit, and then be allowed forty years in which to pay for a homestead. In bad farm years payments should be less, in good years more, the debt might not be paid off in less than twenty years, in order to avoid the evils of speculation, though the client could withdraw at any time by selling to the corporation.

The family-sized, subsistence farm was the ideal set up in the report and later aimed at by the Farm Security Administration. Though it was provided that small proprietors should have the advantage of mechanical equipment and breeding stock owned in common, outright cooperative farming, which would have been more efficient, was not contemplated. The subsistence farm unit was a defeatist counsel, urged because it would avoid additions to the commercial crops. It was nourished by a social-work rather than an economic approach to the problem of insecure farm groups.

The representative of the Southern Tenant Farmers' Union on the President's Committee protested against it, saying that the small cotton farm, at least, belonged to the past. Later on, as a matter of fact, some true farm cooperatives, not unlike the successful ones in the Soviet Union, were developed, but encountered the bitter hostility of large planters and their spokesmen, who did not want to see poor men on the land rising to independence.

It was recommended that the Farm Security Administration, where possible, save owners from dropping into the ranks of tenants and laborers by arranging for scaling down their debts, and by paying off some of what remained in order to make them eligible for loans from the Farm Credit Administration. Retirement of submarginal land and resettlement of the people should be continued at the rate of two to five million acres a year. Proposals for corrective state action included compulsory written leases, giving the tenant ownership of improvements made by him during the lease; complete or partial exemption of small homesteads from taxation; protection of civil liberties, a vain hope where state authorities allowed landlords to break up tenants' union meetings and otherwise habitually invade constitutional rights; further expenditures for relief would be reduced by extension of education and health services among farm people.

The Bankhead-Jones Farm Tenancy Act, passed in 1937 as a result of this report, became the means whereby the Farm Security Administration and associated agencies carried out the scheme of arresting rural decay. Its work may be treated under the heads of (1) rehabilitation and (2) resettlement.

REBUILDING CHEAPER THAN RELIEF

Rehabilitation aimed to take families off relief—or remove them from the danger of falling on relief—and to make them self-sustaining. This program involved not only loans (an average of $500, repayable in five years at 5 per cent interest) to buy tools, equipment, livestock, but also outright grants to buy food, clothes, medical care, and feed, though half of those receiving grants were not rehabilitation families. The loans were made to families that could not get credit anywhere else, simply in the faith that favorable conditions, an earnest desire to succeed, and the promise to cooperate in a new farm plan would bring results. Each plan embraced feeding family and stock from the produce of the place, the development of at least two market products, and the use of tilling methods to preserve soil fertility. In the crop year 1940, standard rehabilitation borrowers increased their annual net income by $75,289,838, or 35 per cent over the year before coming on the program, and the value of all their belongings, minus all debts, by 20 per cent. The average value of goods produced at home by such families—mainly milk, meat, canned fruits and vegetables—was $264, or 62 per cent more than in the year before these families received help. Most of the families got long-term written leases. Since the beginning, committees in every agricultural county scaled the debts of 163,000 farmers by $103,000,000, or 22 per cent. Group medical-care plans were set up in 881 counties, besides separate dental-care plans. Small farmers were enabled to establish or take advantage of co-operatives of several types: for furnishing tractors and purebred sires; for maintaining community cotton gins, storage warehouses, and processing plants; for buying all sorts of farm and home needs; or for leasing land. In the years 1934–1941, a total of 1,477,492 families received $705,939,000 in rehabilitation loans or grants, or both. On the basis of its experience the Farm Security Administration estimated that 80 per cent of all loans will finally be repaid to the government except in the worst drought areas.

Loans, to enable tenant families to buy farms of their own, were repayable over a period of forty years, installments being larger in prosperous years and smaller in lean years. In June, 1941, after four years of the program, 96.5 per cent of maturities had been paid. Twenty times as many applications were received as could be granted, largely from lack of funds but also because both families and farms must give evidence of being good credit risks. About 10,000 new farm dwellings were built at an average cost of $1,383, a similar number were repaired at a third of that cost, and twice as many other farm buildings were constructed or repaired. The average farm thus purchased was 133 acres and the average loan was $5,600.

The Farm Security Administration and its predecessor organization resettled more than 15,000 families on several types of projects in all parts of the country—large cooperative farms, subsistence farms of the community type with or without industries in which cash could be earned for part-time work, and scattered individual farms. More than a million acres were embraced at a capital investment of about $138,000,000, in addition to the cost of irrigation projects in the Far West for 560 families.

Camps for farm migrants were among the most appreciated contributions toward relieving acute rural distress in a dozen states. Usually they were temporary shelters, or good platforms on which tents could be erected, grouped about central sanitary and other community facilities, but a smaller number of permanent homes was erected. In addition, mobile camps shifted location with the harvest. Fifteen thousand families could be accommodated at one time, though a larger number was served in the course of a year. Anyone who saw the deplorable makeshifts endured by the migrant families before the Farm Security Administration constructed its camps knew what this relatively inexpensive service meant in health and morale.

The Farm Security Administration aided defense not only by the many contributions to agriculture that have been described, but by its supervision of the movement of thousands of farm families from extensive areas taken over by the government for troop training. Since the sites chosen for camps, maneuvers, and so on, were generally poor for farming, the families needed help when suddenly required to relocate. The agency also provided much stopgap housing, mostly of the demountable sort, and trailer camps for defense workers.

In the whole period to the middle of 1941, FSA loaned about $574 million to over 900,000 needy farm families for their rehabilitation. The entire rehabilitation program, including probable losses and administrative expense, cost only $75 a year for each family assisted. This is to be contrasted with $350 required for direct relief of a farm family, and relief did little or nothing to improve permanently the economic status of the family.[36] It should be recorded regretfully that, in spite of its achievements, the Farm Security Administration, in 1943, received a drastically reduced appropriation, and much of its personnel with the longest experience left the serv-

[36] *Report* of the Administrator of the Farm Security Administration, 1941 (Washington: Government Printing Office, 1941); U. S. Department of Agriculture, *The Farm Security Administration* (Washington: Government Printing Office, 1941); see also *Resettlement Administration, First Annual Report* (Washington: Government Printing Office, 1936).

ice. The reasons given by its enemies were that the agency had been impractical and extravagant, and that the mounting war budget did not permit continuance of its expenditures on the former scale. These were false and insincere arguments. The FSA was trying, economically, to meet continuing problems. At a time when the nation boasted that it was fighting to protect democracy the world over it was altogether appropriate to secure decent standards for victimized millions at home. The fact was that powerful interests, especially in the South, which did not want to see poor people on the land freed from domination of landlords, finally had their way.

THE THREAT OF THE COTTON PICKER

It has been noticed that one of the conspicuous causes of agricultural distress was the progress of technology on the farm which permitted fewer workers to increase output. Most obvious was the tractor pulling many kinds of improved machinery for preparing the soil, planting, cultivating, and harvesting. Though use of this equipment had spread from the great grain area, the cotton South had been less invaded, among other reasons because of the preponderance of small producers with slender resources. While displacement of farmers in any region posed a problem, the possibility of a mechanical revolution in the cotton economy, with its millions of white and black hand choppers and pickers, was peculiarly disturbing. Therefore while the Secretary of Agriculture was on the whole substantially aided in his program of crop restriction by the droughts, he must have witnessed with mixed feelings a demonstration of the Rust brothers' cotton picker.[37] The invention of a successful mechanical cotton picker has long been an objective, for saving the crop requires the backbreaking work of nearly every man, woman, and child in the cotton country for the months of the ripening season. In the Southwest, where the cotton matures uniformly because of soil and weather conditions, the sled, or stripper, had been used. This trough with bottom slotted like separated fingers of the hand, when pushed down the row of bushes, stripped off the cotton. But where plants varied in height from two to three feet up to three times that, and particularly where the

[37] The New York Times (November 22, 1936).

bolls were ripening from June to November, this method could not be employed. The device had to be selective, or tender unripe bolls would be injured. The cotton picked by each worker was quadrupled by suction machines. These were vacuum tanks with flexible hoses whose valved nozzles were held to the ripe bolls. In one type of machine the suction was supplemented by cones revolving inward in the nozzle; they helped to pull out the cotton. However, any suction machine required numerous human operators with human selection of the cotton ready to be picked.

In 1927 John Daniel and Mack Donald Rust, Texas experimental engineers, invented an automatic cotton picker, and forthwith, in Memphis, set about its improvement and promotion. The principle was that of moist revolving spindles set horizontally in a vertical drum which itself revolved. The spindles passed through the plants, peeling out only the cotton which was ripe. This cotton was mechanically removed from the spindles and carried in a suction pipe to a container. Each drum had more than 1,300 moistened spindles, and the machine picked two rows at a time.[38] First opportunity for informed judgment on the Rust Cotton Picker was furnished in a test demonstration in the Mississippi delta at the end of August, 1936, in the presence of leading cotton experts. The witnesses expressed varying opinions. Some were critical of the amount of cotton left on the bushes, though estimates of this differed widely, from 1 per cent to 33 per cent. Leaf and trash collected by the machine somewhat lowered the grade of the cotton. The general view was that the machine was practical on large plantations with a good yield of cotton, and fears were voiced for the future of small, poor farms. Oscar Johnston, government cotton expert, said that if the machine proved successful in all respects "there would be no point to small-time farming." W. E. Ayres, manager of the Delta Experiment Station, thought the machine should reduce the cost of picking by two thirds. On the basis of a bale to the acre, the machine would pick as much in one hour as eight to ten hand pickers in twelve hours.[39] E. H. Crump, with

---

[38] For general descriptions of the problems and methods of mechanical cotton picking, see Harris Pearson Smith, *Farm Machinery and Equipment* (New York: McGraw-Hill Book Company, Inc., 1937), pp. 305–310; J. Brownlee Davidson, *Agricultural Machinery* (John Wiley & Sons, Inc., 1931), pp. 240–243; *Manufacturers' Record* CXIV (March, 1945), p. 42 ff.

[39] *New York Herald Tribune* (September 1, 1936); *The New York Times* (September 1, 1936).

alarm for the whole cotton economy, urged legislation against the use of the picker.[40]

John Rust at that time was in the Soviet Union demonstrating pickers which that government had ordered. The contrast between foreboding here for impending additions to unemployment because of the machine, and the eager interest of the Soviet Union in a device that would increase output was not lost on the public. As a matter of fact, the Rust brothers, as socially minded as they were ingenious, soon established a foundation to use part of the return from the picker to rehabilitate those thrown out of work by its introduction. Other companies, including established agricultural implement manufacturers, began intensive work on improved cotton pickers. Within a few years the widespread use of mechanical cotton pickers was brought closer by the economies of other labor needed about the growth of cotton, as better choppers thinned the young plants and flame throwers destroyed weeds more effectively.

RISE OF RAYON

Admittedly of serious damage to cotton was the fact that by the end of this period almost a tenth of the world's textile fibers were synthetic. Rayon was the agreed trade name for a variety of yarns made from cellulose substances, usually wood or cotton linters, or from the milk substance, casein. Commercial manufacture of rayon had begun about 1890 in France, a decade later in England, and in 1910 in America. After the expiration of the patents of the Viscose Company in 1921, other companies began operations in the United States. Between 1930 and 1940 American production and consumption of rayon trebled, though Japan outdistanced the United States in rayon production in the middle thirties as the latter had previously surpassed Germany. Rayon was rapidly improved in its properties and multiplied in its uses. Simultaneously, for it could be economically manufactured only on a large scale, it fell in price to the 1932–1937 average of 65 cents a pound. Rayon was not only used in hosiery, dress goods, suitings, and cord tires, but was put to numerous minor purposes formerly filled by cotton. Cotton in mercerized form suffered acutely in competition with rayon.

40 *The New York Times* (September 6, 1936).

Toward the end of the decade of the thirties appeared new synthetic substances employed not only in textiles but in improved plastics in enormous variety. These were derived from neither vegetable nor animal materials, but from chemical ones such as coal, natural gas, air, water, and salt. The most notable of several was "nylon" of the E. I. du Pont Company, first manufactured in quantity in 1939. Besides being stronger than any natural fiber, it seemed to possess none of the defects of many earlier synthetics. Its filaments were more than twice as fine as silk, could be of any desired length, were elastic, resisted heat, were controllable as to luster and shrinkage, and were easily dyed. Nylon took many textile finishes. It was no less adaptable as a substitute for natural bristles, and appeared in shaving, tooth, and hair brushes. "Vinyon" was another all-chemical synthetic of high tensile strength and multiple uses.

INVENTION FOR THE FARM

Advances in farm technology were numerous in the thirties, particularly after the economic position of farmers had improved following the first leanest years and they were supplied with new services and encouraged to benefit from superior methods. The period saw a further use of corn pickers, small combines, and other harvesting and tillage equipment operated with tractors. Extension of rural electrification was rapid. Slow but steady improvement was registered in the productive efficiency of livestock through better breeding, correction of nutritional deficiencies, and disease control. More remunerative crops resulted from widespread use of improved seed, such as hybrid corn, and greater acreage of soybeans. Frozen packing of farm products and canning of juices reduced losses from surpluses of perishables. This progress was not without its penalties. Between 1930 and 1939 the number of tractors in the United States almost doubled to 1,626,000. Three fourths of all tractor sales in 1937 were of the general-purpose type, and by 1940 half of the farm tractors were of this sort. By the end of the decade 1,500,000 farms, or more than a fifth of the total, had tractors.[41]

The Department of Agriculture reported in 1941 that "nearly

[41] U. S. Department of Agriculture, *Technology on the Farm; Report of Inter-bureau Committee* (Washington: Government Printing Office, 1940), pp. 9–10.

every one of these tractors has pushed a few tenants, sharecroppers, or hired hands out of jobs. On one typical Mississippi Delta plantation, for example, the landlord recently bought 22 tractors. He turned off 130 of the 160 sharecropper families which used to work the land, keeping only 30 to handle the new machinery. . . . All this means that fewer people are needed to raise our farm products. . . . We can fill all the normal demands for farm products—both for home use and for export—with 1,600,000 fewer farm workers today than in 1930. Yet most of these surplus farm workers have not been able to find jobs elsewhere; they are still on the land, often with no work at all, or at best a few weeks in harvest time. This overcrowding has led to extreme proverty for millions of farm people." Machinery hit the little farmer hardest. He and his mule and one-row plow had to go. "Tractored off," he migrated in increasing numbers to California or other areas where he was a farm laborer, or he remained nearer home and tried to make a living on land not fit for agriculture.[42] Between 1930 and 1940 there was a decrease of 235,000 cropper families in the South, or a third of the total.[43]

The heavy, cumbersome tractor for draft gave way to the light, small, fast, rubber-tired, relatively cheap models. Rubber tires increased mobility and comfort and decreased gasoline consumption and repairs. Operating at high speeds with trailers, they supplemented or threatened to supplant trucks. They made possible the use of lighter, more maneuverable tillage implements. These developments brought tractors closer to the small farms of southern and eastern states. However, deficient farm incomes of these regions still did not favor the employment of tractors as in the small grain and other areas which were most mechanized. In the deltas of Arkansas and Mississippi, on the black lands of Texas and in western Oklahoma, the use of tractors increased most rapidly; on the high plains of Texas, tractors practically displaced horses and mules. The high speed of the new tractors not only insured timely work; their versatility and power permitted the simultaneous operation of different kinds of equipment. In 1940 the states with the largest numbers of tractors were Illinois (156,347), Iowa (141,774), Texas (113,613), Kansas (103,827), Minnesota (95,552), Ohio (94,-598). The states from which many migrants went to the west coast,

[42] U. S. Department of Agriculture, *The Farm Security Administration*, pp. 4–6.
[43] *Report* of Administrator of Farm Security Administration, 1941, pp. 5–6.

often because they were displaced by machinery, were Oklahoma, with 49,974 tractors, Missouri with 56,034, and Arkansas with 15,-560. The Southeast and New England had the fewest tractors of the farming regions.[44]

The Farm Equipment Institute estimated that in 1935–1939 wholesale sales of farm machinery for use in the United States averaged $408,000,000 annually.[45] An important item was the light combine. In 1938 half the wheat crop was "combined." The machine was adapted to the harvesting of grass seed and soybeans as well as the small grains. Whereas the older large combines had cut a swath 12–16 feet, the "baby" combine cut 5–6 feet, was driven by the power take-off from a tractor, and was operated by one man at a speed of four or five miles per hour. The cost of the baby combine was relatively low; 10,000 were manufactured in 1935–1936. The "midget" combine, cutting a swath of 40 inches, and costing little more than a grain binder, came into use in 1939 and promised to give to small farmers the advantage in harvesting costs theretofore belonging to the largest operations. In 1939 about 80 per cent of the combines sold cut swaths 6 feet or less in width.[46]

Though in 1938 less than 15 per cent of the corn crop was picked by machine, mechanical corn pickers on the market two years later were economical for crops of as little as 100 acres. The picker cut man-hours per acre to a fourth compared to hand work.

For forty years there had been no significant change in haying equipment, until 1940, when several implement manufacturers developed new machines for mowing hay, chopping it up and dumping it into trailer wagons. Then the chopped hay was taken to silos where it was mixed with molasses, ground corn, acid, or other fermenting agent and stored as green feed. Chopped hay requires one third to one half as much storage space as unchopped.

ELECTRIC CURRENT FOR COUNTRY USERS

Rural electrification brought to more of the nation's farms the possibility of 250 different farm uses of current. However, with the exception of the irrigated areas, household appliances made the

[44] Britannica *Book of the Year,* 1941 (Chicago: Britannica Encyclopaedia), p. 280.
[45] *Ibid.*
[46] U. S. Department of Agriculture, *Technology on the Farm,* p. 14.

chief call on electric current on farms. In 1919 little over 100,000 rural homes had electricity from power lines. In June, 1940, some 2,000,000 farms were so supplied, or 29 per cent of the total. From 1926 to 1940 there was a threefold increase in electricity used by farmers. The average electrified farm east of the 100th meridian (roughly midway of the United States East and West) used 1,045 kilowatt hours of current in 1938, while the average electrified farm west of that meridian used more than four times as much. In 1939–1940 about 25,000 more farms were getting current every month.[47]

On June 30, 1941, allotments of the Rural Electrification Administration totaled $369,027,621, and full developments of the systems for which these allotments were made would provide electric services to 1,171,867 rural consumers. A year later, 732 of 823 borrowing organizations had energized part or all of their lines and were serving 780,933 farm families and other rural users. This was in contrast to 549,604 users in 1940, 268,000 in 1939, and 104,528 in 1938. In June, 1941, the REA was advancing an average of $6,-258,988 a month to borrowers with which 7,484 miles of line were being built.[48]

Plant technologists combined to develop varieties of grain to withstand drought, disease, and parasites. Hybrid corn, Thatcher wheat, and rust- and smut-resisting oats gave many ruined farmers a new start. Chinch bugs and root worms were partially routed. Since corn is the most valuable of all American farm crops, improvement of seed corn was the greatest achievement. The first hybrid seed corn was adapted to use in the corn belt in 1929; in 1933 there were 40,000 acres in hybrid corn, and in 1939 some 24,-000,000 acres or one fourth of the national corn acreage. In Ohio and Illinois 55 per cent of the corn acreage was in hybrids, and 75 per cent in Iowa. Hybrid corn added 115,000,000 bushels to the country's corn yield.[49]

Thatcher hard red spring wheat was found in the epidemics of 1935 and 1937 to be more resistant to stem rust than the Marquis and Ceres varieties. The 20,000 acres of Thatcher in 1935 rapidly climbed toward 6,000,000 acres. As Thatcher may yield on the

[47] Ibid., p. 15.
[48] Arthur P. Chew in Americana Annual, 1942 (Chicago: Americana Corp.), p. 21.
[49] Ibid., pp. 21–23.

average 1.3 bushels an acre more than Ceres and 3.3 bushels more than Marquis, the improved variety on 6,000,000 acres would mean 10,000,000 bushels added to the nation's wheat harvest.[50]

Soybean production increased because of the development of better seed-yielding varieties, better harvesting equipment, and new industrial outlets for the product. It was mostly grown in the North Central and Northeastern states. Drought injury to corn encouraged the planting of early-maturing grain sorghums in parts of Kansas, Colorado, Nebraska, and South Dakota after 1930. The yield of cotton was increased 40 to 50 pounds an acre by the choice of a community to grow only one variety. Standardization in 1,500 such communities in 1939 also had the effect of improving the price obtained by the farmers.[51]

SOIL PROTECTION

Use of grasses and legumes in soil building shifted millions of acres from soil-depleting crops, actually increased the output of feed grains by improving fertility, and still more increased the production of total feed. Planting of soil-building crops at the end of the decade was probably 20 per cent above that of 1929–1932. Green manure crops—small grains, grasses, and legumes plowed under—in 1937 were double in acreage those of 1928–1932. The acreage of these green manure crops paid for by the agricultural conservation program in 1938 was almost twice that of the year before. Timothy and clover decreased in favor of alfalfa and lespedeza. The substitution of higher quality legumes for other hays gave increased tonnage and higher food value for the same tonnage. The sowing of cover crops more than doubled in the five years before 1937, preventing erosion of soil from water and wind, and increasing crop yields. Contour plowing, the furrow following the profiles of slopes, had been practiced earlier in parts of the South, but in the thirties came into use in the commercial corn and wheat areas as a soil-conserving measure. The 500,000 acres reported plowed in this manner in 1937 became 5,000,000 acres in 1938. This device held out the prospect of increasing the corn yield by 50,000,000 bushels. The growing of alternate strips of erosion-resisting and erosion-encouraging crops made progress. By the end

[50] *Ibid.*, p. 23.   [51] *Ibid.*, p. 25.

of the decade a half million acres were top-dressed with super-phosphate by farmers participating in the conservation program, increasing by 20 per cent or more the capacity of pasture to support cattle. The western range was improved by a number of practices; deferred grazing was introduced on 12,000,000 acres and limited grazing on 2,000,000, which reduced the overstocked condition of the range.[52]

Increased industrial uses of agricultural products had a beneficial effect on farming. Pulp wood for rayon was a resource, though most of this raw material continued to be imported. More than a fourth of the needed cellulose was from cotton linters. Plastics from vegetable products and proteins, the latter mostly casein from skimmed milk, took on importance. The production of soybean oil increased from 13,000,000 pounds in 1929 to 322,000,000 pounds in 1938, giving America first place in this industry. Peanut oil came into wider use, as did ethyl alcohol in motor fuel. Soon guayule for rubber claimed increased acreage.[53] The pulp paper industry expanded in the South, making mostly the coarse-textured (kraft) paper, though five mills were established there to make bond and book papers. A mill at Lufkin, Texas, was the first to use southern pulp for manufacture of newsprint.

Manganese and other minerals added to poultry feeds produced better broilers and more hatchable eggs. Leafy legumes rich in carotene corrected cattle diseases such as blindness, rickets, sterility, and lameness. By the thirties nearly all dairy and breeding cattle were tuberculin-tested, and bovine tuberculosis was practically eliminated. The areas under federal quarantine against the cattle tick were much reduced, and remained only in Florida and Texas. Artificial insemination permitted the use of proven sires on several hundred females scattered over a considerable area instead of twenty-five to fifty females in a single herd. This device became practicable for horses, cattle, foxes, sheep, swine, and poultry. Seventeen artificial breeding associations for dairy cattle were functioning in ten states in 1939.[54]

Only lack of income prevented farmers' enjoyment of radios, automobiles, and much mechanical equipment. For example, in a southeastern farm section 17 per cent of white families with incomes of $250 to $500 had radios, while among families with in-

[52] *Ibid.*, pp. 28–31.   [53] *Ibid.*, pp. 37–41.   [54] *Ibid.*, pp. 17–20.

comes of $2,500 to $3,000 more than 70 per cent had radios. Of the lower-income families, 28 per cent had cars, while of those with the higher incomes, 96 per cent had cars. Ninety-one per cent of city families had radios, contrasted with only 59 per cent of farm families, though ownership of radios by farmers was higher where electric current was available. Over two thirds of the automobiles bought by farm families in 1935–1936 came from the used-car market, a percentage of used cars larger than that bought by city families.[55]

Most of the improvements in farm production in the thirties threatened to add to burdensome surpluses unless the advances of science and ingenuity were accompanied by conservation, or dropping unsuitable soils from cultivation. Of 415,000,000 acres in cultivation in 1935, the Department of Agriculture judged that only 160,000,000 acres could be farmed by present practices without injury, though 180,000,000 additional acres could be tilled safely if the best-known methods were used. However, 75,000,000 could not remain in use without soil destruction.[56]

OVER-ALL RESULTS FOR AGRICULTURE

Significant summary data for agriculture,[57] 1929–1938, showed that gross income fell from $13,646,000,000 in 1929 (which was higher than it had been since 1920), to a low of $6,286,000,000 in 1932, improved to $6,905,000,000 in 1933 ($131,000,000 of this benefit payments), and continued fairly steadily upward to $11,118,000,000 in 1937. In 1938 there was a drop to $10,016,000,000. The principal overhead charges fell by more than the complaints of farmers led the public to believe. Taxes were higher in 1930 than in 1929 ($567,000,000), and declined to a low of $389,000,000 in 1935, or a fall of 30 per cent. Short-term interest declined from $349,000,000 in 1929 to $170,000,000 in 1937, or 48 per cent. Interest on mortgages went down beginning as far back as 1922. In 1929 this item was $436,000,000 and stood at $268,000,000 in 1938, a decline of 39 per cent. Net rent paid to nonfarmers declined more,

[55] *Ibid.*, p. 206.
[56] *Ibid.*, p. 27.
[57] Simon Kuznets, *National Income and Its Composition, 1919–1938* (New York: National Bureau of Economic Research, 1941), pp. 543–545. Percentages calculated by the author of the present volume.

from $648,000,000 in 1929 to $190,000,000 in 1932, or a fall of over 70 per cent. Thereafter there was steady increase in rent to $593,-000,000 in 1937.

Net income from agriculture in the twenties never reached $8,000,000,000; it was $7,708,000,000 in 1929 and fell to $2,821,-000,000 in 1932. Net income increased then to $6,274,000,000 in 1937, but fell to $5,457,000,000 in 1938. Generally, it was the aim of the government's program beginning in 1933 to increase total payments of agriculture to individuals. These fell from $7,631,000,000 in 1929 to $4,045,000,000 in 1932, with irregular advance to $5,-650,000,000 in 1937, and recession in 1938 to $5,540,000,000. The number of entrepreneurs in agriculture increased throughout the period, from 6,234,000 in 1929 to 6,836,000 in 1938, while the number of wage earners fell from 1,899,000 in 1929 to 1,476,000 in 1934; then there was an increase to 1,624,000 in 1937, followed by a slight decline to 1,619,000 in 1938. Entrepreneurial withdrawals declined much less than wages, from $5,899,000,000 in 1929 to $3,166,000,000 in 1933. Tenants are here included among enterprisers, though for some sections of the country, notably the cotton South, what the commonest type of tenant received was really wages. Wages fell from $1,284,000,000 in 1929 to $517,000,000 in 1933. Entrepreneurial withdrawals by 1937 were $4,546,000,000, or more than they had been in 1931, though wages—$794,000,000 in 1937—were below the 1931 figure. The incomes of both entrepreneurs and wage earners fell from 1937 to 1938.

CHAPTER VII

National Recovery Administration

IF we may speak of what was typical in the New Deal's shifting, improvised program, we may give that character to the National Industrial Recovery Act, including its administration. Not intended to be temporary, like the Banking Act of 1933 and the measures affecting currency, it was designed as a permanent bold improvement. It carried the confusion explicit in the New Deal—the purpose to bolster private enterprise through cooperation of government, business, and labor. It attacked the most conspicuous signs of the depression, industrial stagnation and unemployment. Thus it occupied the central position in New Deal plans. Finally, in colliding with the Supreme Court, it posed the conflict between tradition and experiment. Though abolished, it continued to have influence through certain schemes which it originally contained or helped inspire, such as public works, the National Labor Relations Act, the National Resources Planning Board, and a few specialized and voluntary survivors like the National Coat and Suit Industry Recovery Board. Its concept of the feasibility of increased wages, stable prices, and improved profits through full employment remained to animate future efforts of several sorts.

Like other features of the New Deal, the National Industrial Recovery Act was a composite and adaptation of earlier trends and proposals. In the emergency of depression, the last lingering opposition to collusive action by businessmen was abandoned. With failure of NRA, fear was to revive; the anachronism of laissez faire was paraded in concerted prosecutions by the Department of

Justice, while many who appeared before the Temporary National Economic Committee declared for return to pure competition as an imperative of public policy. The whole episode of attempted reversion to competition was not only futile from the first, but was hypocritical on the part of government, in view of the recent public sanction of business collaboration in NRA, preceded by increasing tolerance of these practices over a long period. Further, repentance for official intrigue with business endured only briefly, for the defense program and the country's progressive involvement in World War II signalized such use of industrial consolidations as had never been known before.

More than forty years of legislation, judicial interpretation, and executive pronouncement had served to show that the antitrust acts could not and should not be enforced, certainly not in the naïve terms of the Sherman law of 1890. The Clayton Act of 1914, while intended to supplement the earlier statute, really weakened it by descending to specific prohibitions. The Clayton amendment amounted to an admission that the Supreme Court had fallen away from the ardor supposed to be inspired in judges by the common-law abhorrence of monopolies. Of this suspicion there had been proof enough in the announcement of the "rule of reason" in the Standard Oil and American Tobacco cases in 1911. Here the Court had declared that mere size in a corporation was not culpable, and that oppression of competitors must be shown. Taken more broadly, this was a transparent admission by the bench that the persistent tendency toward business consolidation might be guided where certainly it could not be prevented.

Not only had conspicuous combinations been treated with increasing tolerance, but the less definable trade association had come to be accepted. Collaboration of business units within a field was as old as the Civil War; practices to maintain prices by a variety of expedients had been furtively followed until the associations boldly stepped into the open. *The New Competition*, by Arthur J. Eddy, a Chicago attorney, published in 1912, coincided with Woodrow Wilson's assaults on business collusion in his crusade for the "New Freedom." Eddy whitewashed the trade associations, urging that by systematic and free sharing of prices, business rivals could rise to a plane of intelligent action amounting to a public benefit. Then, during World War I, the War Industries

Board found the trade associations necessary to its plans for industrial coordination. Only through the trade associations could the board mobilize industries for the war effort. What the associations had formerly done, *sub rosa,* the law now commanded them to do at behest of public authority. As General Hugh S. Johnson, a member of the board, said later: "Conservation, priority, curtailment, price fixing, all required such co-operation and agreement within each industry that the Government was constantly exhibited as requiring in its hour of peril the very things which it had been for years denouncing as criminal."

The war did not put an end to official reliance on trade associations but, if anything, broadened and normalized it. Patriotic participation gave a sanction, and the program of Herbert Hoover, as Secretary of Commerce, for standardizing industrial production, furnished sufficient motive. Further, the "New Economic Era" of the twenties "sublimated" business incentive into a professed passion for public service. With the tacit admission that it could not be uprooted, business collusion was to be policed with the purpose of limiting restrictive elements and protecting rivalries thought to preserve competition. As early as 1919 the Federal Trade Commission began to call "fair-trade practice conferences" which were soon reduced to a system for the self-government of industry under the sympathetic supervision of the commission. Codes of fair competition, drawn up by industry committees and approved by the commission, were enforced against nonsigners by official and industry pressure, and signers, for violation, were cited to the Department of Justice for prosecution.

These agreements of the twenties, except that they did not become legally binding upon nonconsenting units in an industry, were nothing different, so far as trade practices were concerned, from the codes of NRA. They ran back, it is true, to the minimum prohibitions of common law, in which the vitality of competition, as a general rule, was taken for granted; but they also ran forward toward a completeness and detail of solicitude that betrayed the chronic weakness of the competition whose protection was sought. Outlawed were injuries to competitors through selling below cost, through price discrimination, through secret rebates, false branding, defamation, commercial bribery, or enticing away of employees, among other practices. As time passed, provisions and their interpretation conformed more and more to the inevitable designs of the trade associations. "Legislative, statistical and technical aid," it has been said, "may be helpful to business men, but the elimination of over-production and price cutting is vital. The real core of the trade association movement has lain in its attack on free competition. . . ." [1]

Department of Commerce and Federal Trade Commission had been won over. The associations naturally supposed when Hoover became President that they would press their success. They were disappointed, for during Hoover's term, five of eight leading trade associations attacked by the Department of Justice were ordered dissolved. The Federal Trade Commission, thus reproved, revised outstanding rules for sixty-two industries. The trade associations took refuge underground, while their advocates urged that the antitrust laws be liberalized. The depression emboldened them. Heads of "institutes" in cotton textiles, sugar, copper, and rubber in varying degrees declared the antitrust acts obsolete and championed production control by industry. Senators Nye of North Dakota and Walsh of Massachusetts introduced bills which would have hobbled competition. Plans of Gerard Swope, president of the General Electric Company (1931) and of the United States Chamber of Commerce (1931 and 1932), captured wider public attention. Swope wanted trade associations, with compulsory membership, in every industry; through their activities "production and consumption should be coordinated on a broader and more intelligent basis," though this objective would obviously require revision of the Sherman Act. The proposals of Swope and the Chamber of Commerce closely approximated NRA provisions, especially in urging work sharing and adjustment of wages so as to bring purchasing power closer to productive capacity. Later, when much of business turned against the NRA, it was proper to remind that organized business had mainly inspired the measure.

GRADUAL GROWTH OF LABOR PROTECTIONS

Just as the lapse of antitrust legislation had its background, so precedents for the labor provisions of the National Industrial Recovery Act had long been forming in public discussion. We may

[1] Simon N. Whitney, *Trade Associations and Industrial Control; A Critique of the NRA* (New York: Central Book Company, 1934), p. 38.

deal briefly with steps by which the right of workers to organize and bargain through independent unions was recognized, and then touch upon development of proposals for a "floor" under wages and a "ceiling" on hours. General surprise that the Sherman Act, for some years after its passage, was not enforced against business monopoly, became consternation and deep resentment on the part of organized workers when they saw that the law, instead, was being directed against the unions and their methods. The "blanket" injunction against the American Railway Union in 1894 was given this basis. In 1908 the Supreme Court applied the antitrust statute in the Danbury Hatters' case, pointing the moral by assessing heavy damages on account of a boycott. In the same year, in *Adair* v. *United States*, the Court held unconstitutional the provision of the Erdman Act forbidding an interstate carrier to discharge an employee for membership in a labor union. Samuel Gompers and the American Federation of Labor redoubled pressure to relieve organized workers from penalties of the Sherman Act and from the peril of loose injunctions. All political parties in 1912 pledged support which issued in the Clayton Act of 1914. However, uncertainties in phrasing permitted Supreme Court decisions that effectively limited the immunities thought to be granted to labor, though definite net gains remained.

Employers' fight on unions found its aptest instrument in the long-familiar "yellow-dog" or "ironclad" contract, by which workers agreed not to belong to a union during the continuance of employment. Under such a contract a union could be enjoined for attempts to organize the workers or to sustain them in a strike. Numerous state statutes prohibiting the yellow-dog contract were held unconstitutional as fast as passed, a leading case being that of *Coppage* v. *Kansas*, 1915, which rested on the Fourteenth Amendment. The case of *Hitchman* v. *Mitchell*, decided two years later on common-law grounds, held that the union was properly enjoined from inducing workers to breach an anti-union contract. Yellow-dog contracts and use of them in obtaining injunctions became more common.

Hearty support given by organized labor to the government during World War I, chiefly taking the form of the no-strike pledge, resulted in temporary gains: collective bargaining was officially sanctioned, wages were readily raised by employers enjoying cost-plus war contracts, the eight-hour day was established, and the American Federation of Labor and other unions gained 2,000,000 in membership between 1917 and 1920. However, the activity of employers in forming company unions, with 1,500,000 membership by 1920, foreshadowed the reaction against organized labor which characterized the twenties. The steel strike of 1919, for recognition of the union and abolition of the twelve-hour day in a leading industry, was lost because of the savage opposition of the United States Steel Corporation on all fronts, and in the public hysteria against workers, who were confused and even apathetic in their effort. The same year the coal strike was broken by a sweeping federal injunction issued under war powers. The next year the Kansas Industrial Disputes Act forbade strikes and provided compulsory arbitration in employment "affected with the public interest." Despite business prosperity of the twenties, unions lost the membership gained in the war period. Leading industries—steel, textiles, coal mining—ejected unions entirely or crippled them severely, and workers encountered technological unemployment on the one hand and the "stretch-out" and "speed-up" on the other. The Supreme Court itself, and the subordinate courts, had been retreating from the Hitchman decision, refusing injunctions where union persuasion to break a yellow-dog contract was unaccompanied by violence and intimidation. But in 1927 Circuit Judge John J. Parker, of North Carolina, in the Red Jacket case reverted to the primitive Hitchman doctrine. This was a blow which moved labor, on the recoil, to rise against Parker when he was nominated for the Supreme Court in 1930, with the result that the Senate refused to confirm his appointment. This rejection of Judge Parker may be considered a turning point, after which public solicitude for the right to organize, for shorter hours, higher pay, and for limitations on child labor made itself felt. But these favorable developments did not appear until the American Federation of Labor had lost almost 1,350,000 members in a decade, and until the impact of widespread and increasing unemployment was sorrowfully evident throughout the economy.

MAXIMUM HOURS, MINIMUM WAGES

For more than two generations, demand for the shorter work week had been issuing in spasmodic and partial legislation, federal and state. In 1929 the argument was supported by a report of the National Industrial Conference Board that 220 manufacturing establishments, with 400,000 employees, were actually operating on a five-day week. The advocacy and example of Henry Ford were most effective. However, opposition, chiefly of the American Newspaper Publishers' Association, was not wanting. William Green, president of the Federation, beginning in 1930, met objectors with a campaign before Congress and country, declaring that the shorter work week was made imperative by technological unemployment and the need of absorbing labor from the charity rolls. Secretary of Labor James J. Davis, other officials, and influential public groups approved the proposal of work sharing, and in 1932 President Hoover said he favored the five-day week after recovery should begin. The same year the American Federation of Labor, with the resolution, "So long as one workman is unemployed, the hours of labor are too long," determined to have the federal government set the example for industry of a five-day, thirty-hour week.

Then, promptly after Roosevelt's inauguration, the agitation entered the legislative phase with the bill of Senator Hugh L. Black of Alabama prohibiting, with some exceptions, interstate shipment of goods produced by labor working more than six hours a day and thirty a week. The Senate, refusing amendment, swiftly passed this measure, and the House Labor Committee was favorable to the companion bill of Representative Lawrence J. Connery. The concern was not simply for employment, but for continuity of wages as a necessary support for the entire economy. Senator Black said in the debate: "Labor has been underpaid and capital overpaid. This is one of the chief contributing causes of the present depression. We need a return of purchasing power. You cannot starve men employed in industry and depend upon them to purchase." However, the administration stepped in with delaying tactics which frustrated the Black-Connery bill as such.

Of the proposals which contributed to shelving of the Black-Connery measure was one brought forward by Secretary of Labor Frances Perkins that industrial boards should set minimum wages. Minimum-wage laws, mainly covering women workers, had had a checkered career in the nation for more than two decades. In some cases employers had favored them as helping to eliminate unwanted competitors, while organized labor had generally opposed the laws in the fear that legislative protection would weaken union appeal to workers, and with the assertion that minimum wages would surely become the maximum. A third of the states had minimum-wage laws of one sort or another when the movement was arrested by the Supreme Court decision in *Adkins* v. *Children's Hospital,* 1923, which voided the District of Columbia statute in reasoning peculiarly insensible to social demands on industry. Some state laws were cancelled, some were revised, while still others, by common consent, remained in effect, though with impaired application. The depression revived active advocacy. Wages in an increasing number of industries were not only below the level of subsistence, but clearly below the value of services, and even so were intermittent or vanishing. Unemployment insurance and old-age pensions were being urged in localities and states. A national wage-hour statute was bruited. Enactment of minimum-wage laws, mandatory but gradual, and selective in application, received new impulse when Governor Herbert H. Lehman approved a New York law early in 1933, and President Roosevelt urged thirteen states to follow New York's example, with the result that six did so.

Meantime yellow-dog contracts, the principal reliance of employers in injunction suits against unions, had been outlawed. Senator Henrik Shipstead, of the Farmer-Labor party of Minnesota, officials of the American Federation of Labor, and liberal university professors had all borne a hand in a measure which was sidetracked by the Senate until the rejection of Judge Parker for the Supreme Court forced the matter to the front; in 1932 President Hoover signed the Norris-LaGuardia Act upholding the right of unions to induce the breaking of individual-employee contracts if no fraud or violence were used. However, it remained for NRA to seek to block employers who tried to get around the Norris-LaGuardia law by coercing workers into company unions, and by threatening them with loss of jobs if they joined independent unions.

Antecedents of the public works section of the Recovery Act (Title 2) remain to be mentioned. For some years students of the business cycle had increasingly urged that public construction be reduced in times of private business activity and be expanded in periods of depression. A heedless policy, instead of adjusting employment on public construction to that of private, had unwisely intensified demand for labor when business was good and had diminished it when employment was needed. Further, useless work of those on relief had been discouraged because it was wasteful and because it diminished the self-respect of those so engaged. Especially after the onset of the depression the added idea developed that increased public construction could not only take up the slack in employment, but would stimulate private enterprise. The raw materials industries would feel the beneficial effect of increased direct demand for their products, and business of all sorts would profit from the enlarged purchasing power of workers given emergency employment.

Hoover, even while Secretary of Commerce, had wanted large public works appropriations to compensate for lapses in business. When he became President, while employment was still high, he sponsored a study of the benefit of public works. Later he used this policy, though not boldly enough, as exemplified in the restriction that loans of the Reconstruction Finance Corporation must be for self-liquidating projects. He signed a bill under which $2,200,000,-000 was made available for such purposes, but the Democratic House was willing to use the fund for building post offices, and the Senate would not agree to such pork-barrel diversion, so the attempt was brought to nothing. However, Senator Robert F. Wagner of New York continued to urge public works, and, after Roosevelt was elected, was joined in his efforts by the American Federation of Labor.

Thus public works became a part of the recovery bills. Senator Wagner, in the hearings, deplored the shrinkage in public construction, which in 1932 was a billion and a half dollars less than in 1930. Wagner explained the expected benefits of the liberalized program: ". . . the expenditure of large amounts of public moneys upon public works will inevitably induce the investment of substantial amounts of private funds. The construction of a waterworks may make a whole area suitable for residential development. The improvement of a traffic facility may invite the erection of a business enterprise. The fundamental fact to remember is that the distribution of purchasing power and the resumption of investment which this bill involves will have a stimulating effect and help to revive all forms of business activity. Both parts of the bill are designed to provide an immediate impetus to employment and that is the inescapable necessity of the present moment." [2]

It will be seen that the later separation of administration of the public works sections from the remainder of NRA was injurious to recovery. Public construction was intended to prime a pump which was then to be kept going by private industry. But when public expenditure was postponed and limited by decision of the Secretary of the Interior, the stimulating effect was forfeited.

CONTRADICTIONS IN NIRA

There is no need to halt over the planning, drafting, and passage of the NIRA. Several groups, including administration advisers, officials, organized business, organized labor, and others, were systematically at work for the better part of three months on proposals for reviving industry and increasing employment. These groups drew together under pressure of the President and toward the end discussions were under his supervision. The parleys, versions and repeated revisions reached back for inspiration to experience of the War Industries Board, gathered up accumulated impatience of business with antitrust policy, embraced the counterdemands of labor, and relied heavily on the over-all assistance of public works. The interest not represented, except by self-appointed proxies, was that of consumers. While the planning was done to meet an emergency, the formulation was sufficiently deliberate to warrant a judgment of the designers by their handiwork. They framed and Congress approved an act which failed in fact and in law. Whether, in the absence of the Schechter decision holding NIRA unconstitutional, the measure would have persisted, with modifications, is matter for debate. The Agricultural Adjustment Act, similarly struck down by the Supreme Court, rose again in pretty much its former guise. But this scheme had not lost the support of the farmers it was intended chiefly to benefit; on the contrary, they had adhered to it more widely and closely. The AAA did not have the self-imposed disabilities of NRA. Of course AAA adopted the boast that restricted production and public payments to farmers would help invigorate industry and commerce and tend to put the urban population back to work. That

[2] Hearings before Committee on Finance, on S. 1712 and H. R. 5755, U. S. Senate 73 Cong., I Sess., p. 11.

was a theory which could be defended by traditional economic logic. But the AAA, to do it justice, did not depend on public approval of this claim. Organized farmers, as disciplined as clamorous, were frankly out to raise their prices and so their relative purchasing power.

But the corresponding campaign of industry had internal contradictions. Recovery, in the narrow sense, was embarrassed by reform. Restriction of output, hours, and plant capacity was at war with the assumed objective of stimulated investment in heavy industry and increased production, not to speak of the aims of public works. Big business called the tune to which little business was to dance. Labor was to enjoy positive rights under codes which it did not frame or help to administer. More than all else, a whole machinery of control was called competition, and retirement of anti-trust acts and agencies was pretended not to forfeit their salutary protections. In addition, several originators and a larger number of chief administrators of the act must have allowed early loyalty and optimism to quiet, in the beginning, their deeper misgivings. Afterward some of these became outspoken, even abusive, critics; with their choice we are not concerned, except that lack of faith in the project could hardly help make their conduct wavering.

The bill was readily passed in the House, but met more opposition in the Senate, where constitutional scruples, combined with manufacturers' objection to the labor guarantees, delayed approval. Apologists pled emergency, with little effort to answer criticism. NIRA became law June 16, 1933.

As administrator President Roosevelt appointed General Hugh S. Johnson, who gave the early impression that he was "tough," and would "crack down" on recalcitrants. By training and experience he was supposed to be a master of discipline and to have full acquaintance with big business and corporate finance. His energy often degenerated into bluster. His gift for epigram betrayed a fatal tendency to make the complicated simple by calling it so. Before the end it appeared that he was a bull in a china shop, with the difference that after a while the clatter of crockery began to frighten the intruder. He was warm against small delinquents, but did not coerce major objectors, and therefore contributed to the discredit of NRA.

The success of the administrator was jeopardized, perhaps prevented, when the President changed the preliminary plan of organization in two important respects—Johnson was to report not directly to him but to an Industrial Recovery Board composed mainly of cabinet members, and control of public works was given to the Secretary of the Interior. Both provisions made for delay when speed was essential. Through the separation, almost the insulation, of public works from NRA, business and labor in their recovery effort lost the powerful assistance which government spending and initiative could have given them.

What industry wanted, and what it increasingly obtained under NRA, was "self-government." Though the President projected a partnership between industry, government, and labor, industry proved the strongest of the three. The instrument of self-government in each case was a "code of fair competition." Every code, to be sure, had to guarantee freedom of workers to join their own unions, and had to provide for maximum hours and minimum pay. Also, a group offering a code had to be truly representative of the trade or industry involved, and no code could be designed to promote monopoly or to oppress or eliminate small enterprises. If these requirements were met, the approved code became the law of the land, and those who had not assented to it, as well as those who had, were subject to prosecution and penalties for its violation. Thus the codes permitted businessmen practices that had long been furtive and made them not only formal but compulsory on competitors. A code was something between a charter of a medieval guild and the agreement of a modern cartel.

PROCESS OF CODE MAKING

Since the code was so significant, it is useful to describe briefly the steps by which one was formed. Ordinarily, the existing trade association or associations took the initiative; if there was no organization, a promoter, often a lawyer, formed an association for the purpose of submitting a code. The secretary of the sponsoring association was apt to become the central figure in the writing and later in the administration of a code; he became, more than any other one person, lawmaker, judge, and policeman. When a code was first submitted it went to the preliminary inspection of the Control Division, which docketed it and arranged for a deputy administrator, and then to the Code Analysis Division, which checked to see that it contained the mandatory provisions.

Next ensued pre-hearing conferences between the committee of the sponsoring group and the deputy administrator and his advisers. These last were from the Industrial Advisory Board appointed by the Secretary of Commerce, the Labor Advisory Board appointed by the Secretary of Labor, and the Consumers' Advisory Board named by the Administrator, while others were from the Legal Division and the Research and Planning Division of NRA. In the beginning, when codes were few, the deputy administrator and his industry and labor advisers were likely to be men chosen for their special knowledge of the industry concerned, though later, with shortage of personnel, this desirable scheme could not be held to. In the informal pre-hearing conferences chief issues were developed; if the industry was not well organized, and groups within it had submitted rival codes, all were consolidated into a single set of proposals.

The public hearing was held in Washington and was thoroughly advertised in advance. It was presided over by the deputy administrator, assisted by his advisers, and any and all interested groups and persons were invited to give evidence or offer objections. A full stenographic record was made of the hearing. Opposing groups and conflicting purposes, brought into the open at the hearing, remained to be reconciled in post-hearing conferences; these would have dragged on longer except for fear that the President might use his power to impose a code. Moreover, controversial provisions might be inserted in a code for a trial period. The deputy then referred the code with his recommendation, and with any dissent of his advisers, to the administrator. With the administrator's approval, it went to the President, whose signature made the code law.

In the process of code making, the bargaining was primarily between organized industry and organized labor, with the deputy administrator acting as an umpire. It was required that every code must allow collective bargaining, provide for shorter hours, and give increased rates of pay such that the earnings of the worker would not be less than before and, desirably, would be higher. Similarly, it was a foregone conclusion that "fair-trade practices," carrying out a large number of cherished objects of trade associations, were to be written into the codes by industry. The bargaining between industry and labor was for concessions beyond the generally agreed limits. A strong union would exact benefits to labor for every further authority granted over trade practices. The threat to strike was persuasive, especially as business, in anticipation of higher NRA prices, began to pick up. If the union was weak, or if there was no union, labor gains in the code were confined to the mandatory ones.

In this contest over the consumer's dollar, the consumer had little to say. The codes did open the way to wiping out the sweatshop with its hazard of unsanitary products, and the whole of government participation in NRA was supposed to protect the public interest. But the Consumers' Advisory Board lacked organized support; what was everybody's business was nobody's business. The Consumers' Board, comparatively without force in code formation and administration, was the innocent bystander. This board was by-passed in development of NRA policy and, with exceptions, its energies were diffused.

In spite of remarkable efforts, codes at the outset were completed slowly. The first, for the cotton textile industry, was approved within four weeks after the act was signed, and seven more were finished in the following month. But by this time hundreds of proposed national codes had been submitted, and awaited processing. In anticipation of higher code costs of materials and labor, there had been a spurt in industrial production, beginning when NRA was first proposed. Manufacturing output had been increased by some 50 per cent, but factory pay rolls by only half as much. Unemployment was being reduced, but too slowly. There might be a new slump because of inability to sell the fresh surplus at a profit. Industries without codes had an advantage over those already subject to code restrictions. Further, the exhilaration imparted by the announcement of NRA must not be allowed to lapse in the lag of code adoption.

THE BLANKET CODE

At the end of July, 1933, all employers were asked to subscribe to the President's Re-employment Agreement (PRA) and come under a blanket code. Within a few months approximately 2,333,000 employers, with 16,000,000 employees, accepted PRA. The only substantive provisions concerned labor. A signer bound himself to employ no one under sixteen years of age, and to pay clerical and service workers minimum wages from $15 in large cities to $12 in small towns for a maximum 40 hours a week, and factory workers in most cases a minimum of 40 cents an hour for a maximum of 35 hours. Differentials of pay above the minimum were to be kept where possible. Unnecessary price increases were not to be made. All promised to exert themselves to have industry codes submitted promptly. The President's Re-employment Agreement instituted a nation-wide boycott against nonsigners, for every complier covenanted to deal only with firms under PRA or under codes. The boycott was tightened by an executive order requiring that all government contracts for supplies should specify that the contractor conform to the blanket code or his industry code.

The symbol of compliance, and the chief means of arousing public support for the movement toward codes, was the Blue Eagle emblem displayed by all enterprises which conformed. PRA, except for the boycott feature, was voluntary, the federal government having no authority over most of the firms coming under the agreement, their business being intrastate. Voluntary local compliance boards could recommend to NRA that the Blue Eagle emblem be taken away from recalcitrants.[3]

Since signers of the President's Re-employment Agreement accepted higher labor costs and got no compensating control over competition, all had added incentive to hurry submission of codes. The result was a "deluge" of proposed codes, 546 in August and nearly as many more by the end of the year. Beginning in October and running through February, basic codes were approved at the rate of 2 a day. The number of NRA employes had to be increased swiftly from 400 to 4,500, and expenses reached nearly a million dollars a month. In the end NRA approved 557 basic codes, the labor provisions of 19 joint NRA-AAA codes, and 189 supplementary codes.[4]

Each code, when put in operation, was administered by a code authority. In the beginning there was no clear idea of how this cru-

[3] *The National Recovery Administration,* Message from the President of the United States, *House Document* No. 158, 75 Cong., 1 Sess., p. 64. (Cited elsewhere as Committee of Industrial Analysis, The NRA).
[4] Committee of Industrial Analysis, The NRA, p. 21.

cially important part of NRA machinery was to be contrived, and
uniformity was never achieved. The Committee of Industrial Analysis set up by the government, in final critical summary of the whole
NRA experience, said the code authorities "can be properly characterized as the creatures of . . . trade associations" sponsoring the
codes, and that "their personnel and policies were controlled by the
trade associations."[5] In general the members of a code authority
were chosen by a minority of firms in an industry, often by a small
minority of the most powerful. In many cases this resulted from
explicit stipulation in codes; in others it was the consequence even
where safeguards to give representation to nonassociation members
were inserted. The problem of selection was difficult for many reasons; primarily the conflict was between choice on the basis of
volume of business of member firms and choice on the basis of
number of firms. Divisional code authorities, geographic and functional, contributed less than might be supposed to a democratic
result, for these in turn were dominated by the organized and
larger units.

If smaller and scattered business units were underrepresented
on code authorities, labor and consumers were practically not represented at all. Only 3 codes provided for voting members speaking
for interests of consumers, and under only 37 codes were labor
members allowed, and these not always with the right to vote. The
idea of self-government by owners of industry was pervasive and
persistent. In a system of private ownership this was inevitable, but
the exclusion of labor and consumer representation, with much besides, clearly distinguished NRA from a cooperative undertaking,
even from the "partnership" between industry, government, and
labor which the President talked about. True, early in NRA history
government representatives were named to code authorities. Though
these, without vote, were supposed to protect labor and consumer
interests, and indeed had labor and consumer advisers, the hope
was far from realization. Government members were overburdened,
since each was assigned to a number of code authorities. To the extent that they functioned they became embroiled in purely industry
problems in the relation of the code authority to NRA, and, in practice, could at most deal only with critical conflicts rather than exert
constant pressure in the molding of policy. Labor clamored in vain

5 *Ibid.,* pp. 19–20.

for effective voice in the code authorities, while consumers were not sufficiently aware of their exclusion to enter protest, and none in government did it for them.[6]

The code authority was not empowered to enforce provisions of the code on units in the industry. It must report noncompliance to NRA, which might remove the Blue Eagle emblem or refer the infraction to the Federal Trade Commission or the United States District Court. But the code authority enjoyed such discretion in interpretation of code provisions, and such latitude in investigation as made the right of formal enforcement secondary. In practice, the property and liberty of businessmen, not to say the interest of labor and consumers, were placed in the hands of small committees chosen and controlled by dominant industrial groups. NRA and the President could, on review, disallow actions of code authorities, and NRA exercised an increasing oversight of these agencies, but these safeguards, in the bulk of cases, remained nominal.

INDUSTRY DOMINANT IN CODES

Government wanted an increase in purchasing power, and thus insisted on the inclusion in the codes of labor provisions that spread employment and increased total wages. The corresponding concession was industry's control over trade practices. In the beginning industry appeared as the weaker bargainer, but ended as the stronger—so strong that it destroyed the whole compact. The gains of government came at the outset, while those of industry were cumulative. Labor requirements of the codes were few, simple, and early formulated. Industry accepted them, with more or less formal objection, because it must yield, because increased wages could be viewed as beneficial to business, and because prices—despite the President's plea—could and would be increased before wages. The chief reason for acquiescence, however, was that industry was going to make counterdemands of supreme importance to it. Moreover, what government proposed was susceptible of definition. Limits could be set in minimum wages and maximum hours. To be sure, workers, guaranteed the right to organize and bargain collectively, might exert unknown pressure, but this, after all, was a familiar hazard.

[6] *Ibid.*, pp. 18–19, 84–85.

Also, to use a card term, government was discarding from weakness, industry from strength. In conceding control over trade practices, government gave up what it hardly possessed, with only the hope that its demands for labor would prove high trumps. Industry, by contrast, in yielding labor provisions, knew that it consolidated its position. Labor requirements, considering the prevailing volume of unemployment, were artificial, needing conscious support all along the line. Rules of trade practice, on the other hand, were those which industry had long been striving to impose, which needed only the removal of weak legal barriers.

The codes regulated some 150 trade practices by means of more than 1,000 different sorts of provisions. These covered the field of commercial and industrial behavior. "Codes of fair competition" they were called, and in part rightly, for they banned commercial bribery, misrepresentation, and the like, already recognized by law as fraudulent. But in greater part they set aside the antitrust acts by allowing control designed to raise prices and restrict production. The term "fair competition" became largely a misnomer, for the pressure constantly was to reduce or eliminate competition, legal as well as illegal. What had been taken for granted as normal necessary manifestations of competition were to be done away with. The familiar device of recommending a reversal of policy by preserving the old name has rarely had better illustration.

Long hostility of powerful units in business to the antitrust acts was intensified in 1933 by recent technical developments coupled with acute depression. Competition had become destructive. High overhead expense was a prime cause. Where fixed costs are relatively large, the effort to use full plant capacity by capturing a larger share of a diminished market will tend to force prices down to the point where they barely cover variable expense, the slight cost of furnishing the added products. Depression fiercened this force. By March, 1933, wholesale prices on the average had fallen 45 per cent since October, 1929. Idle plants faced impoverished demand. In this situation, ruinous competition could be removed only by agreement to maintain prices. This in itself would have been a benefit, but it promised to be a boon if accompanied by increased purchasing power accomplished through higher wages and expenditure for public works and in direct relief.[7]

[7] *Ibid.*, pp. 27–28.

Naturally, trade practice control was most effective in those industries where rules were most easily policed, as well as imposed, by industry itself. In an industry where units were few and large, the trade association was probably well established, the danger of interlopers was slight, and agreement and enforcement were simple once obstacles in the antitrust acts were removed. Such an industry could increase its share of total demand as much as it was able, and then could be trusted to distribute among its members whatever there was. If, on the other hand, the units in an industry were many, predominantly small, and fluctuating, there was apt to be no trade association or only a weak one, and factional interests made against agreements. Such an industry could not manage its own affairs, no matter how much liberty it was given, and the attempt of government to support rules in the midst of such confusion was not promising from the start.

Thus what was conserved by the codes was collusion rather than competition, unfair rather than fair trade practices. Government tended to be a silent partner to monopoly.

Trade practice provisions frankly aimed at maintaining prices and restricting output, besides many others of varying purposes, were embodied in the codes and became an established part of industry's expectation. Then NRA surveyed what was happening and undertook a general policy of coordination on behalf of industry itself and of supervision in the public interest. The anxiety of government to get codes adopted with the required labor features resulted in an uncritical acceptance of trade practice demands. The individual code as it was negotiated, though the restrictive power it gave to the industry was suspect, seemed relatively unimportant in the whole program, until the number of such codes, each furnishing an incentive to the next, was unmanageable. The first ten codes were most influential in setting policy by precedent. These gave industry significant power over price and production. The first, the cotton textile code, limited machinery operation to two forty-hour shifts per week; the shipbuilding and electrical manufacturing codes contained minimum-price-fixing systems; the corset and brassière code branched out into a long list of prohibitions; the lumber and petroleum codes permitted comprehensive production control, and maintenance of minimum prices in accordance with dangerously vague injunctions for cost determination.

To be sure, at the outset the President had said that wages ought to be raised before prices, and General Johnson, NRA administrator, had briefly warned that while an industry might refuse to sell below cost of production, he would intervene to prevent use of the code to fix extortionate prices. But these caveats, if heard, were not heeded. Industry was fighting on its own ground, where every cover was known. Government, in its ignorance of the complexities of trade practices, and in its haste, exposed itself. The Consumers' Advisory Board and some unofficial organizations protested in vain when protection of consumers was thus being allowed to go by default.

It was late in October, 1933, before the first general policy memorandum of NRA, and that limited in scope, was issued. Next came, early in November, a draft model code, which could have only indirect effect. This was followed by some declarations limiting price fixing. The revision of the model code did not appear until April, 1934, and it was May, when three fourths of the codes had been approved, before a group in NRA specifically charged with formulating policy was set up. By this time the conflicts between codes and within codes, and the demands for exemption and re classification had become formidable. Moreover, as will be seen below, the problem of reconciling and revising trade practice provisions was hopelessly complicated because the task of code administration overwhelmed the belated attempt to chart a general course.[8]

TRADE PRACTICE PROVISIONS

The trade practice features of the codes have been characterized without an enumeration of the kinds of conduct they covered. It is not possible to give the extended list, which amounts to a catalogue of industrial operations, competitive and collusive, with respect to the market. Here was a clinic of the economy. *Required* trade practices that occurred in the largest number of codes or were otherwise most important included minimum price maintenance, uniform methods of cost finding, price filing, specified discount and credit terms, specified standards of products or services, specified transportation terms, standard contracts, specified standards of bids

[8] *Ibid.*, p. 27.

and quotations, classification of customers, specified forms of arbitration, and limitation of machine and plant hours or of industry capacity. Among *prohibited* practices were misrepresentation and deceptive advertising, commercial bribery, defamation of competitors, interference with contracts, false branding and invoicing, specious threats of litigation, spying on competitors, imitation of trade-marks or designs, unjustified price discrimination, substitution of one product for another, making the sale of one product contingent on the sale of another, "style piracy," combination prices, enticement of employees, financing of purchases, repudiation of contracts, dumping, and false receipts. Other practices regulated in one way or another included rebates, consignment sales, premiums, special services, free "deals," and treatment of seconds. These items, in their variety, may be grouped under the three heads of control of prices, control of production, and control of competition. A few illustrative features of each of these will be mentioned.

The prime commercial criminal was the price cutter. He might be the large producer with low costs, or the small producer who could sell his article only by offering it at less than the well-known brands sold for, or one whose plight drove him to sell at less than his own cost. Minimum price provisions were general in the codes, though only 93 codes had minima legally in effect, and in more than a fourth of these control was suspended before the end. In spite of continued clamors by most industries, NRA learned by sad experience that it must limit price control by whatever means attempted.

Sometimes the code authority had power to set specific minimum prices. Oftener members of the industry were forbidden to sell at less than cost of production. At first this seemed a simpler requirement than it proved to be. "Average cost," "lowest representative cost," or "individual cost" all involved complications of cost accounting, of industry structure, of geographical differentials, and of enforcement. No matter what the efforts, demands of competition obtruded, so that, in emergencies, sales below individual cost had to be permitted. Generally, formal consent was not waited for, but evasion was practiced in innumerable ways. The more obvious means of violation were prohibited, only to be followed by ingenious devices which embroiled code authorities and NRA in a multiplicity of petty regulations. Individual plant cost as a determinant of price conflicted with widely used basing point systems that com-pelled plants located nearer a market to include fictitious transpor-tation costs in the price in order to permit remoter plants to com-pete. Rigid enforcement, in many situations, would have drawn NRA into the position of a partisan, which it could not afford to occupy, so that it contented itself with urging, rather than demand-ing, compliance.

In distributors' codes the use of "loss leaders" was frequently forbidden as a method of unfair price competition. A "loss leader" is ordinarily a nationally advertised brand, say of cigarettes or a proprietary drug item, offered by a large department store or chain outlet at less than the usual price and that which must be charged by the smaller dealer. The offender might maintain that his lower price was justified by his lower cost, since he bought a carload lot of the goods in question. Inquiry might reveal that a retailer mak-ing such a bulk purchase was able to do so only because he resold much of the lot to other retailers. It was then objected that he was usurping the function of the wholesaler. To prevent this, manufac-turing codes might require their members to submit lists of their customers classified according to the prices to which each group was entitled. This led to further complications.

Most of the codes provided for price filing, a device for preven-tion of price competition long dear to the hearts of trade associa-tions. Members of the code were required to file their prices with the code authority or with a confidential agent, and these filed prices were made available to all members of the industry and in many cases to customers. The purpose—to permit all to meet com-petition—was best served where there was a mandatory waiting period between the date of filing and the date when the prices were to take effect. In such cases no member could reduce his prices suddenly, all had opportunity to adjust to announced prices, and coercion of many sorts could be brought to compel a member to raise his low prices. The President's review committee concluded that "price filing probably gave rise to more difficulties than any other device in the trade practice field." Government was in an embarrassing position because, though it had made price filing sys-tems in the codes legal, it objected when its own procurement agen-cies, because of price filing, received uniform bids. The result, after a year's experience, was a presidential order permitting bids on government purchases as much as 15 per cent below filed prices. NRA tried, not very successfully, to discourage price control through filing, particularly by disallowing the waiting period.

PRICE AND PRODUCTION CONTROL

It is difficult to pass judgment on the varied policies of price control under the codes, meeting as they did with different degrees of success. In spite of exceptions to satisfy special situations, and more general evasion and violation, they did reduce price flexibility. NRA recognized, too late, that this was a mistake. The competitive system, if allowed to operate, has its virtues. But in order to benefit by these, inevitable penalties must be suffered. It proved impossible to have both penny and pie. NRA as a whole was a compromise between competition and control. The competitive system itself, under modern conditions of technology, tends, paradoxically, toward the reduction or elimination of competition. NRA placed itself in opposition to this development, though there were enough lapses in favor of monopoly or near monopoly. Nothing in NRA gave mandate for frank interference with the structure of industry; lacking this, attempted manipulation of surface manifestations was mischievous, as was nowhere more apparent than with respect to price regulation. When the whole experiment was ended, the question remained whether recovery would not have been hastened by permitting prices to fall rather than by efforts at price support.

If prices were protected against competitive pressures, there was a tendency toward overproduction and accumulation of unsalable stocks. New productive units might be put in operation, as in the lumber and bituminous coal industries; hence "production control" provisions appeared in ninety-one codes. These took the form of maximum quotas for the industry and for individual members, limits on machine hours, and refusal to permit new construction or the operation of equipment that had been idle, besides other measures. The influential cotton textile code set a pattern with its restriction to eighty hours a week. Sometimes, as in the petroleum industry, conservation was an object. Industrial blackmail—pulling down of prices through threat to construct a new plant—could be reduced by requiring code authority, which amounted, of course, to securing permission of producers already in the industry. Production control, like other parts of NRA, involved vexing problems. Where a section of an industry had differential advantages, limitations on production might shift business, as from southern to northern cotton mills. Production control ran counter to the purpose of recovery through new investment and construction of capital equipment. If a new plant was not permitted, was an existing establishment to be allowed to start production in that line to supply its own needs instead of buying in the market? Thinking themselves protected against new producers, existing ones sometimes unjustifiably increased their output. Where demand was elastic and substitute products were numerous, restriction of supply could injure consumers, who got less of the item, and producers, who got no higher price. On the other hand, if production control succeeded in raising price, new plants loomed.

Codes of "fair competition," while including price and production control, were inspired particularly by the desire to regulate a multiplicity of trade practices that were legitimate or illegitimate depending on whose ox was gored. Price filing was a method of limiting competition, and so were many provisions governing production, but, besides, certain "tricks" were especially disallowed. Some of these were already banned by law, but needed the unhampered action of interested groups, freed of antitrust restraints, to make the prohibition effective. Misrepresentation, design piracy, and commercial bribery fell in this class, while rules governing the return of goods were nearly related. Other attempted controls over competition grew out of changes that had taken place in the methods of distribution of goods. The old division of function between manufacturing, wholesaling, and retailing had been confused. Some manufacturers sold direct to retailers, thus eliminating wholesalers, while others went all the way and had their own retail outlets. Besides, the growth of department stores, mail-order houses, chain stores in many lines, and cooperatives contributed further to overlapping, for each of these found economies in being their own middlemen and even their own manufacturers. In this whole area, the initiation and administration of controls within a group with similar aims was simple. Except with respect to cooperatives, the consumer interest was uncertain or obscured or plainly fell in with trade efforts, such as those covering informative labeling and standardization of product. Government, on its part, as a condition of the bargain with industry, assented to code provisions outlawing unfair trade practices.

The trouble came in conflicts between groups, typically between manufacturers and distributors. Here NRA found that it had approved stipulations which clashed. Thus NRA accepted distributive codes that prejudiced manufacturers and manufacturing codes that limited distributors. NRA never chose between the policies of preserving functions distinct, or allowing their integration, and so was involved in incessant adjudication of differences that arose. NRA illustrated the big problem in any system of regulation—how to meet change, and to distinguish between developments which are serviceable and those which are to be checked as degenerative. Here, as elsewhere, NRA was necessarily opportunist, and no principle was worked out. If there had been more time in the beginning, or if the experiment had continued, construction of a clean-cut policy might have proved that the longest way around was the shortest way home.

CODE ADMINISTRATION VEXED

Any estimate of the success of code administration, either by industry or by the NRA, must take account of inherent conflicts between enterprises which, while all were engaged in the same business, contrasted in important ways. Some of these were distinctions in size, in production cost, and in methods of operation, whether integrated or not; concerns producing for export might have a different interest from those serving the domestic market; those with consumer good will, selling standard goods, might have an imperfect sympathy for those with less prestige, pushing substandard goods on a price basis. Classification into this and that "industry" promised a homogeneity that vanished instantly the demands within any group were examined. This variety made administration and enforcement of trade practice provisions difficult. While the problem of securing compliance with labor provisions was simpler, here too were stresses due to foreign elements in large cities, Negro labor in the South, handicapped workers for whom standard wages could not be claimed. There was a broad division between employers with organized and those with unorganized workers, and always there was the tremendous pressure on labor standards due to the mass unemployment. In addition, collective action was new to most small units in American business, and compulsory collective action was certainly novel to all—was so novel, indeed, that NRA was far from sure of its legal grounds, and so was fatally inhibited in pushing prosecution of violators of the codes.

Further, overlapping of codes and differences in code requirements for similar industries and groups of workers increased the problems of enforcement. If a segment of an industry thought it could obtain special advantages, it demanded and too often was granted a separate code; the result was that a large and complex business unit might come under two or more codes, with confusion and contention inevitable. Similarly, an employer with organized and unorganized workers would be paying different wage rates for identical labor in plants which were perhaps adjacent. It is impossible to call to mind, much less to set down here even in barest summary, the multiplicity of vexations which presented themselves in the effort to police the broad field of American industry, particularly when, following years of depression, any sign of recovery tempted individuals to seize the advantage in disregard of collective agreements. Also, as noticed earlier, administrative and enforcement machinery was indirect and was hampered by internal incompatibilities. The code authorities were supposed to represent both industry and the public welfare. Within the code authority, a member was asked to act unselfishly and yet could not forget his individual proprietorship, and his competitors never forgot it. The code authority for an industry could not use coercion, as in removal of the Blue Eagle insignia from a firm, without NRA approval. In turn, as noted before, the legal division of NRA could not itself prosecute violators, but must certify cases to the Department of Justice and the Federal Trade Commission.

The bulk of the codes were still being furiously drafted while problems of administration of earlier codes rolled back on NRA. Thus policy had to be formulated and interpreted, fluid and fixed, at the same time.

NRA machinery for administration altered and expanded rapidly and constantly, so that it would be too much to name the chameleon boards, local, regional, and national. During the first half of the NRA period, emphasis was on adjustment and compliance. But the methods of education, conciliation, and mediation could not, or did not, prevent enlargement of the compliance problem. Unpunished violations provoked organized opposition. NRA itself recognized that some of the code provisions were unwise and unenforceable, and aggrieved members and sections of industries were not long in resorting to the courts to test NRA authority. Inevitable delays in investigation and action encouraged clamors. Compliance was simplest where there was prior organization—as to trade practices in industries with strong trade associations, and as to labor provisions where there were independent unions. Naturally, industries made up of a large number of small units furnished most of the complaints; twenty-five codes of this sort were responsible for 75 per cent of complaints concerning labor requirements.

Jurisdiction in cases of noncompliance involving the collective bargaining provisions of Section 7(a) belonged, except for application of penalties, not to NRA proper, but to the National Labor Board and later to the National Labor Relations Board. In the Compliance Division of NRA there were finally 54 state and branch offices with a total personnel of 1,400. Of the 155,000 cases docketed by the state compliance offices, only about 1 in 100 reached the Litigation Division of NRA, and less than a fourth of these (564) reached the courts.[9]

LABOR IN NRA

The whole of Section 7 concerned labor rights and labor conditions under the codes. Section 7(a) was the crucial part. It declared that every code must provide "(1) That employees shall have the right to organize and bargain collectively through representatives of their own choosing, and shall be free from the interference, restraint, or coercion of employers . . . in the designation of such representatives . . . or in other concerted activities for the purpose of collective bargaining or other mutual aid or protection; (2) that no employee and no one seeking employment shall be required as a condition of employment to join any company union or to refrain from joining . . . a labor organization of his own choosing . . . ." Clause 3 said that employers must comply with labor conditions of the codes.

[9] *Ibid.*, p. 45.

Section 7(b) protected the right of self-organization of workers and collective bargaining in industries where there were no codes, and gave to approved labor standards, so agreed upon, the same binding effect as if they were contained in codes. Section 7(c) provided that where no mutual agreement had been reached, the President might prescribe a limited code fixing maximum hours, minimum wages, and other conditions of labor.

The importance of NRA for labor lay not in the effect of codes on wages and hours, but in the impetus given, through Section 7(a), to labor organization. This section was a charter to independent unions, granting them, legally, an indisputable place in the American economy. The organized labor movement took a fresh start from NRA, in vigor, in numbers, and in acceptance. Enough problems remained—in administrative protection of the right of collective bargaining, in costly splits in the ranks of unionists, in resistance of employers to the new status of their workers. But impetus to unionism was one of the two continuing influences flowing from NRA. The other, less palpable, was recognition that the efficacy of industrial competition was permanently impaired, and that a large measure of business association, with governmental oversight and even partnership, would mark the next phase of economic history in the country.

Inclusion in the codes of the specific labor provisions intended by the President, and their administration, were seriously hampered by a lack of direct labor participation in the formation and operation of codes. In only a score of industries, except through the Labor Advisory Board, may workers be said to have been allowed to help in the drafting of codes. In spite of efforts of NRA officials and of unions to secure for labor equal representation on code authorities, voting membership was obtained in only 23 cases and nonvoting in 28 others. In these instances, true labor partnership was due to the presence of strong unions. But in 85 per cent of the industries covered by NRA, labor organization was weak or, oftener, totally absent, and here any determining influence of labor went by default. NRA tried to justify itself and to console workers with the contention that the Labor Advisory Board, in the formation and administration of codes, protected labor's interests, but without success. Labor representation, over most of the area of NRA, was distant, halting, or *pro forma*.

Thus was again illustrated the fact that, except in the concession of the right of labor to organize and bargain collectively, industry used its position to dominate NRA. The labor provisions of codes, especially in their interpretation, furnished the greatest wrangle in NRA, so it was unfortunate for the objectives of the whole that labor did not have an original and creative part. Government's chief purpose in NRA was the increase of purchasing power by the net reduction of unemployment, by the spreading of work through shorter hours, and by the increase of wages. Thwarting of these ends was due fundamentally to the presence of mass unemployment relieved only partially and belatedly by the auxiliary means of public works, but it owed much to the incessant whittling away of labor standards by industry in the absence of effective labor objection.

In spite of labor's demand, as in the Black-Connery bill, for the 30-hour week, and the administrator's early stand for 32 hours as necessary to the reabsorption of the labor force of 1929, the 40-hour basic week became the NRA standard. This was adopted in 487 codes, for industries employing 13,000,000, or 57 per cent of the total of codified industries; 43 codes had a shorter work week, and 48 a longer. In 64 per cent of the codes, covering 61 per cent of employees, provisions permitted a week of 48 hours or longer for a substantial part of the workers. The standard maximum day was 8 hours for production workers, but nearly half the codes permitted, in one way or another, longer hours for office workers.[10]

The President's Re-employment Agreement, announced July 30, 1933, sought to hasten the code-making process and, by its own superior provisions, to speed recovery through getting "more and fatter pay envelopes to our workers." It proposed a basic 35-hour week for factory workers and a 40-hour week for others. But these shorter hours were greeted by employers with a virtually unanimous demand for exemption. These demands were generally granted by permission to employers to operate under the labor provisions of their proposed codes, so that the 40-hour week, for practical purposes, became the rule for PRA. The spreading of work through shortening of hours, because it added to industrial costs, gave rise to multifarious modifications, which formed a major item in NRA's

[10] Charles F. Roos, *NRA Economic Planning* (Bloomington, Indiana: Principia Press, 1937), Chap. IV.

vexations. In a minority of instances, ironically, better organization under the codes led to increased productivity per man-hour, and to that extent counteracted re-employment.

In spite of all, employment was increased, chiefly through PRA, by reducing weekly hours of work.[11] In the industries covered by the Bureau of Labor Statistics, average hours were reduced from 43.3 to 37.8, or 12.7 per cent, between June and October, 1933. In this period about 2,462,000 workers were re-employed, an increase of 6.8 per cent, the bulk of it occurring in NRA industries. In a sample of industries analyzed, the percentage averaging more than 45 hours per week was reduced from 30 per cent in June to 2 per cent in October.

LAST PHASE

The NRA experiment was weakened by the growing disaffections of both large and small enterprises embraced. The public was most aware of the complaints of the latter that they were oppressed by monopoly, were unable to get the credit necessary to meet the increased costs imposed by NRA, and were injured by the elimination of trade practices that had worked in their favor. The objections of small business were signalized in reports of a National Recovery Review Board, appointed by the President in March, 1934, with Clarence Darrow, the celebrated criminal lawyer, as chairman. The board concluded that in certain industries monopolistic practices existed to the prejudice of the little independents. NRA officials replied that the board had political animus, prejudged the case, was slipshod in inquiry, and encouraged return to wolfish competition. However, so far as attachment to competition was concerned, Darrow and another member of the board declared: "The hope for the American people, including the small business man, not to be overwhelmed by their own abundance, lies in the planned use of America's resources following socialization." The board was soon abolished.

On the other hand, large enterprises, once they tasted sweet immunity from the antitrust acts, were irked by the growing tendency of NRA to return to economic and legal orthodoxy, disallowing tactics that went beyond "fair competition" and were inimical

[11] *Ibid.*, Chaps. V, VI.

to all competition. Also, once recovery had begun, big business was suspicious of the partnership it had entered with government, as it had all along been regretful of the concessions it was obliged to make to labor unionism.

The authority of NRA came to be openly challenged, and in far more cases was simply disregarded. Compliance machinery bogged down, every permitted infraction invited others; NRA was not sufficiently sure of its popular approval or of its legal grounds to take a strong stand. Thus America was not unprepared for the unanimous opinion of the Supreme Court, May 27, 1935, in the Schechter case, which held the NRA unconstitutional. This involved the code of the live poultry industry of the New York metropolitan area. The decision found that the industry was no part of interstate commerce, and thus the commerce power could not be cited to justify congressional control over it. Further, Congress had delegated legislative authority without sufficiently specifying how it should be exercised; that authority had, in fact, been exercised by voluntary associations (the code authorities) which sought to give their mandates the force of positive law. "Without in any way disparaging" the economic motives of the act, the Court declared fatally, "it is enough to say that the recuperative efforts of the Federal Government must be made in a manner consistent with the authority granted by the Constitution." [12]

It is not possible to demonstrate statistically what contribution NRA made to recovery. When NRA lapsed, work hours were lengthened, wage rates fell, unemployment increased. Much of the effect of NRA was emotional, demonstrating the truth of an assumption underlying the whole of the New Deal: social self-confidence and purpose are the stuff of which economic rescue and progress are made. NRA supplied fresh energy to jaded industry and commerce.

But NRA showed, also, that psychological stimulus is not enough. This must be companioned by institutional changes which NRA did not provide for or want. All of the resources, physical and political, for full production and employment and for a rising standard of living were present. But this potential abundance could not be turned into goods and services and security for all the people without deliberate planning for plenty.

[12] See *Schechter v. United States,* 295 U. S. 495.

Planning under NRA was hasty and opportunist. There had been little time for advance design. The urgent task of organizing American industry involved simultaneous scheming and execution. Here was double trouble. The fact that recovery took precedence over reform in the end was fatal, for much of the planning which NRA afforded was, in the first instance at least, for scarcity, not plenty. The hybrid result of social authority and individual incentive was unfortunate. Compromise is the inevitable accompaniment of social reform, but when compromise is the preoccupation, reform becomes incidental.

NRA proved, if anything, that the country had reached a stage in economic development in which old methods would not serve. Private property in the great means of production, and their operation under the profit motive and by reliance on the price system—however overlaid with a spirit of cooperation—could not give full use of materials, machines, and men. Frictions and contradictions inhibited on every hand. Exhortation of government was at first promising, then disappointing, and finally irritating. Instead of forthright planning for a plain social objective, there was circumspect strategy, and that mostly of the moment.

The President was understandably impatient when the Supreme Court invalidated NRA and AAA. But if allowed to run, they could at best have helped the country out of that depression. And in proportion as these expedients seemed to succeed, the fundamental changes in them which would have been necessary to avoid a new breakdown would have been deterred, not assisted. NRA, to the extent that it was a coherent effort, was already falling apart from internal causes when the Court pronounced its end.

Before leaving NRA it is useful to give a brief factual addendum on the behavior of some of the chief forms of business enterprise embraced in the experiment.

INCIDENCE OF DEPRESSION ON INDUSTRY

Gross income from manufacturing fell from $68,468,000,000 in 1929, which was the peak, to $27,635,000,000 in 1932, the low point. Recovery was to $30,557,000,000 in 1933 and thereafter climbed more rapidly to $60,712,000,000 in 1937. The gain in 1936, the first full year after NRA was abolished, was greater than in 1934, the only full year of NRA, though the general progress was bound to be more important than the effect of any particular program. While all major industrial divisions lost income, paper manufacture fared best ($1,909,000,000 in 1929 down to $1,031,000,000 in 1932, a decline of 44 per cent), followed by food and tobacco (45 per cent) and chemicals (46 per cent). Gross income of metals industries went down most (74 per cent), followed by construction materials and furniture (70 per cent). Net income of manufacturing fell from $19,794,000,000 in 1929 by roughly $5,000,000,000 a year to $6,253,000,000 in 1932, recovered to $15,910,000,000 in 1937, but because of the recession was down the next year to $12,574,-000,000.

In terms of their shares in the total payments of manufacturing, wages declined most during the depression, from $10,898,000,000 in 1929 to $4,616,000,000 in 1932, or 57 per cent; property income (dividends and interest) declined from $2,952,000,000 in 1929 to $1,319,000,000 in 1932, or 55 per cent, though dividends alone declined 66 per cent, from $2,743,000,000 in 1929 to $1,110,000,000 in 1932; and entrepreneurial withdrawals declined by slightly less than wages, 52 per cent, from $372,000,000 in 1929 to a low of $176,000,000 in 1934, two years after wages had touched bottom. There was loss in every type of payment between 1937 and 1938, the least percentage drop being in the case of entrepreneurial withdrawals and of interest, which declined scarcely at all. Among major industrial divisions, wage drop during the depression was severest in construction materials and furniture and in metals. Correspondingly, these industries lost the largest proportion of workers. Those in construction materials and furniture fell in number from 1,217,-000 in 1929 to 541,000 in 1932, by 1937 had increased to 1,028,000, but the next year fell again to 845,000, which was below the number for 1936. In metals the drop in number of workers was from 2,687,000 in 1929 to a minimum of 1,345,000 in 1932; there was a small increase in 1933, a much larger one in 1934, reaching 2,796,-000 in 1937, with decline the next year below the number for 1935.

The total number of entrepreneurs in manufacturing declined from 133,000 in 1929 to 72,300 in 1933. The number in 1937 and 1938 was the same, 99,300. Though food and tobacco, and textile and leather divisions of manufacturing were heavy losers in number of entrepreneurs, construction materials and furniture manufacture lost a higher proportion. Metals industries, which behaved much like construction materials and furniture in a number of respects, lost a smaller proportion of entrepreneurs, presumably since metals industries were conducted on a larger scale.[13]

During the depression the share of service industries in the national income, as compared with commodity-producing industries, continued to increase. This was mainly because the prices of services did not fall as much as the prices of commodities. About a third of consumers' outlay went into services, and this proportion increased in terms of current prices, though much less noticeably if the effects of price changes were eliminated. Consumers' outlay on services was at the expense of durable and semidurable goods; perishable commodities continued to claim the same part of the outlay.

The services, running all the way from professional to domestic and embracing new occupations, differed in their behavior during the depression. While total payments to individuals dropped from $10,755,000,000 in 1929 to $7,142,000,000 in 1933 and recovered to $9,348,000,000 in 1937, entrepreneurial net income, for example, fell much more in engineering and advertising than in curative services, recreation and amusement, and the hand trades. The number of employees in service categories decreased between 1929 and 1933 by roughly a million and a quarter, but regained the loss by 1938, while entrepreneurs continued to increase throughout the period. The number of entrepreneurs in recreation and amusement declined by little and then not until 1935, as compared with advertising, which lost heavily and recovered little of the loss. Employees in hotels fell off far more than those in restaurants and garages.[14]

CHANGES IN MERCHANDISING

As NRA embraced retailing, what happened in that field is relevant here. Chain stores and to a less extent large department stores were the focus of developments in wholesale and retail distribution of commodities during the period. While in the twenties chain stores had increased in number of units, in the thirties the trend was toward a smaller number of larger units. The number of chain outlets fell from nearly 160,000 in 1929 to about 123,000 in 1939, or

[13] Kuznets, *National Income and Its Composition,* pp. 576 ff.
[14] *Ibid.,* pp. 212–214, 761 ff.

from 10.3 per cent of the total to 6.9 per cent. Total retail sales
were $49,115,000,000 in 1929, $25,037,000,000 in 1933, $33,161,-
000,000 in 1935, and rose to $42,042,000,000 in 1939. At the begin-
ning and end of this period chain stores had about the same proportion of total retail sales, slightly less than 22 per cent, though
their share had risen to 27 per cent in 1933.

Most independents fought the chains, their trade associations
sponsoring legislation designed to limit the chains' advantages. But
other independents preferred to lay hold on the chief economy in
chain store merchandising, namely the combination of retail and
wholesale functions. These, particularly in the food field, cooperated
in buying, advertising, and warehousing. Usually a wholesaler took
the initiative in forming the voluntary chain, and supplied units
which sometimes remained independent, or others which yielded
much of their autonomy. Among groceries, units in the voluntary
chains were as numerous as units in the regular chains in 1930,
though the sales of the latter were far larger. The thirties witnessed
a striking development of the grouped independent groceries.
Whereas the regular chains declined in number of units from
53,466 in 1930 to 40,350 in 1939, the units of voluntary grocery
chains increased from 53,400 to 113,501. In 1939 the regular grocery chains were estimated to have sales of $2,900,000,000; the
cooperative and voluntary chains, of $2,350,000,000.[15]

Some regular chains, in order to make full use of their buying
and warehousing capacity, sponsored voluntary chains; this was
also a hedge, probably, against increasing taxation of units in regular chains. Outside of the food field, in which they made most
progress, voluntary chains developed among variety, drug, and
hardware stores.

Invalidation of NRA did not mean cessation of efforts to outlaw certain trade practices, particularly discriminatory pricing by
wholesalers and manufacturers and price cutting by retailers. Section 2 of the Clayton Act of 1914 had made it unlawful to practice
direct or indirect price discrimination in interstate trade where the
discrimination lessened competition or tended toward monopoly.
Price differences were allowed in cases of difference in grade, quantity, or quality of merchandise, in selling or transportation cost, and

[15] Delbert J. Duncan and Charles F. Phillips, *Retailing Principles and Methods*
(Chicago: Richard D. Irwin, Inc., 1941), pp. 28 ff.

where they were necessary to meet competition. The principle was that comparable buyers should receive comparable discounts. But this law was more honored in the breach than the observance. Development of large-scale retail outlets, whether individual or in chains, led to honest confusion through partial or complete merger of wholesale and retail functions. To this were added evasions by wholesalers, who allowed advertising and brokerage discounts in cases where such services were in fact not rendered by the retailers.

Therefore the Robinson-Patman Act of 1936 sought to give sharper definition to prohibitions of the Clayton Act and thus permit more effective policing. Differences in price allowed to customers in interstate trade were to be related in specified ways to differences in cost to the vendor. Brokerage fees were made illegal and advertising allowances were banned unless "available on proportionally equal terms to all other customers competing in the distribution of such products." Buyers were made equally guilty with vendors in price discrimination. Numerous states passed similar acts. However, enforcement continued to be difficult, partly because application of the law in a complex variety of cases necessarily involved arbitrary action. Classification of customers defied rule.

The chains and other large retailers were the targets of so-called "fair-trade" laws in practically all the states. Formerly the manufacturer of branded goods who wanted to maintain the retail price of his product had no other course than refusal to sell to violators. The fair-trade acts permitted the manufacturer to sign contracts with retailers to sell at or not below the dictated price; the contracts could contain a "new signer's" clause making the terms of the agreement binding upon other retailers as soon as they were notified.

The Miller-Tydings Act of 1937 legalized retail price maintenance in interstate commerce; the manufacturer might sign a contract with one retailer and notify all the others. Legislation for retail price maintenance was promoted by regular-price retailers and their trade associations, especially the National Association of Retail Druggists. The practice made greatest gains in drugs, toilet goods, cosmetics, books, and liquor merchandising. Manufacturers who embraced the opportunity did so not only to help protect independent retailers and the wholesalers whom these manufacturers needed, but to defend themselves against dictation by the large-scale retailers. Price cutting on nationally advertised products and their use as loss leaders by chains and the largest department stores threatened to reduce profit margins all along the line, and tended to give the goods a bad reputation with consumers. However, there were dangers for the manufacturer in resale price maintenance. Large-scale retailers, if forced into these agreements, might have or develop and push their private brands in vigorous competition.[16]

Resentment of independent retailers, wholesalers, and certain manufacturers against chains found some response among local businessmen generally and even, though to a far less extent, among consumers. These objected to the chains on the ground that they took money out of the local community, refused to share in local civic efforts, were unfair to employees, destroyed independent small merchants, and tended toward monopoly. All of this opposition resulted in discriminatory taxation of chain stores in a score of states and in many cities. The typical tax was graduated by number of stores in the chain, running up to $250 per store where the number was large. The laws were upheld by the Supreme Court of the United States, which said that states might classify property and enterprises for taxation and that differences in tax burden were allowable so long as the classification was reasonable.

A reduction in the number of chain outlets and an increase in average size was partly a consequence of this taxation. A special development was the supermarket. The first of these appeared in the Los Angeles area, where there were 25 in 1929 and 193 by 1935. Similar large food outlets were promptly opened in the East, and by 1939 the country had about 7,000 of them, each doing business of a minimum value of $250,000. At first they were mostly independent ventures which sought low-rent locations, had the crudest fixtures, and employed few salespeople. Their success would not have been possible except for the fact that their customers had automobiles. Before long, however, supermarkets appeared in better locations. Supermarkets formed chains, and the old chains with small outlets began to open supermarkets. Buildings, fixtures, and displays improved, though generally self-service was kept. The owner of an independent supermarket often operated the grocery

---

[16] On the growing power of the large retailer see D. R. Craig and W. K. Gabber, "The Competitive Struggle for Market Control," American Academy of Political and Social Science, *Annals, CCIX* (May, 1940), 84–107.

department himself at small or no profit in order to attract business and permit him to make his return in the form of rents charged for concessions occupying parts of the store. As chains moved into the field of supermarkets they preferred centralized control of all departments and rented few concessions. By 1938 the regular chains were calculated to have 46 per cent of the supermarkets, independents 38 per cent, and supermarket chains 16 per cent. Some supermarkets avoided wholesalers, bought direct from shippers in carload lots, and managed without warehouses.[17]

Chain merchandising proved most successful in "convenience" and other standard goods rather than in "shopping" goods which had style elements or were designed to meet individual demand. While chains, in eligible fields, were apt to give superior competition to independents, by their very growth they encountered the competition of other chains. This cause and others led to the abandonment of many units and to the consolidation of some chains. Retail chains in some cases manufactured or processed part of the merchandise which they sold under their own brand names. In addition to making goods, chains and large mail-order houses frequently dominated manufacturers, who became practically their agents. One of these would set up in business a small manufacturer, say of clothing, take his entire output, dictate its character, and leave him scant profit. If the manufacturer objected to renewing the contract on the previous terms, the powerful customer would threaten to sponsor a new producer, and often did so, leaving the first manufacturer, his workers, and perhaps the whole of a small town in distress.

GROWTH OF COOPERATIVES

The cooperative movement expanded remarkably during the period under review. Agricultural cooperatives were well established earlier, but it was not until 1933 that consumers' cooperatives commenced such gains as left no doubt of their vitality and assured prospects. The parent cooperative, that of Rochdale, England, was established to help meet unusual hardship; likewise its American counterparts, distant in time and place, found their spring in depression conditions. With loans from the Farm Credit Admin-

[17] Duncan and Phillips, *Retailing Principles and Methods*, pp. 32–36.

istration, the federal government aided farmers' and other producers' cooperatives engaged in buying supplies and selling their products. The government directly promoted consumers' cooperation in rural electrification. The most comprehensive effort to supply information was the report of an official commission sent to Europe to study cooperative enterprise there and explore the applicability of cooperation to America.[18] With restrictions, cooperatives of farmers and other producers were exempt from federal income taxes, and consumers' associations were generally embraced in the exemption of cooperatives from state taxes on income, capital stock, and on multi-unit selling organizations.

The volume of business of the cooperatives, as evidenced by the record of the wholesales, rose without a break through 1937, and the slight decline in 1938 was more than overcome in 1939. Net earnings and patronage refunds had dipped in 1933, but the loss was better than retrieved the following year. In 1929 less than 400 retail associations were members of consumers' cooperative wholesales, while six times as many were members in 1939. Sales increased more than seven times, net earnings more than ten times, and patronage refunds more than twelve times. In the eleven-year period, wholesales handling consumer goods did a business of almost $300,000,000 and returned to their members patronage dividends of nearly $5,500,000. It was estimated that at the end of 1939 there were 4,350 retail distributive associations operating stores, buying clubs, and gasoline stations; they had 925,000 members and annual sales of $211,653,000. More than 900 associations, with 576,-450 members, furnished services, such as housing, electricity, and medical care. Credit unions, telephone and insurance associations had additional large memberships.

Retail cooperatives could not grow vigorously until they had formed wholesales. At the end of 1939 there were 13 district wholesales serving 160 retail members in limited areas, 23 regional wholesales with 2,100 retail members, and two interregional associations with regional wholesales as members. The business of the regional wholesales was much the largest, $52,500,000; from net earnings they returned to their member associations $750,000. Some of the wholesales undertook production or processing to supply their

[18] Inquiry on Cooperative Enterprise in Europe, *Report* (Washington: Government Printing Office, 1937), 321 pp.

needs, operating bakeries, coffee-roasting plants, creameries, packing houses, fertilizer factories, and oil and grease plants. Regional wholesales were patronized from time to time by 1,121 nonmember retail associations. Consumers' cooperative societies were concentrated primarily in the West North Central states of Minnesota, Iowa, Missouri, the Dakotas, Nebraska, and Kansas (about 40 per cent of total membership), and in the East North Central states of Ohio, Indiana, Illinois, Michigan, and Wisconsin (30 per cent of total membership). New England and Pacific coast states had each about 7 per cent of the membership, while there were few societies in the South.[19]

In 1940 there were more than 15,500 farmer-owned and farmer-controlled cooperatives of all sorts, including irrigation companies, growers' cotton gins, and fruit, vegetable, poultry, egg, and livestock auctions. Government loans to agricultural cooperatives totaled over $81,000,000 in 1936.[20] During the decade farmers' marketing cooperatives decreased by more than 2,000, but those engaged in purchasing farmers' supplies increased by more than 1,000, and the membership of these purchasing associations grew by more than 400,000. In 1940 there were about 10,700 active farmers' cooperatives, buying and selling, with 3,300,000 members.

[19] *Monthly Labor Review*, LI, No. 4 (October, 1940), 926–933.

[20] Farm Credit Administration, Cooperative Division, *A Statistical Handbook of Farmers' Cooperatives* (Bulletin No. 26; Washington: Government Printing Office, November, 1938), pp. 1, 15, 17.

CHAPTER VIII

Labor under the New Deal

WHEN NRA, particularly its Section 7(a), came to the rescue, labor unionism in America was shattered as it had not been in almost a century, following the panic of 1837. During the prosperous twenties, ironically, unionism had been weakened; the onset and early progress of the depression demoralized it. Between 1920 and 1929 the membership of the American Federation of Labor fell from 4,093,000 to 2,769,700. Practically all unions except those in building construction, public service, printing, and entertainment lost membership. The percentage of workers deemed available for unionization who were organized dropped by practically a half in the decade, from 17.5 per cent in 1920 to 9.3 per cent in 1930. The depression tore at union ranks. Between 1929 and 1933 the American Federation of Labor lost at least 452,200 members, falling to 2,317,500; the unaffiliated unions, despite gains in some, suffered a net loss of 17,400, falling to a total of 655,500. Among the sharpest declines were those in building construction, transportation, textiles, and metals, machinery, and shipbuilding.[1]

Contrary to previous experience in times of brisk business, several influences conspired in the "New Economic Era" to drain the unions of membership and morale. Underlying industrial developments strengthened the opposition of employers and put organized workers at a disadvantage. This was undeserved, certainly unexpected, by labor, which had been loyal to the war effort, forgoing

[1] Leo Wolman, *Ebb and Flow in Trade Unionism* (New York: National Bureau of Economic Research, 1936), pp. 138–139.

the use of the strike, placing Gompers in the closest councils of the government, and investing hopes in the progress of its democratic movement when peace should be won. The International Labor Organization was the contribution of Gompers and his members to the workers of the world, but this most enduring part of the League of Nations was in contrast to baffled struggles at home.

The depression of 1920–1921 brought mass unemployment, with most imperfect machinery of relief in American communities. This was the signal for consolidation of the open-shop drive of employers' associations for the "American Plan." This plausible campaign coincided with and contributed to public and official suspicion of liberal, let alone radical, pretensions. Revulsion of the country toward Russian Bolshevism was matched in the reactionary policies of Republican postwar administrations.

Increased real wages of the twenties relaxed rank-and-file loyalty to the unions, and restricted the vision and damped the ardor of leaders. The cheap automobile helped persuade the worker that he could enjoy a higher standard of living without dependence on the union. A car not only took his leisure time, but took him in many cases to a new home in the suburbs, which was soon equipped with overstuffed furniture, electric refrigerator, washing machine, and vacuum cleaner even more readily bought on the installment plan than with money in his pocket.

Employers capitalized on this mood of their workers with extension of welfare schemes—club houses, athletic facilities, group insurance—which diverted attention from unionism. From these it was but a step to collaboration of labor and management through innocuous shop committees and "industrial democracy" plans, profit sharing, and sale of stock to employees. The Taylor and other systems of industrial engineering revealed the motive in incentive wages and time studies that led on to the labor stretch-out. Ventures of a number of unions into banking and speculative real-estate developments and investment companies took funds which, in most cases, would have been better used in organizing nonunion workers.

Internal dissensions weakened important unions at a time when unity was needed. Opposition leaders often linked Russian communist inspiration, which was alien to the mind of the American worker, with insistence on mass industrial organization, which was

increasingly required by developments in the United States. The
result for several years was harmful factional strife, especially in
garment and textile unions, on the communist issue, and slow
progress in the more hopeful project of industrial instead of craft
unionism in the new mass production industries. Cleavage within
a union was particularly hurtful where, as in cotton manufacture
and coal mining, the industry itself was in a precarious condition
from overexpansion and the threat of substitute products. The consequence was unsuccessful strikes which gained public disapproval,
and governmental intervention which benefited the employers.

Owners moved plants from the better organized North to the
less organized South, or set up branch plants in rural districts
where they could secure nonunion workers. The unions were generally unsuccessful in following these "runaway" employers. Technological improvements, mainly in the substitution of machinery
for human labor, were of a far-reaching significance little understood by old-line union leaders. Craft unionism had been built on
skill, but now skill was being diluted or made obsolete. Ensconced
leaders needed to abandon craft distinctions and to organize the
assembly lines, but they would do neither.

Healthy, expanding unions could not have withstood the on-
slaught of the depression following 1929, and debilitated unions
fell ready victims. Between 1929 and 1933 labor income fell from
$50,964,000,000 to $26,386,000,000, or some 48 per cent.[2] Because
of pay cuts and part-time work, average weekly earnings in manufacturing fell from $25.03 in 1929 to $16.73 in 1933. The index of
the cost of living declined from 99.5 in 1929 to 75.8 in 1933, but
this was less than the decline in wages.[3]

Unemployed union members could not pay dues. Union scales
in many cases became nominal; nevertheless, employers refused to
make new union agreements, or made them on worse terms. While
unionists had the threat of those without work, union employers
were further jeopardized by competition of nonunion firms which
could operate with badly underpaid labor. It was impossible to
sustain wages and union conditions in the same economy with

[2] U. S. Temporary National Economic Committee, *Investigation of Concentration
of Economic Power,* Hearings on Pub. Res. No. 113. 75 Cong., Sess.; *Economic Prologue* (Washington: Government Printing Office, 1939–1941), p. 197.

[3] *Statistical Abstract of the United States,* 1944–1945, p. 161; TNEC, *Economic
Prologue,* p. 61.

mounting millions of unemployed made conspicuous by the beggar, the bread line, the extemporized shack colonies, and the wretched "Bonus Army" and its fate. To be sure, certain unions grew because of the depression. These were composed of workers in upper wage brackets or of white-collar and professional people—teachers, architects, engineers, technicians, journalists, actors, retail and office clerks, even small farmers. But these formed or joined unions as an expedient against their sudden hardship, and their action testified to the worse plight of those in the older labor organizations.

SUDDEN GROWTH OF UNIONS

NRA was to be a partnership between government, industry, and labor; Section 7(a) was "to induce and maintain united action of labor and management under adequate governmental sanctions and supervision." As the antitrust acts were suspended to permit industrialists to take combined action, obviously it was only fair to guarantee the same right to workers, free from interference of employers and courts. Also, collective bargaining would be the means of promoting industrial peace and therefore steady production and the uninterrupted flow of wages and all purchasing power. In the beginning, company unions were not stigmatized except where they embodied coercion on the part of the employer, in the sequel company unions were outlawed.

In their response to the invitation to form independent unions, workers were encouraged by the optimism engendered by the new administration, by the pickup in employment, and by the removal of penalties on union membership and activities. Of less importance was the fact that relief was available for strikers. Not only was prompt expansion of unions spectacular; NRA had laid the foundation for enduring progress of labor organization. Membership of all unions, in and out of the Federation, grew from 2,973,-000 in 1933 to 3,608,600 in 1934, and to an estimated 3,888,600 in 1935. The last figure includes 1,022,100 in the Committee for Industrial Organization, nearly three fourths of these drawn from the Federation; still, the latter's membership rose some 300,000 between 1934 and 1935. Between 1933 and 1934, however, it had gained 712,500.[4] The end of NRA in 1935 marked, for present pur-

[4] Wolman, *Ebb and Flow in Trade Unionism*, pp. xii, 16.

poses, a new period; by 1939 total union strength had been re-
cruited to some 8,500,000, about 4,000,000 in the Federation and
the same number in the C.I.O. In six years nearly 6,000,000 workers
had joined unions.

Over a third of Federation unions increased in membership; a
fourth doubled their membership. Circumstances favored organization of industrial unions; all of the Federation unions that lost
membership were of the craft type. The International Ladies' Garment Workers took NRA as the signal for a militant national organizing campaign and emerged as a major union; in a year it quadrupled its membership to 200,000.[5] The United Mine Workers
gained 135,000 members in three weeks, and went from perhaps
60,000 before NRA to 500,000 or more in 1935. This union organized not only miners, but affiliated to its catchall "District 50"
workers of many industries. The United Textile Workers almost
trebled to 79,200. The oil field workers went from practically nothing to 43,500. The Amalgamated Clothing Workers, long antagonized by the Federation, came in with its 125,000 members.[6] White-
collar and service workers discovered their need of unions. Building
construction lagged, and was responsible for holding back a block
of the old Federation unions.

But the most significant development, during the NRA period,
was the formation of more than 1,100 federal and local unions,
affiliated directly with the Federation, in such mass production industries as automobiles, rubber, aluminum, and lumber. Membership in this group of unions grew from 10,396 in 1933 to 111,489 in
1935.[7] In each industry a federal council served to bind the newly
organized locals together. This could be only a temporary expedient. As will be seen later, large numbers of the craft unions claimed
jurisdiction over workers who often only nominally were painters,
electricians, or machinists, and whose industrial identification was
really with a single product, say automobiles, rather than with a
process or a particular skill. Typically, these workers had not served
apprenticeships, could not handle all of the traditional tools of the
trade, but had been speedily trained to perform a few mechanical
operations. The contest as to whether these workers were to be

[5] I.L.G.W.U. *Report* of General Executive Board to Twenty-second Convention,
1934, p. 10.
[6] Wolman, *Ebb and Flow in Trade Unionism*, pp. xii, 179.
[7] *Ibid.*, p. 66.

permanently organized according to industry, or were to be divided out among the older craft unions, remained in uneasy abeyance until the emergence of the C.I.O. in 1935 after the breakdown of NRA.

If independent unions grew, company unions grew faster. During World War I, shop committees had been established by several supervisory government agencies, especially by the National War Labor Board, to settle grievances and even to engage in collective bargaining. These were viewed with suspicion by employers and with approval by organized labor as being the camel's nose. In the early twenties employers and unions changed sides on the issue. Employers promoted the company unions (erstwhile shop committees) as an open-shop weapon and as an advantageous device for the rising personnel movement.

Over a million and a half workers were covered by the various company representation plans in 1928. Then from the beginning of the depression the number of plans was sharply reduced until NRA put a premium on collective bargaining. Employers, however, wanted a foil to independent unionism. Until the National Labor Relations Act of 1935—or rather its validation by the Supreme Court in 1937—so limited company unions that they were no longer useful to employers, there was no obstacle to their formation as long as the employer's agency in them did not involve coercion. Of 593 such unions in 1935, almost two thirds had been formed since 1933. By 1935 company unions embraced about 2,500,000 workers. The Bureau of Labor Statistics concluded that over two fifths of the company unions were started to oppose progress of independent unions, nearly a fourth were due more generally to the passage of NRA, a fifth were attributable to strikes; only a tenth had as chief motive the improvement of employer-employee relations.

It is not necessary to show how a representation plan, of whatever sort, with members and all of its officers confined to one company, was very rarely indeed independent of the management, no matter what the pretexts. Typically it was inspired and financed by the employer; petty grievances, some of which, if left unadjusted, might have led to trouble, were often effectively dealt with, but legitimate collective bargaining, particularly if it resulted in a contract covering crucial matters, was the distinct exception. Company unions were "kept." They were haunted by fears, lacked strike funds and the outside support of numbers and of expert bargaining agents. Taken all in all, probably not over 20 per cent of workers under NRA were represented by independent unions.

Of course not every employer antagonized the independent unions under NRA. But leaders in important industries did not rely on their ability to circumvent Section 7(a) through company unions, and submitted codes which "interpreted" or nullified the mandatory labor provisions. The example of the automobile industry was the most influential. Its draft code at first claimed the right of employers to continue their traditional open-shop policy. General Johnson, NRA administrator, overruled this, only to approve the code containing wording not different in effect.

NRA and the President were tender of the automobile industry. It was the focus of much raw materials and industrial production; it had been disastrously depressed; it was reluctant to frame a code with Section 7(a), and the Ford Company never did submit; most of all, the automobile industry was depended upon to lead recovery. So NRA backed and filled, while other industries clamored for similar favored treatment and, with cause, were disgruntled when denied it. The further damage to NRA through the mode of settlement of the 1934 automobile strike will be explained below. NRA similarly shifted ground in the bituminous coal code, in this case in deference to growing union strength. The result was constant strife, an injunction forbidding application of the code to Kentucky operators, and the President's plea that Congress should pass the Guffey Coal Bill even though doubtful of its constitutionality. The Weirton Steel Company disregarded the collective bargaining machinery of NRA and secured a decision from a federal district court that held Section 7(a) unconstitutional, and government appeal from this ruling was still pending when the whole NRA was invalidated. No feature of the codes was so controverted as the collective bargaining provisions. Organized labor, in trying to hold NRA to its plain commitment, lost momentum that should have resulted in larger membership gains.

EARLY STRIKES UNDER THE NEW DEAL

The National Labor Board was set up by the President, at the request of the Industry and Labor Advisory Boards of NRA, to supervise labor relations. It was composed of an equal number of representatives of employers and employees, with an impartial chairman. The board had its hands full from the first with the epidemic of strikes which accompanied NRA. The business boomlet which followed the announcement of NRA worked in several ways to injure the prospects and thwart the operations of NRA itself. It provoked unregulated production, at low wages, production which was needed to nourish the undertaking. Prices and profits rose faster than wages. Then, with NRA moving off slowly, industry faltered, re-employment lagged. Workers had been guaranteed rights and would test them. The result was the outbreak of strikes in 1934 and 1935 in a variety of fields, some of them hitherto completely unorganized. Troops were called out in sixteen states, two score workers were killed. Earlier, attempts to unionize the strategic automobile industry had hardly gone beyond the paper stage. The workers were in the main unskilled, many of them fresh from farms. Because of the practice of putting out yearly models, production was seasonal. The employers were solidly phalanxed to maintain the open shop. Detroit had been a Mecca in the era of "automobile prosperity," and the slump produced desperate unemployment. When revival came, these conditions expressed themselves in intolerable speed-up of the assembly lines which turned out cheap cars at the cost of much human scrap.

The workers were ready to respond even to the inept organizing campaign of the Federation. They came in large numbers into federal locals which were viewed by top union officials with mingled satisfaction and suspicion pending the day when the contest between industrial and craft structure would have to be resolved. Early in March, 1934, some 2,000 workers of the Fisher Body Company voted to strike for a 20 per cent wage increase, a thirty-hour week, and recognition of collective bargaining; this decision was followed by a call for 44,000 workers to strike on March 21. General Johnson lived in the air between Washington and Detroit. The day before the strike was to commence President Roosevelt got a postponement, sat long and late with manufacturers and labor leaders in the White House, and forced through a compromise settlement which he declared embodied "a new course in social engineering." This was simply a plan for proportional instead of majority representation of workers in any collective bargaining committee. A special Automobile Labor Board, reporting directly to the President, and therefore outside NRA, was to hold elections which would register the strength of any and every union group. This scheme meant sending to the employer a motley panel speaking discordantly for perhaps as many as ten unions, including one or more fostered by the company and several mere splinter factions; under it the attempt at collective bargaining was the failure that the manufacturers intended. The strike was averted for the time, but the board was regarded by the workers as partial to the employers, labor organizers who had agreed to the compromise were distrusted, and trouble was preparing for the future.

One of America's few approaches to a local general strike paralyzed San Francisco in mid-July, 1934. It began with the longshoremen, who wanted better wages, hours, union recognition, and exclusive union control of the hiring halls. Spreading from the waterfront, the strike soon enlisted 127,000 workers, virtually the whole force of port and city except those permitted to continue essential services. General Johnson tried to rule the storm, but added to the fury; he denounced the Communists who had worked this iniquity. Nine thousand police and militiamen were rendered unnecessary by the more conservative union leaders who called off the strike, securing a compromise settlement for the dock workers.

The cotton textile industry was flatulent from overcapacity. Manufacturers had migrated from older centers to the South, chiefly to get cheap nonunion labor. Even while the rest of the country was prosperous, it was apparent that they had exceeded themselves, and the code had as its prime object reduction of output. The code minimum wages, low as they were, stimulated managers to increase the "stretch-out" by which workers were required to operate more machinery. Complaints brought tardy investigation and unsatisfactory adjustment, several times repeated. A walkout of Alabama mill hands in July, 1934 (against the stretch-out and anti-union discrimination, and for higher wages and collective bargaining) culminated in a call of the United Textile Workers for a national strike of half a million employees in September. Violence was general, but was most conspicuous in the South, where militiamen were ordered to intercept "flying squadrons" of strikers who sped in trucks from one mill·town to another routing out the workers. The National Labor Board had just been abolished, and the new National Labor Relations Board made offers of mediation which the employers refused. After three weeks the President intervened to end the strike; a special textile labor board was set up, new studies of stretch-out and wages were made, but the workers got nothing.

LABOR'S CHARTER OF LIBERTIES

Because of its bipartisan character, the National Labor Board was more likely to compromise cases than to decide them according to the law. Conflicting authority of NRA and of the board over labor relations caused confusion. The statute to be interpreted was vague, the times were tense. The board was guilty of delays which magnified dissension, but it stood for important principles: the majority of the workers were to be allowed to bargain for the whole unit; where there was doubt, a secret election should be held to register free choice between company union and independent union; and last, it was not enough for employers to hear the workers and dismiss their proposals, but instead there must be a bona fide effort to reach an agreement through collective bargaining. The board did not have power to enforce its decisions, but must depend on uncertain action through NRA compliance machinery and referral to the Department of Justice. When strikes produced an impasse, the issue was resolved, as in steel, textiles, and automobiles, by setting up special industry labor boards which fatally weakened the National Labor Board.

Senator Robert F. Wagner, chairman of the board, tried in 1934 to bolster its position by a bill providing for "cease and desist" orders which, on questions of fact, the courts must enforce. But this attempt failed, a substitute measure was mischievous, and the upshot was that in July the President abolished the ill-fated National Labor Board and put in its place a National Labor Relations Board composed of three specialists. This board made progress over its predecessor by ruling that a company union dominated by the employer was not an approved instrument for collective bargaining by workers; since such unions were barred from holding elections, rules of a number of them were revised to remove offensive features.

Two months after NRA was declared unconstitutional Senator

Wagner salvaged and fortified the collective bargaining provisions of Section 7(a) by securing the passage of the National Labor Relations Act. It may be treated here because it grew directly out of the NRA experience. The act rested on the authority of Congress to prevent industrial strife which impeded interstate commerce. Thus large groups of workers—in service trades, agriculture, public employment, and the like—were excluded from protection of the law because they were not engaged in interstate commerce. Soon, however, states began to pass acts modeled more or less closely on the national statute, so that the total coverage was increased.

The Wagner Act declared that "employees shall have the right to self-organization, to form, join, or assist labor organizations, to bargain collectively through representatives of their own choosing, and to engage in concerted activities, for the purpose of collective bargaining or other mutual aid or protection." A new National Labor Relations Board of three experts (the first board of that name having gone out with NRA) was set up to interpret this general provision. The act sought to cure previous shortcomings by the express stipulation that representatives of the majority of the workers in a bargaining unit should have power to speak for the whole, and, crucially important, that the board should determine what was the appropriate bargaining unit—whether the company, the shop, or the craft. Further, the board was empowered to prohibit five "unfair practices" of employers: (1) interference with employees in the exercise of guaranteed rights; (2) financial or other support of a company union; (3) use of hiring and firing to encourage membership in a company union or discourage membership in an independent union; (4) discrimination against a worker because he complained to the board; and (5) refusal to bargain collectively with the representatives of the employees; of course this could not prevent a deadlock where a genuine effort to reach agreement had been made.

Flushed with victory in the recent invalidation of NRA and other New Deal measures, opponents of the administration were primed to discredit the Wagner Act. Fifty-eight prominent lawyers allied with the American Liberty League issued an opinion that the law was unconstitutional, and advised employers to disregard it. Such efforts hampered the work of the board until, in April, 1937, in five test cases involving a variety of businesses, the Supreme

Court upheld the act. In January, 1938, the Supreme Court ended an abuse by deciding that federal district courts might not enjoin proceedings of the board, since by the act enforcement lay with the circuit courts, and no damage to an employer could be shown until the board had made its decision.

The board designated the collective bargaining agency, informally on evidence before it, or formally through an election. The company union, properly so called, was treated as the illegality that the act intended. The procedure of the board for redressing workers' grievances was designed for prompt, informal, and local settlement, in which regional offices and trial examiners, dismissing or adjusting cases, played effective part. In the first five years the board and its officers acted in nearly 30,000 cases involving nearly 6,500,000 workers, two thirds of the cases being concerned with anti-union discrimination and a third with elections. Nine out of 10 cases were closed by agreement of the contenders; 2,161 strikes were settled and 280,168 strikers were reinstated; the board averted 869 threatened strikes involving 202,417 workers; elections numbered 3,492, in which 1,261,130 votes were cast.

Contrary to the belief of many, the National Labor Relations Board did not deal, except indirectly, with substantive matters of dispute between workers and management, nor did it act as mediator. It was charged with protecting the right of independent labor organization and representation, and with forbidding unfair labor practices that would obstruct this right. The steps by which complaints reached the board were gradual, from regional to central authority, and in the process every opportunity was given for withdrawal of cases without merit or for their voluntary adjustment. A complaint was first lodged with the regional office; a field man looked into the matter and half of all cases were dismissed or settled at this stage. If there was evidence of violation of the law, the examiner and regional director urged the employer to conform, and, with the aid of some informal mediation, additional cases were ended at that stage. If the employer was not impressed, the regional director issued a formal complaint, detailing the unfair labor practices found. Some weeks were allowed the employer to answer this before a trial examiner was appointed by the Washington office to hear witnesses on both sides. Less than 6 per cent of cases got this far.

Following the hearing, the trial examiner stated the contentions of both sides in a report which each was invited to criticize. The record, by this time probably voluminous, was then transmitted to Washington for examination finally by the board itself. If the employer was found guilty as charged, the board still used persuasion in the effort to secure compliance. If the employer remained stubborn, the board issued its "cease and desist" order and requested a circuit court to enforce this by an order of its own. Thus the employer had a further opportunity to argue his case, which he might carry, if he chose, to the Supreme Court. However, if the circuit court upheld the board's findings, the employer must obey.

VIOLATIONS OF LABOR'S CIVIL RIGHTS

Many among the largest employers in the country were arrogantly scornful of the protections vouchsafed to labor in Section 7(a) of NRA and later in the National Labor Relations Act. Shown in their open, almost flaunting obstruction of the work of the board, employers' determination to set the new legal guarantees at naught was no less present in industrial spying. Resort to labor undercover men was an old abuse which took on new ubiquity in the twenties and was full blown in the thirties. President William H. Johnston of the Machinists in the twenties had said in private conversation that industrial espionage was in his judgment the chief problem confronting American unions. He went on to tell how a local of boilermakers had discovered that one of their officers was a spy in the pay of a detective agency engaged by the employer. On the next meeting night the members locked the doors of the hall and showed the miscreant their proof, which he could not deny. They then moved the chairs against the wall and after they had finished with the wretch, he spied no more. Clinch Calkins, alluding to the middle thirties, said the spy racket thrives "in times of labor upsurge when workers, compelled and aided by political and economic forces of the moment, feel confidence in their strength to roll away a stone of any magnitude. It is then that spies introduced by management into the labor body multiply and move through it like maggots, corrupting its strength from within." [8]

[8] *Spy Overhead, The Story of Industrial Espionage* (New York: Harcourt, Brace and Company, 1937), p. 22.

Huberman estimated that there was a spy in every one of the 41,000 locals in the United States, and Heber Blankenhorn of the National Labor Relations Board figured that spies cost industry about $80,000,000 a year—40,000 of them at $175 per spy per month.[9]

Gardner Jackson, of Washington, who was the friend of popular rights in many directions, proposed full exposure of the extent and evils of industrial spying through protracted investigation by the La Follette Civil Liberties Committee; the NLRB gave it impetus and constant support.[10] Senator Robert M. La Follette, the chairman, in hearings in several parts of the country, had the assistance of diligent preparation by the subcommittee's attorney, John Abt. Senator La Follette used the novel device of putting on the stand up to a dozen witnesses at once, which made for vivid revelation.

Every sort of employing corporation was represented among the customers of the industrial detective agencies. In the period 1934–1936 the Corporations Auxiliary Company served, among others, Aluminum Company of America, Chrysler, Crane, Diamond Match, Dixie Greyhound Lines, Firestone, General Motors (thirteen plants), Kellogg, Kelvinator, New York Edison, Postum, Quaker Oats, Radio Corporation of America, Standard Oil, Statler Hotels. Pinkerton Agency, 1933–1936, had among its clients Bethlehem Steel, Campbell Soup, Continental Can, Curtis Publishing Company, Endicott-Johnson, Libby-Owens-Ford, Montgomery Ward, National Cash Register, Ohrbach's Affiliated Stores, Pennsylvania Railroad, Shell Petroleum, Sinclair Refining. Railway Audit and Inspection Company had business with Borden Milk, Consolidated Gas of New York, Frigidaire, Western Union, and others.

Spies were either sent into the plants by the detective agencies or were workers found on the job who were solicited to send in regular reports of labor activities. It was found that over a third of Pinkerton spies held offices in unions.[11] The position of recording secretary was one generally sought because this officer took no ac-

[9] Leo Huberman, *The Labor Spy Racket* (New York: Modern Age Books, 1937), p. 6.

[10] U. S. Senate Education and Labor Committee, "Violations of Free Speech and Rights of Labor," Hearings on S. Res. 266, 74 Cong., 2 Sess., (S. Res. 70, 75 Cong., 1 Sess., various dates. 1936–1940.) Convenient summaries of the earlier hearings in Calkins' *Spy Overhead* and Huberman *The Labor Spy Racket*.

[11] Huberman, *The Labor Spy Racket*, p. 24.

tive part in union work, but had the list of members and a record of all that occurred at meetings.

Among the most concrete evidence of oppressive labor practices disclosed by the committee was the use of "industrial munitions." Senator La Follette quoted the committee, which had "learned that there existed an established business of supplying weapons especially adapted for use in industrial disputes. The weapons furnished for such use were principally the various forms of tear and sickening gas, with equipment such as grenades, shells, and guns for discharging them. Submachine guns are also supplied for such use, though to a lesser extent." He continued in his own words: "In investigating the Little Steel Strike of 1937, the subcommittee subpoenaed the Youngstown Sheet & Tube Co. and the Republic Steel Corporation for inventories of munitions kept on hand in their plants. The results were astonishing. The Youngstown Sheet & Tube Co. had 8 machine guns of standard Army tripod type, 369 rifles, 190 shotguns, and 454 revolvers, together with over 6,000 rounds of ball ammunition and 3,950 rounds of shot ammunition. It also had 109 gas guns, with over 3,000 rounds of gas ammunition. The Republic Steel Corporation . . . was . . . the largest purchaser of tear and sickening gas in the United States, purchasing a total of $79,000 worth in the period under investigation. . . . In addition to this gas, the . . . Corporation owned 552 revolvers, 64 rifles, and 245 shotguns, with over 83,000 rounds of ball and shot ammunition. These industrial arsenals far overshadowed the arms and gas equipment in the hands of local law-enforcement authorities in the communities in which they had plants." Senator La Follette said that the arsenals of these two steel companies "would be adequate equipment for a small war." The committee "came to the conclusion that these arms were purchased not for property protection but rather as a part of labor policy."

Half of the sales of over a million and a quarter dollars' worth of tear gas and tear gas equipment were to industrial corporations, and the other half to law enforcement bodies. Also, over two thirds of the tear gas bought by industrial corporations was bought at a time when unions were demanding recognition. The Republic Steel Corporation had a uniformed police force of nearly 400 men equipped not only with revolvers, rifles, and shotguns, "but also with more tear and sickening gas and gas equipment than has been purchased by any other corporation, or by any law-enforcement body, local, State, or Federal, in the country. It has loosed its guards, thus armed, to shoot down citizens on the streets and highways." [12]

RESULTS OF NRA ON LABOR CONDITIONS

The President's Re-employment Agreement gave jobs to about 2,462,000 persons between June and October, 1933, through reducing weekly hours of work. The increase in employment in agriculture in this period was negligible; in other than NRA industries it was 4.4 per cent, but in NRA industries it was 11.4 per cent. Industrial activity in this period declined; hence the increase in employment was the result of shorter hours. In a sample of industries analyzed, those averaging more than 45 hours of work a week were reduced from approximately 30 per cent of the total in June, 1933, to less than 2 per cent of the total in October, 1933; those averaging between 40 and 45 hours were reduced from 38 per cent in June to 5 per cent in October; on the other hand, the percentage of industries with hours less than 40 increased during the period. For all the industries, manufacturing and nonmanufacturing, covered in the monthly reports of the Bureau of Labor Statistics, the reduction in average hours was from 43.3 in June to 37.8 in October, or 12.7 per cent.

However, NRA codes, after they substantially superseded the President's Re-employment Agreement, added very little to the number of jobs between October, 1933, and the first five months of 1935 in spite of a gain in manufacturing production of 14 per cent. This situation was partly due to the fact that half of the industries increased average weekly hours during this period and yet remained within code limits. It was more largely due to tolerances, exceptions, and exemptions that in many cases permitted employers to avoid hiring additional workers. The basic forty-hour week was established in 84 per cent of the codes, in industries employing 13,000,000 or 57 per cent of the total number of workers. But in 64 per cent of the codes, covering 61 per cent of employees in codified industries, provisions permitted a work week of forty-eight hours or longer for many of these workers. Management insisted that flexibil-

[12] Senate Committee on Education and Labor, Hearings on S. 1970, 76 Cong., 1 Sess., pp. 24–29.

ity in the labor force was the necessary means of meeting fluctuations in production, and secured the option of extending hours under certain circumstances with or without overtime pay. The abuse in the application of loosely drawn provisions reduced the re-employment which the codes were intended to accomplish. Flat maximum hour schedules appeared in more than a third of the codes, covering 8,000,000 workers. These limitations in hours were generally effective because the industries favored them as a way to control competition, and strongly organized workers aided enforcement. Several highly seasonal industries operated successfully with hours fixed at forty or below on a flat basis.[13]

Labor contended that codes should at least provide for each worker an adequate annual living wage, minima should be above this level in hazardous and responsible jobs, and wages should be raised to increase mass purchasing power and labor's share in the national income. Efficient management, labor felt, would make this program feasible. However, though NRA continued to give lip service to the concept of the "decent living wage," ideal criteria were not applied. NRA was satisfied if the minimum wage accomplished an increase in total labor income, approximated the minimum in better-paying establishments within the industry, and contributed to equality of wage rates among competing employers. Basic wage minima in codes ranged from 30 to 40 cents an hour; 338 codes covering 55 per cent of all codified workers had the basic minimum of 40 cents or more, and 14 codes covering 5 per cent of all employees had a basic minimum wage less than 30 cents. Particular determining considerations were wages prevailing in 1929, established area differentials, low standards in regions predominantly agricultural, and the supposed financial capacity of the industry. Besides the general limitations in codes, exceptions were frequently granted to individual employers.

More than half the codes had different minimum-wage rates for male workers in different areas or divisions of the industry. The lumber code alone had fifteen different minima. The great line of division in minimum-wage rates ran between North and South. The precedent was set in the initial code, that for cotton textiles, with its $13 weekly wage in the North and $12 in the South. Industrial-

[13] Committee of Industrial Analysis, *The NRA*, pp. 86–96.

ists of the South pled that the differential existed, that it was necessary to compensate for various handicaps of the South, and that
southern workers would not suffer because of lower living costs in
that section. Competing employers in higher-wage areas, labor, and
civic organizations speaking particularly for women and Negroes
answered that the differential was an unjust subsidy for the South,
perpetuated substandard conditions there, and discriminated against
Negroes. In practically all industries with southern establishments
the codes contained wage differentials or a very low flat minimum
which northern employers were expected to exceed. The average
area differential was 6.8 cents per hour, which tended to decrease
the North-South differentials existing before. The amount of the
differential in minimum wages ranged from 1.5 cents (the difference between 16.5 and 15 cents per hour) in the pecan shelling
code to 40 cents in the wrecking and salvaging code. Where differentials were reduced, compliance in the South was hard to secure.
Numerous factors were responsible for southern employers' resistance; perhaps the chief was the pattern of low wages traditionally paid to Negroes, especially in agriculture.

Following strong pressure by labor and women's organizations,
all codes provided that "female employees performing substantially
the same work as male employees shall receive the same rate of pay
as male employees." Nevertheless, 159 codes covering more than 16
per cent of all employees embodied a minimum wage usually 5
cents an hour lower for women workers on the ground that their
work was different from that of men in the industry. Other wage
exceptions were for learners, the aged and otherwise handicapped,
and some casual workers. Exceptions permitting wages below the
basic minimum were responsible for much evasion.[14]

Re-employment under NRA, mainly through spreading of work,
did not represent a burden on the hitherto employed workers as a
whole, though some of the better paid suffered reduction in hourly
earnings and greater reduction in weekly earnings. Principally it
was higher minimum wages that increased total wage payments.
Wages had been severely cut prior to NRA. The average hourly
wage for manufacturing and 13 nonmanufacturing industries rose,
between June and October, 1933, from a low of 43.8 cents to a high
of 52.15 cents, or 19 per cent. In an adequate sample, only about

14 *Ibid.*, pp. 97–103.

3.5 per cent of industries showed decreases. The upward movement of average hourly earnings continued through the proper "code period" of NRA, reaching, by the end of the experiment, 57.2 cents, though in this later period nearly 10 per cent of industries showed decreased average hourly earnings.

Average weekly earnings between June and October, 1933, rose by 3.6 per cent; that is, the 19 per cent increase in average hourly earnings more than offset the 12.7 per cent actual reduction in weekly hours. However, in a sample, about a third of the industries showed reduction in average weekly earnings. In the "code period" from October, 1933, to May, 1935, average weekly earnings increased 8 per cent to $21.86, though in this later period a somewhat larger percentage of industries showed reduction in weekly earnings.

The annual earnings in mining, manufacturing, and construction industries, which had been about $1,367 in 1929, fell to $902 in 1932, and to $874 in 1933. The annual wage income rose to $1,068 in 1935. In accordance with the government's great purpose to increase purchasing power, the money income of workers rose from $1,627,000,000 in June, 1933, to an average of $2,022,000,000 in the last five months of NRA.[15] It must be remembered, however, so far as workers are concerned, that the increase in the cost of living nearly or quite equaled the increase in money wages.

The reduction in child labor was a distinct social gain. The President's Re-employment Agreement forbade in most cases the employment of workers under sixteen years of age; this became the pattern in most of the codes. Reform of child labor has always been easiest in times of heavy unemployment; still, NRA is to be credited with a precedent which was influential until the extraordinary demand for workers during World War II relaxed standards. The President had declared that no sweatshop had a right to exist in the American economy, and NRA gave chief public emphasis to raising the condition of workers. Minimum wages coupled with maximum hours, embodied in NRA and the codes, plus special code provisions in the needle trades and others long cursed with exploitation of homeworkers, accomplished something toward eliminating sweatshops, though the evil was persistent.

[15] *Ibid.*, pp. 108–110.

INDUSTRIAL UNIONISTS SECEDE

A chief by-product of the New Deal, particularly of NRA, was a split in the expanding ranks of organized labor. The right to organize without employer interference, bettered employment, relief that removed the worst threats to labor standards, and the general solicitude of government for the "forgotten man" all encouraged workers in the mass production industries to form unions. They had previously been neglected by the Federation, which was dominated by craft unions jealous of their jurisdictional claims and too little mindful of the effects of the production line in American industry in limiting skills and blurring job divisions. Moreover, in the mass production industries such as automobiles, steel, oil, cement, chemicals, aluminum, electrical appliances, and textiles, the workers, mostly poorly paid, faced great corporate employers. Unionism in these industrial empires was difficult or impossible unless with collective outside help.

But the demand was there, and the Federation responded with its traditional form of interim organization, the federal labor union, which would disappear when the workers were later parceled out to their appropriate craft unions. This had been a serviceable expedient earlier, but no longer applied, since skills were obliterated and there remained only the identification of the worker with an industry. The 307 federal unions of 1932 had grown to 1,788 in 1934. Their instability was patent. Craft union presidents wanted to sift the mass for members, and were supported in their expectations by Federation officialdom. On the other hand, the workers involved felt that their only strength was in industrial solidarity, and they found allies in the existing industrial unions.

The 1934 convention of the Federation, at San Francisco, received a batch of resolutions on industrial unionism, more than a third of the convention favoring it. The result was a decision to organize industrial unions, but since the issue of charters to them was left to the craft-controlled Executive Council, nothing was accomplished. The lines were tighter drawn at the 1935 convention at Atlantic City. John L. Lewis, president of the United Mine Workers, an industrial union, who was especially eager for the similar organization of the closely related steel workers, was again the leader of the minority, now unwilling "to be seduced again." The majority of the resolutions committee, headed by the conservative John P. Frey, president of the Metal Trades Department of the Federation, stood pat, and the minority resolution for an all-out, unqualified drive to organize the mass production workers in industrial unions was defeated. The contest between craft and industrial unionism was signalized for the public by a fisticuff on the convention floor between champions, William Hutcheson of the carpenters and Lewis of the miners.

ROBUST CHAMPIONS

Hutcheson and Lewis were exaggerated prototypes of the contending sides. Hutcheson was head of the largest craft union, Lewis of the largest industrial union in the Federation. Elements of similarity emphasized their difference. Each had used his strength in tyrannous crushing of opposition in his membership. Both were supporters of the Republican party. Both were men of unusual physical size and force. Both were elder statesmen of the Federation's Executive Council.

A dozen years after joining the Brotherhood of Carpenters in his native Michigan, Hutcheson became its first vice-president and swiftly succeeded to the presidency. He felt it his duty to make a specialty of prosecuting the many jurisdictional disputes which confronted the carpenters as new methods and materials were introduced in the building trades. He gained more than he lost, for he made it a habit to absorb defeated smaller unions, thus increasing his membership without the trouble of initial organization. Though he was regularly re-elected for twenty years, his rule was clamorous with protests from the rank and file. The members charged him with sell-outs to employers, with perpetuating his control through his appointed agents, and with illegal expulsion of his enemies. His cordial association with Brindell, racketeering czar of the New York building trades who landed in Sing Sing, drew Samuel Untermeyer's accusation. He was chief labor stalwart in the Liberty League which squared off against the New Deal, and soon resigned from the Executive Council of the Federation because he would not go along with its endorsement of the Roosevelt administration. Hutcheson typically begged the question raised by the young C.I.O., reporting to his 1936 convention that the Brotherhood of Carpenters "being a Craft Organization . . . cannot agree to the organizing of the workers on an Industrial basis." If the Federation gave in, the carpenters would sever their connection with it.

The reactionary Hutcheson was incapable of learning. Not so John L. Lewis, who had profited from the hard schooling of fifteen years at the head of the United Mine Workers. He was born in Iowa of Welsh parents; his father was a black-listed miner, and John entered the pits at the age of twelve. Rising to local union office and attracting attention by his thunderous demands upon the Illinois legislature for greater safety for miners, he was made Federation legislative representative by Samuel Gompers. This position enlarged his knowledge of politics until he resigned the post to become statistician of his own union and to build a firm foundation for a national career as a labor leader. His schoolteacher wife never had another pupil approaching her husband; he acquired vocabulary, logic, and rhetoric as a vehicle, but the power that drove it was his own in plenty.

The United Mine Workers had steady trouble. At times it looked as though they were not united, and more and more of them were not mine workers. Competition within the industry was bad enough, for it had opened far too many mines. Competition of other fuels—oil, gas, electricity—coupled with more efficient uses of coal made the case desperate. Idleness of miners caused chronic restlessness. The dangers of the work, when it was available, spread bitterness that often became rebellion. Under these conditions Lewis's own management, frequently bungling, did not assist toward a solution. He expelled leaders of dissenting districts, only to raise up the rival National Miners' Union. He was guilty of irrelevant Red-baiting. During strikes he signed contracts for certain regions, the coal from which weakened the struggle elsewhere. In the later twenties and early thirties the union lost important fields altogether, and membership fell away by two thirds.

But while he blustered Lewis reflected. His able economic adviser, W. Jett Lauck, helped him plan for stabilization of the industry. Before such ideas were heard in other quarters Lewis proposed to Congress suspension of antitrust acts in favor of federal licensing of mine operators; owners were to be permitted combination in practices that would control production and support prices, while workers were to be specifically guaranteed the right to organize in independent unions. His efforts failed for the moment, but soon came NRA with its labor section, and the Guffey Act for coal. In vigorous organizing campaigns Lewis promptly got back all the miners he had lost, and more. He avoided the bad example of the Federation, which in the mass production industries was setting up federal locals preparatory to parceling out the new members to craft unions. The Federation had not acted on the half-hearted promises made at the 1934 convention to bring belt-line workers into single unions. Lewis in an eight-page memorandum drew up the score of failures and refusals of the Federation to carry out its own commitments.[16]

The weakness could be cured through millions of more members enlisted in industrial unions. If Lewis was to hold his gains in coal, the closely allied and hostile steel industry must be mass organized. He paraphrased Biblical language in pleading for the more generous policy: ". . . whereas, today the craft unions . . . may be able to stand . . . before the gale . . . yet the day may come when this changed scheme of things—and things are changing rapidly now—the day may come when those organizations may not be able to withstand the lightning. . . . Now, prepare yourselves by making a contribution to your less fortunate brethren, heed this cry from Macedonia. . . ." He and his colleagues who opposed fatal loyalty to craft traditions pled with the convention to "adopt a policy designed to meet . . . modern conditions in this industrial nation. . . ."[17]

THE FEDERATION NEEDED REFORM

The American Federation of Labor had grown stale and was overdue for renovation. In parts it was corrupt, and refused or was unable to supply correction from within. Its condition was both cause and effect of the untoward history of the twenties in which the Federation lost almost a third of its membership. Toll had been taken by the open-shop drive, company unions, improved real wages, technological unemployment, rationalization and decentralization of industry, the larger number of women and Negroes seek-

[16] American Federation of Labor, *Proceedings, Fifty-fifth Annual Convention* (1935), pp. 543–560.
[17] *Ibid.*, 541–542.

ing industrial jobs, the wholesale migration of textile and shoe factories from the Northeast, not to speak of a sharp business slump and two briefer relapses which occurred in the decade. Resistance to these developments would have been difficult in any case, but old-line labor leaders had little energy and less insight for the task. Some unions, notably among the Railway Brotherhoods, had diverted effort from necessary labor objects by trying to turn capitalist and share in financial prosperity with speculative investments in coal mines and Florida real-estate developments. Ventures in labor banks were more legitimate but hardly happier in results. In addition, particular leaders were in all degrees of collusion with employers, running from timid conciliation to criminal extortion.

The official labor movement, therefore, entered the depression in more than ordinarily vulnerable state. Demoralizing mass unemployment, with no effective relief until late in 1933, destroyed discipline, played havoc with paid-up memberships, made union scales in many instances mere fictions. Leftist critics of "labor fakers" who were "betrayers of the workers" and had been "domesticated by the bosses" to "degenerate and devitalize" the unions were apt to erect the particular into the general.[18] But even without the animus of these attackers, melancholy evidence was at hand in the successful prosecutions of labor racketeers, in the support which unions sometimes continued to give officials whose criminal activities had been exposed, and in the collaboration of union heads with employers who were prominent labor haters. Exacting bribes and employing gangsters, which were jailable offenses, were far different from joining industrialists in Red-baiting, but all might proceed from the same turn of mind. Neither criminal nor civic collaboration would have had much currency if labor leaders had been attentive to the rank and file and eager to bring into unions the masses of the unorganized. Instead, those who were guilty of these practices traded on the supposed privileged position of the comparatively few skilled workers. Temporary monopoly was the secret of operation. Demanding "strike insurance" of employers, compelling illicit contributions from their own followers, controlling election machinery which kept them perpetually in office, boldly dipping into their

18 William Z. Foster, *Misleaders of Labor* (Chicago: Trade Union Educational League, 1927); Harold Seidman, *Labor Czars, A History of Labor Racketeering* (New York: Liveright Publishing Company, 1938).

union treasuries—all these practices were made possible by the narrow context of craft organization.

Not that labor racketeers lacked the cooperation of "unscrupulous employers, crooked politicians, and professional criminals." Implicated employers paid large sums to labor leaders in order to save larger sums which should have gone in wages. Politicians shared in the booty, saw that prosecutions were quashed or indifferently handled, and referred their henchmen to labor officials for jobs. The end of prohibition set gangsters looking for other fields of endeavor. Some were called in by the unions as strong-arm men and refused to leave, getting such a grip that the unions were made to work for them. It is not necessary to tell the stories of racketeers in food handling, the building trades, cleaning and dyeing, trucking and other fields. The pattern had been set earlier, though it continued into the thirties with special virulence. Until Thomas E. Dewey began his effective prosecutions in New York there had been little check to the discreditable business in its pervasive forms.

Craft unionism in its more selfish and obtuse aspects had long been the complaint of alert labor reformers. William Z. Foster was one of these who could cite chapter and verse from his exasperating experience in trying to organize the consolidated steel industry following World War I. A large number of craft unions participated only nominally in the arduous effort, but were swift enough to assert jurisdictional claims once steelworkers were organized, and demanded that they be parceled out to twoscore loyalties. Foster and others like him demanded that the industrial form should supersede the craft type of union in mass production industries where skills were diluted and old occupational lines of demarcation were blurred. Unfortunately for the effect of their preachment, these protestants within the labor movement often adopted the new Communist allegiance. That was proper enough, but it did invite their conservative or reactionary opponents to brand them as dangerous spokesmen of a foreign power. When the radical group set up dual unions, such as those affiliated with the Trade Union Educational League, the arguments against them seemed conclusive. Many of these dissenters against traditional craft union complacency were inspired first by solicitude for progress of the American labor movement, and second by "instructions from Moscow." To the extent that they were discounted or discredited it was because of their

Communism, not because their criticisms were satisfactorily met.

Fear of Communism, pretended and real, on the part of orthodox American labor leaders in this period is a chapter in itself. As the nation sank into deep, prolonged depression, and the Soviet Union prospered and experienced a chronic shortage of workers, the political attitude of the greatest capitalist nation toward collectivist Russia became distinctly more favorable. The need for securing Soviet orders hushed business anathemas and altered general economic opinion.[19] It is doubtful, however, whether labor suspicion and hostility were mitigated. The substantial triumph over Communist attempts at penetration of the American unions had been accomplished earlier, though watchfulness must be maintained on the propaganda front.

It is fair to say that dominant American labor leaders showed less apprehension of incipient fascism than of the Communist threat. This attitude was in accordance with an old history of minorities, which generally fought harder against friends on the flanks than against foes in front. Craft unionism tempted many into an alliance with big business rather than with the mass of workers or with the interest of consumers.[20] This was something more than commendable cooperation for efficiency and industrial peace. It was forgetfulness of all class contention, a yielding to personal flattery. Elements in the patronage of privileged labor by powerful industrialists and bankers which smacked of fascist method were not perceived, much less resented or rebuffed. Instead, favored labor leaders joined their voices to those of capitalists in deploring energetic labor action. In instances strikes were cried down, compromised, or sabotaged. Self-righteous labor officials, with patriot business executives, hallooed in the hunt of the fervid Congressional Committee on Un-American Activities, of which Martin Dies was chairman.

A term was put to the most enervating form of this labor-capital collaboration when in 1935 Matthew Woll, vice-president of the American Federation of Labor, was compelled to resign from the National Civic Federation of which he was acting president. John L. Lewis for the United Mine Workers introduced a convention resolution aimed directly at Woll: "That no officer of the American

[19] Meno Lovenstein, *American Opinion of Soviet Russia* (Washington: American Council on Public Affairs, 1941).

[20] See Seidman, *Labor Czars*, p. 35.

Federation of Labor shall act as an officer of the National Civic Federation, or be a member thereof." That same day Woll hastened to protest to the convention that he had frequently tried to resign from the Civic Federation and that he was loyal to organized labor; moreover, he read a telegram to Ralph M. Easley, chairman of the Executive Board of the Civic Federation, in which he resigned once and for all. When the resolutions committee of the convention recommended adoption of the resolution, Woll seconded the motion.[21] It is not necessary here to characterize the labor advocacies of the National Civic Federation. Long before Lewis took action, observers of the labor scene had been surprised that an officer of the Federation could sit with comfort in that company, much less join with zest in its assaults.

FORMATION OF THE C.I.O.

In November, 1935, the presidents of eight industrial unions, representing, among others, miners, garment workers, printers, and textile, oil, and refinery workers, formed the Committee for Industrial Organization to promote this form of unionism within the American Federation of Labor. President William Green warned of the threat of dual unionism, but the C.I.O. leaders refused to disband, and went on to appeal to the Executive Council of the Federation in January, 1936, to issue industrial union charters to steel, rubber, auto, and radio workers. The council would do nothing of the kind; on the contrary, it ordered the C.I.O. to break up. Instead, the C.I.O. voted a half million dollars to organize steel, made energetic beginnings in other mass production industries, and received the affiliation within a year of fifteen more unions. In August the Executive Council of the Federation, under a broad interpretation of its authority, suspended the C.I.O. unions, an action which the convention confirmed. The Executive Council of the Federation followed through, and in March, 1937, ordered expulsion of all C.I.O. unions from city and state federations.

The most spectacular organizing and bargaining success of the C.I.O. was in steel, an industry as traditionally hostile to unions as it was powerful and consolidated. Under an agreement with the

[21] American Federation of Labor, *Proceedings, Fifty-fifth Annual Convention* (1935), pp. 438–439, 474–475, 794.

practically moribund Amalgamated Association of Iron and Steel Workers, which was a Federation affiliate, the C.I.O. set up a Steel Workers' Organizing Committee early in 1936 and put $500,000 and skilled leadership into the campaign. Fruitful work was done within the company unions, where strong dissent had already developed. The nation was surprised when the United States Steel Corporation —or, more accurately, its chief subsidiary, the Carnegie-Illinois Steel Company—signed a contract with S.W.O.C. in March, 1937, granting a wage increase, an eight-hour day, a forty-hour week, vacations with pay, and seniority rights. These terms were subsequently improved, after other U. S. Steel subsidiaries and independent firms, to the number of 114, were in agreement with the union. "Big Steel" had its reasons for signing up after years of bitter and successful opposition: the corporation wanted no labor trouble in an impending period of prosperity and increased production; the disaffection of its company unions was probably one factor, as the wisdom of falling in with the evident new industrial policy of the country was another.

The flush of this victory of the workers was suddenly cooled by the determined refusal of four "Little Steel" companies—Republic, Bethlehem, Inland, and Youngstown Sheet and Tube—to recognize the union. The resulting strike, beginning in May, 1937, illustrated time-honored methods of management, made possible by the dominant position of the companies in the communities where they operated. The figure of Tom Girdler, of Republic Steel, suggested a character from Dickens or even one from melodrama. However, Girdler was real enough, and the strike was completely lost. But it was lost on the picket lines only to be fully won, four years later, in the courts and through the National Labor Relations Board, for the last-ditch "Little Steel" companies all recognized the union when it demonstrated its control of the majority of their workers. By the time the United States entered the war, S.W.O.C. had some 600,000 members covered by contracts.

THE OPEN-SHOP CITADEL FALLS

The characteristic achievement of the C.I.O. was in organizing the automobile industry, which stood as the model of mass production, and employed almost entirely semiskilled and unskilled work-

ers, most of these drawn from small towns and rural districts. The
industry had been virtually untouched by unionism; its reputation
for good pay, owing to Henry Ford's influence, had its counterpart
in assiduous anti-union institutions. The greatest single center of the
industry—Detroit—was, more completely than Pittsburgh and more
studiedly than Los Angeles, the embodiment of the open-shop strategy. Further, the automotive industry reached out its tentacles to
many others which were fit subjects for mass organization of labor
—chiefly steel, glass, rubber, and textiles. Also, three huge companies—General Motors, Chrysler, and Ford—dominated the whole,
and had widespread linkages with other areas of American manufacture, mining, transportation, and finance. Automobiles, even
more than steel, would be the test of prowess of the new industrial
unionism.

The C.I.O. structure was built from the badly disintegrated
foundations laid by the Federation in the Detroit area. As soon as
the NRA was announced, a rash of disconnected strikes broke out
in the automobile industry, the result of rank and file protest against
protracted unemployment, wage cuts, attempted domination of the
union by the company, assisted by spies, and an unconscionable
speed-up. Half a dozen unions were formed, besides splinter bodies
that added to the confusion. In this situation, wise policy would
have seen that strength welled up from below, would have respected this and shaped a single great organization that would have
answered the poorly expressed mass demand.

For this opportunity the Federation was badly equipped in tradition, insight, and method. Recalcitrancy of the industry toward
NRA, partial in the case of General Motors and Chrysler, openly
defiant on the part of Ford, hampered the effort. Still, a hundred
federal labor locals were set up by 1934, with membership probably
in excess of 150,000. This was an uneasy accomplishment because
the rank and file found unity among the locals delayed by the Federation leadership. They feared with reason that if a national organization were authorized it would be weakened by old-line Federation demand that the skilled craftsmen, filling critical places, be
separated and assigned to other unions. A threatened general strike
in the industry in March, 1934, which promised to be successful
but which the President and his whole administration feared would
blunt the recovery drive, was averted when Roosevelt called man-

agement and union leaders to Washington. It has been explained elsewhere how a settlement was postponed by the establishment of a special Automobile Labor Board to hold elections and to provide for proportional instead of the majority representation which had been followed as a national rule. The Federation's consent to this was fatal to its future leadership of the automobile workers.

Detroit suffered its own peculiar and long-drawn misery in the depression. It was "automobile prosperity'" in reverse. Unemployment, with merest subsistence, was only the most conspicuous feature of a shattered economy, banks and real estate crying as loudly for relief. The beginnings of improvement increased the discontent of those who received no immediate benefit. Federation organizers were few in the winter of 1934–1935 when the need was for many, and the official in charge was slow in perception and slower in action. After laggard preparation, a convention was called in August, 1935, at which the United Automobile Workers was launched. The Federation imposed the chief organizer as president, though he was anything but popular with the members. Resulting losses within a few months brought the membership down to some 20,000.

In the spring of 1936 Homer Martin became president. He was an ex-preacher turned auto worker, with enthusiasm, oratorical gifts, and the common touch, but he lacked judgment and staying power. Under Martin the new union became militant in organizing and striking, promptly joined the C.I.O., and shortly was suspended by the Federation. At this time, the autumn of 1936, it had 30,000 members. After a year of boldest action it claimed 400,000 members and contracts with 381 companies.

"Quickie" and "sitdown" strikes broke out in the automobile industry in December, 1936. The C.I.O. wanted to continue for a time to put its main strength into steel, but the auto workers could not be restrained. Strikes in glass works and tire factories were proving successful, and sit-downs began in the Fisher Body plant in Cleveland and spread to Flint. Ambitions rose. The officers of General Motors, the Goliath of the industry, were asked for a conference, but referred the union to the superintendents of its individual plants and subsidiaries. The result, in January, 1937, was a concerted strike against General Motors. The sit-down was the chief weapon. A surprise to the corporation, an outrage in the eyes of lawyers and courts, and an insuperable obstacle to police and sheriffs unless they were to provoke bloody battles in assaulting the held plants, this novel union device brought General Motors, as others, to terms. After six weeks Governor Frank Murphy of Michigan, who showed high intelligence and courage throughout, brought about a settlement that was a nearly unqualified victory for the workers and confirmed the C.I.O. in self-confidence and in public respect for its power. The union got exclusive bargaining rights in twenty plants and was to represent its own members in twice as many more. All strikers were rehired, legal prosecutions were stopped, grievance machinery was set up. The corporation did not concede the closed shop, but this was only a temporary and technical loss to the workers. A sit-down against Chrysler ended in capitulation of that company in April, 1937.

FORD BROUGHT INTO LINE

The next campaign of the United Automobile Workers was against Ford. Not only was he against unions in principle, but he had an effective "service" complement of spies and sluggers to keep organization out of his plants. A few assembly shops were quickly gained by the union. The River Rouge plant, a huge industrial concentration with 85,000 workers, just outside Detroit, was another matter. Richard T. Frankensteen, an organizer, and others of the union were badly beaten in May, 1937, when they attempted to distribute leaflets outside the plant gates; Ford maintained they were assailed by "loyal workers," but all the evidence showed the attackers were company guards. A month later the National Labor Relations Board cited the Ford Motor Company for interference with the union; the company disputed the constitutionality of the Labor Relations Act. Violence spread to other Ford plants in Dallas and Memphis, with more citations by NLRB. Progress was slow. The fresh depression of 1937–1938 precipitated a division in the union that led to R. J. Thomas's election as president of the faction recognized by the C.I.O.; Martin affiliated his group with the Federation. The U.A.W.-C.I.O. swept NLRB elections, receiving some 166,000 votes to 37,000 for the U.A.W.-A.F.L.

The Ford Organizing Committee went into full action at River Rouge in the autumn of 1940. As a result of the discharge of eight union leaders in the following April, a strike made 200,000 Ford employees idle. The company met with Philip Murray, C.I.O. president, agreed to a temporary settlement that favored the union, and promised to expedite the election the next month to determine on a bargaining agent. The C.I.O. won by 51,000 to 20,000 over the Federation. Ford then agreed to the closed shop, the check-off, retroactive wage increases, seniority, grievance machinery, and the termination of its "service" department. The U.A.W.-C.I.O. bargained for all Ford workers, and in a new contract with General Motors it assumed the bargaining rights in 81 plants instead of 60, covering 175,000 workers instead of 130,000. The new Chrysler contract was also favorable to the union.

With the country's defense program began the expansion of the union into related industries. In 1941, with a paid membership of 392,000, the union changed its name to United Automobile, Aircraft, and Agricultural Implement Workers of America. As a result of the war this was to become the largest union in the world, with a million members. The growth was not achieved without damaging dissension due to political differences, unauthorized strikes which caused the government to seize aviation factories, and the weakness resulting from the sudden addition of undisciplined, unskilled members. However, intelligent efforts were made to remedy defects by establishing departments and promoting education within the union.

ACCOMPLISHMENTS IN RUBBER AND TEXTILES

Space permits only brief mention of successful C.I.O. invasion of other mass production industries. Earlier attempts to unionize in rubber tires and tubes had succumbed to welfare and employee representation plans of the four great companies, centered at Akron. Encouraged by NRA, however, many federal locals were formed by the Federation, with combined membership of 20,000. Winning of strikes went side by side with resistance to the Federation policy of splitting off many of the rubber workers to craft jurisdictions. Late in 1934, industrial unionists dominated the United Rubber Workers Council and secured a Federation charter in 1935. After a dramatic strike against Goodyear in 1936, ending in union recognition, the Rubber Workers joined the C.I.O. More strikes in and around Akron followed, and Firestone, United States Rubber, Goodrich, and Goodyear signed union contracts. The union had over 80,000 members and represented 60 per cent of the workers of the industry.

Textile workers benefited mightily from the C.I.O. The old Federation union, under stimulus, rapidly increased its membership to 350,000 in 1934. But the big strike in September of that year against low NRA wages and the intensified stretch-out (requiring the workers to tend more machinery), helped by much enthusiasm but hindered by insufficient funds, had been called off. A board appointed by President Roosevelt recommended full study of the issues and that a special Textile Labor Relations Board be established to deal with them. The results were the delay of remedies and the discredit, in the eyes of many, of leaders of the United Textile Workers. Hence the union officers turned over the new drive of the C.I.O., which began early in 1937, to the Textile Workers Organizing Committee, of which Sidney Hillman was chairman. Hillman, president of the Amalgamated Clothing Workers, had a history of success in the mass unionizing, on industrial lines, of low-paid workers in an allied field. He was a skillful and imaginative commander, and had the assistance of an indispensable research chief, Solomon Barkin, and a large corps of organizers with unusual training.

The problem was worthy of the talents summoned to its solution. For years the main cotton branches of the textile industry, as a number of others, had been in migration to the South, where wages were lowest, unionism had a tradition of repeated failure, and the communities, including many of the workers themselves, were strongly prejudiced against intervention from the North. This meant that the basis of the industry in New England and the Middle states was dangerously undermined, for the South presented a solid obstacle of substandard labor conditions, widespread discouragement in the workers, and a sectional chauvinism that was pitted against efforts at betterment. Successes came more readily elsewhere. The South remained the field which had to be taken. The 150 organizers assigned to that region were chosen for their native accent, Protestant faith, and reassuring appearance and manner. They were the equals or superiors of the bosses. A notable instance, as a general public relations officer, was Lucy Randolph Mason, of Virginia, a worthy branch of the noblest family tree. The effort was more than industrial; it was also social and cultural, claiming for this largest group of Southern factory workers full place as citizens. The campaign was well supplied with funds, Hillman's Amalgamated Clothing Workers contributing half a million dollars, the International Ladies' Garment Workers' Union and other C.I.O. units giving generously, so that the mobilization was comprehensive and sustained.

The Textile Workers Organizing Committee strove on all fronts at once, being a main force in securing passage of the Fair Labor Standards Act, which improved minimum wages and maximum hours. This was the best means of abolishing the abuses that had existed as long as southern state legislatures enjoyed autonomy in fixing statutory labor conditions. By 1939 the T.W.O.C. had enrolled 450,000 members, of whom 275,000 were under contract.

PROGRESSIVE LABOR POLITICS

Inevitably, the C.I.O. took an active part in politics. It was a mass movement of workers of less skill whose economic power to protect their jobs and improve their conditions was relatively weak, and needed to be supplemented by favorable legislation and public administration. The C.I.O. came on the scene near the start of the New Deal, when government intervention on behalf of the "forgotten man" was the cry. The C.I.O. opposed the Federation, including the latter's faint and diffused political action. In periods of depression, when industrial force is hard to apply because of unemployment, workers have always tended to rely on political effort. Lastly, the C.I.O., as a new movement needing to recruit large numbers of organizers, educational directors, journalists, and officers of all grades, was able to attract the services of many college men and women, who in better times would have been looking for positions in business and the professions. These were little acquainted with the techniques of unionism as such, and had small patience for the infinite detail of instilling union discipline; rather, they thought in ethical and political terms.

The C.I.O. formed Labor's Non-Partisan League in 1936, with George Berry, head of the Printing Pressmen and later to be United States Senator from Tennessee, as president, John L. Lewis as chairman of the executive board, and Sidney Hillman as treasurer. It was

out-and-out New Deal in allegiance. The Mine Workers contributed
half a million dollars to re-elect Roosevelt that year. The League
gave the President powerful help in the campaign, though just how
much may not be determined. That the aid was more than sentimental in motive was shown in 1937 when Lewis, seeking to have
Roosevelt intervene on behalf of the striking steelworkers, reminded
him of the C.I.O. votes cast in his behalf. The President's "plague
o' both your houses" rejoinder appeared to Lewis ungrateful, not to
say traitorous, and played its part in returning Lewis to his old
Republican loyalty. In the 1940 presidential campaign, Lewis, over
the widest radio hookup ever used by a labor leader to that time,
appealed to C.I.O. members to vote for Wendell Willkie, and promised to resign from the leadership of the C.I.O. if Roosevelt were
re-elected. He did resign, and Philip Murray, a vice-president of
the United Mine Workers, became president of the C.I.O.

Labor's Non-Partisan League sponsored or conducted important
state and local political campaigns, the chief being that of the
American Labor party in New York, which in 1936 mustered a quarter of a million votes for Roosevelt and Governor Lehman, and in
1937 cast almost twice as many in New York City to re-elect Mayor
La Guardia and make Thomas E. Dewey district attorney. The
American Labor party appealed not only to workers but to middle-
class liberals. However, its basis, in organizational strength and in
funds, was the needle trades unions of New York City. Less suc-
cesful local campaigns were conducted by the C.I.O. Non-Partisan
League in Detroit and in Pennsylvania.

The political activities of the C.I.O. alarmed conservative persons, who considered, rightly, that the economic *status quo* was
safest when votes of organized workers were divided between the
candidates of different parties. The prospect of economic demands
joined to political compactness seemed to them dangerous to their
interests and consequently to America. A part of the resulting effort
to discredit C.I.O. political action was the constant allegation that
it was Communist in inspiration. The truth was that a relatively
small number of Communists, ardent in the duties they assumed,
were effective in the organizing work of the C.I.O. and in its political wing as well, but they were far from being the strength of the
movement.

Limited Dividend Housing

Completing Hillside, a WPA development of 1,415 apartments in the Bronx, New York, 1935. (*Acme*)

New Homes for Old

This type of housing project, financed by public money, was constructed on the fringes of industrial areas or on sites cleared of slums. (*Underwood Stratton*)

An Atlanta Slum

Part of the shantytown that once bordered Atlanta University. The wooden houses, crowded together, had few sanitary facilities, few sidewalks, and no paved streets. (*Underwood-Stratton*)

The Same Site after Clearing

The work of the WPA Housing Division in progress on 675 living units of a project costing $2,500,000. (*Underwood-Stratton*)

To Build Soil and People

President Roosevelt dedicating TVA's Chickamauga Dam. (*Acme*)

Irrigation and Power Project

This project on the North Platte River, Nebraska, was typical of large public works which gave employment, directly or indirectly, and permanently served useful purposes. (*Underwood-Stratton*)

Boulder Dam Power
for Los Angeles

The 287,500-volt transmission line required installation of special insulator stacks, shown here. (*Underwood-Stratton*)

"Nonsense, If It Gets Too Deep, You Can Easily Pull Me Out."

A cartoon by Herbert Johnson. (*By permission of the artist's estate*)

PWA Flood Control

Part of the project in the Muskingum watershed, eastern Ohio.
(*Underwood-Stratton*)

For Ocean-Going Ships on the Mississippi

Construction of Lock 26 at Alton, Illinois, part of the PWA program for navigation
and flood control. (*Underwood-Stratton*)

A New Hand

A farmer grinding an axe while he pumps water with a small motor powered by a TVA rural line. (*Acme*)

Contour Plowing

A caterpillar diesel tractor pulling a five-moldboard plow. Further mechanization of agriculture was one of the causes and accompaniments of the depression. (*Underwood-Stratton*)

Bombers for Britain

Production of munitions gave the American economy its first sure revival from the depression. The Lockheed Aircraft Corporation, 1939. (*Acme*)

Urgent War Production Replaced Unemployment

Douglas Aircraft Company's Santa Monica Plant getting a "pep talk" from an officer of the War Department, 1941. (*Acme*)

The Japanese Crisis—December 7, 1941

Ambassador Nomura (*seated*) waiting for a final interview with Secretary of State Cordell Hull. (*Acme*) The Japanese Embassy burning its records. (*Wide World Photos*)

Americans on the Allied War Council, 1941

Major General H. H. Arnold, Secretary of War Henry L. Stimson, Admiral Harold R. Stark, Secretary of the Navy Frank Knox, General George C. Marshall, and Admiral Ernest L. King. (*Acme*)

ABORTIVE ATTEMPTS AT LABOR PEACE

Attempts at reunion of the Federation and the C.I.O., though repeatedly urged by such experienced leaders as David Dubinsky, did not succeed. However, in the progress of these efforts as the Federation lost its original intransigency and arbitrariness, John L. Lewis adopted these qualities and forbade the C.I.O. to proceed with an arrangement in 1937 which promised to be satisfactory to both wings of the labor movement. As peace was delayed, its possibility was further removed. By the time Lewis left the presidency of the C.I.O., and so was no longer an official impediment to reconciliation, the organization had grown to such independent size and strength that it was less likely to make concessions. C.I.O. leaders were entrenched in their separate empire. The Communist minority in the C.I.O. feared unity lest this diminish its influence. The issue of industrial versus craft unionism was no longer the chief, or even a serious, cause of hostility, though dual unionism, in its most aggravated manifestations, had widened the rift.

In 1937 the growing sentiment of the rank and file in both the Federation and the C.I.O. was for a basis of agreement. Lewis so far recognized this as to propose to the Federation convention that year that a committee of one hundred from the C.I.O. meet with a committee of the same size from the Federation to conclude peace. William Green, for the Federation, answered that such a large conclave could not be fruitful. The result was that much smaller committees, three from the Federation and ten from the C.I.O., met in Washington in October. Divergent demands were composed, with the Federation making more concessions. All unions of the C.I.O.—the original twelve and those formed later— were to re-enter the Federation together. In specified industries the industrial form of organization was to apply. The Federation would amend its constitution to declare that only a convention, and not the Executive Council, could suspend or expel a union. Philip Murray, head of the C.I.O. conferees, agreed on this settlement. The C.I.O. was having its greatest success in sweeping in members, and the outlook for unified progress in the labor movement was bright. Then Lewis stepped in, condemned the agreement reached, and disrupted peace plans; Murray issued a statement saying that negotiations were off.

Thereafter, understanding became increasingly difficult. A year later the C.I.O. declared itself, as the Congress of Industrial Organizations, a permanent independent body. The International Ladies' Garment Workers' Union, refusing to be a party to dualism, withdrew from the C.I.O., which meant that its president, David Dubinsky, was no longer in the best position to continue his persistent efforts at peace. C.I.O. leaders had matured to the point of insisting on jurisdictional claims, but had not reached the wisdom of compromise. However, on the plea of President Roosevelt, negotiations were resumed in the spring of 1939. Lewis proposed that the railroad brotherhoods join with the C.I.O. and the Federation, which placed unity out of the realm of practicality. The conferences got nowhere and were discontinued. Lewis's loss of position and prestige in the C.I.O. gave no prospect of conciliation. Instead, as prosperity increased with the defense program, the evil manifestations of civil war multiplied in union scabbing, justified complaints of employers, and profound embarrassment of the Labor Relations Board.

It may be that the rivalry of the Federation and the C.I.O. stimulated organizing efforts and added to the numbers of workers brought into unions. Perhaps the split was the price that had to be paid in order to focus efforts on the mass production industries. Also, the C.I.O., addressing itself to the unskilled and the semiskilled on a broad front, developed a program that expressed a new ambition for unionism. These workers, in addition to organization vis à vis their employers, required legislative protection and stood to benefit by influencing national economic policy. Thus the C.I.O., in the excellent phrase of J.B.S. Hardman, was not content with collective bargaining only, but showed a concern about social engineering. The Federation, to be sure, had long prosecuted legislative and public relations work, with notable accomplishments, but the C.I.O., with its political wing, turned from the defensive to the offensive, and made labor a more constructive force in framing an American design for living.

If these gains from division in "the house of labor" were worth while, they were partial offsets to the greater evil resulting from civil war. It is not possible in small space to begin to recount the losses in the bitter conflict. As the enmity persisted and each camp redoubled efforts to further its own battle, every unworthy method was employed to weaken its opponent. In the process all of organized labor was to a degree discredited. The accusations long flung at foes of unionism now lay against the unions themselves and their leaders. Frequently one or another faction, eager to oust or anticipate its rival, was guilty of such collusion with an employer as no company union could well have exceeded. Too often "raiding" the membership of an opponent took the place of organizing the unorganized. When one great body assumed a position on a public issue, the other was tempted to take a contrary stand with small regard for logic. The anathemas hurled back and forth alienated many whom both needed as friends.

The fierce contest often lodged in the responsibility of the National Labor Relations Board to determine, in a given situation, what was the proper bargaining unit, and to rule on which union was to represent the workers. Especially in the beginning, claims of the C.I.O. embraced all of the employees in a plant without regard to particular processes, while the Federation was jealous of distinctions of craft. This antithesis made the work of the board, operating under a discretionary mandate, difficult in the best case, but the heat and deceptions engendered in disputes rendered it doubly so. The result was that both sides accused the board of flagrant favoritism, and interested employers and their national associations were quick to improve the opportunity to level their own charges. Proposals were made for amendment of the Wagner Act which would have bent it to endorse one form of unionism or the other, or which would have excluded large classes of workers from protection, especially those processing agricultural and forest products. Other changes were urged under the guise of reform when the purpose was to destroy the law. A congressional investigation failed to show favoritism on the part of the board but it showed that some of its agents had been crude and rash; on the other hand, the head of the board's research department was most unjustly persecuted.

In 1939 the board felt obliged to change its practice and permit employers as well as workers to petition for elections to determine representation. It had previously been held that this would allow employers to precipitate the issue prematurely to the damage of the right to organize. But the striking of plants by a rival union, when neither union was sufficiently confident of its strength to submit to an election, created an intolerable situation for the innocent employer; hence he was given relief.

The quarrel between the Federation and the C.I.O. made the jurisdictional dispute a stench in public nostrils. A long stoppage in the lumbering industry of Oregon in 1937–1938 led to a complete antilabor law enacted by referendum. It made union action virtually impossible, and was copied in other states until Supreme Court decisions held such statutes unconstitutional. Labor's internal warfare gave added excuse to the so-called Associated Farmers of California for taking the law into their own hands. The Associated Farmers were composed, not of small cultivators, as the name was intended to imply, but of agricultural corporations operating vegetable and fruit ranches, and of their allies in finance and transportation. The migrant workers found their most elemental rights of protest and organization violated by this combination, which beat and jailed those who would not be grossly exploited.

MODERATE BEGINNING OF SOCIAL SECURITY LEGISLATION

No piece of legislation showed more clearly the break with the recent past than the Social Security Act, approved August 14, 1935. Hoover had inveighed against lapse into the dole—he adopted this disparaging name for public relief—exhorting all to give in organized private charity long after incapacity of the tender heart to meet a tough problem had been demonstrated to most. After initial hesitancy, the New Deal had recourse to widespread work relief through the Civil Works Administration. This was withdrawn in the fatuous belief that sufficient private employment would offer. When this hope was promptly disappointed, direct federal relief was entered upon. Still, these measures were regarded as treatment of an emergency condition. Public relief was bold rather than brave, if this distinction may be made. It did not acknowledge that mass unemployment was a recurring disaster which must be socially provided against on a permanent basis.

Statesmen should not be too much blamed for the tardy maturing of their understanding, or for their reluctance to impose taxes for the novel purpose of social security. As late as 1932 the American Federation of Labor put itself on record as opposed to statutory unemployment compensation. In the United States as a whole, curiosity about European unemployment, old-age, and sickness insurance legislation had remained largely academic. Though intelligent advocacy of state unemployment insurance and old-age pensions had begun to bear fruit, most persons, if they thought about it, were content to rest on pioneer tradition of the self-sufficiency of the individual, or demanded no more than the scattered, well-intentioned, but often insolvent company schemes. Informed and devoted crusaders, such as I. M. Rubinow, John B. Andrews, and Abraham Epstein, were still crying in a wilderness.

The cumulative lesson of the depression set American citizens immensely forward in their appreciation of social hazards. The plan of Dr. F. G. Townsend, of Long Beach, California, for pensioning the aged, relieving unemployment, and restoring prosperity was laughed at in the beginning and sedulously fought by analysts and business interests as its popularity mounted enormously in 1935. The proposal was extravagant—a pension of $200 a month for every person of 60 who agreed to retire from work and spend his pension within the month, the whole to be financed out of a 2 per cent tax on transactions. But, in the absence of promising schemes by the orthodox, it was a natural, creditable, and instructive demand. Those who opposed it had little to offer in its place, which accounted for its vitality, in changing forms, for five years. Its chief service was to take the curse off social security legislation as officially sponsored, since the latter was so much more moderate as to appear safe by comparison.

President Roosevelt disappointed many by his failure to give active support to the Wagner-Lewis and Dill-Connery unemployment insurance bills introduced in Congress in 1934. Instead, he announced in June of that year that a Committee on Economic Security, composed of cabinet members, would study the whole question of social security legislation and report in January, 1935. The promise was swiftly and joyfully accepted in all but obdurate quarters. Indeed, the banner of "social security" was better adapted to public reassurance and to political purposes than to immediate practical performance. The planning stage, congressional course, and initial administration showed a caution which, while natural enough, contrasted with the complacent claims which the President was constantly making.

The central committee had a staff under the direction of Professor Edwin E. Witte, of the University of Wisconsin, and a large Advisory Council with President Frank Graham of the University of North Carolina as chairman. Chief debate in the planning stage revolved about the relative merits of national and federal-state systems, the social hazards to be covered, and whether financing should be through pay-roll taxes or income taxes. The report was made and corresponding bills were introduced in mid-January, 1935. The legislative history brought forward old conflicts and emphasized new ones. In general, it became increasingly clear that this was to be a modest and partial beginning in social security, and the guardians of states' rights—whether on high or low grounds—made headway.

Framers and other friends of the Social Security Act did best in not proclaiming it as a solution but in defending it as a substantial beginning from which further progress would surely be made. Once the institution was accepted, its protections would be extended. At the start it was limited by constitutional inhibitions which divided authority between federal and state powers; roughly half the population was excluded from unemployment and old-age insurance; benefits were small; sickness insurance was omitted. The act embraced five groups: the unemployed, the aged, the handicapped, widows and dependent children, and, through added provision for public health, the general population.

FEDERAL-STATE SYSTEM

The unemployment compensation scheme, or rather schemes, became those of the states, enacted under virtual federal compulsion and subject to a minimum of federal supervision. The federal government taxed all employers in included classes 3 per cent of their annual pay rolls, 90 per cent of which was deductible from any pay-roll tax collected by the state. It was a foregone conclusion that all states would pass approved laws in order to retain the bulk of pay-roll taxes within their own borders. Without such coercion, action of the states would have been slow and uncertain, each refusing as long as possible to burden its own employers. The national government retained 10 per cent to reimburse states for the cost of administration of their laws. The full tax was to be reached gradually—1 per cent in 1936, 2 per cent in 1937, 3 per cent in 1938.

The Social Security Board, set up by the federal government to oversee the most important parts of the law, distributed a model statute for rough guidance of the states in framing their acts. The speed with which states sought and followed this direction was a lesson in the benefit of national pressure. Debate which would have been elaborate in the proportion that it was reluctant was foreshortened, with agreement given promptly before the federal tax gatherer clutched. Still, there were variations in state plans. From the beginning, some states required contributions from workers, though most did not. But the main distinction was between (1) the pooled fund, all employers paying the same percentage of pay roll available for all benefits, and (2) "merit rating" schemes which exacted smaller contributions from employers with less unemployment. Of the second type, the Wisconsin law, existing before the national act was passed, was the most influential example. This provided not for a pooled fund, but for individual plant reserves, each employer paying into his own reserve until it was built up to a supposed safe volume, when he stopped payments until his fund was drawn down. Most states adopted the pooled fund as simpler, more flexible, and surer in benefits to workers. Under the plan of individual plant reserve, the enterprise might fail and leave workers helpless, and most employers would be unable to accumulate a fund large enough to provide against cyclical unemployment. Further, the ability of any one firm to reduce its own unemployment was limited, and, to the extent practicable, each firm already had sufficient incentive to make this reduction without the relatively small gain from differential contribution. To be sure, groups of employers in nonseasonal industries had better claims to preferred treatment, and it was these who, taking advantage of state latitude, were later to insist upon "experience" or "merit rating" to the injury of unemployment compensation in a variety of important respects.

For the first two years under each state law, while a reserve was being accumulated, no benefits were to be paid. The Social Security Board estimated that only about 22,000,000 workers, or less than half of those gainfully employed in 1930, would be embraced. The large groups in agriculture, domestic service, shipping, government jobs, charitable and educational organizations, and those working for small employers were excluded; thus women, on account of the omission of domestics, and Negro men, because agriculture was not covered, were especially discriminated against. Ironically, unemployment itself reduced the numbers of workers entitled to benefit, for only those holding wage credits in jobs for some time before registering as unemployed were eligible to collect. The prospect was that a 3 per cent tax (2.7 per cent remaining to the states) on the average would pay insured workers half their wages for a maximum of 12 weeks if the "waiting period" between the beginning of unemployment and the payment of benefit was four weeks. The caution of planners was evident in the long waiting period which, though it prevented malingering, would sink most working families before they could be rescued. On the other hand, shortening the waiting period would more than correspondingly reduce benefits by including those out of work for short periods.

The Social Security Act required that all funds be held by the federal Treasury, that benefits be paid only through public employment offices or other approved agency, and that no worker be refused benefit because he would not take a job in a nonunion plant or where there was a labor dispute, or in which wages and hours were worse than was ordinary for that kind of work. Beyond this there were no federal standards.[22]

Americans being the most insured people in the world, the notion was that this approved protection was being applied in a new field, that of unemployment. Thus endless calculations, naïve as they were elaborate, undertook to be actuarial. The building up of a reserve fund was lovingly and trustingly regarded. Its proper magnitude, and the means of reaching this magnitude, it was assumed, could be reasonably estimated. The fund became so large that some viewed it with alarm. If conditions of full employment were restored and maintained for a considerable length of time, the fund would be bigger than the annual national income. How could it be invested without inflating values and producing a dangerous boom? Then if depression and unemployment followed, how could the prodigious investments be liquidated without accentuating hard times?

ULTIMATE RELIANCE ON NATIONAL TAX RESOURCES

Obsession with the insurance idea left scant and scornful attention for the chief rival scheme, that embodied in the Lundeen or

[22] Annual Reports of the Social Security Board, 1936, 1937, 1938.

so-called "Workers' Bill," which, after favorable report by the House Committee on Labor, was rejected by Congress. It was based on the contention that unemployment is not a measurable or insurable risk, that unemployment "experience," in any actuarial sense, as the current depression was demonstrating, had no meaning. This bill set up no reserve fund, but instead had recourse to income and inheritance taxes to provide for unemployment and the other hazards covered. Unemployment was a disease of the capitalist system; therefore, let beneficiaries compensate victims. This plan was entirely federal, to be administered by a board of workers; it embraced all of the unemployed, including the professional workers and self-employers, and would pay benefits equal to prevailing local wages from the day of unemployment. Sickness benefits were provided.

Time was to make this stone, rejected by the builders, the head of the corner. The vaunted fund was to prove to be in no sense a segregated reserve, but simply a welcome stream of added income for the federal government, which was spent for many current purposes, chiefly war. This result meant that the unemployed, the "fund" having been diverted and exhausted, were really dependent on the taxing power of government when their claims fell due. Also, within a decade the more generous coverage of the Workers' Bill was to be urged by those who had previously been more conservative. By that time income and profits taxes would have taken on a new magnitude.

The Social Security Act provided for old age through annuities and pensions. Annuities would go to workers in included classes who, with their employers, contributed to a federal fund a percentage tax on wages, rising by periods to 3 per cent each in 1948. The worker, no matter what his wage or salary, if he quit his job at the age of 65 (to make room for younger workers was the idea) would receive an annuity as long as he lived, the amount depending on his earnings, but in no case to be less than $10 a month or more than $85. Of course the first to retire would receive more than they had paid in, the difference being made up from contributions on account of younger workers, which would be higher from this cause. However, every worker, or his estate, would get back more than he himself had paid in—that is, 3 per cent of earnings plus .5 per cent interest. The calculation was that a laborer with average monthly earnings of, say, $50 for forty years would get at age 65 an annuity of $35 per month, a clerical worker who earned $100 a month would receive $53.75, and a mechanic making $150 a month would have $65 a month. The act was amended in 1939 to provide benefits for members of the retired worker's family and for his survivors.[23]

As with unemployment compensation, the same large classes of workers were omitted from the federal annuities scheme. To care for these, and for others who were not workers, a pension plan applied in any state passing a pension law and contributing from taxes. The federal government would pay 50 per cent of the monthly pension or $20, whichever was less. The charitable pension, like the contractual annuity, was intended to abolish the degrading poorhouse, substituting self-respecting maintenance of otherwise dependent old people in their own homes. Abraham Epstein, particularly, through his Association for Old Age (later Social) Security, had made the country poorhouse-conscious, or self-conscious. Much was accomplished, but some of the states, mainly in the South, because of financial incapacity and lenient federal standards, paid miserably small pensions—even when doubled by the federal contribution they would not support life. In many parts of the country humiliating qualifications were imposed for those receiving pensions. The framers of the act were cautious about national supervision of a state, even where this was accompanied by national assistance. Especially in the case of Negroes in the South, but of whites also, decent pensions and other relief allowances would often approach, equal, or exceed wages, provoking the cry that government was subsidizing idleness. Minimum living standards should have been demanded at any cost, economic or political.

The other features of the social security program may be treated briefly. The federal government would match state pensions to the needy blind up to $20 a month, as also state expenditures on training for those otherwise physically handicapped. The annual sum of $3,000,000 was appropriated to assist states in the care of crippled children. The national Treasury would give a third of monthly pensions to widowed mothers supporting needy children, as also $1,-500,000 a year to states for help in the care of dependent children in institutions. Sickness insurance being omitted from the act, a mere token took its place—$2,000,000 annually for extension of the

[23] Fifth Annual Report of the Social Security Board, 1940.

United States Public Health Service, and $8,000,000 annually to help the states in similar work, with an additional $3,800,000 going to the states for maternity and child health treatment. These small sums stood in contrast to the enormous amounts spent by the federal government to destroy and otherwise limit food and fiber which, if distributed to the poor, would have contributed far more to health. This irony was tardily and partially recognized in distributions by the Surplus Commodities Corporations and in other ways.

CHAPTER IX

Public Works

UNEMPLOYMENT, with resulting dependency, remained the country's reproach throughout the depression; indeed, after the depression, by many accepted signs, had been overcome, heavy unemployment continued. Unlike other problems, it was not susceptible to specific treatment. Unemployment had to be reached indirectly through economic revival, for unemployment *was* the depression. Some of the human suffering and some of the injury to the economy could be lessened through public assistance of several kinds. Beginning with 1932 there was an awkward progress from federal direct relief to indirect relief through works projects and on to measures attempting rehabilitation. The causes of unemployment and destitution in the midst of plenty were not corrected. The chief institution, new in America, to come out of the efforts was social insurance. This, while partially remedial, is in the main ameliorative, and at best a compromise with a problem held by some to be insoluble.

Direct governmental relief, in money or in kind, need not detain the narrative. It has been seen that the Hoover administration, after too long insistence that the "dole" would be degrading to recipients, finally acknowledged its necessity. While the New Deal deserved credit for promptly acknowledging this responsibility and hugely expanding appropriations, the Roosevelt administration, after two years, sought to end the practice, not because it was disgracing millions of individuals, but because this form of relief was burdensome to the federal government. To be sure, there were programs to displace direct relief, but these were begun only after sad delays, and their purposes were but imperfectly accomplished.

The Emergency Relief Act of 1932 provided for federal loans to help local communities carry their loads. The act of 1933, establishing the Federal Emergency Relief Administration in May, gave grants-in-aid to the states, and it was soon ruled that only public agencies might dispense relief funds. This decision was a gain, because it gave impetus to public welfare work and opened the way to requiring minimum standards in states and political subdivisions as the condition of continued federal assistance. Progress, however, was never more than partial, and to the end there was discrimination in relief allowances between racial groups and between sections of the country. The federal government never assumed the duty of removing, through relief, substandards of living. From April, 1934, to the end of that year, though some FERA funds were used for public works and rural resettlement, direct relief was dominant. An average of four million families was receiving $150,000,-000 a month, which is to say that a sixth of the population was on the rolls. Usually enough was given in food and fuel, but clothing, household supplies, and shelter were provided intermittently or not at all. Much of the burden of the jobless was borne by landlords, and many of these came on relief. Organizations of the unemployed sprang up, with informed leaders who tried, with considerable success, to improve relief standards. The bread lines, as visible evidence of destitution, had disappeared, but picket lines of the unemployed before local relief offices often took their place. Pickets' placards announcing "No Money for Toilet Paper," or "We Can't Buy Razor Blades" were more effective than volumes of general protest.

In January, 1935, the President declared that "the Federal Government must and shall quit this business of relief." The method was to abandon federal grants to the states for unemployment relief and to substitute a joint program of public works for "employables" and resumption of local care for "unemployables." This was the program under the Emergency Relief Appropriation Act of April, 1935. The law wisely permitted relief grants to the states until public works were actually started, but beginning in July, FERA restricted grants, assuming that works projects would take over. There were painful delays, in which administrative discomfiture was nothing beside the undeserved suffering and humiliation of relief clients. Old local relief projects had been liquidated before the new joint projects were in motion. Rural relief families were dropped from the rolls, but for some months did not get help from the Resettlement Administration, to which they were referred. No new applicants were accepted at the centers for transients after September 20. The $4,880,000,000 appropriation for public works seemed a magnificent illusion. However, relief demobilization was finally set for December. The result was to place additional burdens on the states and localities, which not only were to care for the unemployables and for those eligible for works projects though not in fact taken on, but were to supplement the so-called "security" wage.

In public works, as in the broader field of industrial recovery and re-employment, it was soon evident that careful plans for substantial projects could not be prepared quickly, much less put in prompt execution. When the program of codifying industries was moving off slowly, the President's Re-employment Agreement was promoted to hasten the process of spreading work and raising hourly wages. Similarly, when the Public Works Administration was retarded by its character and method, the Civil Works Administration was improvised as a speedier means of putting men to work, stimulating the materials industries, and increasing purchasing power. CWA, like PRA, was an *apéritif* for recovery.

CWA was created by the President on November 9, 1933, and began giving employment in one week. Despite the fact that the undertaking was substantially over by the end of March, 1934, and was finished by the middle of July, it reached an employment peak of 4,264,000 (January, 1934), and spent over $951,000,000 on 180,-000 projects.[1] Speed and size were possible because appropriation was entirely federal, while approval of projects was left to the state CWA authority, and practical supervision was assigned to the sponsoring agency, usually local. That is, the complications of co-operative federal-state-local financing and administration were largely eliminated. The projects were "quickies," chosen to reduce the volume of unemployment which was again mounting with the

[1] National Resources Planning Board, *Security, Work and Relief Policies,* Appendix 5 (Washington: Government Printing Office, 1942).

lapse of the boomlet of the summer and with the onset of winter. While "leaf raking" was not absent, CWA was more productive than the work relief which until then had been carried on with FERA, state, and local funds. The 1,500,000 from the old stopgap relief projects, together with 500,000 more employables from the relief rolls, were transferred to CWA, and more than 2,000,000 workers not on relief were also employed. Projects were intended to be limited to public property. A third of the expenditures were on repair of 255,000 miles of roads and streets. School buildings and grounds were improved; stadiums, swimming pools, parks, and airports (over 450 landing fields) were constructed; 3,000 artists and a large number of professional and clerical workers in great variety were given suitable assignments.

WORK RELIEF LONG NECESSARY

CWA began by offering minimum hourly wages running, for the skilled, from $1.00 in the southern zone to $1.20 in the northern, and for the unskilled from 40 cents to 50 cents, with the provision that where prevailing or union rates were above the minima, the higher rates should be paid. Maximum hours were 30 per week and 130 per month. In January, 1934, maximum hours were reduced so far that some workers had to seek supplementary relief, and in March, to conserve dwindling funds and to meet the criticism that CWA paid more than private employment in some sections, particularly the South, minimum wages were put at a flat 30 cents. It was calculated that average weekly earnings on CWA were $14.72.[2]

As little as possible was spent for materials and equipment, even a smaller proportion than that spent by the later Works Progress Administration. This policy, besides putting the bulk of the funds directly into the hands of workers who would spend them forthwith, made the start and completion of projects swift. However, it conspicuously reduced the efficiency of the work, as in projects where rock for roads was broken by two-pound hammers instead of by rock crushers, and was tamped by hand instead of being packed by steam rollers. Other even more imbecile devices were used for increasing the ratio of labor cost, as in projects that required trenches for electric lines to be dug to unnecessary depth.

[2] *Ibid.*

CWA was terminated because the winter hardship was past; criticism of the large outlays, especially for other than destitute workers, was loud; it was believed that the Public Works Administration would soon take over, and that the purchasing power already injected would revive private employment. Harry Hopkins, the relief administrator, would not be dissuaded from the fatuous conviction that the millions of workers suddenly discharged from CWA were going to find ordinary jobs. The fact was that nine years more, the last two actually after the United States had entered World War II, must come before public works, as a means of assisting the unemployed, could be done away with.

Still, CWA proved that huge numbers could be brought into a works program in minimum time, and it afforded experience which was valuable in the long efforts that were to follow.

After CWA was cut off, the Federal Emergency Relief Administration established, in cooperation with the states, the Emergency Work Relief Program. This makeshift was cheap, taking workers from the relief rolls at relief wages (which reached a peak of $30.45 per month in January, 1935), but it was not economical, being uncoordinated and producing few tangible results. Ever since May, 1933, when the first federal relief act was signed, it had been the professed design of the administration to use federal funds only for the relief of those unemployed by the nation-wide depression, leaving the unemployables to local succor. In fact, however, this had not been possible, and FERA was carrying at least a million and a half persons who could not take work if it were offered them. In September, 1934, dissatisfaction with this state of confusion was expressed in the recommendation of the Conference of Mayors that the federal government assume responsibility for the unemployed only, turning back those who were mentally or physically unfit for work (except veterans) to the states and localities.

President Roosevelt made this division conclusive in a message to Congress early in January, 1935, in which he proposed that a new works program should put the central government out of the business of direct relief. He said of the supposed unemployables: "Such people, in the days before the great depression, were cared for by local efforts—by States, by counties, by towns, by cities, by churches and by private welfare agencies. It is my thought that in the future they must be cared for as they were before. . . . Local responsibility can and will be resumed. . . ." The security legislation then planned would help the localities bear their burden. Then he went on to say of the employables on relief, estimated by him to number 3,500,000: "With them the problem is different and the responsibility is different. This group was the victim of a nation-wide depression caused by conditions which were not local, but national. The Federal government is the only governmental agency with sufficient power and credit to meet this situation. We have assumed this task and we shall not shrink from it in the future." [3]

The Committee on Economic Security echoed this distinction, though many social workers felt and said that poverty and misfortune were so generalized in their causes that unemployment could not be made the criterion of federal obligation. Masses of people not considered employable had been brought to destitution by the depression or other pervasive forces. The President's estimate of the number of needy employables was a minimum one. Not only social workers but the general public was sensible of the claims of those who had been rendered unemployable, if they were so, because they had been so long without work. The President's allocation of several millions to the ranks of unemployables was called in question by the experience of the good years in the twenties when nearly the whole of the labor force worked, and was more conspicuously invalidated by World War II, which reduced unemployment from 9,000,000 to a few hundred thousands and put halt and maimed, old and young, in jobs. Federal direct relief, for wider classes than those embraced under mothers' pensions and aid to the aged and the blind, was not discontinued until December, 1935.

RELIEF VERSUS RECOVERY THROUGH PUBLIC WORKS

The Works Progress Administration was created under the Emergency Relief Appropriation Act of 1935 which made available $4,713,000,000. The main idea was that employment on public projects, as distinguished from acceptance of doles, would preserve the workers' precious self-respect, conserve skills, and utilize vast resources for the creation of wealth. The works program was set up by executive order of May 6, 1935. WPA was intended to

[3] Address of the President . . . before a Joint Session of . . . Congress, Jan. 4, 1935, *House Document* No. 1, 75 Cong., 1 Sess.

coordinate the efforts of the Public Works Administrations (PWA, provided for in Title II of the National Industrial Recovery Act of 1933), the Bureau of Public Roads, and many other federal agencies furnishing work. It was at first planned that the small number of workers not thus absorbed would be engaged by WPA on limited supplementary projects of its own. In any event, for those looking to the federal government, real jobs, it was announced with some drama, were to supersede debilitating relief. Men and women who were employable could lift up their heads again with the assurance of earning wages. The shrewdness of the masses of the people has rarely been better exemplified than in their incredulity from the beginning. A long history of paring down work income, of exclusion from employment, and of other policies which related public works to relief, was to confirm their doubts.

Now came a conflict of purposes, sharpened by opposing personalities. Harry Hopkins, who had been relief administrator, headed the WPA, which was charged with "the honest, efficient, speedy, and coordinated execution of that program in such manner as to move from the relief rolls to work on such projects or in private employment the maximum number of persons in the shortest time possible."[4] Incidentally, as noted above, WPA could recommend and carry out "small useful projects designed to assure a maximum of employment in all localities." Secretary of Commerce Harold Ickes was chairman of the Advisory Committee on Allotments; it was soon apparent that in this capacity he would try to extend to the whole works program the aims that had characterized the Public Works Administration over which he had presided from the beginning. Ickes wanted the funds used for heavy construction projects which eventually would pay for themselves in money, and which would be executed often by private contractors and on other than public property. Not only did he insist on a clear *quid pro quo,* but he had in mind recovery rather than relief. He was not saving potential assets in workers' self-respect and capabilities so much as he intended to create present assets in bridges, buildings, and railroad overpasses. But Ickes' public works were slow in maturing, for they entailed legal and engineering delays; they required that a large proportion of funds be spent on materials and equipment rather than on direct labor; and much of the skilled labor they

[4] Executive Order No. 7034, May 6, 1935.

needed had to be sought without reference to relief rolls. Hopkins, who kept pressing for his quicker, more expansible projects, won a victory when more than a third of the appropriation was allocated for his light operations, and it was WPA which furnished most of the jobs and dominated the public works program. Hopkins remained administrator of WPA until he became Secretary of Commerce in 1939; in the same year WPA and PWA were merged in the Federal Works Agency.

First to describe WPA. By its own decision, within the provisions of the law, WPA determined that projects must (1) have authorized local sponsors; (2) have a general public usefulness; (3) not interfere with private employment; (4) be susceptible of execution by the available supply of workers eligible for WPA; (5) not demand excessive expenditure on material as compared with labor; (6) be capable of completion by the end of the fiscal year, since WPA lived on annual grants; (7) except in rare circumstances, be on public property. Congress itself laid down prohibitions against production of war material, promotion of prison industries, and construction of public buildings costing the federal government more than a specified amount. Beginning in 1939, after a chorus of criticism had been raised from many quarters, WPA was restricted in a number of other ways; particularly theater projects were flatly forbidden, and projects for artists, writers, and musicians narrowly escaped the axe. Each of these limitations had a history of conflicting interests. Several added to the vexations and reduced the usefulness of WPA without conferring corresponding benefits on private enterprise or the American people.

WPA paid what were termed "security wages," higher than relief allowances, but generally lower than were current in private employment. There were exceptions to the last comparison, for WPA refused to lower its rates to meet the substandard ones prevailing in certain districts, notably of the South, though on occasion workers were forced off WPA as a means of compelling them to take worse-paying jobs in agriculture. Where there were, in fact, no private jobs to be had, there was no justification, so far as the motive of transfer was concerned, for keeping security wages so low.

WPA wage rates differed according to classification of workers —unskilled, intermediate, skilled, and professional or technical;

according to four national regions; and according to the degree of urbanization of the particular county within the region. In the beginning the rates ran from a low of $19 to a high of $75 in southern states east of the Mississippi and north to Virginia and Kentucky, and from a low of $40 to a high of $94 in New England, the Middle Atlantic, the East North Central and Far Western states, and Minnesota and Iowa. However, after 1935, differentials against the South were lessened by the requirement of Congress that distinction in wage rates for similar work in various sections of the country should not be greater than could be justified by differences in the cost of living. But removal of discrepancies should not change the monthly average wage for the country as a whole, a requirement which meant in practice that some northern wages had to be lowered to bring up the South. In August, 1939, the extremes of the range were $31.20 and $94.90. The assumption long made that the cost of living was markedly lower in the South than in the North was disproved by findings of the Wage and Hour Division of the Department of Labor in 1938. Variations in the cost of living between cities in the same region, North or South, were greater than those between regions. However, the cost of living was found to be slightly less in southern than in northern cities, running from 1.4 per cent less for towns and small cities to something under 6 per cent less for larger places. Later studies of the Textile Workers Union, with Labor Department supervision, showed no significant differences in northern and southern textile towns. Probably more influential than any scrutiny of relative costs of living was the willingness of national relief authorities to take as an empirical guide the lower *level* of living in the South. Many whites in the South objected to relief wages which would lift Negroes out of their customary minimum standard.

Wages on work projects were reduced by sickness, bad weather when some projects could not be operated, layoffs to distribute work, limitation of hours, employment of workers at less than their rated skills, and in other ways which in the total seemed to call in question whether public work, so far as the recipients were concerned, was different from direct relief. Indeed, the wages might not be as good as relief, for relief and the old work relief program made grants proportional to the number of dependents, whereas

WPA officials rejected such a consideration. Harry Hopkins said in 1935, "I believe that all families should receive the same wages regardless of their size." Private employment was not remunerated on the basis of family size "and there is no reason why government work should be."

LOW BUDGETS, LOWER RELIEF WAGES

WPA made some studies of the relationship of its scheduled rates to costs of defined standards of living. Lowest was an "emergency" standard and somewhat higher was a "maintenance" standard. WPA explained that "those forced to exist at the emergency level for an extended period would be subjected to serious health hazards. From the point of view of the long-time well-being of workers' families, a desirable standard of living would be one in which the concepts of maintenance and emergency have no place." The scheduled WPA wage for unskilled labor in May, 1935, would buy from 39.5 per cent of the emergency budget for a family of four in Atlanta (and hardly more in other southern cities) up to 76.8 per cent in Indianapolis. By August, 1939, the workers worst off were able to buy more of the budget—from 64.3 per cent in Atlanta to 75.5 in Indianapolis. The percentage in New York was 67.2 in 1935 and 65.2 in 1939. Of course the maintenance standard, averaging $30 above the emergency standard, was hopelessly out of reach. Also, those quoted are the scheduled *rates*, not the lower wages actually received.[5] A study in 1940 of a small sample of workers who had been eligible for WPA for an average of 39 months showed that they had in fact worked only 57 per cent of the time. After review of the whole program, a recent careful student said "the alleged security of the security wage gradually vanished into thin air" and that "the 'security' aspect of WPA employment had been pretty well liquidated by 1940. . . ."[6] Average monthly earnings of WPA workers ran from $52.14 in 1936 to $58.79, or 12.7 per cent higher, in 1941. In December, 1935, when WPA workers averaged $41.57, a third received less than $30, the same proportion between $30 and $50, and a third $50 or more. At the top only 2.7 per cent

[5] Donald S. Howard, *The WPA and Federal Relief Policy* (New York: Russell Sage Foundation, 1943), p. 178.
[6] *Ibid.*, p. 171.

got $90 or more, while 4.9 per cent got from $10 to $15 and 5.7 per cent got less than $10.[7] Throughout WPA history the unskilled workers comprised from 60 to 70 per cent of the total.[8] Comparison of WPA earnings with relief grants is necessarily rough for many reasons, but it may be said that a majority of relief clients transferred to WPA benefited considerably. This was intended. In the beginning of 1935 it was expected that monthly earnings on the works program would average $50, whereas the dole then averaged only $30.43 per family, ranging from about $48 in Massachusetts, New York, and Nevada to less than $12 in South Carolina, Kentucky, and Oklahoma. However, it must be realized that those gaining by transfer from relief to WPA were not a cross section of the relief population, for often those in greatest need were chosen.

Through the first six years of the WPA (to July, 1941) total expenditures on projects were $11,365,000,000. Seventy-eight per cent (8,869,000,000) was spent on construction and conservation projects, embracing more than $4,000,000,000 on highways, roads, and streets, and more than $1,000,000,000 each on public buildings, and publicly owned or operated utilities. The remaining 22 per cent ($2,497,000,000) was devoted to community service programs, including education, recreation, art, music, writing, historical surveys, public health, sewing, school lunches, distribution of surplus commodities, and vocational training for defense industries. The construction and engineering projects accounted for more than 75 per cent of the employment provided.[9]

WPA did not begin to give work until August, 1935. By 1941 WPA had employed over 8,000,000 different individuals, or one fifth of all workers in the country. Counting dependents, WPA earnings had been of direct benefit to 25,000,000 or 30,000,000 persons. The average monthly number on the WPA pay roll—about 2,112,000—varied considerably from month to month and from year to year; the most conspicuous variations were the decline in the second half of 1937, the subsequent increase which made 1938 the heaviest year of the program (2,717,000 monthly average with an

[7] *Ibid.*, p. 184.

[8] Federal Works Agency, Work Projects Administration, *Report on Progress of the WPA Program* June 30, 1941, p. 49. This whole series with varying titles, 1935–1942 (Washington: Government Printing Office) gives the most detailed account of WPA, in text, figures, pictures, and graphs.

[9] *Security, Work, and Relief Policies*, Appendix 3.

all-time peak of 3,238,000 in November), and the generally down-ward trend after the spring of 1940. In the month in which World War II commenced (September, 1939) there were still 1,654,000 on WPA (2,243,000 in February, 1940), and the program was not finally liquidated until four years later. Beginning with 1937, WPA ranked ahead of general relief in number of individuals and house-holds aided. Average WPA earnings, 1936 through 1941, were $1,-383,666,000 per year, or more than three times the amount dis-tributed in the second largest assistance program, that of general relief.[10]

President Roosevelt said, "The provision of work for . . . people at occupations which will conserve their skills is of prime im-portance." Consequently the task assigned to WPA was occupation-ally about as inclusive as was unemployment. How the attempt was made to meet that demand was told in an inscription on the WPA building at the New York World's Fair:

WPA seeks to employ at their own skills: accountants, architects, bricklayers, biologists, carpenters, chemists, dentists, draftsmen, dieti-tians, electricians and engravers, foresters and firemen, geologists and gardeners, hoisting engineers and housekeepers, instrument men and iron workers, inspectors, jackhammer operators and janitors, kettlemen and kitchen maids, librarians and linotypers, locksmiths and lumbermen, millwrights and machinists, musicians, nurses and nutritionists, oilers and opticians, painters and plasterers, plumbers and pattern makers, pho-tographers and printers, physicians, quarry men and quilters, riveters and roofers, roadmakers and riggers, sculptors and seamstresses, stone-masons and stenographers, statisticians, teamsters and truck drivers, teachers and tabulators, upholsterers and ushers, veterinarians, welders and wood-choppers, waiters and watchmen, X-ray technicians.

In spite of limitations imposed upon it—the chief of which was that it should avoid work conflicting with private employment—WPA undertook more than a quarter of a million different projects ranging over nearly all fields of economic and social activity and varying in size from a $40 million airport to trifling repairs to a country schoolhouse. The phenomenal list embraced everything "from the construction of highways to the extermination of rats;

[10] WPA Progress Report, June, 1941.

from the building of stadiums to the stuffing of birds; from the improvement of airplane landing fields to the making of Braille books; from the building of over a million . . . privies to the playing of the world's great symphonies. . . . One might . . . contrast sewing garments and rip-rapping levees; draining swamps and painting murals; repairing wharves and mending children's teeth; . . . sealing abandoned mines and teaching illiterate adults to read and write; and planting trees and planting oysters." [11]

Among the most distressed of the unemployed were the transients, most of them unattached men but large numbers moving in families. Those on interstate wanderings got little help before September, 1933, when FERA grants for centers and camps were certified. Obligations of nearly $106,517,000 were incurred for all types of transient relief from January, 1933, to March, 1937. The peak load of 302,000 cases, costing $5,038,270, was reached in April, 1935. Able-bodied men cared for at the urban centers—often hastily converted warehouses—were expected to work thirty hours a week. They put up partitions, installed plumbing in the centers, worked in the stock rooms that gave out clothing; some were orderlies in the hospital wards and others cleaned the quarters. Assignments to projects away from the centers included pest control, chiefly setting traps for rats on public premises. The morale of the men, after their life on the road, responded remarkably to the good care given them —hot showers, warm dormitories with clean beds, decent clothing, plenty of wholesome food, and medical attention. Their own possessions were, of course, practically nil, though each was apt to carry with him a few trinkets which he prized out of all proportion to their intrinsic worth because they stood for him as a person in a moving mass of misfortune. Families were provided for in the camps, but in the cities they were lodged outside the centers. In February, 1935, when the unattached numbered 158,353, there were also under care 142,107 members of transient families. In September, 1935, intake at the centers was terminated and the program was curtailed. Some were cared for outside the centers while they worked on WPA projects; others were given transportation to their homes if jobs were assured on their return. [12]

[11] Howard, *The WPA and Federal Relief Policy*, p. 126.
[12] U. S. Federal Works Agency, Federal Emergency Relief Administration, *Final Statistical Report* (Washington: Government Printing Office, 1942), pp. 70–74.

THE ARTS IN WPA

The Works Progress Administration, getting away from the easy but wasteful lumping of all kinds of people in direct relief, tried to devise employment that would permit the jobless to be engaged at their particular skills. Such a program would not only tend to preserve morale, but would prevent special proficiency from rusting out and turn it to the uses of the country. WPA faced a challenge in the unemployed actors, musicians, artists, writers, and, to a less extent, teachers. All art and much education had been regarded in America as a luxury, so that depression, with decreased spending, struck these groups a hard blow. Their skills being highly developed, they could not readily shift to other occupations and were at a disadvantage in competing with laborers. Actors and musicians had suffered their own severe technological unemployment because of the advent of moving and talking pictures and radio. Estimates of the numbers unemployed in these callings differed widely, though their need was unquestioned. Imagination and courage were required to organize special programs for them in WPA; peculiar administrative problems were involved, and many were ready to criticize an indulgence in "frills" in what was, after all, a relief undertaking demanding strict economy.

The drama projects in connection with relief from 1933 to 1935 had been local and made little call on the creative capacities of the few embraced. The Federal Theatre Project, inaugurated in the autumn of 1935 at the instance of Harry Hopkins, was comprehensive, dignified, and discriminating in plan, and the results justified what was invested in it. While control was kept in Washington, execution was vested in state authorities. Except for necessary supervisors, who were paid slightly more, workers in the theatre project—actors, scene painters, stage hands, and mechanics—received local WPA wages. Efforts were made to have presentations reflect regional life, and in many cases they unobtrusively dealt with themes having current social application.[13]

As late as April, 1941, some 6,200 unemployed musicians on WPA projects gave musical performances for 2,800,000 persons. Besides public performances by orchestras, bands, and choruses,

[13] For a full account by the National Director of the Federal Theatre Project see Flanagan, Hallie, *Arena* (New York: Duell, Sloan and Pearce, 1940).

varied activities included development of community music. Under the art program thousands of easel paintings, murals, prints, and works of sculpture were executed and exhibited or placed permanently in schools, hospitals, libraries, and other public buildings. The writers' projects produced hundreds of books and pamphlets dealing with life in the United States, notably elaborate descriptions of most of the states in the American Guide series. Research and records projects accumulated and arranged large quantities of historical and other material. In addition, adaptations of work relief embraced many women in welfare services such as public health and hospital assistance, school lunch programs, and distribution of surplus commodities.[14]

PROVISION FOR YOUTHFUL UNEMPLOYED

Depression unemployment fell with disproportionate severity upon young workers. The enumerative check census of 1937 found that while only 8.3 per cent of all workers were in the 15–19 age group, 18.5 per cent of the totally unemployed were in this age bracket; the 20–24 age group composed 14.8 per cent of the labor force, but 19.2 per cent of the unemployed. The 1940 census returns were similar. Different surveys showed from 2.6 to 3.1 millions under the age of 25 unemployed in the spring of 1940, and 4.1 millions in the summer of that year. During the depression, about 1,750,000 young people were coming on the labor market annually. Youth formed a third of all the unemployed, and a third of the youth could not find work; further, a fifth of the young people who had work were employed only part time. Nor were long periods of unemployment reserved for the older workers; for instance, 39 per cent of unemployed youth in Michigan in January, 1935, had been out of work for at least a year, and 18.4 per cent for three or more years. Unemployment was worse among girls than among boys, and the incidence was heaviest among the children of the poor.

The ill effects of frustration at the outset of life need no elaboration. Two programs attempted to deal with the problem, those of the Civilian Conservation Corps and of the National Youth Administration. In these the objects of relief, removal from the labor market (made work), and training for later jobs were combined.

[14] Federal Works Agency, *Report on Progress of the WPA Program*, June 30, 1941.

The Civilian Conservation Corps was the more concrete, the less diffused of the two schemes. It was commenced in March, 1933, and in seven years enrolled more than 2,250,000 young men in 1,500 camps located in every state. The maximum strength of the corps was over 500,000 in August, 1935. Most of the time 17–25 were the age limits, none could remain in the program more than two years, and all must be capable of hard physical labor. The work of the camps, of 200 men each, was in a variety of outdoor improvements—structural, such as bridges and fire towers; transportation, such as trails, emergency roads, landing fields; erosion and flood control; forestry and forest fire prevention; the making of recreation facilities; range improvement; and conservation of wild life. The boys worked consistently on useful public projects under intelligent planning and supervision; their health improved from good food, plenty of exertion in the open air, medical care, and regular hours.

In selection, supposing they met the physical qualifications, economic need was the prime consideration, but later on a larger proportion were taken from nonrelief families. Wages were $30 a month, $22 being sent to family or other dependents. Generally the enrollees must be unmarried except for veterans, of whom there could be a maximum of 30,000 in the corps. Camp administration, including education, was under the War Department, though the army officers in charge were not allowed to impose military training; the Departments of Interior and Agriculture laid out the work projects, which were determined by the needs of the community.

The work contributed conspicuously to the conservation and productiveness of the national domain. The training acquired by the enrollees was of two sorts, on the job and after hours. Most of the jobs were unskilled or semiskilled, but others invited or demanded knowledge and expertness in use and maintenance of tools and equipment, and in methods. The largest proportion of enrollees came from and returned to cities, and there was question how much of their work experience in the camps could be of direct service to them in urban employment. Education during leisure time received, naturally, imperfect stress. Many thousands were taught to read and write; more attended classes in vocational than in academic subjects, though suitable equipment for the former was often limited. Teachers, though well intentioned, were not well qualified for their difficult task, chiefly because they were poorly paid and had brief tenure. Vocational guidance was given generously, though against a background of near futility because of the persistent unemployment. As the defense program grew, instruction took on a semimilitary character.

The CCC was inadequate in the numbers embraced. In the beginning of 1938, when the program was well developed, only a sixth of the applicants could be accepted, and in the middle of 1940, when defense employment and selective service had come to the rescue, fewer than two thirds of the applicants were taken; in the Southeast and Southwest, where need was greatest, the smallest proportions of applicants were accepted. Moreover, many most requiring physical rehabilitation were not enrolled because of the rigorous standards. The CCC involved an expenditure per youth of from $995 to $1,244 per year. Negroes formed about the same proportion in the CCC as in the population. The minimum enrollment period was for six months and, though desertions were disconcertingly high, after 1937 the average stay in a camp was never less than nine months.[15]

The National Youth Administration was authorized by the Federal Emergency Relief Appropriation Act of 1935 and, in 1940, became a part of the Federal Security Agency. It gave part-time work to students in high school, college, and university to enable them to remain at their studies and off the labor market, and to young people 18 to 25 who had left school; 90 per cent of the out-of-school projects were for those living in their own homes, while the other 10 per cent, in sparsely settled rural areas, were conducted in resident centers. Need was the chief criterion of eligibility.

High school students were allowed to work no more than 3 hours on school days and 7 on Saturdays and received a maximum of $6 a month. Undergraduates and graduate students could work a maximum of 8 hours a day, the first group receiving $10 to $20 a month and the second group $20 to $30. In June, 1940, average monthly earnings of 212,647 high school (and some elementary school) students were $4.74, those of 99,657 college undergraduates were $12.68, and those of 1,655 graduate students were $21.72. The work done was designed to further education, and was typically

[15] See Annual Reports, Director of Civilian Conservation Corps, 1935–1940, also National Resources Planning Board, *Security, Work and Relief Policies,* pp. 261–265.

in the laboratory, in the library, in school administrative offices, or in connection with research projects of teachers. In most cases the value of the work, to the students themselves, to the institutions, and to the communities, was lessened because it was irregular, for short periods, and poorly supervised. However, this criticism was by no means universally valid, for many of the assignments were rewarding to all concerned. By the end of 1940 some million and a half young men and women had taken part in the student work program.

Those in the out-of-school program did work similar to that of the Civilian Conservation Corps, except that more of it was in urban communities. They built or repaired schools, libraries, hospitals, constructed bandstands, stadiums, swimming pools, tennis courts, roads, airports, levees, and dams; repaired furniture and tools; served over 77 million school lunches; raised and canned food; did a large volume of clerical work. Although related class training was often encouraged for those in nonresident projects, it was a regular part of the program in resident projects. Hours worked on the out-of-school projects were naturally longer than those on the in-school projects; in June, 1940, they averaged 57 per month and earnings ranged from $8.62 in Kansas to $28.75 in New York City. Those in resident projects worked 90 hours a month at an average wage of 25 cents an hour and, after deductions for maintenance, had $8 to $10 a month for their own use. The average annual cost of the student program varied from $65 to $83 per worker, and for the out-of-school program from $212 to $242.[16]

INCEPTION OF THE HOUSING AUTHORITY

The efforts of the Housing Division of the Public Works Administration formed the curtain raiser to the superior and more widely accepted accomplishments of the United States Housing Authority. Its basis was in a few words in the National Industrial Recovery Act which empowered the administrator to include "low-rent housing and slum clearance projects. . . ." No one has claimed authorship of the provision, perhaps because PWA housing was a

[16] Security, Work and Relief Policies, pp. 265–276. See also Betty Grimes Lindley and Ernest K. Lindley, A New Deal for Youth: The Story of the National Youth Administration (New York: The Viking Press, 1938).

good deal reviled. However, the shyness was justified only in part. Some blame was deserved by Secretary Ickes' inveterate insistence that each undertaking of his Housing Division, like all public works under his control, be painfully economical in the narrow sense, while neglecting the prime purpose of giving speedy relief to unemployment. He required exhaustive, and exhausting, preliminary investigation, a precious regard for legality in every particular, and was patient with endless delays which produced few jobs and no more than a dent in the physical reduction of slums. On the other hand, he did lengthen his stride as he went along. After three months of disappointing attempts to stimulate private demolition and construction, through limited-dividend corporations, Secretary Ickes launched a new PWA Housing Corporation which would itself engage in the business of providing low-cost housing; when this corporation was disallowed by the Comptroller General, Ickes was prompt in giving the intended mandate to the existing Housing Division.

The PWA Housing Division began in July, 1933, and continued until superseded in November, 1937, by the United States Housing Authority. It made possible 7 limited-dividend projects, lending 85 per cent of their cost at 4 per cent interest for thirty years; and 51 public projects in 36 cities, accommodating 22,000 families, contributing outright $150,000,000, or 45 per cent of their cost, the remainder to be repaid over 60 years at 3 per cent interest. The loss of time, and of attendant preparatory expenditures, was mainly due to inexperience with public housing on the part of the division, of the communities it sought to help, and of the country generally. Hardly more than 1 per cent of the proposals by limited-dividend corporations could be accepted, because they were not suitable to the purpose of the law, or because the sponsors could not contribute the required 15 per cent of equity. Then action by the Housing Division itself was interrupted, since the courts forbade it the power of eminent domain which in practice was usually necessary to assemble many small plots of land for slum clearance. Later it was established that local housing authorities could employ eminent domain, but in the beginning there were no local authorities through which the division could work. Private greed had to be detected and foiled, the enthusiasm of honest citizens redirected, political hostility countered. Public realization that the lowest income groups cannot be decently housed by private enterprise at rentals which they can afford, and that consequently subsidy is needed, came slowly.

However, as a result of Housing Division advocacy, thirty states, the District of Columbia, Hawaii, and Puerto Rico had passed enabling legislation for local authorities by the time the division went out of existence, and some fifty local authorities had been set up. The division succeeded, by pamphlet, platform, and example, in educating the nation to the means and benefits of public housing. Despite charges of extravagance and waste, construction costs compared favorably with similar private building, and were sometimes lower. On a representative sampling, the Bureau of Labor Statistics found that the average cost for each dwelling unit was $3,549—or $979 a room if recreational and other public facilities were included. Shelter rent (without utilities) in September, 1937, averaged $5.37 a room a month, or only 37 cents more than the rent of incomparably inferior slum quarters which included, moreover, no advantages of sunlight, air, or playgrounds. With heat, hot water, electricity, gas, and refrigeration the PWA monthly rental for each room was $7.50. Naturally, vacancies were negligible. Of course, prices paid by PWA for sites varied widely with location—from $4.30 per square foot in a congested New York City area to $.004 per square foot in the outskirts of Miami, Florida; they averaged 44 cents.[17]

The United States Housing (Wagner-Steagall) Act, was approved September 1, 1937, after another measure, in important respects superior, introduced by Senator Wagner in 1936, failed of passage. The new law set up the United States Housing Authority (USHA) in the Department of the Interior, though it was given its own administrator. The program of the USHA, as compared with that of the PWA and of other public housing efforts in the country to that time, was wider and more mature: its purpose was primarily "the provision of decent, safe, and sanitary dwellings for families of low income" and "the eradication of slums," and only secondarily "the reduction of unemployment and the stimulation of business activity." The PWA had itself cleared slums, erected, owned, and operated the new housing; it had provoked criticism for being too

[17] See Margaret H. Schoenfeld, "Progress of Public Housing in the United States," *Monthly Labor Review* LI, No. 2 (August, 1940), pp. 267–282.

centralized. Consequently, the USHA was empowered to work only indirectly, giving financial assistance to state and local housing authorities; not more than 10 per cent of the available funds was to be used in any one state.

NEW HOMES FOR OLD

By 1940 the original $500,000,000 allowed the USHA had been increased to $1,600,000,000, which could be employed in three forms of aid—loans, annual contributions, and capital grants. Loans for acquisition and construction could be supplemented by capital grants or, after completion of the project, by annual contributions; both were for the purpose, where necessary, of bringing the rents down to the paying capacity of the low-income groups to be served. If a loan was all that was required, it could amount to 100 per cent of the cost of the development. If a capital grant or an annual contribution was made in addition, the loan was limited to 90 per cent of the cost. Outright subsidy by the federal government entailed subsidy by the local housing agency—in the case of contributions, 20 per cent of that of the federal government; in the case of capital grants, 20 per cent of the cost of the project. The local subvention was made, in practice, in the form of tax exemption. The USHA was limited, in any capital grant, to 25 per cent of the project's cost, but an annual contribution to operation was preferred, and no capital grants were made. Contracts for annual contributions could be re-examined after ten years, and at five-year intervals thereafter, and modified to meet changed conditions. Loans were made for sixty years at interest not less than the current federal rate plus .5 per cent. There were other similar precautions; for example, projects, excluding land, must not cost more than $5,000 per dwelling unit or $1,250 per room in cities of over half a million, or more than $4,000 per dwelling or $1,000 per room in smaller places. Moreover, where an annual contribution was made, it was on the condition that the project include the elimination of substandard dwellings equal to the number of new ones erected, though demolition could be deferred where demand for housing required. USHA took over the projects of PWA and began disposing of them to local housing agencies, which increased rapidly to some 400 by 1940.

The law stipulated that tenants in USHA developments be in

the lowest income third of the population in that locality, and come from substandard housing. The average income of all families in USHA projects on December 31, 1941, was $837 a year; in small towns of the South and Southwest the top of the range was lower than this; in large cities of the North it was higher by several hundred dollars. The act limited occupancy to tenants whose income was five times the rent, or, if there were three or more minor dependents, six times the rent. The average shelter rent in USHA projects was $12.64 a month for each dwelling unit, ranging from $10.51 in the South and Southwest to $14.47 in the North. Payment for utilities brought the average up to $17.82 a month; rents in USHA projects were in all cases less than those charged in the slums from which the tenants came. The frequent charge that public housing competed with private housing was false. Private enterprise, unaided, could not meet the needs of low-income groups, being obliged to charge about twice the rent paid for substandard quarters. In the last year of the USHA, before the program was interrupted by the war, the rent scale was made flexible to meet the needs of large families which required more bedrooms. More children did not mean more income; hence USHA recommended to local authorities that they rent some large dwelling units at hardly more than smaller ones, though these larger units might be in the less desirable locations in the projects. The plan worked admirably, causing no resentment among tenants and helping to hold delinquencies in rent payments down to a fraction of 1 per cent in the great majority of projects. Some local authorities accepted into the projects families on relief. Construction cost of the 130,000 homes erected by USHA averaged $2,720, or about one-fourth less than the cost of privately erected housing. USHA developments cost less per dwelling unit than the PWA projects which had been erected in the same localities, often by several hundred dollars, sometimes by a thousand dollars or more, and USHA rents and average family incomes were correspondingly less. Efficiency improved as public housing began to strike its stride.

USHA succeeded in persuading numerous local housing authorities that the best attack on the slum was indirect, by the erection of the development on low-cost vacant land where there could be low density of population. This relieved the community from paying high prices to slum owners for their crowded sites and dilapidated buildings, prices based on exploitation. It avoided driving the surplus population of the slum, which could not be housed in the slum clearance project, to other substandard dwellings, and thus spreading the slum evil. Where the project was built on the city's outskirts, owners of slum properties began to lose their tenants. Once the latter had found superior homes which they could afford, local government would compel owners of slum buildings to rehabilitate or demolish them. The latter course was usually chosen, and the land was put to legitimate use‾ after its value had been thus deflated. Of 78,750 unsafe or unsanitary dwellings eliminated up to the end of the USHA program, less than half (38,735) were on the project (slum clearance) site, and 40,015 were off the site as a result of suburban siphoning of tenants. Slum owners objected with every argument. Those more honestly solicitous for the municipal tax rate could only be told that the cities must find income in some other source than the enforced misery of part of their people. As a matter of fact, the loss of taxes from abandoned slums or from exemption on slum clearance was more apparent than real. Many slum properties, while occupied, were tax delinquent, and slum areas often cost the communities, in added expense for jails, hospitals, firehouses, and so on, considerably more than was derived from these areas in public revenue. In four years USHA, in one way and another, cleared more slums than had been possible in the nation in the previous forty years, and the total of slum areas began to shrink.[18]

REHOUSING RURAL FAMILIES

Those familiar with housing needs knew that, contrary to popular supposition, the proportion of substandard dwellings was larger in small towns than in cities, and was largest of all (probably 40 per cent) in rural areas. Farm homes were overcrowded, for the depression had backed up on the farms large numbers who would normally have sought opportunity in urban places. There had been, too, a return flow from the cities, families that camped on rural relatives or packed themselves into tar-paper shacks of minimum size. Few country habitations that had not collapsed were vacant. A mere beginning in alleviating these deplorable conditions was

[18] See Annual Reports of the United States Housing Authority, 1937–1941.

made by the Rural Rehabilitation Section of the Federal Emergency Relief Administration and by the Subsistence Homesteads Division of the Department of the Interior. The projects so started were inherited by the Resettlement Administration, established in 1935 (later the Farm Security Administration). Those of the industrial-agricultural type did nothing to lighten the burdens of the legatee. They were designed to furnish food to the inhabitants from their small agricultural plots, while the necessary cash income was derived from part-time work in an industry purposely planted in the community. The idea was romantic, but, where several other difficulties were overcome, at best lent itself to the evils of the "sheltered workshop"—that is, the labor, all unskilled to begin with, under patronage, and lacking a union and alternative cash employment, was apt to be exploited to the disadvantage of those dependent on jobs in that industry elsewhere. Also, some of these communities were unnecessarily costly in construction.

Resettlement did better in its own program. Incident to its object of rehabilitating submarginal rural families, it was charged "to administer approved projects involving . . . resettlement of destitute and low-income families from rural and urban areas, including the establishment, maintenance, and operation in such connection of communities in rural and suburban areas." [19] Most of the communities were purely agricultural; to them were transferred families from worn-out lands bought by the federal government and converted to recreational, reforestation, or wild-life areas. The new communities, widely scattered throughout the country, were on inexpensive land which yet was susceptible of agricultural improvement. Some were self-contained, with their own schools, stores, churches. Generally they had cooperative features, as in the ownership of breeding stock, tractor stations, purchase of fertilizer, and the like, and some were entirely cooperative in farming method.

The dwellings, farm buildings, and, indeed, all improvements were economical but expertly designed. The influence of these communities, both in housing and in social institutions, spread beyond their own confines. Critics, chiefly southern politicians who, it is to be feared, did not want to see the living standards of the poor in

[19] Resettlement Administration *First Annual Report* (Washington: Government Printing Office, 1936).

planting districts improved, in some cases succeeded in having inside plumbing and even cellars omitted from construction plans. On completion, the projects were turned over to local nonprofit associations responsible for supervision, collection of purchase installments, and payment of taxes. The homes and small farms were sold to carefully selected occupants on a forty-year basis, with interest at 3 per cent. Payments fell due at times when farm operations made them most convenient. In addition to the resettlement communities, individual farm dwellings were built beginning in 1939 in cooperation between the Farm Security Administration and the USHA. They cost between $1,500 and $1,800 each, and, erected on plots deeded to the local housing authority, were rented (at about $72 a year) or sold over forty years to families which moved from substandard (a restrained description) homes. Sanitary privies are to be classed under health rather than housing, but the many thousands of them built on farms, replacing abominations or placed where no facility existed before, were not the least contribution of the New Deal. From lack of privies the soil, particularly of the South, had become contaminated and spread hookworm disease.

Resettlement Administration built three "greenbelt" towns near Washington, Milwaukee, and Cincinnati, housing 2,300 low-income families, the working members of which had jobs in the cities. These were successful experiments in suburban planning and community self-management. The dwellings were rented, not sold, on a basis to meet most capital cost over 60 years and all carrying charges, including interest at 3 per cent. The federal government, in order to keep rents low enough, was prepared for a subsidy or "write-off" as high as 25 per cent of capital cost.

CHAPTER X

Tennessee Valley and
Reciprocal Trade

BEFORE it flooded the Clinch River area with water back of the Norris Dam, the Tennessee Valley Authority transferred more than five thousand bodies from country cemeteries. It was a pity that the damage done by these dwellers to their country in two hundred years could not be so swiftly and completely removed. They had almost brought the land down to death with them. The forest had been slashed, the hillsides plowed for corn, the topsoil in great part washed away by the fifty-inch rainfall; the streams were converted in dry weather to trickles, and in wet to destructive torrents. The Clinch is only one of many mountain rivers and creeks making for the Tennessee, and the watersheds of all of these, and of the Tennessee as well, told the same story of despoilment. The Scotch-Irish were self-reliant but ignorant, spirited but stubborn.

Part of their poverty had been caused by the physical isolation of the mountains, but more of it was due to the social isolation into which they had been driven by slavery. To the westward and southward, where the mountains flattened, their fellows had similarly been victims of the competition of black chattels. The whole of Tennessee and the parts of six other states embraced in the great valley—Virginia, North Carolina, Georgia, Alabama, Mississippi, and Kentucky—had all been exploited, drained by man as completely as they had been drained by the river system. All had been exhausted, with no restoration. Families which came over the mountains to found and defend free homes, had kept the names and the speech of ancestors while sacrificing a rich heritage. If the quaintness of the eighteenth century had survived into the twentieth, modern reforms might have been asked to enter respectfully, but the picturesque and amiable obsolete had been sullied by perverse ruination. Mere antiquity had no claims against stupidity and destitution.

So much for indictment. Praise must be given for the response of four and a half million people to rescue. Dogma had always belonged to them, whether issuing in the constitution of frontier Watauga, flaming in family feuds, or persisting in the deadly doctrines of country preachers. But in spite of this, the ancient practicality of the Scotch had not been killed. Indeed, it was so nimble that it could leap two sorrowful centuries from the log dam and little overshot water wheel to millions of cubic yards of concrete with the imbedded turbines, from the apple-butter kettle to the quick-freezing plant and sanitary cannery, from the sievelike shack to the tasteful cottage, from superstition to science.

Of all the works of the New Deal, that undertaken and wrought by the Tennessee Valley Authority may live longest for bold simplicity of conception and honesty of execution. Here hurtful tradition was not deferred to, but was displaced. Here patching did not substitute for planning. Here greedy private claims were set aside for the common good. Here people came before politics. Here abundance was not expected somehow to profit from induced scarcity, but "the fuller life" was translated from a hopeful phrase into more food, clothing, shelter, conveniences, and recreation. The TVA addressed itself to the greatest public works project in history, with the engineer, the architect, the chemist and men of a score of other sciences commanded to lead the way. It was and is literally a down-to-earth experiment, with all that we know from test tube and logarithmic table called on to help. It was a union of heart and mind to restore what had been wasted. It was a social resurrection.

If this seems a flight of fancy, grant something to the gratitude —and the knowledge—of one who was born within hailing distance of the scene, and whose family all but surrendered there before surviving to witness the miracle. If the Civil War rejoined this area to the Union, a better campaign, of construction instead of destruction, has rejoined it to the economy of America, and made not one region but a whole nation richer. It was, in large little, what Soviet Russia undertook in a vaster fashion.

The act creating the Tennessee Valley Authority was signed May 18, 1933, bringing to an end a tedious and wasteful controversy over what should be done with the power dam and two nitrate plants built by the government at Muscle Shoals in the period of World War I at a cost of $129,000,000. The successive congressional bills, investigations, and presidential vetoes marked a history of inhibitions gradually overcome by accumulating sentiment in favor of government operation of the properties in a unified plan of development. For years during prosperity and depression, objection to public competition with private fertilizer and power interests blocked all but meager use of the installations. At length it became clear that fertilizer companies did not think the plants could be advantageously operated by them, and that it was the power privilege which was coveted by would-be lessors, including Henry Ford. From 1921, Senator George W. Norris steadily pressed for government operation on an ever more comprehensive scale. When Congress had come to his view in 1928, President Coolidge gave the bill a pocket veto. When another measure came before Hoover in March, 1931, he showed that presidential appreciation of the drift of opinion had not improved. For the Coolidge silence, Hoover substituted a written veto message which was among the most unfortunate of his efforts. His dogmatic opposition to government generation and transmission of power led him to miss entirely the regional and national potentialities of Muscle Shoals. As has appeared often in these pages, President Hoover set up a number of government agencies for overcoming the depression which approximated, in form, the bolder expedients of the Roosevelt New Deal. But they were lacking in scope and spirit, and the best of them waited for his successor to make them coherent and effective. On the power issue, however, Hoover lagged woefully behind the remainder of his own program.[1]

REGIONAL REBUILDING REVIVES DEMOCRACY

In 1929, Roosevelt, as Governor of New York, had urged public development of power sites on the St. Lawrence, the transmission

[1] *Hoover State Papers*, I, 521–529.

and distribution lines to be privately owned if the companies would guarantee to give consumers the lowest rates consistent with fair return on actual investment. When monopoly of the lines loomed, Roosevelt proposed that these too be publicly owned, and the New York Power Authority was established in 1931. He advocated the St. Lawrence Treaty between the United States and Canada, signed in 1932, looking to joint development of power and navigation. President Hoover, with "no taste for federal government operation and distribution of power," delayed action on this project, but Roosevelt carried his crusade into the election contest. In his speech at Portland, Oregon, he discussed government development of power in four great regions, "the St. Lawrence River in the Northeast, Muscle Shoals in the Southeast, the Boulder Dam . . . in the Southwest, and the Columbia River in the Northwest." These would give the country "a national yardstick to prevent extortion against the public and to encourage the wider use of that servant of the people—electricity."

All along he was thinking of more than abundant power at low rates, which was to be only the central feature of comprehensive economic and social planning for an area. He explained this in a speech at Montgomery after visiting Muscle Shoals with Senator Norris and others in January, 1933, and in a message on April 10 proposed a Tennessee Valley Authority which should enter "the wide fields of flood control, soil erosion, afforestation, elimination from agricultural use of marginal lands, and distribution and diversification of industry. In short, this power development of war days leads logically to national planning for a complete river watershed involving many States and the future lives and welfare of millions."

The Tennessee Valley Authority Act of 1933, as amended in 1935, set out the specific objects of flood control, navigation, power generation and sale, proper use of marginal lands, and reforestation; in addition there was the mandate to make and execute plans "for the general purpose of fostering an orderly . . . physical, economic, and social development" of the area. The act speaks of "the general welfare," the "well-being of the people living in [the] river basin," and says the statute "shall be liberally construed to carry out the purposes of Congress. . . ." It is mistaken to suppose that any one part of the TVA program claims chief solicitude. From the first, river, land, and people were embraced in a unified scheme.

The development of each bore, physically and socially, an organic relation to all the others. The degenerative process was to be reversed, and a recuperative one put in its place. Denuded hills and helplessly exposed topsoil had meant sheet erosion and a recurrently flooding river. Therefore the watershed was to be protected by planting forests and cover crops, and by a sensible tillage which let the rains sink in and thus make the flow of the river more even. If dams had been built, and there were no erosion control, the lakes would have silted up. As it was, dams would permit further flood prevention, facilitate navigation, and produce electricity. The power generated would allow the river, so to speak, to flow up hill. For the electricity would be used to manufacture fertilizer that would produce leguminous crops impossible without it; clover, alfalfa, vetch, and lespedeza, thus helped by phosphates, would store nitrogen in the soil and aid in recovering its fertility, which, in a beneficent interaction, would further limit surface runoff of rainfall. Outside this circle of regenerative forces were others similarly contributing to the rebuilding of the region. Cheaper transportation, varied industry, and better farming would all add to income, which, by improving education and health, would contribute again to productivity. Man was to work with nature, not against it as before.

This principle of cooperation has been invoked, also, in the realms of political, economic, and social management. The unit of operation has been the region. The river system knows no town, county, or state boundaries, and thus the lawmaking and administrative agencies of each have been invited to work together under federal sponsorship. Many said, and some honestly feared, that national assumption of responsibility would weaken or destroy local response, but the fact is that democracy has been enlivened instead of killed. The power companies and their well-disciplined following flung the reproach that private business enterprise would be discouraged and restricted, but the result was that it expanded and flourished. All elements in society were impoverished together when production was meager, and prospered together when opportunities were enlarged. States' rights and local and individual autonomy were never expressions of democracy so long as near destitution ruled; instead, the few exploited the many, and drained what was left of the common heritage. Discrimination against the weak in voting, in working, and in the enjoyment of public services, which resulted from the strains of desperate competition, was lessened when the people laid hold on a higher standard of living. Democracy had become despotism and decay in the small unit of production and government, but was revived by national and regional effort.

The machine age, introduced by the Industrial Revolution, had decreed corporate business enterprise, while the power age, ushered in by the electric turbine, had compelled the public corporation. From Watt to kilowatt was the step from private to public enterprise. The plan of TVA was the vision without which the people perished. The whole of the New Deal was a reflection of the stage to which economic society had arrived, a recognition—however imperfect—that individual rights could be preserved only as collective responsibilities were discharged. Some have declared, frequently for their own purposes, that the South is the last bulwark of democracy in this country. Nowhere was recoil from the New Deal sharper than in the conservative southern wing of the Democratic party. But such objections are not heard very long. In spite of false claims of power companies and politicians, the people of the Tennessee Valley have welcomed public benefits which have enabled them to develop institutions worthy of their early democratic traditions. The democracy of the physical frontier, long since dwindled, has been revived in the democracy of the social frontier, and the second is stronger and richer than the first. A group of farmers in a county council, consumers of electricity meeting to manage their cooperative, construction workers making a wage bargain with the TVA— these are all more democratic than anything that has happened in a Tennessee, Alabama, or Mississippi courthouse in a round century.

THE LOSING FIGHT OF PRIVATE POWER COMPANIES

By means of a score of dams which it built or bought, besides others, privately owned, which it supervised, TVA provided flood control, navigation, and power production. The Army Corps of Engineers had recommended low dams, but TVA was sustained by Congress in its decision for high dams as warranting the quadruple cost. High dams give more storage space, a deeper and straighter channel, fewer locks, and vastly greater hydroelectric power. Annual flood damage on the river, worst at Chattanooga, used to average over $1,775,000, all of which will be eliminated, plus much more in the lower Ohio and Mississippi, when the entire 10,000,000 acre-feet of controlled storage is completed. In the management of the reservoirs, their multiple purpose is constantly in mind. For the sake of flood control, an empty reservoir is desirable, and for the object of power production, a full one is best, and this conflict has to be reconciled. Generally, the reservoirs are drawn down before the winter and early spring rains, and are filled for the dry summer season. The control system is expertly devised to serve all needs to the maximum extent.

In order to hold the water in the land, as the very best kind of storage, TVA has set out millions of trees (much of the work done by twenty CCC camps), built check dams large and small and cut diversion ditches, and made it possible for farmers to manage their cultivated lands in a way to conserve moisture in the soil. This last has been through the furnishing of fertilizer free to 20,000 farms, 1 in 10 of the total in the valley, covering 3,000,000 acres, in return for an engagement of these demonstration farmers to follow directions in growing cover crops and in contour plowing. Besides, TVA fertilizer, in this program, went to farmers in twenty states outside the area. The fertilizer is triple superphosphate, concentrated from the low-grade ore abundant in middle Tennessee; it is cheaper to transport than the ordinary commercial fertilizer, which is mostly worthless filler, and, used according to the TVA plan, is far more effective. Hillsides that had been in corn, to the injury of farm and farmer, were turned to green with the hay crops.[2]

When completed, the dams will give a nine-foot channel in the 652 miles of river from Knoxville, Tennessee, to Paducah, Kentucky. But with six feet as far as Chattanooga, 100,000,000 ton-miles of freight are estimated to have moved on the river in 1941; this was almost five times as much as in 1933, when transport on the lower stretches was uncertain, and on the upper river was impossible at seasons when the minimum depth was only one foot. The effect of the dams has been to convert the stream into a staircase of lakes

[2] David E. Lilienthal, *TVA, Democracy on the March* (New York: Harper & Brothers, 1944), pp. 26–27.

bearing gasoline, grain, ore, cement, iron, and steel. Inland towns have become ports, with dock and elevator facilities. This inland waterway is an important part of the Mississippi system, planned to be 5,700 miles of nine-foot channel.[3]

Probably no sector of American business, in the New Economic Era of the twenties had developed more concentration of control and more abused the interests of consumers and legitimate investors than the power companies. The pyramided utility holding company became the symbol of promotional success through financial trickery. Too often a superstructure of legal claims without economic or ethical warrant was erected on a base of operating properties which received little benefit and were compelled to overcharge the customers they had, and to neglect potential users who could not pay the exorbitant rates. This "power empire" began to crumble with the depression, and found itself further threatened by the public exasperation embodied in the intention of TVA to make and sell power at low cost. TVA was authorized by statute to dispose of all surplus electricity, giving preference to public bodies—states, counties, municipalities—and to cooperative nonprofit organizations of citizens and farmers; it could construct transmission lines, and distribute to farms and villages not served at reasonable rates; not least, it could prescribe retail rates to be charged by bodies buying its current at wholesale.

The private power companies of the area began their suits in variety and pressed them with diligence and ingenuity, the cost of all being charged up to their customers in the rates. Nevertheless, TVA in 1934 signed contracts with two holding companies—the Commonwealth & Southern Corporation and the National Power & Light Company—for acquisition of many of their properties in the valley, but legal obstructions prevented actual transfer of most of these at the time. One of these suits furnished the first significant test of the constitutionality of the TVA power policy. In September, 1934, minority stockholders of the Alabama Power Company sought to prevent the sale of certain of its properties to the TVA. District Judge William I. Grubb, in February, 1935, held that while TVA might dispose of surplus current unintentionally created, its

[3] *TVA Annual Report*, 1940 (Washington: Government Printing Office, 1940), p. 3; Lilienthal, *TVA*, pp. 12, 44, 101–104.

deliberate creation of additional surplus was an "illegal proprietary operation," and seventeen municipalities were enjoined from buying power from TVA and from spending PWA funds to construct distributing systems for this purpose.

This decision was reversed by the Circuit Court and later by the Supreme Court in the Ashwander case (February, 1936), which, however, dealt only with the Wilson Dam power, and left the constitutionality of broader operations of TVA undetermined. Therefore, in May nineteen utilities, operating in nine states, brought an injunction suit to prevent TVA, except as to the Wilson Dam, from carrying out its power program. A three-judge district court in November, 1937, after a long trial, dismissed the complaint, finding that "the dams and their power equipment . . . must be taken to have been authorized, constructed and planned in the exercise of the constitutional functions of the Government." On appeal, the Supreme Court held that the companies had no standing there, and went on to say that TVA competition with private companies was legal, and that municipalities might construct distributing systems with loans from PWA. While the constitutional question was not squarely met by the Supreme Court, the legality of TVA electricity practices was taken by the companies as established. Soon the companies, in rapid succession, were selling to TVA and the municipalities of the area jointly, TVA buying the generating plants and transmission lines, and the cities the distribution systems with the proceeds of electric revenue bonds readily floated at low interest rates. Thus TVA power sales to municipalities, which had amounted to only 63,914,000 kilowatt-hours in 1938, were 2,038,-211,000 in 1941, bringing a revenue of $8,633,000.[4] Mr. Wendell Willkie, president of Commonwealth & Southern, had made himself the chief protagonist of the private companies, first in posing the issue of the entrance of the federal government into the field, and then in demanding that if the properties were to be bought, it must be at their value as going concerns, and not at the depreciated value of the physical plant. He lost on the first count, but only partially on the second, for TVA concluded, wisely, that the economies it would enjoy justified a liberal bargain in the interest of public relations.

[4] *TVA Annual Report, 1941.*

ECONOMY OF ABUNDANCE

A chief service of TVA has been its demonstration that, in the use of electricity, abundance is cheaper than scarcity. Director David Lilienthal said in the beginning, "The rate charged for electricity, within wide limits, determines its cost." The furnishing of electric current obeys the principle of decreasing cost. Once the expense of the installation has been incurred, the greater the consumption of electricity, up to a point not yet encountered, the less the unit cost. Generating of current is a small part of total cost of delivering it to the consumer, from one tenth to one sixth. The problem, then, was to cut unit distribution costs. This was done mainly by low "promotional rates," which stimulated the generous use of current, turning it from a luxury, dearly bought, into a true utility, so cheap as to be universally demanded. Besides offering lower rates as an inducement to fuller use, TVA extended and interlinked transmission and distributing lines. Rural lines, of improved construction, were run at much less cost than those of the private companies, which had been prohibitively expensive for all but closely settled farm districts. A necessary part of the promotional policy was to make available electrical devices for farm and home use at prices and on credit terms which a low-income population could afford.[5]

Except for an increasing number of industries, and a small number of private users who would later form their own cooperatives to buy the current, TVA did not sell directly to ultimate consumers. In order, therefore, to make sure of the advantages of fuller use, the law required that companies, municipalities, and cooperatives contracting for TVA current should sell it at retail at specified low rates. An average wholesale rate of seven mills per kilowatt-hour was set, with the condition that residential customers should be charged 3 cents per kilowatt-hour for minimum use, the rate going down to four mills per kilowatt-hour for maximum use. The wholesale rate was lower for large contractors, so that in 1941 the cities of Memphis, Nashville, Chattanooga, and Knoxville paid TVA for their power an average of 3.9 mills per kilowatt-hour, smaller cities paid slightly over 5 mills, and cooperatives 5.8 mills. The public

[5] Lilienthal, *TVA*, pp. 21–24; Joseph S. Ransmeier, *The Tennessee Valley Authority* (Nashville: Vanderbilt University Press, 1942), pp. 132ff.

utilities (private companies) got the lowest wholesale rates, an average of 3.8 mills, because they could take much interruptible and secondary power; industries paid an average of 4.3 mills. The private power companies reduced their retail rates partly because of TVA contract provisions, partly to meet TVA competition, and partly because they found out that lower charges to consumers increased gross and net revenues. The Alabama Power Company reduced rates 31 per cent, with the result that residential use increased 44 per cent; the Georgia Power Company, for a rate cut of 35 per cent, got increased consumption of 47 per cent; the Tennessee Electric Power Company reduced rates most, by 46 per cent, and was rewarded with the largest increase in consumption, of 92 per cent. In addition to the enormous social gains, the gross and net income of the private companies have increased.[6]

Of course TVA power sales increased slowly in the first years, while dams and transmission lines were being constructed, cities were acquiring distribution systems, rural electrical cooperatives were being formed, and industries were being developed. The marked increases began in 1939. Between 1934 and 1941, sales to municipalities increased from 2,913,000 kilowatt-hours to 2,038,-211,000; to cooperative associations from 4,251,000 (1935) to 223,-826,000; to electric utilities from 386,964,000 to 626,654,000, naturally a smaller increase than the others since the adjacent companies were being bought out. Sales of power to industries grew from 5,548,000 kilowatt-hours in 1938 to 1,809,664,000 in 1941. Direct sales, pending formation of cooperatives, were never large, and declined after 1940. Revenue from power sales increased from $826,-000 in 1934 to $20,254,000 in 1941. The bulk of this revenue was from municipalities ($8,633,000) and from industries ($7,780,000), sales to utilities amounting to $2,361,000, to cooperatives to $1,-300,000; direct sales accounted for $180,000.

By the end of 1941 TVA generating capacity was more than 1,000,000 kilowatts, and this power was serving virtually the whole of Tennessee and large areas in Mississippi, Alabama, Georgia, and Kentucky. The President, and TVA itself at first, having emphasized that the agency was to furnish a "yardstick" for judging the rates and service of electric utilities, there was inevitable debate over comparability of cost accounting methods of the public and

[6] Ransmeier, The Tennessee Valley Authority, pp. 160–165.

private enterprises. The contest—in court cases, congressional investigations, and elsewhere—was fierce and clouded by the smoke of battle. In the end it was settled what part of total TVA investment should be allocated to power, and that interest payments to states in lieu of taxes, and charges for amortization of indebtedness should be included among TVA expenses. The last item was really gratuitous, for private power companies do not amortize, but issue new securities; still, the charge was included out of deference to the view that TVA power, though public, was a business, and must supply grounds for judging whether the investment was profitable. Before 1939 the power service was operated at a deficit, but in that year the return was 1.6 per cent, in 1940 was 2.3 per cent, and in 1941 was 3.7 per cent. The majority of a congressional investigating committee concluded that "the total cost charged to power, together with a reasonable interest thereon, will be recoverable to the Treasury of the United States within a period of 50 years."

Later it was realized, however, that TVA did not provide a yardstick for measuring the efficiency and fairness of privately owned electric companies, for its vast size, its control over the flow in an entire river system, and its other means of coordination placed it beyond comparison in engineering and economic respects. Mere adjustments in accounting could not compensate for the superiorities possessed by TVA. There had been a time when municipally owned plants were able to supply current cheaper than those privately owned; then private enterprise, linking a number of plants and distribution networks in systems, superseded all but a few of the public efforts; finally TVA turned the tables again. Low TVA "promotional" resale rates worked wonders in increasing consumption and at the same time proved financially sound. The town of Tupelo, Mississippi, was only the most striking case: average residential consumption before TVA was 49 kilowatt-hours per month at an average rate of 7.4 cents per kilowatt-hour, but after five years of TVA power, average consumption was 164 kilowatt-hours at an average charge of 1.67 cents. In Athens, Alabama, consumption trebled under the lower rates. While residential consumption in 1941 averaged 81 kilowatt-hours per month in the nation as a whole, at a rate of 3.79 cents, TVA customers averaged 120 kilowatt-hours, and paid only 2.06 cents. TVA municipal and cooperative distributors made net revenue of more than 15 per cent of gross income;

all but three of the seventy-six municipal contractors for TVA power made money, though more of the thirty-eight cooperatives, which have special problems in serving rural districts, showed losses. The gains from low TVA rates have been extended, by force of example, far beyond that region.

LIBERAL LABOR POLICY

The Tennessee Valley being predominantly rural, the bringing of current to farmers and small communities was more than a legal mandate on the agency. Only 1 Mississippi farm in 100 had electricity, 1 out of 36 in Georgia, 1 out of 25 in Tennessee and Alabama. When TVA was ten years old, 85,000 farms in seven states were being served, or 1 out of every 5; the rate of increase had been three times as fast as for the country as a whole. Much of this was accomplished with the help of the Rural Electrification Administration, though TVA did its own missionary work earlier, and a number of towns taking TVA power ran their lines out to the surrounding country. From the first the object was to give the farmers the benefit of as many as possible of the many uses of electricity on the farm, the Electric Home and Farm Authority furnishing credit for the purchase of electric stoves, water heaters, refrigerators, hay driers, feed grinders, pumps, saws, milking systems, and many more. Manufacturers were persuaded to offer these at special low prices. One of the most primitive areas in the country, where all was done with sweat, suddenly led the nation in the sale of electric appliances. The president of the Florida Power and Light Company had the candor to say to the Edison Electric Institute that "the TVA is the grandest piece of promotion that has ever broken on the electrical industry. Imagine the President of the United States standing up and saying that every house in America ought to be completely electrified!" Besides large farm refrigerators for keeping all sorts of foods in quantity, rural cooperative freezing lockers, capable of saving fresh meats, fruit, and vegetables indefinitely, did much to improve the diet of the farm people, particularly by encouraging the raising of beef and dairy products. Quick-freezing units took on commercial importance for berries and the like.[7]

[7] Lilienthal, *TVA*, pp. 19–20.

The meetings of rural electrical cooperatives are schools of democracy, in which for the first time the people pridefully promote their own material welfare. It is to be remembered that low rates for current, and appliances bought at low prices and on time, would not in themselves have been enough to speed this transformation. The income of the rural people had to be raised through many activities of TVA before they could avail themselves of the new opportunities. That is where the unity of the TVA scheme came into play. Employment was given on construction projects, farm output was increased through fertilizer and instruction, transportation was improved, and the general level of intelligence and efficiency was raised.

In order to dispose of its increasing surge of power as new dams were built, at a time when municipalities were not prepared to take it, TVA began to sell directly to some industries and indirectly to others by supplying privately owned utilities. This policy was criticized as favoring business interests instead of consumers of the region. The reproach was undeserved, because the power in question would otherwise have been wasted then, and encouragement given to manufacturing meant a healthy diversity in production and more employment opportunities. TVA at no time solicited industries established elsewhere to come to the valley, and much less did it spread the lures of cheap power, low wages paid to docile unorganized labor, and tax exemption such as had long baited the appeals of southern chambers of commerce. This abstention was a national service, for it departed from the tradition of robbing Peter to pay Paul.

On the contrary, the whole purpose of TVA was to improve industrial standards in the heart of the South, and thereby protect the higher standards obtaining elsewhere. To begin with, TVA has a liberal policy toward its own workers, who numbered almost 14,000 in June, 1940. The statute obliges the agency to pay not less than the rates of wages prevailing in the vicinity for similar work, with due regard to be given to rates secured through collective bargaining. These rates are settled at annual conferences between representatives of management and labor, most of the construction and industrial workers being members of fifteen American Federation of Labor unions, which together formed the Tennessee Valley Trades and Labor Council. Some workers, mainly white-collar, belong to C.I.O. unions, but they nowhere have a bargaining majority.

Until 1940 the labor policy of TVA, while collectively arrived at and definite in all important features including settlement of disputes, was not embodied in a signed agreement. Indeed, President Roosevelt had said that "the process of collective bargaining, as usually understood, cannot be transplanted into the public service." But in that year the Trades and Labor Council signed with TVA an agreement "to set up . . . conference machinery and procedures to determine rates of pay . . . as well as hours of service and conditions of work of the employees; to adjust all disputes growing out of grievances or out of the interpretation or application of established labor standards agreed upon between the Council and the Authority; and to promote intensive labor-management cooperation between the Authority and its employees." The Trades and Labor Council wanted the closed shop, but this TVA felt itself legally forbidden to concede, for, while exempt from civil service, the agency must make appointments on the basis of merit and efficiency. There were only four strikes in eight years, and all of these were of short duration. The successful record of collective bargaining in TVA has gone far to refute the charge that great extension of public employment will destroy or limit independent collective action of workers.

TVA has employed Negroes in about the same ratio in which Negroes prevail in the areas of the projects; in the total it has slightly exceeded, in its employment, the 10 per cent which Negroes constitute of the population of the region. TVA makes no discrimination in wages, and has put a few Negroes in positions of more authority than they ordinarily occupy in that part of the country. But TVA has practiced segregation in construction crews and housing, has not given Negroes the same opportunity as whites for training and advancement, and generally has been unwilling to displease local white prejudice by equal treatment of all employees without regard to race or color. TVA, as a national agency offering tutelage to a lagging district, was in a difficult position. But the certainty of much lessened employment for Negroes when the big construction projects should be completed seemed to recommend every action designed to integrate the Negroes into the economic and civic life of the valley.[8]

[8] *TVA Annual Report,* 1940, p. 37; Lilienthal, *TVA,* pp. 94–96.

Mainly because unified control was necessary to make every part of the program contribute to every other part, TVA chose to do all its work itself—the designing, the assemblage of labor force and materials, and the actual construction—rather than let it out on contract as is the usual custom with public projects. For example, housing for workers built at dam locations was intended to furnish an example to adjacent communities, and the health and recreational services organized for construction crews were expected to persist in the neighborhood after the construction gangs had dispersed. All parts of the region were to be drawn upon for workers, and the skills acquired were to be useful in the future development of production in the valley. Instead of the traditional "hell on wheels" construction camps, the TVA workers' towns, even where most temporary, left behind them local betterment instead of demoralization.

ADMINISTRATIVE PROBLEMS SUCCESSFULLY MET

The TVA, in total, was the biggest engineering and building job in history and, planned and executed throughout by a public agency, established records for low accident rate, low unit costs, and precision in keeping to construction schedules. This success was the more remarkable because typically the work had not a single purpose, but a number of objects which must be combined, frequently by means of compromises. TVA has been free of political appointments to its force; this is quickly written, but is an achievement when one considers the combined effects of the character and magnitude of the enterprise, national party habit, and deep and prolonged depression.

TVA undertook, by definition, a regional development of "the Tennessee River drainage basin and . . . such adjoining territory as may be related to or materially affected by" the work. The area comprises more than 40,000 square miles in seven states, and is over 400 miles long from east to west and from 50 to 200 miles broad. The population is 2,500,000. As the region was a physical unit, conditioned by the central river and its tributaries, so it was, more or less, an economical and social unit. A political unit it was not, for nowhere else were claims of county and state autonomy more traditional and insistent. But the low level of economic competence in the area called for national assistance. In this task political dangers of two sorts were overcome—the selfishness and recalcitrance of local governments, and overcentralization that might have resulted from national authority. The solution lay in a regional agency, deriving its power from the central government, but autonomous within its area, and charged to enlist the cooperation of state and local bodies and officials. TVA did not have to run to Washington for every decision, nor did it have to defer to local prejudice in every policy. The economic depression, and the special exhaustion of the area in question, which amounted to a permanent depression there, facilitated initiation and operation of the scheme, quieting political and business protests which would otherwise have been more vocal.

TVA was set up as an administrative agency, the board of directors of three reporting to the President. The directors were responsible for both making and executing policy. To the board the President appointed as chairman Arthur E. Morgan, hydraulic engineer and educator; Harcourt A. Morgan, agriculturist and President of the University of Tennessee; and David E. Lilienthal, specialist in utilities regulation. Broadly, A. E. Morgan had charge of construction, H. A. Morgan of agricultural programs, and Lilienthal of electric power operations. Not until 1937 was a general manager, John Blandford, given authority under the board of directors, and expected to coordinate the many aspects of the huge enterprise.

The plan of combining federal, state, and local powers in a regional agency worked well, as the whole course of rapid and widespread accomplishment proved. Dissension which developed in the board of directors got more attention than it deserved so far as the success of the experiment was concerned. The notice which this episode attracted owed something to objections of private utilities to being superseded by public enterprise, and had encouragement from both local and congressional political jealousy.

Arthur E. Morgan, in an American setting, was a little like one of the "old Bolsheviks" in the Soviet Union, a man more talented in bold creation of social machinery than in its subsequent day-to-day operation. On a regional scale, he would have been a veritable George Washington if he had been able to combine both gifts. Chairman Morgan's complaints of his fellow directors came to a head, in 1937, in his objection that they favored certain private claims against the public interest, and, more vaguely, that in another quarter they pressed public claims too far against private rights. He considered that his colleagues on the board conceded too much to Major George Berry (later Senator from Tennessee), who wanted damages because the Norris reservoir had flooded his marble quarries. At the same time Chairman Morgan was saying that the legitimate interests of the private utilities in the region, represented by Wendell Willkie, chairman of the Commonwealth & Southern Corporation, were being invaded by the power policy of the majority of the TVA board. When Chairman Morgan would neither retract nor consent to substantiate his insinuations against the integrity of his colleagues, President Roosevelt removed him, in March, 1938, appointing to the board James P. Pope, former Senator from Utah, and making Harcourt A. Morgan chairman. The deposed chairman pursued the matter unsuccessfully through a congressional investigation and a court suit. Retrospect will show that his disabilities, while justifying his eventual removal, were minor as compared to his initial contribution to a great social achievement. The private marble claims were disallowed, the private power interests were satisfied with the price and other conditions they received, and TVA was hardly more than interrupted in its progress.

TVA encouraged establishment of small scattered industries, using native materials and supplying, in many cases, special local demand. Laboratory experiments undertaken by TVA developed means of processing the clays, woods, and metals of the region, and all of the knowledge and models were furnished free to enterprisers seeking to use them. Of course electric current made this program of industrial decentralization especially feasible. While there were some large industries in the valley, and these expanded under TVA stimulus, it was not until the defense program after the outbreak of World War II that emphasis on small units gave way to demand for large plants. Supply of power to industries leaped forward in 1938, revenues from this source more than trebling between that date and 1941; soon thereafter most of TVA's vast amount of electricity was going directly into the production of aluminum, explosives, and other war production. The crowning achievement was the manufacture of atomic bombs at Oak Ridge, Tennessee, an entire new city built for this purpose. David E. Lilienthal, the chairman of the

TVA, in his otherwise excellent book,[9] seemed unaware of the irony of turning to destruction the energies of a region that had been entered for the express purpose of conservation and development.

RECIPROCAL TRADE AGREEMENTS

Between 1929 and 1932 the value of the foreign trade of the United States declined faster than did that of the world as a whole, dropping from $9,640,000,000 to $2,934,000,000, or nearly 70 per cent. During the year 1932 the steep descent was halted, and a moderate improvement took its place. Beginning with 1933 the recovery was sharper, continuing at about the same rate of increase until 1936.

The Trade Agreements Act of May 12, 1934, amending the Hawley-Smoot Tariff Act of 1930, furnished the basis of the New Deal's correction of former high protection and its world repercussions. Twenty-six reciprocal trade agreements (including four supplementary ones) were signed under this act and its extensions in 1937 and 1940 to the end of our period, beginning with the agreement with Cuba, effective September 3, 1934, and embracing, as the last, that with Argentina, effective only three weeks before Pearl Harbor, November 15, 1941. It is impossible to say what the history of the nation's foreign trade would have been in these seven years in the absence of the agreements program. As it was, the rate of improvement did not increase, except for the year 1936, which was countered by a corresponding decline in 1937, until the effect of armaments orders became conspicuous with the outbreak of war. Even then, until 1940 the rate of gain was not as great as in 1936, after which the curve was steeper. By the end of 1941 the nation's foreign trade was above that of 1929 and equal to that of the middle of 1920.

The law provided an intelligent procedure of ample hearings before the final composition of the list of commodities on which this country would seek and those on which it would be willing to grant concessions. A Committee for Reciprocity Information was to gather and supply information to an interdepartmental Trade Agreements Committee, which made recommendations to the President through the Secretary of State; both committees comprised

[9] Lilienthal, TVA.

representatives of the Tariff Commission and the pertinent government departments of State, Treasury, Agriculture, and Commerce. The elaborate administrative machinery was to safeguard the delegation of congressional authority, about which opponents had raised question. As a matter of fact, there were ample precedents, in law and public practice, for the delegation, as also for the promulgation of agreements by the President without reference to the Senate.[10]

Of the agreements here considered, twelve and one supplement were with Latin-American countries, including Brazil, Venezuela, and Argentina, and negotiations were preparing with Chile and Uruguay. The political effects of these agreements with Latin America, toward Western Hemisphere solidarity, were important in addition to the trade results. Of agreements with other countries, those with Canada, effective January 1, 1936, and with the United Kingdom, including Newfoundland and the British colonial empire, effective January 1, 1939, were of greatest consequence, Canada being the chief exporter to the United States and Britain the largest importer from the United States.

The act empowered the President, in order to obtain from other countries concessions on American exports, to reduce existing United States tariff rates up to 50 per cent, to bind existing rates against increase, and to guarantee continued duty-free entry of products on the free list. Nearly two thirds of the nation's total foreign trade, and a higher percentage of that with Latin America, was carried on with countries covered by reciprocal agreements. Perhaps of equal importance with the direct concessions obtained was inauguration or confirmation by the agreements of the most-favored-nation provision. This protected American exporters against subsequent lowering of import duties by an agreement country to producers elsewhere, generalized the concessions to all countries which did not discriminate against the United States, and tended to break down the constricting system of quotas, exchange control, and purchases by government monopolies which had grown up in the world and was at that moment serving the military purposes of

[10] House Committee on Ways and Means, *Report* on H.R. 3240, 79 Cong., 1 Sess.; U. S. Department of State, *The Reciprocal-Trade-Agreements Program in War and Peace* (Publication 1893, Commercial Policy Series 73; Washington: Government Printing Office, 1943); U. S. Committee for Reciprocity Information, *Rules of Procedure, Trade Agreements Act, Section 350, Tariff Act of 1930, and Executive Orders Affecting the Committee* (Washington: Government Printing Office, 1940).

countries with which the United States was soon to be at war. The most-favored-nation feature had the particular admiration of Secretary of State Cordell Hull, who was the incessant promoter of the trade agreements program.

The economic results of the trade agreements as such are hard to appraise because of the nation's recession in 1937–1938, export subsidies on certain agricultural staples, war for the two years 1939–1941, and rearmament abroad and in the United States before that; these influences distorted the country's foreign trade in volume, nature, and direction. The major changes came beginning with December, 1939, when the outbreak of war was felt. United States imports were exceptionally low in 1938, but began to recover in 1939. In 1939, exports to trade agreement countries increased, while exports to nonagreement countries decreased, widening a difference which was evident earlier. So there is reason for comparing the average of the first eleven months of the two years 1938 and 1939 with the same periods for the pre-agreement years 1934 and 1935. This shows an increase of exports to agreement countries of 60.5 per cent, and to nonagreement countries of only 29.6 per cent. Imports from agreement countries increased 22.1 per cent against 10.6 per cent for nonagreement countries. In these comparisons the nation's trade with the United Kingdom is omitted, since that agreement was not in effect until 1939.

United States export of armaments was chiefly to the trade agreement countries, and import of raw materials needed for munitions was mainly from these. The first eleven months of 1939, compared to the same period of 1938, showed an increase in exports to agreement countries of 4.9 per cent, and to nonagreement countries a decrease of 7.9 percent. Imports from agreement countries increased 17.5 per cent, and from nonagreement countries 13.2 per cent. Even before the war showed its startling effects, the first eleven months of 1939 included marked increases in exports of aircraft, metalworking machinery, and aluminum for military purposes, principally to the United Kingdom and France. However, the increase in shipments of iron and steel scrap to Japan and Italy alone, nonagreement countries, was greater than the increase in total shipments.

Then during December, 1939, United States exports reached the highest monthly figure since March, 1930. Thus the full year 1939

showed an increase in exports to agreement countries over 1938 of
8.1 per cent as compared to 4.9 per cent without December, and to
nonagreement countries a decrease of only 4.9 per cent as compared to 7.9 per cent. Imports from both groups of countries increased sharply.

The Trade Agreements Unit of the Department of Commerce,
in announcing comparisons of 1941 with 1935 and 1940, cautioned,
"Conclusions on the effect of trade agreements on our trade should
not be drawn from figures for abnormal war years." Anyhow, the
basis of the figures had been changed. The forces at work were no
longer commercial, but mainly military and political. Of course,
United States exports and imports, particularly to and from agreement countries, continued to increase, and were destined to go
higher before there was any slowing of the rate of advance.[11]

[11] U. S. Committee for Reciprocity Information, *Rules of Procedure* (Washington:
Government Printing Office, 1940).

CHAPTER XI

War to the Rescue

LAMENT FOR LAISSEZ FAIRE

A SINGULAR interlude in the New Deal was the "Investigation of Concentration of Economic Power" by the Temporary National Economic Committee. The committee enjoyed the blessing, perhaps the inspiration of the President, who in April, 1938, sent a message to Congress "calling attention to the need for a thorough study of the concentration of economic power and its injurious effects on the American system of free enterprise." Authorized June 16 of that year, the committee began hearings December 1 and continued them intermittently for eighteen months.

This was a full-dress inquisition, testimony of 552 witnesses consuming 775 hours and being published, with 3,300 technical exhibits, in 31 volumes, 6 supplements, and 43 monographs. Senator Joseph C. O'Mahoney of Wyoming was chairman, Leon Henderson was executive secretary (afterward "executive coordinator"), and relevant government departments had representatives, such as Thurman Arnold, Assistant Attorney General, Isador Lubin, Commissioner of Labor Statistics, and others from Commerce, the Federal Trade Commission, the Securities and Exchange Commission, and so on. The New Deal administration had done far more than any other in the country's history to practice collective control and enterprise, through government alone and in cooperation with private interests. Here it was making an about-face, vehemently accus-

361

ing its erstwhile business collaborators. Greater frankness, or a better sense of humor, would have required the administration to blame itself for past actions. Why this sudden evangelism for "free enterprise," this surprising reversion to the reformist zeal of veritable Grangers of sixty years before?

A guess would be that the "recession" beginning in the autumn of 1937 had disillusioned the President and his advisers with former New Deal interventionist policies, and persuaded them that another crusade, however contradictory to the old one, was indicated. The President himself, and several leading participants, such as Henderson, who had been intimately involved in government encouragement of business combination, confessed no embarrassment in now damning what they had helped produce.

The committee X-rayed and roundly denounced the familiar means and manifestations of business combination, such as price leadership, market control, basing point systems, patent pools, and many others. It concluded that "monopoly has greatly increased in American industry during the last fifty years because of the lax enforcement of the anti-trust laws, the impetus to price-fixing given by World War I, the tremendous development of trade associations during the twenties which increased price-fixing, the NRA experiment in 1933, and the great merger movements from 1898 to 1905 and from 1919 to 1929. . . . In those industries which appear normally to be competitive, competition is constantly breaking down." [1] In unlimited detailed evidence, summary figures of the Bureau of Internal Revenue for 1935 stood out. They showed that of all corporations reporting from every part of the nation, .1 per cent of them owned 52 per cent of the assets of all of them. Less than 5 per cent of them owned 87 per cent of the assets of all of them. Also, .1 per cent earned 50 per cent of the net income of all. Of all manufacturing corporations reporting, less than 4 per cent earned 84 per cent of the net profits of all. [2]

The preachment of the whole vast exposé was that the depression could be blamed in good part on the concentration of economic power that had nefariously administered prices ordained, in the

[1] U.S. Temporary National Economic Committee, *Final Report of the Executive Secretary* . . . . (Washington: Government Printing Office, 1941), p. 26.

[2] U.S. Temporary National Economic Committee, *Investigation of Concentration of Economic Power. Final Report and Recommendations . . . to the Congress . . .*, Senate Document No. 35, 77 Cong., 1 Sess., p. 11.

natural competitive order, to be sensitive and self-adjusting. The enormity of this crime was illustrated in the losses of the American people in nine years of depression, 1929–1938, as given by Isador Lubin in opening testimony. Assuming that the total amount of salaries and wages paid out in 1929 had remained unchanged, workers lost $119,000,000,000, farmers lost $38,400,000,000, and investors $20,100,000,000. The national income forfeited equaled $1,000 for every man, woman, and child in the country. With no allowance for population increase, which in the period had made 6,000,000 more workers available, 43,435,000 man-years of employment had been lost; this meant that all workers could have taken a vacation of a year and two months with no greater subtraction from national income.[3]

In light of the elaborate evidence and long experience with ineffectiveness of anticombination efforts, the committee might have concluded that the choice for the future was between concentration of economic power in private hands or in public hands. Such a choice—falling, one would hope, on the strategic extension of government economic authority—was too obvious to be called bold. But the committee was unprepared for this recommendation. Loyal to the President's purpose "to preserve the system of private enterprise for profit," the committee proposed that where private initiative was degenerative, government should reinvigorate it. The committee seemed unconscious of the touching quality of a faith in private enterprise that required government inducement. However, the TNEC was embarrassed by fresh manifestations of concentration of economic power which were accumulating at the time the final report was offered. These belonged to armament for World War II. With mixed shame and boasting, it said: "To marshal the resources of America in defense of democracy there has been set up in Washington in the Office for Emergency Management and under the Council of National Defense an instrumentality of economic concentration the like of which the world has never seen. Not even Mr. Hitler commands industrial power and resources comparable to those directed by one central authority in the massive effort of America to protect the free peoples of the world against totalitarian aggression. In this organization and its work is to be

[3] TNEC, Hearings, Part I, *Economic Prologue* (Washington: Government Printing Office, 1939), pp. 12ff., 196.

found the epitome of the problem this Committee was directed to study." [4]

Already defense contracts showed the extent to which economic concentration had proceeded in the United States. In the interest of efficiency the government had been obliged to favor giant private enterprise. Of defense contracts awarded from June 1, 1940, to March 1, 1941, four states received 39.32 per cent, six states got 53.75 per cent, and fifteen states got 82.25 per cent. Of all contracts, 45 per cent (some $13 billion) were awarded to six closely interrelated corporate groups, and sixty-two companies or groups received 80 per cent of the total.[5] (This pattern was to be continued and emphasized after the United States declared war.) A smile-provoking sequel was the prompt departure from the committee of Messrs. Henderson, Lubin, and others to assume leading roles in war economic concentration, Henderson becoming "Price Administrator," no less!

However embattled, the TNEC avowed its final "faith in free enterprise. Every recommendation which it makes is intended to keep enterprise free. . . . We must . . . not only stop the process of concentration by the action of government and business under the antitrust laws, but the government should actively encourage the development of new private enterprise by positive programs designed to foster and protect it. . . . If the opportunity for the employment of idle men and idle money is to be found in a free, private enterprise system then, obviously, we must find the way to stimulate that enterprise by encouraging the investment of private savings in new private enterprise. It is only thus that business and industry can be decentralized, either socially or geographically, and the danger of final concentration in Government avoided." [6] The committee recognized that the lowest-income third of the population could be relieved and made to contribute to the health of the economy only through government initiative and help.

The resulting proposal for a program amounted, on the one hand, to enormous government supplement to private enterprise, and, on the other, to new prohibitions on private abuses, after the manner of the Clayton Act. To the whole equivocal episode of the Temporary National Economic Committee may be appended Presi-

[4] TNEC, *Final Report and Recommendations*, p. 3.
[5] *Ibid.*, pp. 3–4.   [6] *Ibid.*, pp. 7-10.

dent Roosevelt's doubtful but dogged commendation: "It is a program whose basic thesis is not that the system of free private enterprise has failed in this generation, but that it has not yet been tried." [7]

AN ESTIMATE OF THE NEW DEAL

What were the relative advantages offered by the New Deal to various interests in the American economy? We may answer the question with rough accuracy. Agricultural proprietors conceded least for what they received. Banks and other financial institutions came off next best as beneficiaries. Industry and commerce, embraced in NRA, were third; they granted labor's right to collective bargaining, agreed to minimum wages and maximum hours, and got in return suspension of the antitrust acts, or "industrial self-government."

Labor received guarantees which were more important for the future than at once. Unequivocal establishment in law of the right of organization and independent collective bargaining offered opportunity of which labor availed itself. The Fair Labor Standards Act set national minimum wages and maximum hours which were to be improved upon. In addition to legal sanctions, the New Deal gave organized labor strong moral encouragement which helped launch it on a larger career in the economy. Still, anti-injunction legislation had already, before NRA, gone far to establish the freedom of independent unions; shorter hours of the individual worker and the throwing out of child labor were no great inconvenience in a period of huge labor surplus, while higher hourly wages had long been urged by enlightened employers as a means of ensuring profits and industrial stability. Further, though the President begged that prices should not be raised until some time after wages had been increased, this was never more than a pious hope. Industry held out its hands to have bonds of stout rope taken off, and to accept in return wrappings of packthread.

At the outset, labor fared not so well as employers. In order to benefit by government liberality, a sector of the economy must be tolerably organized to deal with its problems with or without public assistance. "To him that hath shall be given. . . ." Producers of the

[7] *Ibid.*, p. 20.

great farm staples had their associations which, despite disappointment in previous legislative attempts, continued vigorous lobbying; the masses of small farmers, though they took no part in the work of the Grange or the Farm Bureau Federation, were accustomed to being corralled by government farm agents scattered through every locality. Banks, as compared with the other groups here discussed, were few in number, interdependent, organized officially and unofficially, and enjoyed the solicitude not only of the Secretary of the Treasury but of every counselor of the President, for all parts of economic society were felt to hang on an able banking system. Considering the distress of the banks, it is a question whether they did not get even more than the farmers. The best assets, surrendered to the Reconstruction Finance Corporation in return for cash elsewhere unobtainable, were frozen so long as the banks remained closed, and would have shrunk to a fraction of their value had the banks dared reopen except according to government plan with government support.

Industry had the benefit not only of such over-all organizations as the Chamber of Commerce of the United States and the National Association of Manufacturers and their local divisions, but of a thousand trade associations which had at least escaped, if not the notice, the effective hostility, of the Federal Trade Commission, and antitrust prosecution. The concentration of control in industry was equally or more important in facilitating united action, since the habit of following leaders spread influence beyond the bailiwick of absolute authority. Besides, if depression had eliminated weak units of industry and commerce, it left the remaining stronger ones in a better position.

In contrast, organized labor had never numbered more than 10 per cent of American workers, had suffered losses of membership in the prosperous twenties, and was critically weakened by three years of depression and unemployment. The masses of workers had been no more than touched by organization, and when, in millions, they lost their jobs, instead of improving the case of those still drawing wages, the unemployed were a constant threat to standards of hours and pay and to unionism.

Thus we may venture the summary that farmers and bankers came into the New Deal as preferred claimants; industry obtained the opportunity, in return for certain concessions to labor, to do

openly what it had already been doing secretly; while labor must
first organize to lay hold on what was offered it, and needed all of
the defense that the National Labor Board and the National Labor
Relations Board could give it, and more. We have not considered
here the remaining distinguishable economic interest. What was the
quid pro quo of consumers? Being least organized, consumers were
least capable in the grand bargaining, if indeed, it may be said that
consumers could bargain at all. The higher prices and the reduced
output, which were to be the main means to recovery, must fall on
their devoted heads, with only the assurance that whatever started
the economy going again must benefit the buyers of goods and
services, and that, after all, consumers were inextricably confused
with all elements receiving direct advantages. If labor was little
consulted by NRA, consumers were present only by proxy. However, *pro forma* recognition was progress, and doubtless prepared
the way for more serious wartime protection, as in the Office of
Price Administration.

The New Deal failed, if we judge by its ability to bring about a
fully functioning economy, for at the end of six years of effort the
nation still had some 10,000,000 unemployed. The New Deal reduced unemployment, both absolutely and relatively, as compared
with what it had been when the administration took office in the
spring of 1933. But the 10,000,000 remained as a stubborn reproach.
A companion purpose had been to increase the measure of social
justice. Success in this would necessarily be slower, and the means
of gauging achievement are less definite. It is not surprising that
President Roosevelt, midway in his reform program, was obliged to
describe one third of the nation as ill fed, ill clothed, ill housed.
Nor should one expect this condition to be removed in another
three years; perhaps thirty years would not be too long an interval
to allow for such a widespread renovation. To produce something
like social justice, much preliminary work had to be done that
would not show quick or concrete results. The situation of those
worst off had been ameliorated, and glaring abuses had been more
or less corrected. The unemployed had relief, direct or through public works, and half the labor population had some guarantees in the
new social insurance. The farmers' plight had been notably lessened, hard-pressed homeowners had been assisted or rescued, here
and there slum spots had been cleared. Looseness of banks, decep-

tions of financial promotion, and harmful conduct of holding companies had been rebuked and restrained, while labor unions were recognized in law and in practice.

However, these tangible accomplishments, excellent in themselves, were not as significant as the hope, indeed self-confidence, which the New Deal had aroused in the nation. The New Deal proclaimed, and went a distance to prove, that we need not be frustrated by inscrutable misfortune, but could be masters of our future. This mental candor and moral lift formed the true contribution, and for them all praise is due.

REVERSALS OF ECONOMIC POLICY

Reviewing the whole performance from 1933 to the outbreak of war in Europe in 1939, we find that the New Deal took full advantage of the President's promise, early given, that efforts were experimental, that if one expedient proved faulty, another would be tried. The New Deal was grandly opportunist. The term might be used as a condemnation, but is here employed as a description. The administration did not stop at change of emphasis, but resorted to reversal of plans. Attempted inflation was abandoned for policing of prices. Profuse government spending was followed by restriction and spending again. Business collusion was at first promoted, later prosecuted. Economic nationalism was embraced, then rejected. These were the conspicuous about-faces; minor vacillations need not be mentioned.

Holding to the intention of rehabilitating the accepted economic system—call it capitalist, private profit, individual enterprise, what you will—the New Deal twisted and turned to shake off the burden of mass unemployment. Success in this was bound to be the test of validity. Failure was especially vexing because the goal seemed near with the economic improvement of 1937, only to recede with the fresh slump later in that year which continued into 1938. "Recession" it was called instead of "confirmed depression," but the softer word did not cure the discrediting fact. Lost ground was painfully regained, but the country did not see its way out of the woods until the advent of World War II.

Despite all efforts—Hoover's orthodoxy tempered with boldness, and Roosevelt's boldness mixed with orthodoxy—the nation did not emerge from the decade of depression until pulled out by war orders from abroad and the defense program at home. The rescue was timely and sweet, and deserved to be made as sure as possible. Whether the involvement of the United States in the war through progressive departure from neutrality was prompted partly by the reflection that other means of extrication from economic trouble had disappointed, nobody can say. No proponent did say so. Instead, advocates of "all-out aid to Britain," convoying of Allied shipping, and lend-lease took high ground of patriotism and protection of civilization. History may see a causal connection, conscious or not, between dull times and democracy vindicated.

In any event, the declaration of war in Europe marked the end of the New Deal as a group of domestic policies. Though it was years later that the President announced that the New Deal was dead, after the German march into Poland a different stimulus— war production for the United States and its friends—was supplied to the nation's economy. Not all progressive social measures at home were abandoned; the old momentum continued in some directions. But, broadly, there was a change of front, with other objects subordinated or incidental to defense and the fashioning of America into "the arsenal of democracy." Two evidences of the change were notable. The protracted inquiries of the Temporary National Economic Committee had prepared the way for a concerted attack on monopoly, and the Department of Justice was being staffed for this purpose. This campaign, except for token efforts, was scrapped, because it was promptly apparent that the great industrial consolidations must be chiefly relied upon to take and execute munitions contracts. Thurman Arnold, the Assistant Attorney General who was to have scourged monopoly before the bar, was translated to the calm of the bench, while the enemies of competition were reprieved.

The second instance of distraction from reform was no less significant. This was the denial by Congress of further appropriation to the National Resources Planning Board. The board, somewhat beyond its deserts, had become the symbol of intended large-scale intervention of government in economic life, and as such had drawn the fire of foes of the New Deal among businessmen and politicians. Its destruction removed a rallying point for progressive forces within the administration, and served notice that deliberate long-range planning was adjourned for the duration. The National Resources Planning Board's first publications had been remote from the present or hortatory, but later it made most serviceable investigations into problems of population, water and fuel resources, technology, consumer income and expenditures, and the means of regional development.

When war orders were increasingly pouring in upon industry, it was not necessary to ponder different means of furnishing employment, for it was clear that before long the problem would be one of workers, not of jobs. Further, Roosevelt was less and less obliged to rely on a New Deal backing, for the defense program and prospect of frank entry into the war strongly tended to blur economic and political lines to the advantage of the administration. Wendell Willkie, Roosevelt's Republican opponent in the campaign of 1940, was in agreement with the President on all-important foreign policy, so much so that points of difference on domestic design faded in the public mind. After the election, Willkie was virtually to read himself out of his party by his closer approximation to the President's purposes. The defense effort required that business become the active partner, instead of the suspicious protégé or hostile observer of the federal government. This did not immediately prove so simple as the promises of enormous war orders would seem to ensure. For a time some vocal businessmen were inclined to refuse to be wooed by Washington. They feared the Greeks though bearing gifts. Were munitions contracts just another New Deal dodge? Preparation for war, or war itself, would probably magnify the power of government over them. At best, they reflected, war prosperity would have its costly aftermath.

Important industrialists hung back, staged a "sit-down strike of capital" until assured that government would bear the major part of financial risk if they accepted defense orders and expanded their plants. But business objections were withdrawn as guarantees—RFC help, cost-plus contracts, carry-back of losses—came thick and fast. Before long these skeptics were boasting that private enterprise had accomplished "the miracle of war production," and they so far plucked up courage as to believe that they could again control national economic policy.

TONIC EFFECT OF WAR

Economic revival in the United States dated from the outbreak of war in Europe in September, 1939. Progress, except for a brief lapse, was accelerating. Every force of degeneration gave way to concerted effort; dejection was jolted into alertness, which became purpose and system. Fatigue was replaced by high national morale which developed private and public economic inventiveness. It was like watching blood drain back into the blanched face of a person who had fainted. Problems remained before recovery would be full, but all had obviously been placed in the way of solution.

The Price Administrator, Leon Henderson, reviewed the grateful signs of resuscitation: "The impact [of war in Europe] upon American markets was immediate. Memories of the first World War —memories of insatiable demand, of shortages, of inflation—were rekindled and there was an immediate and sharp increase in buying. The businessman who customarily bought one carload put in an order for three. Prices rose precipitately, basic commodities and basic raw materials both jumping about 25 percent in the single month of September. The rise of prices itself evoked widespread accumulation of inventories that further fed the stream of buying. A speculative boom was on.

"Employment in manufacturing increased almost 10 percent by the end of the year. Pay rolls rose 16 percent. The Federal Reserve index of industrial production, which stood at 106 percent of the 1935–1939 average in August, rose to 125 in December. This was an all-time high, exceeding the peak level of 1937 by 3 percent and the peak level of 1929 by 9 percent." Then in the period of the "Sitzkrieg," when many half believed the smoldering fire would not after all set the world aflame, speculation in basic commodity markets slumped; employment, pay rolls, and production receded toward August levels and nine months after the German demolition of Warsaw the general economic situation in the United States was not much different from its status before the war. This was only the calm before the storm. Henderson continued: "The period of the 'phony war' ended abruptly with the invasion of Denmark and Norway on April 9, 1940. A month later, on May 10, 1940, the German armies invaded the Low Countries. Within 38 days the French had been conquered and the British driven back across the Channel. The American people awoke to realization of their peril." [8]

President Roosevelt sounded the tocsin in his message to Congress, May 16, 1940: "These are ominous days—days whose swift and shocking developments force every neutral nation to look to its defenses in the light of new factors. The brutal force of modern offensive war has been loosed in all its horror." Thus the defense program was launched. From this time forward the gathering of America's economic energies was vehement and planful. By July, Congress had authorized defense expenditures of $12 billion; nine months later the appropriations had grown to $35 billion, an amount in excess of the entire cost of World War I. "The tasks confronting the [Advisory] Commission were formidable. For 10 years the American economy had limped along, operating at a fraction of its productive capacity." The index of industrial production which in 1930–1939 had averaged 87 by April, 1940, reached 112 but two years later had sprung to 174. "Expansion of production to the limit of our capacity was . . . the first task of the Defense Commission. . . . Millions of men whose skills had been neglected had to be trained. Production of raw materials, which had been geared to the requirements of a half-idle economy, had to be expanded. Industrial plant facilities, long unused, had to be brought back into operation. More than this, it was necessary to expand these facilities enormously to provide tools for the men being put to work." [9]

ADMINISTRATIVE ORGANIZATION FOR DEFENSE EFFORT

Responsibility for mobilizing the resources of the United States for defense and lend-lease production fell upon a succession of agencies created by statute and by executive order. Changing organization, functions, and relative emphasis were dictated by administrative experience and by progress of the war. The shifting array of agencies, with numerous false starts, betrayed more confusion and ineptitude than could be assigned to haste and pressure of the emergency. Bernard M. Baruch, who had been chairman of the War Industries Board in World War I, protested against repeating earlier mistakes; he urged that the War Department's industrial

---

[8] U.S. Office of Price Administration, *First Quarterly Report,* For Period Ended April 30, 1942 (Washington: Government Printing Office, 1942), pp. 1-2.

[9] *Ibid.,* pp. 2-4.

plan, which had been arrived at as a result of previous trial and error, should be followed without further loss of precious time. Mr. Baruch's reports on war industry were republished, with an introduction by General Hugh S. Johnson, vigorously critical of current "fumble and blunder." [10]

The War Production Board "with full and final authority over all American production" was not created until January 13, 1942.[11] This had been preceded, first, by a War Resources Board, appointed in September, 1939, with Edward R. Stettinius, Jr., to make an over-all survey. After invasion of the Lowlands and the fall of France revealed Germany's full power, the President created, May 25, 1940, the Office for Emergency Management. This agency later took over prime authority in the defense program, but for eight months its activities were minor while a National Defense Advisory Commission carried chief responsibility. This was appointed May 29, 1940, with seven members: William S. Knudsen, in charge of industrial production; Edward R. Stettinius, Jr., industrial materials; Sidney Hillman, labor; Leon Henderson, price stabilization; Harriet Elliott, consumer protection; Chester Davis, agriculture; and Ralph Budd, overseeing transportation. Nominally it was advisory to the revived Council of National Defense composed of six cabinet members, but it formed and executed policy.

The Office for Emergency Management was made superior to the National Defense Advisory Commission by an administrative order of January 7, 1941, when the defense effort was moving into a new phase, with the introduction in Congress three days later of the lend-lease bill. OEM progressively absorbed the functions of the Advisory Commission, retaining its main divisions with changes and setting up new specialized sections to meet developing needs. The attenuated Advisory Commission gradually became inoperative. Two principal agencies were subordinate to the Office for Emergency Management. One was the Office of Production Management "to plan, stimulate, and direct the manufacture of planes, tanks, ships, guns, and the building of the plants that make them." [12]

10 Bernard M. Baruch, *American Industry in the War*, Richard H. Hippelheuser, ed. (New York: Prentice-Hall, Inc., 1941).

11 U.S. Office of Facts and Figures, *Report to the Nation: The American Preparation for War* (Washington: Government Printing Office, 1942), p. 3.

12 U.S. Office for Emergency Management, Division of Information, *Handbook: Functions and Administration* (Washington: Government Printing Office, 1941), p. 5.

OPM came to have divisions of Production, Priorities, Purchases, Materials, Labor, Contract Distribution, and Civilian Supply. The other chief branch of the Office for Emergency Management was that of Price Administration which, later relieved of the duty of civilian supply, retained the subsections of Price Operations and Consumer Services.

Priorities, or the assignment of orders of preference in the use of scarce materials and equipment, became the chief means of production control in World War II as in World War I. As war demands grew with unexampled rapidity and yet the claims of essential civilian production were ever present, a Supply Priorities and Allocation Board, under the chairmanship of Vice-President Henry A. Wallace and composed of his colleagues from other chief federal departments and war agencies, was established in the Office for Emergency Management. Among other agencies whose work was coordinated through OEM were those of Civilian Defense, Transportation, Defense Housing, Health and Welfare Services, Inter-American Affairs, Scientific Research and Development, and the National Defense Mediation Board. The Office of Agricultural Defense Relations was in the Department of Agriculture. Alterations in defense administrative organization, while frequent, were in the direction of centralized oversight of an increasing number of specialized services.[13]

NATIONAL WEALTH IN SOCIAL CAPACITY

The defense period of eighteen months before Pearl Harbor, and more acutely the participation of the United States as a belligerent in World War II, demonstrated the principle that national wealth consists not so much in ready assets as in economic capacity, and that ability to exploit resources depends upon national will and organization. What are termed economic processes are rather, in their creative aspect, moral purpose and political application. The defense and war experience stood in contrast to national efforts during the depression. The demand of war was superior, for the crisis was immediate and the issue would be decisive. War furnished incomparable economic aids and inducements as well as obstacles. The United States doubled production and called out

13 *Ibid.*, pp. 4-8, and diagram pp. 36-37.

every social energy in order to defeat foreign enemies. While efforts to overcome the depression showed remarkable spirit beginning with 1933, they did not match, in ingenuity or devotion, the total exertion of war. For this discrepancy there were many reasons, one being that institutional changes in wartime were accepted as temporary, with the promise of return to familiar custom, while equally effective attack upon economic breakdown would involve important permanent alterations in social structure. Nevertheless it may be that deep and protracted depression, ended by war but not prevented from recurrence, threatens dangers equal to those of armed assault. In fact, war is only the most likely result of depression. And just as peace must be maintained by international concert, so prosperity within countries cannot be ensured except on a world basis.

The progress of defense mobilization, which involved overweening government initiative in organizing the economy, owed much to lessons learned by the people of the United States during the depression. The superior role played by public appropriations and explicit official decisions and directions was only part of the story. The indirect influence of government construction, contracts, and controls was increasingly powerful. Perhaps, faced by the peril of war, the country would have acquiesced in these uses of government authority in any event. As it was, there were objections to progressive deliberate involvement of the United States in the war, but these arguments were offered on moral and military grounds rather than arising from economic and political inhibitions. The mass of the people had become accustomed, during the depression, to look to the federal government as the responsible operative organ in American life. The depression had made them familiar with a proliferation of federal agencies which touched their daily doings. The executive function, expressing itself in administration, had grown in importance out of proportion to legislative and judicial departments. The theory of a central government of limited powers, preoccupied with checks and balances, had yielded much to the emergency of economic collapse. The implied powers of the federal government had been summoned and put into action as never before. National resources had rescued the whole banking system, loaned as generously to distressed industrial enterprise, come to the relief of farmers, rebuilt the Tennessee Valley, protected home-owners, and fed millions of the unemployed. The inability of private capacity, whether in the greatest business or the humblest worker, to cope with general peril had been demonstrated.

ROLE OF GOVERNMENT IN DEFENSE PRODUCTION

The expansion of defense production is crudely measured by the increase of public expenditures for this purpose. On July 1, 1940, with the British debacle at Dunkirk fresh before American eyes, the United States was spending for defense at the annual rate of $2 billion. On January 1, 1941, on the eve of lend-lease, defense spending had risen to the rate of $6.2 billion a year. By July 1, 1941, as the Germans invaded Russia, the rate of United States defense spending had reached $10.6 billion annually. By December 1, 1941, just before the attack of the Japanese on Pearl Harbor, United States spending had reached the annual rate of almost $20 billion, and already plans were calling for expenditure of $4 billion a month in 1942.[14] By December 1, 1941, government and private industry had committed themselves to spend $5.1 billion and $1.2 billion respectively to expand old plants and to build new ones.[15]

These figures, large and swiftly increasing though they are, give slight notion of the invigorating effect of defense contracts on a languid economy. Orders for every sort of construction, equipment, and product made not only the immediate impact in the industries and localities where placed, but spread themselves at accelerating rate throughout the fields of manufacture, commerce, transportation, credit, and agriculture. The certain prospect of ever-larger demands, which counted no cost except that of time, was an important sustaining force in the process of conversion from peace to war. By the end of October, 1941, War Department supply contracts of $50,000 or over had been reported from all states except Arkansas, Montana, Nevada, New Mexico, and the Dakotas. A sample of orders placed in Connecticut, an early center of defense production because of its brass, other metal, and textile industries reveals cables, flexible, $137,226; cores, armor-piercing, $55,000; cloth, under collar, $55,330; fuses, bomb, tail, $114,495; hats, service, $90,110; ditto, $57,200; webbing, $58,406; wire, $228,035; springs, operating rod, $72,947; components, ammunition, $484,000; fuses, bomb,

[14] U.S. Office of Facts and Figures, *Report to the Nation: The American Preparation for War*, p. 4.
[15] *Ibid.*, p. 44.

$59,400; plugs, fuse, $118,125; guns, submachine, $2,176,360; ditto, $3,108,855; ditto, $416,655; ditto, $2,576,123. So they ran for four large pages of fine type for Connecticut; five pages for Illinois, and shorter but substantial lists for Indiana, California, Alabama, to mention a few of the chief.[16]

After ten months of the defense effort, over 1,600 war production plants were being constructed or enlarged at a cost of $2,839,-503,000; some were completed and in operation, and most were nearing completion. Plants were built and operated by the government, were built by government and operated by private industry on lease or not, and in other cases government made loans for defense plant expansions.[17] Government financing accounted for 84 per cent of the total, private financing for the remaining 16 per cent; government financed more than 84 per cent of facilities for guns, ship construction and repairing, ammunition, shells, and bombs, while furnishing two thirds of the funds for tank production.[18] As an inducement to private expansion, under the Second Revenue Act of 1940 (October), plants certified as being used for defense purposes could be amortized in a five-year period regardless of the life of the plant, a valuable concession particularly because it had the effect of reducing high war-profits taxes. However, for price purposes the plant owner was limited to the normal depreciation allowance.[19] The benefit, though generous, was not sufficient to persuade private investors to build munitions and other plants not convertible to peacetime production.

EFFORTS TO DISTRIBUTE WAR CONTRACTS

The British had "exploded" their war production into "bits and pieces," using as many plants as possible to manufacture parts to be assembled. Small British factories were more readily converted than those in the United States because less specialized and there-

[16] U.S. War Production Board, *Listing of Major War Department Contracts by State*, June, 1940, through September, 1941, with October, 1941, Supplement. Compiled by OPM Bureau of Research and Statistics . . . (Washington: Government Printing Office, 1942), p. 4.

[17] U.S. Office for Emergency Management, *Defense, One Year* (Washington: Government Printing Office, 1941), p. 11.

[18] *Ibid.*, p. 12.

[19] U.S. Office for Emergency Management, *Address Delivered by David Ginsburg . . . before the Practicing Law Institute, New York City, . . . the Amortization Deduction* (Washington: 1941, mimeographed).

fore more flexible. However, from an early stage in the American defense program efforts were made to encourage subcontracting by the large firms which were primarily favored with orders. Inevitably the big producers of known competence, resources, and responsibility were the first recourse. Beginning in September, 1940, the Office of Small Business Activities, the Defense Contracts Service, and the Division of Contract Distribution were successively spreading production so as to incorporate small-scale enterprises. Such a spread was evidently desirable because it utilized existing facilities, avoided migration of workers, and reduced after-war readjustments. Trains were sent through the country with exhibits of parts to be made, regional "defense production clinics" gave more specialized information, and numerous agencies assisted in bringing prime contractors and subcontractors together. However, from the beginning, the largest firms and plants received the overwhelming proportion of orders and executed about 70 per cent of the work. Most of the subcontracts were let to companies which were themselves large. The defense and war periods increased the dominance of the industrial giants which was conspicuous beforehand. Officials who had so recently launched a fresh campaign to break up business consolidation, where they said anything, excused current developments on the score of the emergency, but in numerous ways evidence showed that preference in war contracts added permanently to concentration of control.[20]

It was confessed that "the biggest problem of all is finding the best ways to bring the little man into the defense program." In spite of obstacles, feats were performed in converting small plants to war production. When he found that his materials had gone to war the owner of a 20-man plant that made merry-go-rounds "stepped out and talked himself into a subcontract from an airplane company. . . . Men who had spent years carving horse heads went to work on lathes. Those who had painted designs on thrill rides took to casting dies. Special training was given the men. The staff of 20 was doubled. Now men and machines who made dizzying Ski-Hi rides are making metal towers used by repair crews to reach the noses of bombers. . . . Versatile men and machines of a mid-

[20] See U.S. Smaller War Plants Corporation, *Economic Concentration and World War II, Report . . . to the Special Committee to Study Problems of American Small Business, United States Senate.* Senate Committee Print No. 6, 79 Cong., 2 Sess., pp. 1–64, especially pp. 32–33.

western factory, which used to make thermostats for stoves, are now making the intricate devices that fire artillery shells." A safe and lock plant converted to producing tank parts, mines, and complete gun units.[21]

Defense production required the supply of critical and strategic materials through new production, stockpiling, and conservation. Metals like magnesium, tungsten, copper, aluminum, and lead stood high on the list. New plants for the extraction of these were built or financed by government, and private interests were assisted by every means to expand their output. High-cost copper producers were subsidized, an economical method, since it increased production without raising the price of most of the supply. Supplementing separate actions to increase imports and restrict less essential uses, General Metals Order No. 1 was issued by the Director of Priorities of the Office of Production Management May 1, 1941; it established inventory control over sixteen scarce metals and alloys to prevent accumulation in private hands beyond current defense production demands.

The Production Division of OPM had responsibility for estimating total defense needs in aircraft, ordnance, tools, construction, and shipbuilding, recommended plant expansions, and passed upon foreign and domestic defense orders. The Purchases Division reviewed major proposals for defense and construction projects to avoid competitive bidding of services and to ensure that the right quantities were available at the correct time and at reasonable prices.

CONTROL BY PRIORITIES

This much done, the Priorities Division of the OPM set up and supervised a system to put "first things first." The priorities machinery was the heart of production control, and it became increasingly comprehensive, not to say intricate, as time went on. The priorities scheme, which applied to both military and necessary civilian production, had the double purpose of making materials, equipment, transportation, and labor available in the order of defense needs and at the times required to keep the enormous national production line moving. Some industries, such as aluminum

[21] U.S. Office for Emergency Management, *Conversion: America's Job* (Arsenal of Democracy Series; Washington: Government Printing Office, 1942), pp. 5, 18–19.

and machine tools, had been placed on mandatory priority status earlier, but a law in June, 1941, specifically provided for the use of priorities. The Priorities Critical List embraced about three hundred items on which Army and Navy orders could be given automatic preference; contracting officers simply assigned the designated ratings, thus eliminating separate consideration of each case. The highest rating in the priorities system was AA, reserved for extreme emergencies, after which came A-1-a, A-1-b, A-1-c, and so on down to A-1-j, when a new series began with A-2 and continued to A-10. Some civilian ratings were designated B-1 down to B-8.

Limited blanket ratings, avoiding numerous individual certificates, covered vital industries such as tool-building, and project ratings similarly applied to materials for defense plant construction. Public services and essential industries such as mining, railroads, and food-processing plants could secure an A-10 rating for repair parts. However, for production as a whole the individual preference rating certificate was the typical form. Issued to a manufacturer, he sent it to his materials supplier with his order. It showed the delivery date and the rating, thus determining how the order was to be scheduled. Innumerable practical problems were involved for producers as well as administrators. Particularly as blanket ratings were used without report to the central authorities, it became impossible to keep supplies equal to the volume of materials ordered with the benefit of preference ratings. The saying came to be that a low priority was nothing but a "hunting license." This situation of serious shortages, even for military requirements, was partially cured by M (Materials) orders which directly allocated production. All suppliers were obliged to report their expected production for the month, and specific quantities were assigned to specific users, so that these were sure of being served, no matter how many preference orders were outstanding.

L (Limitation) orders were issued by the Priorities Division, on recommendation of the Civilian Supply Division, and conserved scarce materals by reducing the amounts devoted to civilian goods such as automobiles, refrigerators, washing machines, and vacuum cleaners.[22]

22 On stockpiling of scarce materials see Office for Emergency Management, *Materials for Defense* (The Arsenal of Democracy Series; Washington: Government Printing Office, 1941); for a succinct description of the defense priorities system, see

The Office of Defense Transportation was created in 1941, when freight and passenger traffic on the railroads was increasing for the third successive year. Half the increase in traffic volume from the 1938 low occurred in 1941. That the railroads were not taken over by government in World War II as in World War I was due to their more efficient management and their ability to move the loads, supplemented as they were with means of transport which had developed in the interval. The efficiency of freight service was increased 20 per cent in the defense period; the average net ton-miles per freight train-hour increased from 12,473 in 1938 to 14,938 in 1941.[23]

PROGRESS OF PRICE STABILIZATION

The Advisory Commission early saw that the war and rearmament program "would bring acute pressures to bear upon the price structure, which if unchecked would work severe hardship upon our people and seriously impede the program itself." [24] The first protection against this danger was in expanded supply. Three arrangements were devised to meet the inability or unwillingness of individuals to bear the risk of financing wartime plants and equipment. The first was the Emergency Plant Facilities Contract, under which enterprises financed expansion and were reimbursed by the Army and Navy in not more than five annual installments. An act passed by Congress, October 9, 1940, permitted war contractors to borrow on these contracts from banks and the Reconstruction Finance Corporation. The second plan was that under which corporations were allowed to write off wartime plant investments in five years or retroactively in a shorter time if the emergency did not last so long. A special committee was set up to certify that the plant facilities were essential to the national defense. The third method was construction by the Defense Plants Corporation, a

---

Office for Emergency Management, *Handbook, Functions and Administration* (Washington: Government Printing Office, 1941), pp. 18–25, 31; Office for Emergency Management, *War Facts* (Washington: Government Printing Office, 1942), pp. 15–23 is fuller, though containing some developments in the period of war production proper, as does also War Production Board, *Priorities in Force* (Washington: Government Printing Office, 1942) compiled to March 6, 1942.

[23] J. J. Pelley, president Assn. American Railroads, in *American Year Book,* 1941, pp. 518–519.

[24] U.S. Office of Price Administration, *First Quarterly Report,* 1942 (Washington: Government Printing Office, 1942), p. 4.

subsidiary of the ubiquitous RFC, after which the war production facilities were leased to private firms for operation.

The chief duty of the Price Stabilization Division of the Advisory Commission was to prevent price increases directly. The problem at first was specific and local, for most industries began far below capacity. Only where government war demand was concentrated did production rise toward capacity and threaten price increase. Consultations with industries sought to choke off speculative excesses and restrained price rises in critical metals and other materials, farm implements, machine tools, and textiles. Help was given to Army and Navy procurement officers on the timing of purchases and the spreading of orders to match existing capacities. These measures were felt to be successful; while between May, 1940, and February, 1941, the increase in total industrial production was 24 per cent and in durable manufactures affected by the defense program the increase was 43 per cent, the rise in the general wholesale price index was only 3 per cent and this was partly on imported materials.[25]

As defense production and demand advanced, shortages in one key industry spread to another and began to create "bottlenecks" farther along the line in industries which had not reached capacity output. The commission attempted to cope with the stringency by a system of voluntary priorities, but it was soon clear that advisory powers were not enough. In January, 1941, the President bestowed particular powers by establishing the Office of Production Management, with three divisions to care for production, materials, and labor supply. OPM soon imposed emergency compulsory priorities to make sure that defense production secured the necessary materials.

Moreover, price pressures proved too strong to be controlled by mere agreements and warnings. Price increases of key products threatened to start whirlwind spirals as with metals in 1916 and 1917. A turning point in prices came in February, 1941. While the general wholesale price index and that of 28 basic commodities began to move upward in August, 1940, it was not until February, 1941, that acceleration became serious, spreading to embrace retail prices. The danger of a universal price rise became clear with enactment of lend-lease in March, 1941, as the "arsenal of democ-

[25] *Ibid.*, p. 5.

racy" would do "no worrying about the dollar sign or the terms of repayment." [26]

Already in February, 1941, the Price Stabilization Division had begun issuing maximum price schedules, the first for secondhand machine tools and four others covering certain metals, metal scrap, and bituminous coal. Now the President on April 11, 1941, replaced the Price Division by the Office of Price Administration and Civilian Supply, "to take all lawful steps necessary or appropriate in order to prevent price spiralling, rising cost of living, profiteering, and inflation . . . ." Not yet was the need for furnishing sufficient goods to the civilian population as a means of holding down prices separated from Price Administration and treated as a production problem. Though OPACS received additional power to issue maximum price schedules, it could impose no direct penalties for violations. Withdrawal of priority privileges was not effective punishment, and the agency had no control at the retail level. Voluntary action continued the principal reliance. Suggestions were given, fair prices were reported, and adherence to them was requested. "Freeze letters" went to those with prices out of line urging that prices must be held, and industry groups entered into informal agreements to limit prices of metals, paper and pulp, rubber products, textiles, foods, hides and leather, fuel, lumber and building materials, chemicals, and house furnishings. However, by August 1, 1941, it was found necessary to issue formal price ceilings for combed cotton yarn, fine cotton grey goods, nickel and brass scrap, hides, and pig iron. By this time 12.5 per cent of the total wholesale value of minerals, manufactures, and imports had been brought under informal price control, and an additional 10 per cent was under formal control, so that almost one fourth of the wholesale price structure was under some regulation by midsummer.

MORE AUTHORITY OVER PRICES REQUIRED

In spite of this, wholesale prices rose during the spring and summer by 2 per cent a month. The administrator said that "far-reaching changes were taking place in the underlying situation and it was clear that pressure upon the price structure would grow month by month and place impossible burdens upon the office as at that

[26] *Ibid.*, p. 7.

time constituted." Statutory powers were demanded for price control. "The single dominant factor in the changing economy was the volume of defense expenditures." When the defense program was launched, monthly expenditures for war materials totaled $200 million, but ten months later, in April, 1941, expenditures were $1 billion a month. In the following eight months they were to double to the rate of $2 billion. "It was this rapid expansion of defense outlays that was the dynamic element in the developing economic situation and was the source of the increasing pressure on prices." [27]

From the standpoint of price control and defense production, consumers were becoming too well supplied with certain manufactures embodying scarce labor and metals. Income payments rose .5 per cent a month from August, 1939, to April, 1940; 1 per cent a month from then till November, 1940; 1.5 per cent till April, 1941; and for the balance of the year increased 2 per cent a month, bringing total income payments to $104 billion in December, 1941. Consumers, long starved for money with which to buy much-wanted conveniences, promptly laid out their increased incomes at the rate of $78 billion a year in August, 1941, as compared with $65 billion in May, 1940, when the defense program began. Between 1939 and 1941 the increase in sales of automobiles was 35 per cent; vacuum cleaners, 45 per cent; incandescent lamps, 61 per cent; electric washing machines, 63 per cent; household refrigerators, 69 per cent; and kitchen ranges, 110 per cent. Investment also increased with income, and contributed to swell the volume of consumer demand. Fortunately, the industrial slack making possible increase in supply prevented prices from rising in proportion to demand; industrial production rose by 20 per cent in the single year 1941, bringing the index to a level almost twice as high as the average for 1930–1939.[28]

The advance in production as a percentage of capacity was spectacular in certain industries which were in midstream of war demand. Thus from August, 1939, to October, 1941, the production of steel ingots rose from 61 per cent of capacity to 99 per cent—indeed, production reached 97 per cent of capacity as early as February, 1941. Pig iron production rose from 65 to 98.1 per cent of capacity; copper refinery production, from 57.6 to 86.7 after reaching almost maximum capacity nine months earlier; cotton spindle activity, from 85.1 to 125.8 per cent; passenger cars, from 10.9 to 58.9 per cent;

[27] *Ibid.*, p. 9. [28] *Ibid.*, p. 10.

cement, from 56.6 to 78.6; bituminous coal, from 62.6 to 95.8 per cent; furniture production, from 59 per cent to 90 per cent. In the last month before the outbreak of war in Europe, none of these industries was operating at more than 86 per cent of capacity, and every one was well below full capacity when the defense program began; however, by February, 1941, pig iron, steel ingot, copper refining, cotton and rayon textile production were at or above 95 per cent of capacity.[29] For years of depression every effort had been made to restore production in key industries, and in vain; now war revived them in a trice.

AGREEABLE FEATURES OF DEFENSE ECONOMY

The defense period was a delightful economic interlude, full of pleasures and with few penalties. Incomes of most segments of the population rose, work was increasingly abundant and better paid, the numbers of the unemployed were being gradually reduced. Wholesale prices increased, imparting an exhilaration to business, while for a time these increases were not reflected, or not fully reflected, in retail prices, a fact which gave consumers a sense of benefit. Farmers were enjoying an increase in prices of their staple crops far greater than the advance in prices of things farmers bought. Trade and transportation picked up with production, and private investment again appeared attractive. War was the cause of all, but war was as yet far from American shores, and the people were assured on the highest authority that they were privileged to aid free nations with their output and would not be called upon to give their lives. The frustration of the depression was dissipated by the sense of contributing to a worthy object. Alarm over totalitarian aggression was genuine and increasing, but it had not yet become national dread or acute fear for American safety. The defense program induced a glow, economic and emotional, and only later did tensions and sacrifices enter.

By summer of 1941 it appeared that the defense economy was facing an inflation problem of wartime proportions "and that it would be necessary to strengthen the apparatus of price control with full and explicit statutory authority."[30] The President asked this power from Congress in a message of June 30. Lengthy hear-

[29] *Ibid.*, p. 11.   [30] *Ibid.*

ings were held on bills in House and Senate. In his supporting testimony the Price Administrator relied on the experience of the United States in World War I and on that of foreign countries in both world wars. He urged that direct control in particular areas of price pressure be supplemented by fiscal measures designed to siphon off excess purchasing power. Wages would have to be restrained, but this duty should be given to another agency than that charged with price stabilization. While congressional consideration of more effective price control proceeded into the autumn, in September and October Axis submarines attacked United States destroyers patrolling the Atlantic, and in November the President received authority to arm merchant ships sailing to belligerent ports. The House of Representatives passed the Emergency Price Control bill on November 28, 1941, just nine days before the Japanese attacked Pearl Harbor.

In the four months that the bill was under discussion in Congress the Office of Price Administration and Civilian Supply, relying on executive authority, had taken about a hundred informal actions covering almost every field except that of farm products; these actions brought an additional 12 per cent of the wholesale price structure under control.[31] Since the price of raw cotton had been rising, the Price Administrator was obliged to announce a sliding scale of ceiling prices on cotton yarns and grey goods, tying the maximum prices of these to the market price of spot cotton. This device was dropped when the General Maximum Price Regulation was issued. Formal ceilings held firmly, and informal controls, apart from their application to automobiles and petroleum products, were also successful. Uncontrolled prices, on the contrary, continued to rise; this was a constant threat to maintenance of price ceilings and in fact forced upward revision of these in a number of cases.

Between February and December, 1941, retail prices of foods, clothing, and household furnishings rose by 15 per cent.[32] Firms were so numerous and so widely dispersed geographically that control over retail prices could not be exercised except on the basis of statutory power of enforcement. The Price Administrator complained of the rise in prices of farm products which breached his ceilings on other goods. Between August, 1939, and March, 1942, prices received by farmers increased by 66 per cent, much exceed-

31 *Ibid.*, p. 12.   32 *Ibid.*, p. 13.

ing prices that farmers paid, with the result that the parity ratio rose from 70 to 99. However, beginning in October, 1941, the upward trend in farm prices was matched by a rise in prices farmers paid, so the farmer, like the city worker, was caught in the inflationary spiral.[33]

In the two years from August, 1939, to August, 1941, production of consumers' goods increased about 25 per cent, the automobile industry having completed its 1941-model year with an output of 4,325,000 cars, while the supply of household equipment advanced generously. From August, 1941, however, the production of consumers' goods, particularly durable goods requiring metals, reflected the increasing war demands for materials and equipment. The automobile industry was obliged to reduce the output of 1942 models by half, and similar restrictions were imposed for refrigerators, washers, ironers, vacuum cleaners, stoves, and automatic phonographs. Soon it was apparent that with 50 per cent of the national production converted to war needs, there would be no more consumers' goods using significant amounts of metals.[34]

The attack on Pearl Harbor ended the period of selective price controls. By calls to the commodity exchanges the Price Administrator moved quickly to prevent increases in domestic prices of rubber, tin, Australian wool, copra, kapok, and other materials imported from the Far East. The first formal wartime emergency schedule and the first at the retail level was issued to halt rapidly rising prices of flashlights on the Pacific coast, where air raids were expected. The War Production Board froze all sales of automobile tires and directed their rationing by the Office of Price Administration; this action brought OPA back into the field of civilian supply from which it had been separated in August, and its responsibility for rationing was progressively developed. Industry was rapidly approaching capacity in plant and manpower; the slack was being taken up and more production could be had only from overtime work, multiple-shift operation, and new plants.

The Emergency Price Control Act was signed by the President on January 30, 1942, and for the first time the Office of Price Administration had undisputed statutory power to regulate prices and rents and punish violators. However, advertising was not called a commodity and so was not included in the provisions of the act.

[33] *Ibid.*, p. 31.   [34] *Ibid.*, p. 27.

What was more important, the Price Administrator's authority was severely limited with respect to agricultural commodities; he could not set ceiling prices on these until they had reached at least 110 per cent of parity. The prices of farm staples still had a great way to rise before this minimum limit was reached. Moreover, since the increase of farm prices contributed powerfully to the advance in prices of goods which farmers bought, the magnitude of the permitted rise in farm prices was difficult to foresee.

The General Maximum Price Regulation was issued April 28, 1942, along with a series of orders paving the way for rent control. GMPR, as the order was known, applied at manufacturing, wholesale, and retail levels to virtually everything that Americans ate, wore, and used. Each manufacturer and seller, including those supplying services, was limited to prices which he charged in March, 1942.

LABOR MOBILIZED FOR DEFENSE PRODUCTION

The way in which war, at a price, invigorated the economy was shown in the improvement of employment and of labor conditions generally in the defense period from the spring of 1940 through the year 1941. With respect to labor, however, more than in some other sectors of the economy, long neglect during the depression made rapid recovery difficult. In branches of work most necessary to defense production, skills had deteriorated and apprentices had not been trained. Many new jobs opened, requiring special capacities, could not be quickly filled even from the large body of the unemployed. Numbers of defense workers with lesser skills did not come from the ranks of the unemployed, but shifted from other industrial jobs, came from agriculture or casual labor, or were domestics or young persons and women not ordinarily seeking employment. In fact, sudden conversion to war production in some instances caused "priorities unemployment" in civilian industries which could not secure critical materials. Emergency employment projects built up during the depression, such as WPA, CCC, and NYA, combed their rolls for individuals possessing skills or aptitudes most needed in defense work and as far as possible applied the labor of others to constructing induction centers, airfields, or community works in war centers. Accelerating migration of workers to war centers raised problems of housing, educational, and health facilities, particularly where war industries were established in places with small or no previous population.

Rapid as was the increase in nonagricultural employment—from 35,321,000 in April, 1940, to 41,036,000 in December, 1941—pay rolls increased faster, especially in durable goods industries. In this group the index of employment (1923–1925 = 100) increased from 104.3 for 1940 to 144.2 in December, 1941, while the index of pay rolls advanced from 107.8 to 195.4; wage earners in durable goods numbered 4,015,100 in 1940 and 5,553,100 in December, 1941, while the weekly pay roll in the same period advanced from $108,008,000 to $195,794,000. In addition to new jobs available, the work week was lengthened, overtime made itself felt, and many workers shifted into better-paying jobs. In the durable goods industries average weekly hours increased from 39.2 in 1940 to 42.8 in December, 1941, while average hourly earnings increased from 73.4 cents to 87.1 cents and average weekly earnings went up from $29.88 to $38.62.[35] The rise of pay rolls above employment was particularly striking in blast furnaces, steel works, and rolling mills, foundry and machine shops, petroleum refining, and cotton mills. In wholesale and retail trade, payrolls lagged behind employment. The advantage to all manufacturing workers in the defense period was not so much from advances in wage rates as from fuller employment and pay rolls. While the index of weekly pay rolls between the year 1940 and December, 1941, increased 62 per cent, the cost of living (or more precisely the cost of goods purchased by wage earners and lower salaried workers in large cities) increased slightly less than 10 per cent—from 100.2 in 1940 to 110.5 in December, 1941.[36]

An important element underlying the whole employment situation was the increase in numbers in the armed forces, which grew from 822,000 in November, 1940, to 2,071,000 a year later.[37] The Selective Training and Service Act had been signed September 16, 1940. In addition to the larger number of draft deferments because of specialized skills, some men actually inducted into the military

[35] U.S. Department of Commerce, *Survey of Current Business,* 1942 Supplement (Washington: Government Printing Office, 1942), p. 38; U.S. Bureau of Labor Statistics, *Chart Series,* II, No. 2 (June, 1941), A2; III, No. 1 (March, 1942), A6.

[36] U. S. Bureau of Labor Statistics, *Chart Series,* III, No. 1 (March, 1942), A3, A32.

[37] U. S. Department of Commerce, *Survey of Current Business,* 1942 Supplement, p. 38.

service were placed in an enlisted reserve and released for war work.

In the eighteen months from July, 1940, to December, 1941, some 2,500,000 persons received instruction, to fit them for war work, in 1,200 public vocational and trade schools, in more than 150 colleges and universities, and in 1,000 shops set up in public schools. Over 200,000 workers in war contract plants received "in-plant" training, and several hundred thousand on Youth Administration and Civilian Conservation rolls completed defense training courses.[38] A Federal Committee on Apprenticeship of the Department of Labor, in cooperation with the Labor Division of the Office of Production Management, organized apprenticeship features of in-plant training.

The month before Pearl Harbor a plan was announced for the training of 200,000 "lead men" of superior skill, while at the same time operations in war plants would be broken down into their simplest components to permit the less skilled to perform them.

Workers of forty or fifty and above, who had been regarded as constituting a special problem during the depression because of their age, suddenly came industrially alive. Large numbers, especially those with scarce skills, came out of retirement, often surrendering old-age assistance and annuities to return to work. In September, 1941, it was estimated that 30,000 women were at work in arms and munitions plants alone, and women were being eagerly taken in aircraft, radio, electrical instrument, and other light industries such as those requiring assembly of small parts.[39]

PROBLEMS OF NEGRO WORKERS AND MIGRANTS

A Negro Employment and Training Branch of the Labor Division of the Office of Production Management was established in April, 1941, but opportunity to draw Negroes into war work, particularly in skilled occupations, was persistently neglected by government and obstructed by employers and white workers. Here was a large labor resource which in defiance of defense needs and democratic principles was being disregarded. Not until an impressive "March on Washington" of indignant Negroes was threatened did

[38] Witt Bowden, of the Bureau of Labor Statistics, in *American Year Book*, 1941, p. 600.   [39] *Ibid.*, p. 601.

the President issue an executive order, June 25, 1941, creating in OPM a Committee on Fair Employment Practice. The committee was to investigate complaints of discrimination in employment by reason of race, creed, color, or national origin, and all defense contracts were directed to contain an antidiscrimination clause. The work of the committee encountered many embarrassments but became increasingly effective, though not until long after Pearl Harbor, when the labor market had much tightened, were its objects anything like achieved. Before Pearl Harbor the shift to war industries did not reduce aggregate employment in civilian industries.

The chairman of the House Committee on Defense Migration said that prior to Pearl Harbor about 2,000,000 people above the normal movement had been attracted to war boom towns. In January, 1941, the Division of Coordination of National Defense Housing was created in the Office for Emergency Management; in eleven months 100,000 defense homes were built or building, and 6,500 dormitory units and 200,000 FHA privately financed homes had gone into construction. In June, 1941, Congress appropriated $150,-000,000 to assist the suddenly crowded wartime communities to expand their facilities in schools, hospitals, water, sewage disposal, and milk pasteurization.[40]

The Office of Production Management Labor Division had a Mediation and Conciliation Section operating in war industries to prevent disputes and stoppages which were numerous because of job shifts and disturbance of craft lines. Rapid labor turnover was a conspicuous feature of the defense period. The rate of discharges increased, perhaps partly because under the Fair Labor Standards Act passed in October, 1940, all weekly hours beyond forty became overtime, and employers had additional incentive for securing the best workers. However, voluntary departures increased more rapidly than discharges. The rate of layoffs in 1941 dropped toward half what it had been in 1940. Total separations in representative factories in 135 industries rose from 40.27 per hundred employees in 1940 to 46.68 in 1941, while accessions increased from 52.72 to 64.51.[41]

This conciliation section of the Labor Division of OPM was fol-

[40] *Ibid.*, p. 608.
[41] U.S. Bureau of Labor Statistics, *Chart Series*, III, No. 1 (March, 1942), A41.

lowed by the establishment in March, 1941, of the National Defense Mediation Board composed of four members representing employers, four representing workers, and three members from the public. The board handled cases certified to it by the Secretary of Labor and undertook to reduce the number of stoppages, which had increased rapidly; whereas in 1940 2.3 per cent of all workers were involved in strikes, 8.4 per cent were involved in 1941.[42] Late in December, 1941, a specially called management-labor conference promised no stoppages and peaceful settlement of all disputes. The War Labor Board was set up later.

REVIVAL OF EXPORTS

The increase in United States foreign trade was an important part of economic improvement in the defense period. Exports not only engaged labor and plants and absorbed raw materials, but removed the goods from American markets. The following table shows the sudden advance in 1940:

INDEXES OF CHANGES IN QUANTITY, UNIT VALUE, AND TOTAL VALUE
OF EXPORTS AND IMPORTS OF MERCHANDISE, SELECTED
YEARS 1926–1930 TO 1941
(1923–1925 average = 100)

Source: Adapted from U. S. Department of Commerce, Bureau of the Census, *Foreign Commerce and Navigation of the U. S. for the Calendar Year 1941* (Washington: Government Printing Office, 1944), p. xv.

	1926–30 av.	1931–35 av.	1936	1937	1938	1939	1940	1941
Exports, including re-exports, value	105	44	54	73	68	70	88	113
Exports of U. S. merchandise								
Quantity	122	76	82	105	105	110	129	154
Unit value (price)	86	59	66	70	65	64	68	73
Value	105	45	54	74	68	70	88	112
General imports, value	104	44	62	80	51	60	68	86

It is apparent that the increase in exports was accounted for almost entirely by United States merchandise rather than by re-exports. Advance in United States exports to Canada, beginning in 1940, was striking, as seen in the following table:

[42] *Ibid.*, p. A37.

U. S. EXPORTS, INCLUDING RE-EXPORTS, SELECTED
YEARS 1938 TO 1941
(*In thousands of dollars*)

	1938	1939	1940	1941
Total	$3,094,440	$3,177,176	$4,021,146	$5,147,154
North America, Northern	475,572	498,170	724,612	1,012,331

Source: Bureau of the Census, *Foreign Commerce and Navigation of the U. S. for the Calendar Year 1941*, p. xii.

There were large increases in exports to Europe and Africa, but not to Asia. However, as late as the year 1941 United States exports of domestic merchandise to Japan were as follows: total agricultural, $9,816,556; total nonagricultural, $49,295,932; nonagricultural semimanufactures, $17,582,507; and finished manufactures, $24,009,-458.[43] Japan received in 1941 from the United States only 289 tons of iron and steel scrap, worth $4,580, while the United Kingdom received 91,577 tons worth $1,878,223, the largest shipments of iron and steel scrap going to any country.[44] In 1941, Germany had virtually nothing from the United States.[45]

However, in 1940 the United States exported to Japan 958,778 tons of scrap worth $16,971,450, and in addition 3,151,793 barrels of motor fuel and gasoline worth $16,230,881, of which 199,540 barrels were high-grade (presumably airplane) motor fuel valued at $576,659. Japan received from the United States in 1940 total petroleum and petroleum products valued at $55,125,351. In this year the United States exported slightly less of these commodities to the United Kingdom, which received 3,126,610 barrels of motor fuel and gasoline valued at $10,008,082, and total petroleum and petroleum products valued at $51,097,733; however, Canada received a larger total of these products.[46] In 1940 the United States exported to Japan 24,691 tons of potassic fertilizer materials worth $933,315, and in 1941 the quantity of these products exported to Japan was 22,388 tons worth $673,028. Japan got no explosives from the United States in either year.[47]

[43] U.S. Department of Commerce, Bureau of the Census, *Foreign Commerce and Navigation of the U.S. for the Calendar Year 1941* (Washington: Government Printing Office, 1944), p. xxi.   [44] *Ibid.*, p. 394.   [45] *Ibid.*, p. xxi.
[46] *Ibid.*, 1940, pp. 467, 483.   [47] *Ibid.*, 1940, p. 576; 1941, p. 480.

Though starting on a very small scale in the third month of 1941 and not reaching before Pearl Harbor the volume afterward achieved, what the United States shipped under the Lend-Lease Act of March 11, 1941, even in that year provided a sharp fillip to exports.

LEND-LEASE EXPORTS, BY MONTHS, 1941
(Value in dollars)

March	$ 1,316,550	August	$ 66,663,424
April	$ 5,631,469	September	$ 85,848,371
May	$16,471,658	October	$166,674,045
June	$34,693,311	November	$136,810,906
July	$71,817,607	December	$154,975,547
		Total	$740,902,888

Source: Bureau of Census, *Foreign Commerce and Navigation of the U.S. for the Calendar Year 1941*, p. xxxvi. For a fuller treatment see U.S. Lend-Lease Administration Office, *Report on Lend-Lease Operations, 1941–42* (Washington: Government Printing Office, 1943).

VARIETY OF LEND-LEASE EXPORTS

The total of lend-lease exports, even in less than ten months of the opening year, was almost a fourth of the United States total exports in value in 1938 and 1939 and between a fifth and a sixth of the total value of exports in 1940. Lend-lease exports in 1941 went to practically all countries except those with which the United States was later at war, as appears below:

LEND-LEASE EXPORTS, BY COUNTRIES, 1941
(Value in dollars)

North America	$ 14,259,490	Asia	$40,547,851
South America	$ 347,390	Australia	
Europe		and Oceania	$14,480,695
United Kingdom	$572,620,342	Africa	$93,520,393
U.S.S.R.	$ 544,932		
Other countries			
in Europe	$ 4,554,795		

Source: Bureau of the Census, *Foreign Commerce and Navigation of the U.S. for the Calendar Year 1941*, p. xxxvi.

The variety of lend-lease exports, making good the President's promise that the United States would be the "arsenal of democracy," is partially seen in the table following:

LEND-LEASE EXPORTS, BY SELECTED SUBGROUPS, 1941

Meat products $82,626,539
Animal oils and fats, edi-
ble $25,902,843
Dairy products $56,394,216
Eggs in shell. . . . . $ 6,671,151
Egg products $38,022,205
Grains and preparations . . $12,034,946
Vegetables and prepara-
tions $18,519,295
Tobacco, unmanufactured $23,030,999
Raw cotton $34,103,567
Nonmetallic minerals:
Motor fuel and gasoline. $34,333,850
Lubricating oil $11,177,467

Metals and manufactures,
except machinery and
vehicles:
Iron and steel semi-
manufactures $36,087,378
Copper and manufac-
tures . . . . $ 9,970,326
Machinery and vehicles:
Power-driven metal-
working machinery . . $ 7,293,929
Tractors and parts. . . . . $ 7,401,126
Automobiles:
Motor trucks, busses,
and chassis $27,147,296
Passenger cars and
chassis . . . . $ 2,782,887
Other automobiles, parts
and accessories . . . . . $ 3,377,479
Other machinery and ve-
hicles $77,804,037

Source: Adapted from Bureau of the Census, *Foreign Commerce and Navigation of the U.S. for the Calendar Year 1941*, p. xxxvi.

A notion of the increase in total exports of United States merchandise, of concentrated foods and some other items in 1941, after lend-lease commenced, as compared with 1940, is obtained from the table below:

EXPORTS OF DOMESTIC MERCHANDISE, BY ECONOMIC CLASSES, 1940 AND 1941
(Value in thousands of dollars)

	1940	1941
TOTAL	$3,934,181	$5,019,877
Manufactured foodstuffs	$166,872	$418,457
Meats	16,809	94,591
Lard	12,724	38,567
Milk, condensed, evaporated, and dried	14,177	62,053
Egg products	68	38,307
Wool noils (inferior combings) and wastes	5,340	125
Wool tops (good wool)	—	2,027
Coal	82,043	113,704
Fertilizers, phosphate rock	3,845	5,854

Source: Adapted from Bureau of the Census, *Foreign Commerce and Navigation of the U. S. for the Calendar Year 1941*, p. xxii.

In the spring and summer of 1940 the funds in the United States of countries conquered or overrun by Germany and the Soviet Union were frozen—those of Norway and Denmark on April 8, of the Netherlands, Belgium, and Luxembourg on May 10, of France on June 17, and of Latvia, Estonia, and Lithuania on July 14, 1940. The funds in the United States of the Soviet Union and of Japan were not frozen until a year later, both on the same day, June 14, 1941. Most of these actions were taken under Executive Order No. 8389, regulating transactions in foreign exchange and foreign-owned property. Under a presidential proclamation of July 17, 1941, the same purpose was served of preventing supplies from going to aggressors by issuance of lists of "blocked nationals," firms abroad with which no commercial or financial dealings were permitted.[48]

WAR BRINGS "FULL EMPLOYMENT"

It remains to mark the stages by which the United States entered the war. This subject may appear to many to belong in the sphere of political and military considerations, and to call for no emphasis in an economic history of the period. But the war, including the participation of the United States, was part and parcel of the depression. Most would agree that without the depression, itself a consequence of World War I, there would have been no World War II. Amidst the economic strains which led to the destruction of international morale it is enough to remember the burden of unemployment in Germany, which more than any other one thing was responsible for dictatorship there and the chain of fatal consequences. Only the heedless will draw a line at the outbreak of war in Europe in the opening days of September, 1939, and say: Here began a new historical chapter.

Actually, in the crucial respect of waste of economic resources, human and physical, the war was, particularly for the United States, a deepening of the depression. If the nation had ten million unemployed when the war began, a few years later, when it was well into the conflict, it had three times as many not productively employed. Count eleven million in the armed forces, twenty million in war

[48] U.S. Treasury Department, *Documents Pertaining to Foreign Funds Control* (Washington: March 30, 1942), p. 5.

production, plus others, not so conveniently separable, who were supplying the demands of battle, and it is clear that "full employment" was a flattering unction. Their concentrated efforts for ruin the world around were for purposes which, by very definition, could have no place in a normal economy. Mere idleness of the thirty odd million, if the economic view could be separated from other considerations, would have been vastly preferable.

In his second campaign for the Presidency, in August, 1936, Roosevelt declared: "If war should break out again in another continent, let us not blink the fact that we would find thousands of Americans who would be tempted for the sake of fool's gold to break down or evade our neutrality. . . . To resist the clamor of that greed, if war should come, would require the unswerving support of all Americans who love peace." He was himself, in three short years, to lead the clamor to break down and evade the nation's neutrality. Often—whether self-deceived or not—he was less than candid in his acts and reasoning, and committed the nation against its will, or at least in advance of its will.

We know from experience that the origins of a war do not appear accurately until long afterward, with full publication of documents and calm appraisal of all environing circumstances. The allusions here to events preceding the declared entry of the United States into World War II are taken from the chronology issued by the government.[49]

It is not necessary to go further back than the special session of Congress called by the President September 21, 1939, to repeal the arms embargo of the Neutrality Act of 1937. The "cash and carry" device of the Neutrality Act of November 4, 1939—belligerents could take away their war supplies, previously paid for, in their own ships—was the result of the fateful debate. Because of Britain's supremacy on the sea, this meant that munitions and war materials of the United States went—with the exception of Japan, not yet in the war—only to the Allies. It was the first of a crowding succession of violations of the neutrality proclamation of two months before, which recited that "the laws and treaties of the United States . . . impose upon all persons who may be within their territory and

[49] "Events Leading up to World War II," *House Document* No. 541, 78 Cong., 2 Sess., p. 217.

jurisdiction the duty of an impartial neutrality during the existence of the contest" and that "it is the duty of a neutral government not to permit or suffer the making of its territory or territorial waters subservient to the purposes of war . . . ." President Roosevelt, in calling the special session of Congress, had assured his audience in these words, "I give you my deep and unalterable conviction, based on years of experience as a worker in the field of international peace, that by the repeal of the embargo the United States will more probably remain at peace than if the law remains as it stands today." [50] That hopeful belief was by degrees to be actively abandoned.

JAPANESE IN EAST INDIES WOULD BLOCK CRITICAL IMPORTS

Omitting intervening events of similar tendency, on April 17, 1940, Secretary of State Hull issued a formal statement that any change in *status quo* of (read Japanese attack on) the East Indies "would be prejudicial to the cause of stability, peace, and security . . . in the entire Pacific area." He noted that the Indies "produce considerable portions of the world's supplies of . . . essential commodities such as rubber, tin, quinine, copra, et cetera. Many countries, including the United States, depend substantially upon them for some of these commodities." [51] Though this solicitude for the safety of the Netherlands Indies as the unique source of war materials was the commencement of the nation's active hostility toward Japan, the United States did not even then freeze Japanese funds within its borders or discontinue its large shipments of oil and scrap which had assisted Japan's attack on China.

On May 16, 1940, in asking Congress for new defense appropriations, President Roosevelt used expressions which forecast much in his changing policy: "Defense cannot be static. Defense must grow and change from day to day. Defense must be dynamic and flexible, an expression of the vital forces of the nation and of its resolute will to meet whatever challenge the future may hold." [52] This anticipated later suggestions that the defense of the United States might lie three thousand miles from its own shores. On June 10 the President condemned Italy's entrance into the war, and prom-

[50] *Ibid.,* p. 218.   [51] *Ibid.,* p. 235.   [52] *Ibid.,* p. 239.

ised to "extend to the opponents of force the material resources of this Nation . . . ." [53] July 31 the United States embargoed aviation gas except to the Western Hemisphere, an action that drew a quick protest from Japan, against which the embargo was aimed. On August 18, the United States established a Joint Defense Board with Canada, though Canada was, of course, an active belligerent.

Soon followed (September 2, 1940) a major event in this sequence drawing the nation farther from even the name of neutrality —the exchange of fifty "over-age" United States destroyers for British air and naval base sites reaching from Newfoundland to South America.[54] The President informed Congress of the accomplished fact. This deal, which had been wrapped in secrecy, would seem to have been a stretch of the President's authority, legal and moral. Before this the government had furnished its planes to the Allies by turning them back to the manufacturers to be credited on new planes, the manufacturers, nominally, then selling the old ones to the democracies.

The Selective Service Act was approved September 16, 1940. This was the first peacetime conscription law in the United States; under it was required the registration of all men, citizens and aliens, between the ages of 21 and 36, from whom up to 000,000 were to be taken annually for a year's training and military and naval service.[55]

Relations with Japan, which on September 27 had signed a military and economic alliance with Germany and Italy, became increasingly strained. Ambassador Kensuki Horinouchi declared that the refusal of export licenses for aviation gasoline, machine tools, and the impending embargo of scrap to Japan were unfriendly acts, as Japan had been a principal buyer of scrap, and the prohibition did not extend to Britain. President Roosevelt had been calling for additional armaments, military and naval, of all sorts, and repeated his assurance that "great strength of arms is the practical way of fulfilling our hopes for peace and for staying out of this war . . . ." Both Roosevelt and his chief opponent in the presidential campaign, Wendell L. Willkie, promised that no American boys would be sent to fight beyond the nation's own shores.

[53] *Ibid.*, p. 243.   [54] *Ibid.*, p. 255.   [55] *Ibid.*, p. 256.

LEND-LEASE SWELLS EXPORTS

The British ambassador, Philip Kerr, Lord Lothian, begged for more aid in planes, munitions, ships, and money, warning that if the British ramparts fell, "the war will inevitably cross the oceans and roll up against your shores." [56] Four days later President Roosevelt echoed the idea that Britain was defending the United States: ". . . it is important from the selfish viewpoint of American defense that we should do everything to help the British Empire defend itself." The slogan of "all-out aid to Britain" rapidly gained popularity. Lend-lease was preparing, notably in the President's message to Congress, December 29, 1940: "The people of Europe who are defending themselves do not ask us to do their fighting. They ask us for the implements of war . . . which will enable them to fight for their liberty and for our security. . . . There is no demand for sending an American Expeditionary Force outside our own borders. There is no intention of any member of your Government to send such a force. You can . . . nail any talk about sending armies to Europe as deliberate untruth. . . . We must be the great arsenal of democracy." [57] Roosevelt recommended lend-lease to Congress on January 6, Secretaries Hull, Stimson, and Knox urged it, and on March 11, 1941, the Lend-Lease Act to extend aid to countries whose defense was vital to that of the United States was approved. The President had said that the time was near when the countries resisting aggression could no longer pay for weapons in cash. The United States would not lend them money— the Johnson Act forbidding loans to defaulted governments still stood—but would lend them billions of dollars worth of munitions, and be repaid in time in similar materials or other goods. Munitions orders from home and abroad had powerfully stimulated the nation's languid economy. It was set dancing when waning foreign resources were replenished by the enormous demand which the democracies were now invited to exercise. The nation had come a long way, in a short time, from "cash-and-carry."

Ambassador Joseph C. Grew on January 27 warned the State Department from Tokyo of the report that the Japanese military intended a mass attack on Pearl Harbor in case of "trouble" between the two countries.

[56] *Ibid.*, p. 264.   [57] *Ibid.*, pp. 265–266.

In March the United States appropriated $7,000,000,000 for lend-lease. The next month was signed with the Danish minister an agreement for defense by the United States of Greenland, since "defense of Greenland against attack by a non-American power is essential to the preservation of the peace and security of the American continent . . . ." [58]

President Roosevelt proclaimed an unlimited national emergency. "The war is approaching the brink of the Western Hemisphere itself. It is coming very close to home." At this time, despite Germany's inability to invade England across the Channel, the Atlantic Ocean was represented as a small obstacle, even an easy highway to attack on the United States. It was arranged to train British fliers in the United States. Roosevelt branded the sinking of the S. S. *Robin Moor* by Germany as "the act of an international outlaw." [59]

Events now moved rapidly. Germany invaded Russia June 22, 1941, and strong distaste of the United States for the Soviet Union since its barter agreement with Germany January 10 was modified to permit release of Russian credits and a promise of aid. On July 7, following agreement a week before, the American navy landed forces in Iceland "in order to supplement, and eventually to replace, the British forces which have until now been stationed in Iceland," the purpose being to protect Iceland from becoming a German base against the United States, whose frontiers had sprung far out into the North Atlantic. [60]

Two weeks later, France having been obliged to give in to Japanese demands for military control of French Indo-China, Acting Secretary of State Summer Welles told Ambassador Kichisaburo Nomura that there was no basis for pursuing the conversations between Japan and the United States, since clearly Japan had occupied Indo-China "for purposes of offense against the South Sea area." United States differences with Japan, it would seem, were not due to her aggressions as such, for these were old and American exporters had been long allowed to assist them with raw materials, but were due to the fact that Japan was threatening the United States sources of rubber and tin. The government expressed concern about tin and rubber the next day. Roosevelt sought to avoid trouble with Japan by arranging for neutralization

[58] *Ibid.*, pp. 275–277. [59] *Ibid*, pp. 283–285. [60] *Ibid.*, p. 288.

of Indo-China if Japan would get out. But promptly the United States froze Japanese assets.[61]

The "Atlantic Charter" of August 14, 1941, was a joint statement by President Roosevelt and Prime Minister Winston Churchill of the purposes of the war. The document all but made the United States the declared ally of Britain. Late in August Pan American Airways agreed to ferry planes from this country direct to the British forces in the Middle East via West Africa. The older, more inhibited way had been to take them to the Canadian border.

ABORTIVE NEGOTIATIONS WITH JAPAN

Beginning with August 27, 1941, Premier Konoye of Japan on numerous occasions tried to arrange a meeting between himself and President Roosevelt, avowedly to reach an understanding that would prevent war between the two nations. Roosevelt declined the conference. The United States was discussing with Great Britain mutual aid in the event of a Japanese move against the East Indies. The United States was prepared to repel hostile action in the Atlantic as well. Following German attack on the destroyer *Greer*, carrying mail to Iceland, the President ordered the navy to "shoot on sight" German war vessels in "defense waters." Later Roosevelt called for the arming of American merchant ships. Secretary of State Hull wanted it too. If the Neutrality Act stood in the way, Hitler's depredations demanded that it be changed.

Finally Konoye declared that if he could not have a meeting with Roosevelt to restore peaceful relations, he would be obliged to resign and would probably be succeeded by "a less moderate leader." Prince Konoye's government did resign October 16, and two days later a general, Hideki Tojo, became premier with a military cabinet. On November 3, Ambassador Grew, in Tokyo, informed the State Department that Japan was preparing to attack the United States if peace parleys failed, and four days later Hull told the Cabinet that relations with Japan were critical. Churchill promised that Britain would be at war with Japan "within the hour" should America become involved.[62]

The remainder of the story is quickly told. For a few days after the middle of November it looked as though perhaps some accom-

[61] *Ibid.*, pp. 289–290.   [62] *Ibid.*, pp. 295 ff.

modation might be reached between the United States and Japan. But the Japanese were unwilling to give, as Hull required, "some satisfactory evidence that their intentions were peaceful." Hull warned Army and Navy officials that a Japanese surprise attack was imminent. The United States outlined for Japan a program which would have taken her out of the war, and "urged further effort . . . . to resolve our divergencies of views in regard to the practical application of . . . . fundamental principles . . . ." The Japanese ambassador replied that these demands put an end to negotiations, as his government would reject them. The United States wanted to know whether the concentration of so many troops by Japan in Indo-China did not portend further aggression. The Japanese said they were taking precautionary measures only.[63]

On November 26, a council of the President, Secretaries of State, War, and Navy, and chiefs of staff expected war and desired that "the Japanese fire the first shot" so that the administration would have "the full support of the American people." There would then be "no doubt in anyone's mind as to who were the aggressors." Two days after this, in a meeting with the President, the Secretary of War "was inclined to feel" that we were justified in "an attack [on the Japanese] without further warning." However, the decision of the War Cabinet was for more warning and waiting, and on December 6 President Roosevelt appealed to the Japanese Emperor to preserve the long peace between the two countries.[64]

On December 7, Japanese warplanes attacked the great United States naval base at Pearl Harbor, Hawaii. The Japanese note rejecting the proposals Washington had made for a solution of the situation was given to Secretary of State Hull nearly an hour after the attack had occurred. The note said that the United States had clearly been conspiring with Britain and other countries to obstruct Japan's objects in East Asia, and that hope of peace was at an end. The next day the United States, with only one dissenting vote, declared a state of war with Japan, as did England. On December 11, Germany and Italy declared war on the United States, and this country on them.

[63] *Ibid.,* pp. 304–307.
[64] Testimony of former Secretary of War Henry L. Stimson in Pearl Harbor investigation, *The New York Times* (March 22, 1946); Division of Public Inquiries, Government Information Service, *U.S. Government Manual* (Washington: Government Printing Office, spring, 1942), p. iv.

Summary

IN a review of the depression years distinct divisions of progress and of policy appear. The first was from the stock market crash in October, 1929, to the end of Hoover's term. Most indexes worsened until the summer of 1932, which may be called the low point of the depression economically and psychologically. Improvement in the next few months was said by Hoover and his supporters to be the beginning of a true recovery, which, alas, was checked and turned downward by business fears of the inflationary intentions of the new President-elect. Probably the charge proceeded from political pique rather than from economic insight. Later, when Roosevelt was in office, departure from gold was accompanied by business betterment; further, despite the earlier emergence of most European countries, what the people were to learn of the stubbornness of the depression in the United States warrants the belief that matters had not commenced to mend by the autumn of 1932.

The Hoover treatment of the depression was founded on outmoded tenets, false optimism, and inertia. This approach was not due simply to Hoover's attachment to the sufficiency—almost the sacredness—of free economic forces. Time was a factor. The experience of business exuberance was so fresh. Coolidge had shown, or so it was felt, that government could coast while prosperity smiled all around. Hoover, so auspiciously placed in the driver's seat, had no need to use the engine, for the car gathered speed. The sudden blow-out left all with a sense, mocking though it was, of continued forward motion.

Much that was later ascribed to Roosevelt daring was made possible by instructive observation of Hoover's failure. Roosevelt in his first campaign was not so far ahead of Hoover, in the seriousness of his apprehensions or the boldness of his proposals, as his later policies imply. Nor was Hoover's reaction to the depression all of a piece. Reluctantly but steadily, as forced by circumstances, he departed from his predilections, devising numerous government aids to recovery. As more or less developed, not a few of these were patterned after by the New Deal. Hoover's still waters ran deeper than he has been given credit for. Relative to the period and the party, Hoover was experimental and adaptable. The moratorium on intergovernmental debts was a courageous stroke. The Federal Farm Board plainly pointed to the more effectual curbing of agricultural surpluses. Federal relief to the states was small in amount but big in what it portended. The Reconstruction Finance Corporation was taken over bodily by the New Deal, expanded in function during the remaining depression years, and grew into even greater vigor in the war economy.

Still, Hoover never grasped the magnitude of the problem or summoned resources to meet it. His inhibitions while in office, if not proved then, spoke loud in his criticisms of his successor.[1]

Roosevelt, called upon to lead just when the banking crisis had rapidly matured, lacked plans but possessed what was of greater immediate importance—a superb purpose. Confident of his own powers, he poured strength into the people. His inaugural assurance was a moral triumph, outweighing in influence the legislative improvisations of the next "hundred days." Someone has said that economic law is what a country decides it wants. The aphorism was illustrated then. Hearts beat again, minds went to work. There was a grandeur in the promise, albeit not always borne out in the performance.

Roosevelt's course falls, roughly, into four stages: (1) Intimate government participation in banking, currency management, industry, and agriculture. Erring bankers were reproached; the currency was cut loose from gold and controlled for national ends; industry and labor, through NRA, were drawn into a partnership with government which had collusive as well as merely cooperative features; staple crops were restricted when the AAA paid farmers not to produce. Other projects were included, such as more generous federal relief through CWA, FERA, and WPA. This effort, or combination of efforts, came to an end with the Banking

[1] For example, in his *Challenge to Liberty* (New York: Charles Scribner's Sons, 1934).

Act of 1935 and the revolt of the Supreme Court when it invalidated NRA and AAA. The President's stigmatic "horse and buggy" outburst and his thwarted attempt suddenly to change the composition of the Court were expressions of disappointment followed by a change of tack.

(2) The next stage, 1935–1937, took the wind on a new quarter, but the sails of government were to be filled by the same breeze of higher prices at all costs. The NRA was a wreck and had to be abandoned, but the AAA was patched up and still served its turn, while fiscal freedom had been happily vouchsafed by liberal Supreme Court decisions covering currency powers. Though government was no longer allowed to be the partner of business, it could and must be the patron of business. The method was to support private enterprise, even superseding it where necessary, through robust spending and lending. This was the period of "pump priming," as it was fondly called, the instruments being RFC subventions, and vast public works including TVA and public housing.

This was the high tide of the New Deal in its recovery rather than its reform phase. Perhaps the administration lacked the courage of its convictions. Maybe the doubts which it developed were the results of the cries of those alarmed over deficits. More likely the New Dealers concluded from the gratifying business indexes that the spend-lend pump priming had turned the trick, that the depression was conquered, and that therefore the government could resign its efforts. Whatever be the case, expectations were premature. The "recession" or relapse of the autumn of 1937 was bitterly disappointing to New Dealers and, in the eyes of the critics, discredited the policies used.

(3) The President and his strategists, never committed to consistency, recovered poise faster than did the country. Refusing to resume their price-raising program, or to deprecate it as having been a mistaken policy on their part, they pretended innocence of the error, and sent up the hue and cry after the culprits, now designated as private concentrations of economic power which deserved to be exposed and prosecuted. One miscreant had donned tunic and badge of policeman, and pointed to the others—monopolies and all their cohorts—as the public enemies. This was the New Deal's nimblest shift of role. The solemn investigation by the Temporary National Economic Committee into the evil lapse of competition

was the sequel. This third policy of the New Deal in attacking the depression was at length abandoned in mingled minor chagrin and major relief of mind.

(4) The passing embarrassment was caused by the fact that chief inquisitors into the wickedness of price and production control scampered from the committee hearings to assume command of OPA and Emergency Management. And a vast anxiety was overcome because to the benefits of the "arsenal of democracy" had been added America's full engagement in World War II.

CHAPTER XII

The Literature of the Subject

WORLD ECONOMY BETWEEN WARS

INTERNATIONAL developments, including those which came before the great depression and helped cause it, are found in League of Nations, *World Economic Survey*, annually 1931–1941 (Geneva: League of Nations, 1932–); a briefer treatment, good for background, is League of Nations, *Report on Inquiry into Course and Phases of the Present Economic Depression* (Geneva: 1931). Lionel Robbins, *The Great Depression* (London: Macmillan & Co., Ltd., 1934) is one of numerous competent works giving an English view. Bearing immediately on the part played by this country is Hal B. Lary, *The United States in the World Economy, The International Transactions of the United States during the Inter-war Period* (U. S. Bureau of Foreign and Domestic Commerce, Economic Series No. 23 Washington: Government Printing Office, 1943); of course a good many of the sources mentioned below, dealing with particular aspects of the depression, hark back to the pre-depression period.

MARKET CRASH AND COURSE OF THE DEPRESSION

The "Pecora Investigation" into the 1929 stock market crash and the operations of investment bankers is reported in the U. S. Senate Banking and Currency Committee, Hearings on S. Res. 84 *et al.*, 72, 73 Cong., April 11, 1932–May 4, 1934, various dates, Parts 1–20. The evidence of J. P. Morgan is in Parts 1 and 2, that of the Chase Securities Corporation in Parts 5–8; Parts 15–16 concern the Securi-

ties Exchange Act. For a résumé by the chief government prose-
cutor see Ferdinand Pecora, *Wall Street under Oath* (New York:
Simon and Schuster, 1939). See New York Stock Exchange, *Year
Book*, 1929–1930 (New York: 1930); *ibid.*, Report of the President
(New York: 1930). Irving Fisher, *The Stock Market Crash—and
After* (New York: The Macmillan Company, 1930). U. S. Bureau
of the Budget, *The Budget of the United States Government*
(Washington: Government Printing Office, annually) gives the
effects of the depression on government income and outgo. U. S.
Bureau of the Census, *Statistical Abstract of the United States*
(Washington: Government Printing Office) gives significant in-
dexes of economic fluctuations in the period. *The New York Times*,
January 2, 1942, contains that paper's "Weekly Business Index" in
graphic form, affording an excellent at-a-glance picture of the depression.

PRESIDENT HOOVER'S POLICIES

As a holdover with Hoover, the Coolidge complacency for some
months excluded admission that there was a depression; William
Allen White, *A Puritan in Babylon; The Story of Calvin Coolidge*
(New York: The Macmillan Company, 1938) is built on slight acquaintance with Coolidge personally, but on far ampler political
knowledge and social observation, and is shrewd in places. As this
country sank into depression while the Soviet Union forged ahead
in production, economized labor, and became a market for our
goods the attitude toward the U.S.S.R. became more favorable.
This reflection of the depression is documented in Meno Lovenstein, *American Opinion of Soviet Russia* (Washington: American
Council on Public Affairs, 1941). Gilbert Seldes, *The Years of the
Locust: America, 1929–1932* (Boston: Little, Brown & Company,
1933) is a lively and acute account of the opening years. The part
of the federal government before the New Deal, beginning with
timidity but reaching relative temerity, is conveniently traced in
William Starr Myers, ed., *The State Papers and Other Public Writings of Herbert Hoover* (New York: Doubleday, Doran & Co. 1934,
2 vols.); William Starr Myers and Walter H. Newton, *The Hoover
Administration; A Documented Narrative* (New York: Charles
Scribner's Sons, 1936) is partisan but a useful source; Ray Lyman

Wilbur and Arthur Mastick Hyde, *The Hoover Policies* (New York: Charles Scribner's Sons, 1937) brings much to the support of a frankly friendly view. William Starr Myers, *The Foreign Policies of Herbert Hoover, 1929–1933* (New York: Charles Scribner's Sons, 1940) deals with efforts on which Hoover placed great emphasis. Herbert Hoover, and Calvin Coolidge, *Campaign Speeches of 1932* (New York: Doubleday, Doran & Co., 1933) is marked by some dignity, more irony, and still more dullness. Rexford G. Tugwell, *Mr. Hoover's Economic Policy* (New York: The John Day Company, 1932; John Day Pamphlets No. 7) is more substantial than the usual campagin criticism, and furnishes a marker for the place where the road forked into Old Deal and New. For a conspicuous episode in which President Hoover was an actor, see W. W. Waters, *B.E.F., The Whole Story of the Bonus Army* (New York: The John Day Company, 1933). Herbert Hoover, *The Challenge to Liberty* (New York: Charles Scribner's Sons, 1934) is a reiteration of faith and stubborn rejoinder of the ex-President to Roosevelt's first year.

TARIFF AND THE DEPRESSION

On the tariff, see Joseph M. Jones, *Tariff Retaliation: Repercussions of the Hawley-Smoot Bill* (Philadelphia: University of Pennsylvania Press, 1934); Hsu Chao Ho, *A Study of the Probable Effects of the Hawley-Smoot Tariff of 1930* (New York: Free Trade League, 1931); U. S. Tariff Commission, *Computed Duties and Equivalent ad Valorem Rates on Imports in the United States from Principal Countries, 1929 and 1931* (Washington: Government Printing Office, 1933). Numerous materials are available on the reciprocal trade agreements. See U. S. Committee for Reciprocity Information, *Rules for Procedure, Trade Agreements Act, Section 350, Tariff Act of 1930, and Executive Orders Affecting the Committee* (Washington: Government Printing Office, 1940); Senate Finance Committee, "Extension of Reciprocity Trade Agreements Act," Hearings on H.J.Res. 407, 76 Cong., 3 Sess., February 26–March 6, 1940. A review covering the period is James Constantine Pearson, *The Reciprocal Trade Agreements Program: The Policy of the United States and Its Effectiveness* (Washington: The Catholic University of America Press, 1942).

House Committee on Ways and Means, Report to accompany H.R. 3240, A Bill to Extend the Authority of the President under Section 350 of the Tariff Act of 1930, as amended . . . Union Calendar No. 158, House Report No. 594, 79 Cong., 1 Sess., reviews procedure, results, and opinions of various interests in industry, business, agriculture, labor, and the public concerning the reciprocal trade agreements; see also U. S. State Department, *The Reciprocal-Trade-Agreements Program in War and Peace* (Publication 1893, Commercial Policy Series 73; Washington: Government Printing Office, 1943). Alonzo E. Taylor, *The New Deal and Foreign Trade* (New York: The Macmillan Company, 1935) examines the commercial policies of Henry A. Wallace.

RECONSTRUCTION FINANCE CORPORATION

The source for operations of the Reconstruction Finance Corporation is the *Quarterly Report* (Washington: Government Printing Office, 1932–); see, for a summary, RFC, *Seven-Year Report to the President and the Congress,* by Jesse H. Jones, chairman (Washington: Government Printing Office, 1939). On the origin of this important agency see Senate Banking and Currency Committee, "Creation of a Reconstruction Finance Corporation," Hearings on S.1, (a bill to provide emergency financing facilities for banks and other financial institutions), 72 Cong., 1 Sess., December 18–22, 1931; and House Committee on Banking and Currency, Hearings on H.R. 5060, 5116 (H.R. 7360, the Steagall bill, was reported), 72 Cong., 1 Sess., December 18, 1931, January 7, 1932. On the continuation and extension of functions of the RFC, consult House Committee on Banking and Currency, Hearings on H.R. 2301, 75 Cong., 1 Sess., January 15, 1937; H.R. 4240, S. 1175, 74 Cong., 1 Sess., January 21–25, 1935; Senate Committee on Banking and Currency, Hearings on S. 1175, 74 Cong., 1 Sess., January 23, 1935; S. 1102, 76 Cong., 1 Sess., February 14, 21, 1939. Herbert Spero, *Reconstruction Finance Corporation Loans to the Railroads, 1932–1937* (New York: Bankers Publishing Company, 1939) contains a bibliography on the problem of railway finance in the depression. Obligations of the RFC for unemployment relief were set forth, among other places, in House Committee on Banking and Currency, Hearings on H.R. 9360, 75 Cong., 3 Sess., February 8, 1938.

THE NEW DEAL

General economic works published in the period, with the exception of textbooks, grew out of the stressful times and were related to current policy by way of apology or attack. Paul H. Douglas, *Controlling Depressions* (New York: W. W. Norton & Company, 1935) assumes liberal government intervention; U. S. National Resources Committee, *The Structure of the American Economy* (Washington: Government Printing Office, 1939–1940, 2 vols.) is by a group of economists closely associated with the New Deal. Carl Snyder, *Capitalism the Creator; The Economic Foundations of Modern Industrial Society* (New York: The Macmillan Company, 1940) is of contrary tendencies, with animadversions. A book which anticipated much in the reform program of the next years is Stuart Chase, *A New Deal* (New York: The Macmillan Company, 1932).

A guide to the material of the period is *The New Deal, A Selected List of References*, Compiled by Florence S. Hellman (Washington: U. S. Library of Congress, 1940, mimeographed). An earlier list is Arthur Sydney Beardsley, and Oscar C. Orman, *Bibliography of Selected Materials Relating to the Legislation of the New Deal* (Seattle: University Book Store, 1935). An essential source for the New Deal period is Franklin D. Roosevelt, *The Public Papers and Addresses of Franklin D. Roosevelt*, compiled and collated by Samuel I. Rosenman (New York: Random House, Vols. I–V, 1938; The Macmillan Company, Vols. VI–IX, 1941). The first volume begins with his acceptance of the nomination for the governorship of New York in October, 1928, and the last runs into January, 1941. Each volume has an introduction by Roosevelt reviewing briefly but pointedly the period represented by the papers in it.

Of numerous books on the New Deal many are limited in the period or topics covered, some are solicitous, some splenetic. Among those by scholars and observers using detachment are *The Recovery Problem in the United States* (Washington: Brookings Institution, 1936), a symposium by numerous specialists; Arthur Meier Schlesinger, *The New Deal in Action, 1933–1939* (New York: The Macmillan Company, 1940); Louis M. Hacker, *A Short History of the New Deal* (New York: F. S. Crofts & Co., 1934); Charles A. Beard and George H. E. Smith, *The Future Comes; A Study of the New*

Deal (New York: The Macmillan Company, 1933) and the same authors' *The Old Deal and the New* (New York: The Macmillan Company, 1940). An early account is Schuyler C. Wallace, *The New Deal in Action* (New York: Harper & Brothers, 1934). New Republic, *Balance Sheet of the New Deal*, Prepared by the Editors (New York: New Republic, 1936, special supplement) and the Editors of the Economist, *An Analysis and Appraisal of the New Deal* (New York: Alfred A. Knopf, Inc., 1937) are by acquainted critics. Ernest K. Lindley's *Half Way with Roosevelt* (New York: The Viking Press, 1937, rev. ed.) is by a strong admirer. Raymond Moley, *After Seven Years* (New York: Harper & Brothers, 1939) is a narrative of a close participant who afterward discovered what Charles Lamb would have called an "imperfect sympathy" for the New Deal. Wholly opposed are William McDonald, *The Menace of Recovery; What the New Deal Means* (New York: The Macmillan Company, 1934) and David Lawrence, *Beyond the New Deal* (New York: McGraw-Hill Book Company, 1934). Henry Hazlitt, *Economics in One Lesson* (New York: Harper & Brothers, 1946), fighting a rearguard action, fires away at government intervention in the economy in the thirties. Lesser efforts of the opposition are Alexander Jay Bruon, Jr., *The New Deal with Mephistopholes; Heading for Disaster.* . . . (New York: [Dutton, Inc.], 1935); Burton Braley, *New Deal Ditties; or, Running in the Red with Roosevelt* (New York: Greenberg, Publisher, 1936). Of different character are Anthony Wayne Rosinia, *The New Deal under the Microscope; An Economic Discussion* (Chicago: L. W. Arkin and Associates, 1939); Arthur Krock, *A New Deal Aide-mémoire. A Chronological Account of Many of the Major Activities of President Franklin D. Roosevelt . . . and of Developments . . . in . . . Policies . . . 1932–1935* (New York ? 1935); and Unofficial Observer (John Franklin Carter), *The New Dealers* (New York: Simon and Schuster, 1934). Viewing the subject from special angles are Henry James Whigham, *The New Deal; English and American* (New York: G. P. Putnam's Sons, 1936) and Carroll Atkinson, *The New Deal: Will It Survive the War?* (Boston: Meador Publishing Co., 1942). Frances Perkins, *The Roosevelt I Knew* (New York: The Viking Press, 1946) is one of numerous books of reminiscence and fuller record which will come from the President's close collaborators.

UNEMPLOYMENT AND RELIEF

The fields of direct relief and work relief are not clearly separable in fact, and the most useful summary reports deal with both areas. Consult U. S. Work Projects Administration, Research and Statistical Division, *Catalog of Publications* (Washington, reproduced from typewritten copy, 1941) and Doris Carothers, *Chronology of the Federal Emergency Relief Administration, May 12, 1933 to December 31, 1935* (WPA Research Monograph VI; Washington: Government Printing Office, 1937). Comprehensive statements are U. S. Federal Works Agency, Federal Emergency Relief Administration, *Final Statistical Report*, Prepared under the direction of Theodore E. Whiting (Washington: Government Printing Office, 1942); slightly earlier are U. S. Work Projects Administration, *Summary of Relief and Federal Work Program Statistics, 1933–1940*, by Theodore E. Whiting and T. J. Woofter, Jr. (Washington: Government Printing Office, 1941); *Average General Relief Benefits, 1933–1938*, by Enid Baird and Hugh B. Brinton (Washington: Government Printing Office, 1940); and *Analysis of Civil Works Program Statistics* (Washington, 1939). When it appeared, U. S. National Resources Planning Board, *Security, Work and Relief Policies*, 78 Cong., 1 Sess., *House Document* No. 128, Part 3 (Washington: Government Printing Office, 1942), was referred to as the American counterpart of the Beveridge Report on Social Security in Britain; it is the most inclusive record of welfare efforts of the New Deal, reviewing experience and projecting new plans, but is vexingly arranged. More specialized is U. S. National Resources Planning Board, *Development of Resources and Stabilization of Employment in the United States* (Washington: Government Printing Office, 1941).

U. S. Work Projects Administration, *Report of Progress of the WPA Program* (Washington: Government Printing Office, 1935–1942); these reports appeared at varying intervals and give a detailed account of developing experience. Important phases are treated in *Five Years of Rural Relief* (U. S. Work Projects Administration; Washington: Government Printing Office, 1938); *ibid., Urban Workers on Relief* (Washington: Government Printing Office, 1936–1937, 2 vols.) considers occupational characteristics. Doak Sheridan Campbell and others, *Educational Activities of the*

Works Progress Administration (Washington: Government Printing Office, 1939) and National Conference of Social Work, *Proceedings* (Chicago: University of Chicago Press, 1929–1938; New York: Columbia University Press, 1939–1941) contain much material on relief in all its aspects. Tracts of the times but serviceable are U. S. Work Projects Administration, *Questions and Answers on W.P.A.* (Washington: Government Printing Office, 1939) and *The Realities of Unemployment*, by Harry L. Hopkins, Administrator (Washington: Government Printing Office, 1937). The same agency's *Construction Expenditures and Employment*, by Peter A. Stone (Washington: Government Printing Office, 1937), and *Hourly Wage Rates for WPA and for Private and Other Public Construction, 1938, Selected Occupations* (Washington: 1939) deal with particular problems. See further, *Family Unemployment; An Analysis of Unemployment in Terms of Family Units* (Washington: Government Printing Office, 1940) and *Youth on Relief* (Washington, photolithographed, 1936). Other treatments of young people in the programs are Betty Grimes Lindley and Ernest K. Lindley, *A New Deal for Youth: The Story of the National Youth Administration* (New York: The Viking Press, 1938) and Lewis L. Lorwin, *Youth Work Programs, Problems and Policies*, Prepared for the American Youth Commission (Washington: American Council on Education, 1941).

Many WPA publications were themselves relief projects, the work of professional writers and research students, and ranged over varied fields. In most popular use is the "American Guide" series, each volume describing the history, geography, and culture of a state, an example at the other extreme is U. S. Work Projects Administration, *Sino-Tibetan Linguistics* . . . Produced on a WPA Project Sponsored by the University of California Department of Anthropology (Berkeley: 1937–1941, 16 vols. in 15).

Of course the congressional hearings on unemployment and unemployment relief give the flux and formation of opinion as reports of administrative agencies do not. The following list of hearings is arranged chronologically: Senate Committee on Commerce, Hearings on S. 3059, 3060, 3061. 71 Cong., 2 Sess., March 18–April 1, 1930, on unemployment in the United States; House Committee on the Judiciary, Hearings on S. 3059, 3060, H.R. 8374, 8655, 9560, 11,414, 12,550, 12,551, 71 Cong., 2 Sess., June 11, 12, 1930, on regulation of public work to prevent unemployment; Senate Committee on Manufactures, "Unemployment Relief," Hearings on S. 174 and S. 262, 72 Cong., 1 Sess., December 28, 1931–January 9, 1932 (various dates) gives a picture of relief needs at the time as testified to by representative social workers, bankers, labor leaders, and government officials; what was reported out was S. 3045, the La Follette-Costigan bill; House Committee on Labor, Hearings on H.R. 11,055, 11,056, 12,097, 72 Cong., 1 Sess., April 29–May 6, 1932; Senate Committee on Manufactures, "Federal Cooperation in Unemployment Relief," Hearings on S. 4592, 72 Cong., 1 Sess., May 9–June 4, 1932.

Senate Banking and Currency Committee, Hearings on S. 4632, S. 4727, S. 4755, and S. 4822, 72 Cong., 1 Sess., June 2–13, 1932, has testimony of William T. Foster, director of the Pollack Foundation and author of *The Road to Plenty*, and of Benjamin C. Marsh, who spoke for a joint committee on unemployment of sixteen national organizations; S. 4755 was introduced by Senator Robert F. Wagner of New York, and others. See also Senate Committee on Manufactures, Hearings on S. 5125, Parts 1 and 2, 72 Cong., 2 Sess., January 3–February 3, 1933. Senate Committee on Banking and Currency, Hearings on S. 5336, 72 Cong., 2 Sess., February 2, 3, 1933, is on unemployment relief through the Reconstruction Finance Corporation; Senate Committee on Education and Labor and House Committee on Labor, Joint Hearings on S. 598, 73 Cong., 1 Sess., March 23, 24, 1933, contains testimony on unemployment relief by Herbert Benjamin of the National Committee of the Unemployed Council; Lewis W. Douglas, Director of the Budget; Frances Perkins, Secretary of Labor; William Green, president of the A.F.L.; and Owen R. Lovejoy, of the Children's Aid Society of New York. Senate Committee on Education and Labor, "Additional Public Works Appropriations," Hearings on S. 3348, 73 Cong., 2 Sess., April 24, May 30, 1934, contains testimony of Charney Vladeck, member of New York Housing Authority; Harry B. Dalzell, of the American Water Works Association; Harry L. Hopkins, Federal Emergency Relief Administrator; and C. A. Dykstra, City Manager of Cincinnati. Later hearings are House Committee on Appropriations, "Investigation and Study of the Works Progress Administration," Hearings on H.R. 130, 76 Cong., 1, 3 Sess., April 11–May 1, 1939; Special Senate Committee to Investigate Unemployment and

Relief, Hearings on S. 1265, 76 Cong., 1 Sess., February 24–March 10, 1939; U. S. Senate Committee on Banking and Currency, "Works Financing Act of 1939," Hearings on S. 2759, 76 Cong., 1 Sess., July 12–14, 18–20, 1939.

Interpretive works by careful students are E. Wight Bakke, *The Unemployed Worker* (New Haven: Yale University Press, 1940) and Donald S. Howard, *The WPA and Federal Relief Policy* (New York: Russell Sage Foundation, 1943), which reduces voluminous material to usable form and supplies valuable judgments; Arthur Whittier Macmahon, John D. Millett, and Gladys Ogden, *The Administration of Federal Work Relief* (Chicago: Public Administration Service, 1941), and Lewis Merriam, *Relief and Social Security* (Washington: Brookings Institution, 1946).

The extent of unemployment, as variously ascertained or interpreted, is reported in U. S. Bureau of the Census, *Census of Partial Employment, Unemployment, and Occupations, 1937* (Department of Commerce; Washington: Government Printing Office, 1938); "Extent of Waste from Depression Unemployment," *Monthly Labor Review*, XLIX, No. 5 (November, 1939), 1076, is a summary of a part of U. S. National Resources Committee, "The Structure of the American Economy"; Paul Webbink, "Unemployment in the United States, 1930–1940," *American Economic Review*, Papers and Proceedings of Fifty-third Annual Meeting, No. 5 (February, 1941), 248–272, contains a review of the treatment of unemployment by government.

HOUSING

Housing, public and private, is treated in a number of official and unofficial surveys. First may be mentioned U. S. Bureau of Foreign and Domestic Commerce, *Real Property Inventory* (Washington: Bureau of Foreign and Domestic Commerce, 1934, 65 numbers in 8 vols.); this put a factual floor under many proposals. Similar and later is David L. Wickens, *Residential Real Estate, Its Economic Position as Shown by Values, Rents, Family Income, Financing, and Construction* (New York: National Bureau of Economic Research, 1941, Publication No. 38). See also U. S. Bureau of Foreign and Domestic Commerce, *Financial Survey of Urban Housing* (Washington: Government Printing Office, 1937) and U. S. National Resources Planning Board, *Housing; The Continuing Problem*

(Washington: Government Printing Office, 1940). A case history is contained in City of Atlanta, Housing Authority, *Annual Report* (Atlanta: 1939–). Other treatments scattered over the decade are Edith Elmer Wood, *Recent Trends in American Housing* (New York: The Macmillan Company, 1931); the same author's *Introduction to Housing: Facts and Principles* (Washington: Federal Works Agency, U. S. Housing Authority, 1940); Editors of *Fortune, Housing America* (New York: Harcourt, Brace and Company, 1932); Catherine Bauer, *Modern Housing* (Boston: Houghton Mifflin Company, 1934); Clarence Arthur Perry, *Housing for the Machine Age* (New York: Russell Sage Foundation, 1939); Stella K. Margold, *Housing Abroad up to World War II; Supplemented by Comparisons with Conditions in the United States* (Cambridge: Massachusetts Institute of Technology, 1942); and Nathan Straus, *The Seven Myths of Housing* (New York: Alfred A. Knopf, Inc., 1944) is a mature book by a creative public servant reviewing depression experience. The National Housing Act was the subject of inquiry in Senate Committee on Banking and Currency, Hearings on S. 3603, 73 Cong., 2 Sess., May 16–24, 1935, and House Committee on Banking and Currency, Hearings on H.R. 9620, 73 Cong., 2 Sess., May 18–June 4, 1934.

Several works treat of government spending during the depression. Arthur E. Burns, and Donald S. Watson, *Government Spending and Economic Expansion* (Washington: American Council on Public Affairs, 1940) discuss policies and give tables of critical data. Another study is Charles F. Phillips and J. V. Garland, *Government Spending and Economic Recovery* (New York: H. W. Wilson Co., 1938. Harold G. Moulton, *The New Philosophy of Public Debt* (Washington: The Brookings Institution, 1943) is not favorable to deficit financing. U. S. Bureau of the Budget, *The Budget of the United States Government* . . . (Washington: Government Printing Office, annual, series begins 1922–1923) consists of the budget, preceded by the message of the President transmitting it and by various explanatory statements.

BANKING AND CURRENCY PROBLEMS

Much of the banking and currency legislation of the New Deal period was passed without hearings because of the emergency, and even debate, as reported in the *Congressional Record*, was often brief. That was not true of the depression years before the crisis of 1933. The following references will be found useful: branch, chain, and group banking were investigated in House Committee on Banking and Currency, Hearings on H.R. 141, 71 Cong., 2 Sess., February 25—June 11, 1930, Parts 1–15 in 2 vols. U. S. Senate Committee on Banking and Currency, Hearings on S. Res. 71, 71 Cong., 3 Sess., January 19—March 2, 1931; *ibid.*, Hearings on S. 4115, 72 Cong., 1 Sess., March 23—April 29, 1932, Parts 1–3 reports the "Glass" inquiries into "Operation of the Federal Reserve and National Banking Systems"; the same committee, "Restoring and Maintaining the Average Purchasing Power of the Dollar," Hearings on H.R. 11,499 and S. 4429, 72 Cong., 1 Sess., May 12, 13, 18, 1932 contains testimony of B. M. Anderson, Morris A. Copeland, Irving Fisher, T. Alan Goldsborough, Willfred I. King, Eugene Meyer, George F. Warren, and Edward A. O'Neal; Professor Warren said, "When the wholesale price level falls it is due to money. . . . If the wholesale prices of all commodities . . . could be raised . . . to 1929 . . . that would restore employment. Then people would begin to buy. . . ." The previous high price level was from our ownership or control of so large a part of the world's gold. Now that the world wanted its gold back, we had arbitrarily to increase the price of gold in paper. In these times of crisis, pet schemes, if propitiously presented to distressed officials, might become policy or were given a whirl. The formula of Professors George A. Warren and Frank A. Pearson was a case in point; it is explained in their *Prices* (New York: John Wiley & Sons, 1933) and *Gold and Prices* (New York: John Wiley & Sons, 1935); see on this question Charles O. Hardy, *The Warren-Pearson Price Theory* (Washington: Brookings Institution, 1935, Pamphlet Series, No. 17).

League of Nations, *The Program of the World Economic Conference; The Experts' Agenda and Other Documents*, with introduction by James W. Angell (Boston: World Peace Foundation, 1933) is a highly intelligent and sincere piece of work, necessary to an understanding of the hopes—destined to disappointment—invested in the conference; on the Silver Purchase Act of 1934, which was an outcome of the conference, see Senate Special Committee on the Investigation of Silver, Hearings on S. Res. 187, 74 Cong., 1 Sess., and hearings held 76 Cong., 1 Sess., February 7—April 8, 1939, Parts

1–8, on the administration and commercial and economic effects of the Silver Purchase Act of 1934; on repeal of the act, see Senate Committee on Banking and Currency, Hearings on S. 785, 76 Cong., 1 and 3 Sess., April 19–27, 1939 (Part 1), March 19, 1940 (Part 2).

Basic material on the Banking Act of 1935 is in House Committee on Banking and Currency, Hearings on H.R. 5357, 74 Cong., 1 Sess., February 21—April 8, 1935, and in Senate Committee on Banking and Currency, Hearings on S. 1715, Parts 1 and 2, 74 Cong., 1 Sess., April 19—May 22, 1935. On voiding of the gold clause in securities of the United States, see Senate Committee on Banking and Currency, Hearings on S.J. Res. 155, 74 Cong., 1 Sess., July 11–17, 1935, and House Committee on Banking and Currency, Hearings on H.J. Res. 339, 348, 74 Cong., 1 Sess., July 10, 11, 1935. House Committee on Banking and Currency, "Policy of Monetary Plenty Instead of Scarcity," Hearings on Goldsborough Bill, H.R. 7188, 75 Cong., 1 and 3 Sess., July 8, 1937—March 10, 1938, various dates.

Arthur Whipple Crawford, *Monetary Management under the New Deal; The Evolution of a Managed Currency System, Its Problems and Results* (Washington: American Council on Public Affairs, 1940) is an accurate and comprehensive account, with illuminating detail; it was valuable in the preparation of the present volume. B. Griffith Johnson, Jr., *The Treasury and Monetary Policy 1933–1938* (Cambridge: Harvard University Press, 1939) and James Daniel Paris, *Monetary Policies of the United States, 1932–1938* (New York: Columbia University Press, 1938) cover much of the same ground. O. M. W. Sprague, *Recovery and Common Sense* (Boston: Houghton Mifflin Company, 1934) is a straightforward statement of views which led to the author's resignation from the post of Treasury adviser. Frederick A. Bradford, *Money and Banking* (New York: Longmans, Green & Co., 1935) has a brief, clear treatment of the depression period; the same author's *Monetary Developments Since 1932* (New York: Longmans, Green & Co., 1934) has a selected bibliography. American Bankers Association, *Economic Policy Commission, Banking after the Crisis* (New York: 1934) has value as a contemporary document. C. D. Bremer, *American Bank Failures* (New York: Columbia University Press, 1935), a careful piece of work, shows how classification affects the count.

Board of Governors of the Federal Reserve System, *Federal Re-*

serve Bulletin (Washington) is essential as a continuing record of economic experience in the period; see also Federal Reserve Bank of New York, *Monthly Review of Credit and Business Conditions,* its *Annual Reports,* that for 1933 being valuable for the banking crisis at the outset of the New Deal; and its *The Federal Reserve System Today* (New York: 1936).

SECURITIES REGULATION

Operations of the Securities and Exchange Commission are given in the *Annual Report* (Washington: Government Printing Office, 1935–). On public-utility holding companies see House Committee on Interstate and Foreign Commerce, Hearings on H.R. 5423, 74 Cong., 1 Sess., February 19–April 13, 1935, Parts 1–3; Senate Committee on Interstate Commerce, Hearings on S. 1725, S. 2796, 74 Cong., 1 Sess., April 16–29, 1935, Parts 1–2, with supplemental statement. Securities and Exchange Commission, *Report of Public Utilities Division* (Washington: Government Printing Office, 1939) has charts showing location of operating utilities and subsidiaries of registered holding companies. The same commission's *Report on Fixed and Semifixed Investment Trusts,* 76 Cong., 3 Sess., *House Document* No. 567 is supplemented by its *Report on Investment Trust and Investment Companies,* pursuant to Sec. 30 of the Public Utility Holding Company Act of 1935 (Washington: Government Printing Office, 1939) which examines investment counsel, management, supervisory, and advisory services. See also Gerhard Alden Gesell, *Protecting Your Dollars; An Account of the Work of the Securities and Exchange Commission* (Washington: National Home Library Foundation, 1940).

AGRICULTURAL PLIGHT AND POLICIES

U. S. Federal Farm Board, *First [–Third] Annual Report . . . for the Year Ending June 30, 1930 [–1932]* (Washington: Government Printing Office, 1930–32) show how the problem was revealed without being resolved; *The Farm Board* by E. A. Stokdyk and Charles H. West (New York: The Macmillan Company, 1930) has some of the background of the distress of agriculture but was written too early to do more than project the work of the board;

see also Ann Berkelbach and D. C. Hutton, *The Pinch of Plenty; The World Agrarian Crisis* (London: Sidgwick & Jackson, Ltd., 1932). The official account of New Deal efforts is in U. S. Department of Agriculture, *Agricultural Adjustment; A Report of Administration of Agricultural Adjustment Act* (subtitle varies. Washington: Government Printing Office, 1933–1941). On agricultural adjustment legislation of 1937 and 1938 see Senate Committee on Agriculture and Forestry, Hearings on S. 2787, S.R. 158, 75 Cong., 1 Sess., May 18–June 11, 1937; House Committee on Agriculture, Hearings on H.R. 8505, 75 Cong., 1 Sess., May 17–June 10, 1937; Senate Committee on Agriculture and Forestry, Hearings on S. 2787, S. Res. 158, 75 Cong., 2 Sess., October 15–November 1, 1937, Pts. 1–20.

The best general account is E. G. Nourse, Joseph S. Davis, and John D. Black, *Three Years of the Agricultural Adjustment Administration* (Washington: Brookings Institution, 1937). Related works are Sherman E. Johnson, *Wheat under the Agricultural Adjustment Act* (Washington: Brookings Institution, 1934); Henry Irving Richards, *Cotton and the AAA* (Washington: Brookings Institution, 1936); Joseph S. Davis, *On Agricultural Policy, 1926–1938* (Palo Alto: Stanford University Food Research Institute, 1939), composed of pieces written at different times; Donald C. Blaisdell, *Government and Agriculture; The Growth of Federal Aid* (New York: Rinehart & Company, Inc., 1940). O. V. Wells, "Agriculture Today: An Appraisal of the Agricultural Problem," in *Yearbook of Agriculture,* 1940 (Washington: Government Printing Office, 1941) pp. 385–97, is a good summary, showing prices received and paid by farmers.

The story of the start of AAA is told in Henry A. Wallace, *New Frontiers* (New York: Reynal & Hitchcock, 1934), and reasons for the program were succinctly given in the same author's pamphlet, *America Must Choose; The Advantages and Disadvantages of Nationalism, of World Trade, and of a Planned Middle Course* (New York: Foreign Policy Association, 1934); in this connection see William A. Wirt, *America Must Lose—by a "Planned Economy," the Steppingstone to a Regimented State* (New York: Committee for the Nation, 1934). Mordecai Ezekiel and Louis H. Bean examined *Economic Bases for the Agricultural Adjustment Act* (Washington: Government Printing Office, 1933). Peter Molyneaux, *The Cotton*

South and American Trade Policy (New York: American Peace Conference, 1936) became a classic among the calls on behalf of the farmers for an end of high protection. George N. Peck (with Samuel Crowther), *Why Quit Our Own?* (New York: D. Van Nostrand Company, 1936) is the defense of his stand by the first Agricultural Adjustment Administrator, who soon resigned.

The agricultural adjustment programs operated in ways not anticipated, often injurious to renters. The best single source of information on nonowners in their various categories and in all parts of the country is U. S. Special Committee on Farm Tenancy, *Report,* Prepared under the Auspices of the National Resources Committee (Washington: Government Printing Office, 1937, including illustrations, maps, and tables); see also Paul V. Maris, "Farm Tenancy," in *Yearbook of Agriculture,* 1940 (Washington: Government Printing Office, 1941), pp. 887–906. Several books by unusually qualified writers picture the plight of southern sharecroppers (in fact, insecure contract laborers) and other farm renters in that section. Among them are Charles S. Johnson, Edwin R. Embree, and W. W. Alexander, *The Collapse of Farm Tenancy* (Chapel Hill: University of North Carolina Press, 1935); Arthur Franklin Raper, *Preface to Peasantry* (Chapel Hill: University of North Carolina Press, 1936); Arthur Franklin Raper and Ira De A. Reid, *Sharecroppers All* (Chapel Hill: University of North Carolina Press, 1941). An early pamphlet which did much to bring the dispossessed to public notice, stimulate organized relief, and lead to defense by formation of their own union is Norman M. Thomas, *The Plight of the Share-Cropper* (New York: League for Industrial Democracy, 1934). A sequel was Howard Kester, *Revolt among the Sharecroppers* (New York: Covici Friede, 1936); a human document is Southern Tenant Farmers' Union, *The Disinherited Speak; Letters from Sharecroppers* (New York: published by The Workers' Defense League for the . . . Union, 1936); see also Fred Frey and T. L. Smith, "The Influence of the AAA Cotton Program upon the Tenant, Cropper, and Laborer," in *Rural Sociology,* I (Baton Rouge: 1936), 483–505. Erskine Caldwell and Margaret Bourke-White, *You Have Seen Their Faces* (New York: The Viking Press, 1937) is not confined to tenants, but is a book of southern poor folks, mostly in poignant photographs.

On the whole subject of migrant workers during the depression consult U. S. Bureau of Labor Statistics, *Handbook of Labor Statistics* (Bulletin No. 694; Washington: Government Printing Office, 1941 ed.; pp. 557–589; pp. 578–582 cover "Refugee Labor Migration to California." See also House Select Committee to Investigate the Interstate Migration of Destitute Citizens, Hearings on H. Res. 63 and H. Res. 491, 76 Cong., 3 Sess., July 29–December 11, 1940, various dates and published in 10 vols. The *Preliminary Report* was issued in 1941. This inquiry by the committee of which John H. Tolan was chairman continued in the next Congress on the subject of migration of defense workers: House Select Committee Investigating National Defense Migration, Hearings on H.R. 113, 77 Cong., 1 Sess.; pagination and volume numbers of the 13 vols. published in 1941–1942 are continuous with those from previous hearings. The last hearings prior to Pearl Harbor were those at St. Louis, November 26, 27, 1941, reported in Part 23, though some evidence in later hearings refers to the period before Pearl Harbor.

On "Okies" and "Arkies" migrating to California see Paul S. Taylor and Edward J. Rowell in *Monthly Labor Review*, 47, No. 2 (August, 1938), 240–250. Carey McWilliams, *Factories in the Field; The Story of Migratory Farm Labor in California* (Boston: Little, Brown & Company, 1939) is a work by an on-the-spot investigator, who treats the highly commercialized agriculture of California, the procurement and exploitation of labor under it, and documents John Steinbeck's novel, *The Grapes of Wrath* (New York: The Viking Press, 1939). This tells the story of a family, "tractored off" the land in Arkansas, which tried its unhappy fortunes on California fruit and vegetable ranches. See also George Thomas Miron, *The Truth about John Steinbeck and the Migrants* (Los Angeles: Haynes Corporation, 1939) and Marshall V. Hartranft, *Grapes of Gladness, California's Refreshing and Inspiring Answer to Steinbeck's Grapes of Wrath* (Los Angeles: DeVorss & Co., 1939).

NATIONAL RECOVERY ADMINISTRATION

The National Industrial Recovery Act and National Recovery Administration left a large literature of description, praise, and dispraise. The most authoritative short account is Committee of Industrial Analysis, *A Report on the Operation of the National Recovery Administration*. Message from the President of the United States,

March 2, 1937. *House Document* No. 158. This is condensed from four much longer summary studies which in turn followed NRA *Evidence Study*, Nos. 1–52 (Washington: 1935–1936, mimeographed), dealing with industries, and NRA *Work Materials*, Nos. 1–87 (Washington: Government Printing Office, 1935–1936, partly mimeographed and partly lithographed). These *Work Materials*, based on prodigious files, give the fullest, though sometimes uncritical, survey of all phases of NRA experience. Individual numbers are superior in interest of subject matter and treatment; among others may be mentioned *Summary of Analysis of Trade Practice Provisions in NRA Codes*, 1935 (No. 2); *Code Authorities and Their Part in Administration of NRA*, 1936 (No. 46); W. H. Edmonds and W. W. Swift, *The Basic Code*, 1936 (No. 33); I. S. Moise and G. B. Haddock, *Manufacturers' Control of Distribution; A Study of Trade Practice Provisions in Selected NRA Codes*, 1936 (No. 62). Special studies in this series on labor and NRA are given under another head in this bibliography. U. S. National Recovery Review Board, *Report to the President by Chairman Clarence Darrow* (Washington: 1934, mimeographed) is critical of NRA as fostering concentration of economic control. Charles Frederick Roos, *NRA Economic Planning* (Bloomington, Ind.: Principia Press, 1937) is an informing account, though with rather too much rescue of intramural history. Leverett S. Lyon, Paul T. Homan, Lewis L. Lorwin, and others, *The National Recovery Administration; An Analysis and Appraisal* (Washington: Brookings Institution, 1935) is a good study by neutral observers; Brookings Institution, *The ABC of the NRA* (Institute of Economics Publication No. 54; Washington: 1934) is to much the same effect, but briefer.

LABOR UNDER NRA

Labor under NRA is treated in several studies of NRA Division of Review, *Work Materials* (Washington: Government Printing Office, 1935–1936), among others Anne Page, *The Labor Program under the NIRA* (No. 45); Raymond S. Rubinow, *Section 7(a): Its History, Interpretation, and Administration* (No. 45); Solomon Barkin, *Wages and Hours in American Industry; NRA Source Material* (No. 10). Other treatments are Leon C. Marshall, *Hours and Wages Provisions in NRA Codes* (Washington: Brookings Institution, 1935); NRA Research and Planning Division; *Hours, Wages, and Employment under the Codes* (Washington: 1935); National Recovery Administration, *Geographic and Population Differentials in Minimum Wages,* Prepared under supervision of L. C. Marshall (Washington: 1935), a collection of maps gives main features of wage differentials in the first 500 codes. National Recovery Administration, *Tabulation of Labor Provisions in Codes Approved by August 8, 1934* (Washington: 1935), covers the first 517 NRA and AAA codes. A brief study by Lois MacDonald, Gladys Palmer, and Theresa Wolfson, *Labor and the NRA* (New York: Affiliated Schools for Workers, Inc., 1934) gives valuable background as well as labor aspects of NRA.

Charles Aikin, ed., *National Labor Relations Board Cases* (New York: John Wiley & Sons, Inc., 1939) sets forth in effect "the growing law of the national administrative control of labor relations"; "Arguments in the Cases Arising under the Railway Labor Act and the National Labor Relations Act," 75 Cong., 1 Sess., *Senate Document* No. 52, contains fewer cases than the foregoing. Robert R. R. Brooks, *Unions of Their Own Choosing; An Account of the National Labor Relations Board and Its Work* (New Haven: Yale University Press, 1939); Joseph Rosenfarb, *The National Labor Policy and How It Works.* Preface by Senator Robert F. Wagner, Foreword by J. Warren Madden (New York: Harper & Brothers, 1940), and Louis G. Silverberg, *The Wagner Act; After Ten Years* (Washington: Bureau of National Affairs, 1945) are appraisals.

The record of the so-called La Follette Civil Liberties Investigation of numerous forms of interference with the rights of labor is in Senate Committee on Education and Labor, Hearings on S. Res. 266, 74 Cong., 1 Sess., and S. Res. 70, 75 Cong., 1 Sess., April 10, 1936–January 29, 1940, various dates; preliminary hearings and 61 parts. An earlier and more localized inquiry is reported in Senate Committee on Manufactures, "Conditions in Coal Fields in Harlan and Bell Counties, Kentucky," Hearings on S. Res. 178, 72 Cong., 1 Sess., May 11–19, 1932; this reviews a disgraceful chapter in operator domination with profitable connivance of public officials, the kind of thing which the National Labor Relations Act soon went far to prevent. About the time of the official investigations several books on labor spies appeared, among them Edward Levinson, *I Break Strikes! The Technique of Pearl L. Bergoff* (New York: Rob-

THE LITERATURE OF THE SUBJECT 427

ert M. McBride & Company, 1935); Leo Huberman, *The Labor Spy Racket* (New York: Modern Age Books, 1937) is a summary of results of the earlier part of the La Follette inquiry by an experienced reporter; Clinch Calkins, *Spy Overhead; The Story of Industrial Espionage* (New York: Harcourt, Brace and Company, 1937) draws upon the same material.

On the rise of the Committee for Industrial Organization see American Federation of Labor, *Proceedings* Fifty-fifth Annual Convention, 1905 (Washington: Judd & Detweiler); Robert R. R. Brooks, *When Labor Organizes* (New Haven: Yale University Press, 1937). C.I.O., *The Case for Industrial Organization* (Washington: 1936) is an example of the popular pamphlets which issued in a stream from the C.I.O. See also American Federation of Labor, *A.F. of L. vs. C.I.O.; The Record* (Washington: 1939) as well as Herbert Harris, *Labor's Civil War* (New York: Alfred A. Knopf, 1940). *Men Who Lead Labor*, by Bruce Minton and John Stuart (New York: Modern Age Books, 1937) has candid, sometimes acidulated appraisals of personalities in A.F.L. and C.I.O. by authors with inconvenient memories; Harold Seidman, *Labor Czars, A History of Labor Racketeering* (New York: Liveright Publishing Corp., 1938) has a bias in good part justified. William Z. Foster, *Misleaders of Labor* (Chicago: Trade Union Educational League, 1927) is an older account of stagnation and corruption as seen by a renovator who had become a leader of the Communist party; the same author's *Industrial Unionism* (New York: Workers' Library Publishers, 1936) restated what had long been his advocacy. In Benjamin Stolberg, *Tailor's Progress, The Story of a Famous Union and the Men Who Made It* (New York: Doubleday & Company, 1944). Chapters VIII–X are informing on the New Deal impetus to unionism and the A.F.L.-C.I.O. split as illustrated by the International Ladies' Garment Workers. Joel Seidman, *The Needle Trades* (New York: Rinehart & Company, 1942) treats of unions which took a leading part in the revival of organized labor beginning with 1933. Carl Raushenbush, *Fordism; Ford and the Workers, Ford and the Community* (New York: League for Industrial Democracy, 1937) concerns an employer who defied NRA and the National Labor Relations Board. Leo Wolman, *Ebb and Flow in Trade Unionism* (New York: National Bureau of Economic Research, 1936) gives the most reliable figures of membership. Orme Wheelock Phelps,

The Legislative Background of the Fair Labor Standards Act; A Study of the Growth of National Sentiment in Favor of Governmental Regulation of Wages, Hours, and Child Labor (Chicago: University of Chicago Press, 1939) treats a development which grew out of NRA.

During part of the depression ominous noises off-stage were made by the Dies Committee (Representative Martin A. Dies, of Texas, chairman) investigating un-American activities; most of the evidence was far-fetched and the enquiry underemphasized organizations and propaganda of a fascist nature; see Special Committee to Investigate Un-American Propaganda and Activities, Hearings on H. Res. 282, 75 Cong., 3 Sess., August 12, 1938–May 21, 1940, various dates.

SOCIAL SECURITY

The literature of Social Security in the United States grew rapidly. For a guide see U. S. Social Security Board, *A Brief Reading List on the Social Security Act, Including References on the Amendments of 1939* (Washington: Government Printing Office, 1930). A good starting place is U. S. Advisory Council on Social Security, *Final Report* (Washington: 1939). For the first congressional consideration see House Committee on Ways and Means, Hearings on H.R. 4120, H.R. 7260, 74 Cong., 1 Sess., January 21–February 12, 1935; Senate Committee on Finance, Hearings on S. 1130, 74 Cong., 1 Sess., January 22–February 20, 1935; House Committee on Labor, "Old Age and Social Insurance," Hearings on H.R. 10, 185, 2827, 2859, 74 Cong., 1 Sess., February 4–15, 1935; the Lundeen or "Workers'" bill was H.R. 2827. The official running account of operations is in U. S. Social Security Board, *Annual Report*, 1935–1936– (Washington: Government Printing Office); the first *Annual Report* of the U. S. Federal Security Agency was issued by the Government Printing Office, Washington, 1941. In framing their laws the states made ready use of U. S. Social Security Board, *Draft Bills for State Unemployment Compensation of Pooled Fund and Employee Reserve Account Types* (Washington: Government Printing Office, rev. ed., January, 1937). U. S. Social Security Board, *Proposed Changes in the Social Security Act. A Report . . . to the President and to . . . Congress . . . January 1939* (Washington: Government Printing Office, 1939; appeared also as *House Document* No. 110, 79 Cong., 1 Sess.) was one of the board's most important reports, having effect on subsequent legislation liberalizing the act. U. S. Social Security Board, *A Handbook on Federal Old-Age and Survivors Insurance as Provided in the Social Security Act* (Washington: Government Printing Office, 1941) is convenient. Eveline M. Burns, *Towards Social Security; An Explanation of the Social Security Act and a Survey of the Larger Issues* (New York: McGraw-Hill Book Company, 1936) and Paul H. Douglas, *Social Security in the United States, An Analysis and Appraisal of the Federal Social Security Act* (New York: McGraw-Hill Book Company, 2nd ed., 1939) were among the first treatments to appear; Professor Douglas's book has a good discussion of the legislative history of the act. Abraham Epstein, *Insecurity, A Challenge to America; A Study of Social Insurance in the United States and Abroad* (New York: Harrison Smith and Robert Haas, 1933) by a devoted student and advocate, was an influence; the 1941 edition (New York: Random House) contains an analysis of the Social Security Act, the status of state legislation, and a discussion of health insurance problems.

A spirited account of Dr. Francis E. Townsend's O.A.R.P. (Old Age Revolving Pensions) and of Upton Sinclair's E.P.I.C. campaign (End Poverty in California) is contained in Carey McWilliams, *Southern California Country, An Island in the Land* (New York: Duell, Sloan, and Pearce, 1946). See also Francis E. Townsend, *A Ready Reference Book Presenting . . . the Townsend Plan . . .* (Chicago: Townsend National Weekly, 1941). For a destructive analysis, see National Industrial Conference Board, *The Townsend Scheme* (New York: National Industrial Conference Board, Inc., 1936).

CONSUMPTION AND PRODUCTION

Consumption as a field for economic study received new stress in this period because of the importance of consumption in sustaining production, public responsibility for relief, and the increase in consumer cooperatives. The underlying survey is U. S. National Resources Committee, *Consumer Incomes in the United States: Their Distribution in 1935–36* (Washington: Government Printing Office,

1938). This was followed by *Consumer Expenditures in the United States: Estimates for 1935–36* (Washington: Government Printing Office, 1939), and by *Family Expenditures in the United States* (Washington: Government Printing Office, 1941). Maurice Leven, Harold G. Moulton, and Clark Warburton, *America's Capacity to Consume* (Washington: Brookings Institution, 1934) did much to make the country conscious of inequality in the distribution of income, and its results. Spurgeon Bell examined *Productivity, Wages, and National Income* (Washington: Brookings Institution, 1940) and Simon S. Kuznets published the results of his careful research into *National Income and Its Composition, 1913–1938* (New York: National Bureau of Economic Research, 1941, 2 vols.).

Several works deal with production in the period. One that showed underuse of installed plant, even in the best times, is E. G. Nourse and others, *America's Capacity to Produce* (Washington: Brookings Institution, 1934); see also Simon Kuznets, *National Income and Capital Formation, 1919–1935* (New York: National Bureau of Economic Research, 1937), his *Commodity Flow and Capital Formation* (New York: National Bureau of Economic Research, 1938), and his *National Production, War and Prewar* (New York: National Bureau of Economic Research, 1944). Arthur F. Burns, *Production Trends in the United States Since 1870* (New York: National Bureau of Economic Research, 1934) stops with 1930 but gives valuable background material. Another early account is Frederick C. Mills, *Recent Economic Tendencies* (New York: J. J. Little & Ives Company, 1932). Cabinet Committee on Cotton Textile Industry, Message from the President of the United States to Congress, 74 Cong., 1 Sess., *Senate Document* No. 126, reviews the sorrows of this industry, which were acute again after lapse of NRA; means are recommended for meeting overcapacity through "an organization set up within the industry with governmental assistance and cooperation."

On Technocracy, which drew ominous conclusions from the advances in productivity, see Howard Scott and others, *Introduction to Technocracy* (New York: The John Day Company, 1933), which is the authorized version, so to speak; Frank Arkright, *The A B C of Technocracy, Based on Authorized Material* (New York: Harper & Brothers, 1933); Graham A. Laing, *Towards Technocracy* (Los Angeles: The Angelus Press, 1933). Paul Blanshard, *Technocracy and Socialism* (New York: League for Industrial Democracy, 1933) is a pamphlet putting the new proposal in an old perspective. U. S. National Resources Committee, *Technological Trends and Labor Policy, Including the Social Implications of New Inventions* (Washington: Government Printing Office, 1937) is prosy considering the dramatic nature of the subject. See also House Committee on Labor, "Investigation of Unemployment Caused by Labor-Saving Devices in Industry," 74 Cong., 1 Sess., February 13–March 2, 1936. U. S. Department of Agriculture, Interbureau Committee, explored *Technology on the Farm* (Washington: Government Printing Office, 1940) and U. S. Temporary National Economic Committee, "Technology and Concentration of Economic Power," Part 30 of Hearings on Pub. Res. 113, 75 Cong., April 8–26, 1940 (Washington: Government Printing Office, 1940, pp. 16,207–17,599) treat other aspects.

TENNESSEE VALLEY AUTHORITY AND OTHER PLANNING

The Tennessee Valley Authority gave rise to a large literature listed in U. S. Tennessee Valley Authority, *Congressional Hearings, Reports, and Documents Relating to TVA, 1933–1940,* Compiled by Alice M. Norwood (Knoxville: 1941); a later bibliography is Tennessee Valley Authority, *A Selected List of Books, Theses, and Pamphlets on TVA,* Compiled by Ernest I. Miller (Knoxville: 1942); See also F. D. Roosevelt, *Power Views of Franklin D. Roosevelt,* Compiled . . . for National Power Policy Committee (Washington: 1934). The TVA *Annual Report* (Washington: Government Printing Office, 1933–1934–) is the fullest record; much detail is given in Investigation of U. S. Tennessee Valley Authority, Hearings on S. J. Res. 277, 75 Cong., 3 Sess., May 25–December 19, 1938, various dates, Pts. 1–14 in 7 vols., index included in Pt. 14; these hearings led to Joint Committee to Investigate U. S. Tennessee Valley Authority. *Report pursuant to Pub. Res. 83,* 75 Cong., together with Minority Views in 3 vols.; 76 Cong., 1 Sess., *Senate Document* No. 56. Controversy over the TVA introduced Wendell Willkie to politics; see his *The Other Side of the TVA Program,* Address of . . . President . . . Commonwealth and Southern Corporation before the Rotary Club of Birmingham, Alabama, November 7, 1934 (Birmingham: 1934); also Commonwealth & Southern

Corporation, *Analysis of the Annual Report of the Tennessee Valley Authority Released on December 31, 1936* (New York: 1937).

The TVA did a good job of public relations in popular pamphlets. An example is *The Development of the Tennessee Valley* (Washington: Government Printing Office, 1936), which contains a summary of the various phases of the work, with pictures, and basic rates for residential and farm use of current in TVA contracts. Others are TVA, *How Cheap Electricity Pays Its Way: TVA* (Washington: Government Printing Office, 1938), which explains the operation of municipal and cooperative electric systems distributing TVA power; *Recreational Development of the Southern Highlands Region* (Knoxville: TVA, 1938); *Fifty Inches of Rain, A Story of Land and Water Conservation* (Washington: Government Printing Office, 1939); *Forests and Human Welfare . . . With Special Reference to the Tennessee Valley Region* (Washington: Government Printing Office, 1940); *TVA, Its Work and Accomplishments* (Washington: Government Printing Office, 1940); *Tennessee Valley Authority Act . . . May 18, 1933 . . . as Amended to November 21, 1941* (Washington: Government Printing Office, 1942). David E. Lilienthal, *TVA; Democracy on the March* (New York: Harper & Brothers, 1944), being by the director of the undertaking, shows peculiar insight. Treatments by visitors include R. L. Duffus, *The Valley and Its People; A Portrait of TVA*, Illustrations by Graphics Department of TVA (New York: Alfred A. Knopf, Inc., 1944); Wilson Whitman, *God's Valley; People and Power along the Tennessee River* (New York: The Viking Press, 1939); Julian S. Huxley, *TVA Adventure in Planning* (Cheam, Surrey: The Architectural Press, 1943). Joseph Sirera Ransmeier, *The Tennessee Valley Authority; A Case Study in the Economics of Multiple Stream Planning* (Nashville: The Vanderbilt University Press, 1942) is technical, but repays examination. Charles Herman Pritchett, *The Tennessee Valley Authority, A Study in Public Administration* (Chapel Hill: University of North Carolina Press, 1943) deals with an important aspect. Talbot Faulkner Hamlin, *Tennessee Valley Authority Architecture* (Knoxville: TVA, 1940) presents a significant by-product of the project.

The National Resources Committee and its successor Planning Board increasingly furnished materials for economic and social design, though events did not favor their use for this purpose. See

National Resources Planning Board, *Functions of the . . . Board* (Washington: Government Printing Office, 1941); U. S. National Resources Committee, *Progress Report* (Washington: Government Printing Office, 1936–1939), its *Regional Factors in National Planning and Development* (Washington: Government Printing Office, 1935), *Energy Resources and National Policy* (Washington: Government Printing Office, 1939), and *The Problems of a Changing Population* (Washington: Government Printing Office, 1938).

TEMPORARY NATIONAL ECONOMIC COMMITTEE AND CONCENTRATION

An extensive and intensive survey of the operation of the American economy and the pass to which it had come is in U. S. Temporary National Economic Committee, "Investigation of Concentration of Economic Power," Hearings on Pub. Res. 113, 75 Cong., 3 Sess. (hearings held in 75 and 76 Cong.) December 1, 1938–January 19, 1940, various dates; Parts 1–25 and 43 monographs. Two official reports undertake in different ways to summarize the voluminous evidence: the *Final Report of the Executive Secretary*, Senate Committee Print, 77 Cong., 1 Sess. and the *Final Report and Recommendations of the . . . Committee*, Senate Document No. 35, 77 Cong., 1 Sess.

An introduction to the TNEC inquiry is contained in Part 1, *Economic Prologue*, December 1–3, 1938 (Washington: Government Printing Office, 1939). A competent book reporting the origin and purpose of the Temporary National Economic Committee, summarizing its hearings, and appraising its findings, is David Lynch, *The Concentration of Economic Power* (New York: Columbia University Press, 1946). The way in which these same tendencies of the largest companies toward aggrandizement were abetted by government and other forces in the defense and war periods is startlingly evident in U. S. Smaller War Plants Corporation, *Economic Concentration and World War II; Report . . . to the Special Committee to Study Problems of American Small Business*, Senate, 79 Cong., 2 Sess., Committee Print No. 6. See also Arthur R. Burns, *The Decline of Competition; A Study of the Evolution of American Industry* (New York: McGraw-Hill Book Company, 1936).

A sample of numerous inquiries into consolidation in merchandising is U. S. Federal Trade Commission, *Chain Stores; Invested*

Capital and Rates of Return in Retail Chains, Letter from chairman transmitting report in response to S. Res. 224, 70 Cong.; see in this connection E. T. Grether, *Price Control under Fair Trade Legislation* (New York: Oxford University Press, 1939).

THE DEFENSE ECONOMY

Within little more than three years the country moved from abhorrence of war to preparation for war. Pacifist sentiment was assisted by substantial and sensational news flowing from a public inquiry by the Nye Committee (Senator Gerald P. Nye, of North Dakota, chairman) into the manufacture and sale of arms. Readers were struck by the impartiality of munitions makers between countries so long as lucrative orders were to be obtained; see Senate Special Committee to Investigate the Munitions Industry, Hearings on S. Res. 206, 73 Cong., 2 Sess.; S. Res. 8, 74 Cong., 1 Sess.; Sen. Res. 221, 74 Cong., 2 Sess., September 4, 1934–February 20, 1936, various dates; Parts 1–40 in 13 vols.; see also Senate Special Committee to Investigate the Munitions Industry, *Report,* 74 Cong., 1 Sess., *Senate Report* No. 946, 7 parts.

A good review of government controls and of the economy generally in the defense period is U. S. Office of Price Administration, *First Quarterly Report; For period ended April 30, 1942* (Washington: Government Printing Office). U. S. Office of Production Management, *Duties and Functions* (Washington: March, 1941) explains an intricate organization. U. S. Office of Facts and Figures, *Report to the Nation; The American Preparation for War* (Washington: Government Printing Office, 1942) is a summary of accomplishments. U. S.War Production Board, *Listing of Major War Department Supply Contracts by State, June 1940 through September 1941 with October 1941 Supplement,* Compiled by Office of Production Management Bureau of Research and Statistics . . . (Washington: Government Printing Office, 1942) shows concretely how defense spending was reviving the economy. U. S. War Production Board, Division of Information, *Converting Industry; Turning a Nation's Production to War.* Transcript of Conference of Business Paper Editors and Publishers with War Production Board Officials (Washington: 1942) gives some description and more exhortation by Donald M. Nelson, chairman of the WPB. Edward S.

Mason, J. M. Clark, Charles O. Hardy, and others, an unpublished manuscript *Price Problems in a Defense Economy,* Prepared for the Conference on Price Research (New York: 1941, typewritten copy at National Bureau of Economic Research and microfilm in New York Public Library) considers questions which became increasingly academic as war controls were imposed. Harry S. Truman was chairman of the U. S. Senate Special Committee Investigating the National Defense Program, "Investigation of the National Defense Program," pursuant to S. Res. 71, 77 Cong., 1 Sess., April 15–July 9, 1941, Parts 1–5. U. S. Congress, *Events Leading Up to World War II,* 78 Cong., 2 Sess., House Document No. 541, omits little but treats nothing at length.

A part of the story of economic improvement in the defense period is furnished by U. S. Lend-Lease Administrator, *Report to the 78th Congress on Lend-Lease Operations from the Passage of the Act, March 11, 1941, to December 31, 1942* (Washington: Government Printing Office, 1943).

Appendix

STOCK PRICES: DOW-JONES & CO., INC., AND *NEW YORK TIMES*
AVERAGES: 1929 TO 1941

(Dollars per share)

Year	Dow-Jones & Co., Inc.[a] (65 stocks)	*New York Times* [b] (50 stocks)
1929	$125.43	$251.08
1930	95.64	199.59
1931	55.47	125.09
1932	26.82	57.81
1933	36.00	74.63
1934	39.16	85.52
1935	41.97	96.92
1936	58.98	127.87
1937	58.08	121.57
1938	43.10	93.67
1939	48.01	102.05
1940	45.28	98.52
1941	41.22	87.94

[a] Dow-Jones list includes industrials, public utilities, railroads; averages of daily closing figures.

[b] *New York Times* list includes industrials and railroads; averages of Saturday closing prices.

Source: Standard and Poor's Corporation.

SALES ON NEW YORK STOCK EXCHANGE: VOLUME, 1929 TO 1941

Year	Stocks, Millions of shares	Bonds, par Value *(millions of dollars)*
1929	1,125	$2,982
1930	810	2,764
1931	577	3,051
1932	425	2,967
1933	655	3,369
1934	324	3,726
1935	382	3,339
1936	496	3,576
1937	409	2,793
1938	297	1,860
1939	262	2,046
1940	208	1,669
1941	171	2,112

Source: *Commercial and Financial Chronicle.*

COMMERCIAL AND INDUSTRIAL FAILURES, NUMBER AND
LIABILITIES, 1929 TO 1941

Year	Number of Failures	Current Liabilities (*1,000 dollars*)
1929	22,909	$483,252
1930	26,355	668,282
1931	28,285	736,310
1932	31,822	928,313
1933	20,307	502,830
1933 [a]	*19,859*	*457,520*
1934	12,091	333,959
1935	12,244	310,580
1936	9,607	203,173
1937	9,490	183,253
1938	12,836	246,505
1939 [a]	*11,408*	*168,204*
1939	14,768	182,520
1940	13,619	166,684
1941	11,848	136,104

[a] Figures in italics comparable with preceding years.
Source: *Dun & Bradstreet, Inc.*

CAPITAL ISSUES, SUMMARY BY CLASSES, 1929 TO 1941

(In millions and tenths of millions of dollars)

Year	Total Issues[a]	New Capital	Refunding	Railroads	Corporate			Farm Loan and Government Agencies
					Public Utilities	Industrials	Miscellaneous	
1929	$11,592.2	$10,182.8	$1,409.4	$817.2	$2,442.8	$2,459.8	$4,306.6	.....
1930	7,677.0	7,023.4	653.7	1,026.5	2,566.2	1,151.9	728.6	$86.5
1931	4,022.9	3,115.5	907.4	516.5	1,538.9	329.6	204.0	125.6
1932	1,730.3	1,192.2	538.0	61.0	540.3	20.9	21.8	169.6
1933	1,053.7	709.5	344.2	99.9	92.7	186.6	2.3	90.2
1934	2,212.3	1,386.3	825.9	249.2	158.4	53.2	30.2	721.7
1935	4,752.3	1,412.1	3,340.2	196.7	1,283.8	706.5	80.4	1,137.1
1936	6,254.3	1,973.3	4,281.0	796.1	2,125.3	1,258.0	452.6	375.2
1937	4,001.3	2,100.7	1,900.6	356.7	827.5	1,036.9	212.5	437.7
1938	4,459.2	2,355.0	2,104.1	72.4	1,222.6	798.1	47.3	1,146.0
1939	5,853.1	2,298.4	3,554.7	185.6	1,327.0	512.2	171.4	2,461.6
1940	4,805.9	1,950.5	2,855.4	372.3	1,274.1	764.2	352.0	804.3
1941	5,545.9	2,853.9	2,692.0	365.3	1,383.0	675.5	195.0	1,969.0

[a] Issues of states and municipalities, and of foreign governments included.

Source: Commercial and Financial Chronicle.

BANK DEBITS TO DEPOSIT ACCOUNTS (EXCEPT INTERBANK); VOLUME
REPORTED BY BANKS IN 141 LEADING CITIES, 1929 TO 1941

(Millions of dollars)

Year	Total	Year	Total
1929	$935,030	1936	$428,605
1930	661,956	1937	433,043
1931	481,356	1938	373,522
1932	322,365	1939	389,677
1933 (11 months)	282,708	1940	408,535
1934	331,503	1941	491,649
1935	374,173		

Source: Board of Governors of Federal Reserve System, *Reports, Federal Reserve Bulletin.*

RECONSTRUCTION FINANCE CORPORATION: LOAN AND OTHER AU-
THORIZATIONS, BY CHARACTER OF LOANS; PURCHASES OF SECURITIES
FROM PWA; AND ALLOCATIONS TO OTHER GOVERNMENTAL AGENCIES,
FEBRUARY 2, 1932, TO DECEMBER 31, 1941

(In thousands of dollars)

	Total Feb. 2, 1932, to Dec. 31, 1941		Outstand-ing Dec. 31, 1941
	Disbursed	Repaid [a]	
Loan and other authorizations, by character of loan, total	$9,465,950	$6,527,667	$2,938,283
Banks and trust companies	$3,342,253	$2,827,492	$514,851
Loans to aid in the reorganization or liquidation of closed banks [b]	1,035,530	1,003,087	32,443
Loans to open banks [c]	1,138,252	1,082,585	55,667
Loans on and subscriptions for preferred stock, and purchases of capital notes or debentures	1,168,471	741,730	426,741
Export-import banks: Loan and subscriptions for preferred stock	201,500	27,500	174,000
Federal home loan banks: Purchase of stock	124,741	. . . .	124,741
Agricultural financing institutions, etc.	1,450,652	1,448,941	1,711
Loans to federal land banks	387,236 [d]	387,236	. . . .
Loans to federal intermediate credit banks	9,250	9,250	. . . .
Loans to regional agricultural credit corporations	173,244	173,244	. . . .
Loans to Commodity Credit Corporation	767,717	767,717	. . . .
Loans to Secretary of Agriculture to acquire cotton	3,300	3,300	. . . .
Loans to joint-stock land banks	24,667	23,389	1,278
Loans to agricultural credit corporations	5,644	5,644	. . . .
Loans to livestock credit corporations	12,650	12,650	. . . .
Authorizations for financing exports of agricultural surpluses	47,301	47,301	. . . .
Loans for financing agricultural commodities and livestock	19,644	19,211	433
Other financial institutions	837,101	595,820	241,281
Building and loan associations (including receivers)	125,275	122,115	3,160
Insurance companies: Loans	90,693	89,863	830
Loans on and subscriptions for preferred stock	34,475	12,555	21,920

Source: Federal Loan Agency, Reconstruction Finance Corporation; *Report* for the Fourth Quarter of 1941.

[a] Exclusive of repayments, unallocated, pending advices, as of Dec. 31, 1941.

[b] Includes loans to receivers, liquidating agents, and conservators; loans through mortgage loan companies to aid closed banks; and loans on assets of closed banks under Sec. 5e of the RFC Act, as amended.

[c] Excludes loans through banks to business enterprises.

[d] Includes $193,618,000 representing refinancing of previous loans by the corporation to these banks.

RECONSTRUCTION FINANCE CORPORATION, ETC.—*Continued*

	Total Feb. 2, 1932, to Dec. 31, 1941		Outstand-ing Dec. 31, 1941
	Disbursed	Repaid [a]	
Mortgage-loan companies: [e]			
Loans	245,131	220,973	24,158
Loans to The RFC Mortgage Company	165,462	111,480	53,982
Loans to Federal National Mortgage Association	140,065	38,834	101,231
Subscription for stock of The RFC Mortgage Co.	25,000	....	25,000
Subscription for stock of the Federal National Mortgage Association	11,000	....	11,000
Railroads (including receivers and trustees)	828,167	365,671	462,496
Business enterprises—loans and participations (except to aid in National Defense) [f]	271,848[g]	162,328	109,520
National Defense—loans, participations, and purchase of stock of corporations created by the RFC to aid in National Defense	1,000,447	173,152	827,295
Mining, milling, or smelting of ores—loans	6,899	3,127	3,772
Self-liquidating projects	605,221	546,450	58,771
Drainage, levee, and irrigation districts	98,211	25,397	72,814
Repair of damage by earthquake, flood, etc.	12,003	10,976	1,027
Loan to a foreign government	350,000	4,844	345,156
Other	336,907	336,059	848
Loans to credit unions	600	600	....
Loans to processors, or distributors subject to processing taxes	15	15	..
Loans to state funds for securing repayment of deposits of public moneys	13,065	13,065	....
Loans to refinance public-school district obligations	942	94	848
Loan for payment of teachers' salaries	22,300	22,300	....
Amounts made available for relief, under the Emergency Relief and Construction Act of 1932, as amended	299,985	299,985 [h]	....
Purchases of securities from Public Works Administration	652,563	538,194	114,369
Allocations and loans to other governmental agencies	2,899,711	2,552,029[i]	347,682

[e] Excludes loans through mortgage loan companies to aid closed banks and to business enterprises.

[f] Includes loans to business enterprises through banks and mortgage loan companies.

[g] In addition, participating banks had disbursed $87,607,000 on immediate and deferred participations as of Dec. 31, 1941.

[h] Includes $17,159,000 representing repayments and other reductions by states and political subdivisions; and $282,826,000 representing cancelation of the corporation's notes, pursuant to the provisions of the act approved Feb. 24, 1938, equivalent to the balance of the amounts disbursed.

[i] Of this amount, $2,455,898,000 represents cancelation of the corporation's notes, pursuant to the provisions of the act approved Feb. 24, 1938, equivalent to the balance of the amount disbursed for allocations to other governmental agencies and for relief by direction of Congress and the interest paid thereon. The remaining $37,000,000 is held by the corporation in a revolving fund (capital of regional agricultural credit corporations) pursuant to Sec. 84 of the Farm Credit Act of 1933, as amended. An additional $2,500,000 of the foregoing revolving fund is held by the United States Treasury, such amount having been paid subsequent to the cancelation of the corporation's notes.

FARM REAL ESTATE: LAND TRANSFERS AND VALUES, 1929 TO 1941

| Year | Estimated Number of Farms Changing Ownership per 1,000 Farms | | | Index of Estimated Value per Acre (*1912–14 equals 100*) |
	Total ª	Voluntary Sales and Trades	Forced Sales and Related Defaults	
1929	58.0	23.5	19.5	116
1930	61.5	23.7	20.8	115
1931	61.9	19.0	26.1	106
1932	76.6	16.2	41.7	89
1933	93.6	16.8	54.1	73
1934	78.6	17.8	39.1	76
1935	69.1	19.4	28.3	79
1936	72.9	24.8	26.2	82
1937	74.0	31.5	22.4	85
1938	65.4	30.5	17.4	85
1939	63.8	29.7	17.0	84
1940	63.0	30.2	15.9	84
1941	63.7	34.1	13.9	85

ª Omits miscellaneous transfers.

Source: U. S. Department of Agriculture, Bureau of Agricultural Economics, *Annual Report, Agricultural Finance Review.*

EXPORTS AND IMPORTS OF MERCHANDISE, 1929 TO 1941
(*In thousands of dollars*)

Year	Exports	Imports	Excess of Exports
1929	$5,240,995	$4,399,361	$841,634
1930	3,843,181	3,060,908	782,273
1931	2,424,289	2,090,635	333,654
1932	1,611,016	1,322,774	288,242
1933	1,674,994	1,449,559	225,435
1934	2,132,800	1,655,055	477,745
1935	2,282,874	2,047,485	235,389
1936	2,455,978	2,422,592	33,386
1937	3,349,167	3,083,668	265,499
1938	3,094,440	1,960,428	1,134,012
1939	3,177,176	2,318,081	859,095
1940	4,021,146	2,625,379	1,395,767
1941	5,147,154	3,345,005	1,802,149

Source: U. S. Department of Commerce, Bureau of Census and Bureau of Foreign and Domestic Commerce.

GROSS AND NET PUBLIC DEBT, 1929 TO 1941

(In billions of dollars)

	1929	1930	1931	1932	1933	1934	1935	1936	1937	1938	1939	1940	1941
Gross public debt													
Federal and federal agencies	18.2	17.9	19.6	23.4	28.2	38.0	41.5	45.1	47.8	47.5	49.9	53.1	66.5
Federal government	16.3	16.0	17.8	20.8	23.8	28.5	30.6	34.4	37.3	39.4	42.0	45.0	58.0
Federal agencies	1.9	1.9	1.8	2.5	4.4	9.5	10.9	10.7	10.5	8.0	9.9	8.1	8.5
Net public debt													
Federal and federal agencies	15.7	15.4	17.1	18.7	21.0	23.1	26.0	29.5	31.3	32.6	34.8	36.7	47.6

Source: U. S. Department of Commerce, Bureau of Foreign and Domestic Commerce, *Survey of Current Business* (July, 1944).

PHYSICAL VOLUME OF INDUSTRIAL PRODUCTION, 1929 TO 1941
(Index numbers 1935–39 average = 100)

Year	Index	1941, Month [a]	Index [a]
1929	110	February	144
1930	91	March	147
1931	75	April	144
1932	58	May	154
1933	69	June	159
1934	75	July	160
1935	87	August	160
1936	103	September	161
1937	113	October	163
1938	88	November	166
1939	108	December	167
1940	123		
1941	156		

[a] Adjusted for seasonal variation.
Source: Federal Reserve Board.

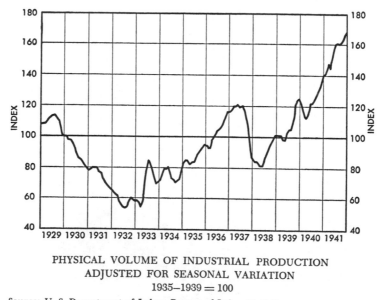

PHYSICAL VOLUME OF INDUSTRIAL PRODUCTION
ADJUSTED FOR SEASONAL VARIATION
1935–1939 = 100

Source: U. S. Department of Labor, Bureau of Labor Statistics.

EMPLOYMENT AND PAY ROLLS
ALL MANUFACTURING INDUSTRIES

Source: U. S. Department of Labor, Bureau of Labor Statistics.

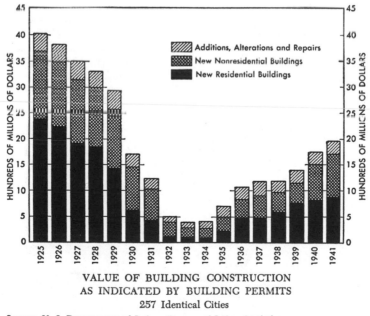

VALUE OF BUILDING CONSTRUCTION
AS INDICATED BY BUILDING PERMITS
257 Identical Cities

Source: U. S. Department of Labor, Bureau of Labor Statistics.

WHOLESALE PRICES, AGRICULTURAL AND INDUSTRIAL, 1929 TO 1941

(Index numbers 1926 = 100)

Year and Month	All Commodities Other than Farm Products	Farm Products	All Commodities
1929	93.3	104.9	95.3
1930	85.9	88.3	86.4
1931	74.6	64.8	73.0
1932	68.3	48.2	64.8
1933	69.0	51.4	65.9
1934	76.9	65.3	74.9
1935	80.2	78.8	80.0
1936	80.7	80.9	80.8
1937	86.2	86.4	86.3
1938	80.6	68.5	78.6
1939	79.5	65.3	77.1
1940	80.8	67.7	78.6
1941	88.3	82.4	87.3
1941: January	82.7	71.6	80.8
February	82.7	70.3	80.6
March	83.6	71.6	81.5
April	85.0	74.4	83.2
May	86.6	76.4	84.9
June	88.0	82.1	87.1
July	89.3	85.8	88.8
August	90.7	87.4	90.3
September	91.9	91.0	91.8
October	92.8	90.0	92.4
November	92.7	90.6	92.5
December	93.3	94.7	93.6

Source: U. S. Bureau of Labor Statistics.

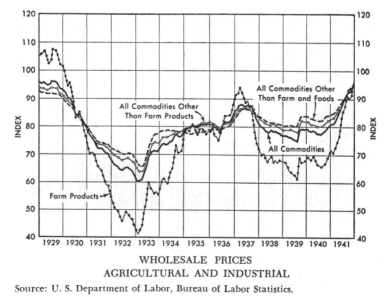

WHOLESALE PRICES
AGRICULTURAL AND INDUSTRIAL

Source: U. S. Department of Labor, Bureau of Labor Statistics.

COST OF GOODS AND SERVICES: PURCHASES BY WAGE EARNERS AND
LOWER-SALARIED WORKERS, AVERAGE FOR LARGE CITIES OF
THE U. S., 1929 TO 1941

(Index numbers 1935–39 = 100)

Year	All Items	1941, Month	All Items
1929	122.5	January 15	100.7
1930	119.4	February 15	100.8
1931	108.7	March 15	101.2
1932	97.6	April 15	102.2
1933	92.4	May 15	102.9
1934	95.7	June 15	104.6
1935	98.1	July 15	105.3
1936	99.1	August 15	106.2
1937	102.7	September 15	108.1
1938	100.8	October 15	109.3
1939	99.4	November 15	110.2
1940	100.2	December 15	110.5
1941	105.2		

Source: U. S. Bureau of Labor Statistics.

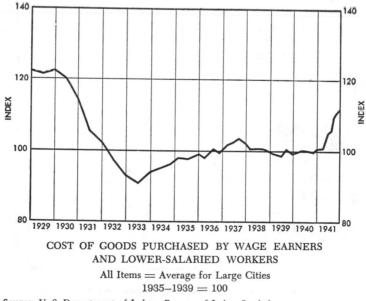

COST OF GOODS PURCHASED BY WAGE EARNERS
AND LOWER-SALARIED WORKERS

All Items = Average for Large Cities
1935–1939 = 100

Source: U. S. Department of Labor, Bureau of Labor Statistics.

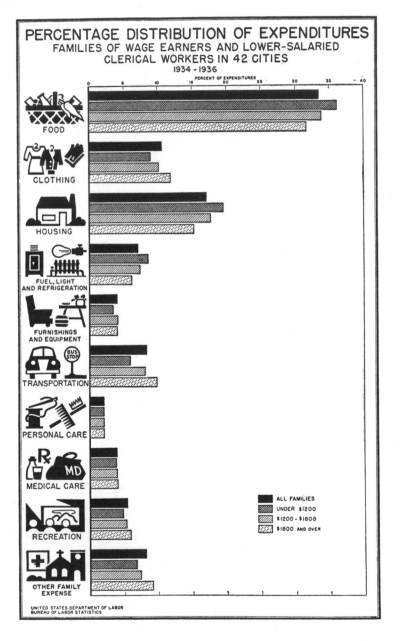

PERCENTAGE DISTRIBUTION OF EXPENDITURES
FAMILIES OF WAGE EARNERS AND LOWER-SALARIED
CLERICAL WORKERS IN 42 CITIES
1934-1936

PERCENT OF EXPENDITURES

FOOD

CLOTHING

HOUSING

FUEL, LIGHT AND REFRIGERATION

FURNISHINGS AND EQUIPMENT

TRANSPORTATION

PERSONAL CARE

MEDICAL CARE

RECREATION

OTHER FAMILY EXPENSE

ALL FAMILIES
UNDER $1200
$1200 - $1800
$1800 AND OVER

UNITED STATES DEPARTMENT OF LABOR
BUREAU OF LABOR STATISTICS

PRELIMINARY ESTIMATES OF LABOR FORCE, EMPLOYMENT, AND
UNEMPLOYMENT IN THE U. S., 1929 TO 1940 [a]

(*In thousands*)

Year	Total Labor Force	Armed Forces	Civilian Labor Force	Unemployment	Employment						Adjustment for Duplication and Incomparabilities	Unemployment as a Percentage of the Civilian Labor Force
					Total	Agricultural	Nonagricultural					
							Employment	Employees	Self-employed	Employees in Non-Agricultural Establishments		
1929	48,065	262	47,803	1,499	46,304	9,972	36,332	29,343	6,989	30,502	−1,177	3.1
1930	48,683	263	48,420	4,248	44,172	9,869	34,303	27,551	6,752	28,655	−1,104	8.8
1931	49,270	260	49,010	7,911	41,099	9,829	31,270	24,867	6,403	25,864	−997	16.1
1932	49,830	254	49,576	11,901	37,675	9,725	27,950	21,958	5,992	22,837	−879	24.0
1933	50,403	252	50,151	12,634	37,517	9,658	27,859	22,013	5,846	22,904	−891	25.2
1934	51,032	258	50,774	10,968	39,806	9,484	30,322	24,247	6,075	25,246	−999	21.6
1935	51,663	269	51,394	10,208	41,186	9,698	31,488	25,264	6,224	26,317	−1,053	19.9
1936	52,273	301	51,972	8,598	43,374	9,598	33,776	27,183	6,593	28,328	−1,145	16.5
1937	52,849	322	52,527	7,273	45,254	9,437	35,817	28,940	6,877	30,170	−1,230	13.8
1938	53,465	335	53,130	9,910	43,220	9,322	33,898	27,213	6,685	28,377	−1,164	18.7
1939	54,095	369	53,726	8,842	44,884	9,252	35,632	28,633	6,999	29,869	−1,235	16.5
1940	54,479	535	53,944	7,476	46,468	9,192	37,276	30,051	7,225	31,388	−1,337	13.0

[a] *1929–1940*—Total Labor Force: Armed Forces (from BLS) plus Civilian Labor Force (Census interpolated by BLS), Unemployment: Civilian Labor Force minus Total Employment. Total Employment: Agricultural Employment (Census interpolated by BAE) plus Nonagricultural Employment (Census interpolated by adjusted BLS). Employees: MRLF level estimates fluctuated by BLS. Self-employed: Preliminary BLS Employees in Nonagricultural Establishments: Preliminary BLS. Employees in Nonagricultural Establishments: Preliminary BLS level employees because of duplication and statistical incomparabilities.

Source: U. S. Department of Labor, Bureau of Labor Statistics, Employment and Occupational Outlook Branch, Occupational Outlook Division, June 29, 1945. *Technical Memorandum* No. 20, July 4, 1945.

ESTIMATED CIVILIAN LABOR FORCE, EMPLOYMENT, AND
UNEMPLOYMENT, 1941, BY MONTHS

Month	Estimated Number (*Millions of persons*)		
	Labor Force	Employed	Unemployed
January	52.8	45.2	7.6
February	52.7	45.5	7.2
March	52.4	45.6	6.8
April	53.3	46.7	6.6
May	54.0	48.3	5.7
June	55.7	49.8	5.9
July	56.0	50.4	5.6
August	55.8	50.5	5.3
September	54.3	49.8	4.5
October	53.5	49.6	3.9
November	53.3	49.4	3.9
December	53.3	49.5	3.8

Source: *Monthly Labor Review*, LIV, No. 1 (January, 1942), 266; *ibid.*, No. 2 (February, 1942), p. 547.

ESTIMATES OF UNEMPLOYMENT IN THE U. S., 1929 TO 1940

(In thousands)

Year	Preliminary BLS	A.F.L.	C.I.O.	N.I.C.B.	Robert Nathan	Alexander Hamilton Institute	Corrington Gill	Daniel Carson	National Research League	Labor Research Association[a]	Cleveland Trust
1929	1,499	1,864	1,831	429	1,752	3,456	1,850	1,910	2,473	.....	.....
1930	4,248	4,735	4,710	2,896	4,645	6,929	4,750	4,825	5,325	.....	.....
1931	7,911	8,568	8,322	7,037	8,118	10,939	8,410	8,725	9,539	.....	4,124
1932	11,901	12,870	12,120	11,385	11,630	14,728	12,480	13,100	14,220	.....	8,777
1933	12,634	13,271	12,643	11,842	11,942	14,394	12,840	13,700	14,723	16,783	13,416
1934	10,968	11,424	10,845	9,761	9,993	12,419	11,130	12,115	13,288	16,138	14,098
1935	10,208	10,652	10,050	9,092	9,102	11,629	11,140	11,240	13,073	16,824	12,130
1936	8,598	9,395	8,756	7,386	7,723	10,008	9,780	10,200	12,614	16,658	12,372
1937	7,273	8,282	8,109	6,403	6,855	8,366	8,860	9,235	.....	14,751	.....
1938	9,910	10,836	11,030	9,796	9,865	11,934	11,870	.....	.....	14,825	.....
1939	8,842	9,979	10,813	8,786	9,835	10,696	.....	.....	.....	16,368	.....
1940	7,476	9,104	10,276	7,607	9,552	9,379	.....	.....	.....	.....	.....

[a] Estimates as of November except 1938, which is as of April.

Source: U. S. Department of Labor, Bureau of Labor Statistics, Employment and Occupational Outlook Branch, Occupational Outlook Division, June 29, 1945. *Technical Memorandum* No. 20, July 4, 1945.

Index